Applying Predictive Analytics Within the Service Sector

Rajendra Sahu
ABV-Indian Institute of Information Technology and Management, India

Manoj Dash
ABV-Indian Institute of Information Technology and Management, India

Anil Kumar
BML Munjal University, India

A volume in the Advances in Business Information Systems and Analytics (ABISA) Book Series

IGI GLOBAL
DISSEMINATOR OF KNOWLEDGE
www.igi-global.com

Published in the United States of America by
IGI Global
Business Science Reference (an imprint of IGI Global)
701 E. Chocolate Avenue
Hershey PA, USA 17033
Tel: 717-533-8845
Fax: 717-533-8661
E-mail: cust@igi-global.com
Web site: http://www.igi-global.com

Library of Congress Cataloging-in-Publication Data

Names: Sahu, Rajendra, 1964- editor. | Dash, Manoj Kumar, editor. | Kumar, Anil, 1980- editor.
Title: Applying predictive analytics within the service sector / Rajendra Sahu, Manoj Dash, and Anil Kumar, editors.
Description: Hershey, PA : Business Science Reference, [2017]
Identifiers: LCCN 2016054820| ISBN 9781522521488 (hardcover) | ISBN 9781522521495 (ebook)
Subjects: LCSH: Management--Statistical methods. | Decision making--Statistical methods. | Big data. | Service industries--Data processing.
Classification: LCC HD30.215 .A67 2017 | DDC 658/.0557--dc23 LC record available at https://lccn.loc.gov/2016054820

This book is published in the IGI Global book series Advances in Business Information Systems and Analytics (ABISA) (ISSN: 2327-3275; eISSN: 2327-3283)

British Cataloguing in Publication Data
A Cataloguing in Publication record for this book is available from the British Library.

All work contributed to this book is new, previously-unpublished material. The views expressed in this book are those of the authors, but not necessarily of the publisher.

For electronic access to this publication, please contact: eresources@igi-global.com.

Advances in Business Information Systems and Analytics (ABISA) Book Series

Madjid Tavana
La Salle University, USA

ISSN:2327-3275
EISSN:2327-3283

Mission

The successful development and management of information systems and business analytics is crucial to the success of an organization. New technological developments and methods for data analysis have allowed organizations to not only improve their processes and allow for greater productivity, but have also provided businesses with a venue through which to cut costs, plan for the future, and maintain competitive advantage in the information age.

The **Advances in Business Information Systems and Analytics (ABISA) Book Series** aims to present diverse and timely research in the development, deployment, and management of business information systems and business analytics for continued organizational development and improved business value.

Coverage

- Business Information Security
- Legal information systems
- Data Strategy
- Strategic Information Systems
- Performance Metrics
- Information Logistics
- Big Data
- Data Analytics
- Statistics
- Management information systems

IGI Global is currently accepting manuscripts for publication within this series. To submit a proposal for a volume in this series, please contact our Acquisition Editors at Acquisitions@igi-global.com or visit: http://www.igi-global.com/publish/.

The Advances in Business Information Systems and Analytics (ABISA) Book Series (ISSN 2327-3275) is published by IGI Global, 701 E. Chocolate Avenue, Hershey, PA 17033-1240, USA, www.igi-global.com. This series is composed of titles available for purchase individually; each title is edited to be contextually exclusive from any other title within the series. For pricing and ordering information please visit http://www.igi-global.com/book-series/advances-business-information-systems-analytics/37155. Postmaster: Send all address changes to above address.

Titles in this Series

For a list of additional titles in this series, please visit: www.igi-global.com

Business Analytics and Cyber Security Management in Organizations
Rajagopal (EGADE Business School, Tecnologico de Monterrey, Mexico City, Mexico & Boston University, USA) and Ramesh Behl (International Management Institute, Bhubaneswar, India)
Business Science Reference • copyright 2017 • 346pp • H/C (ISBN: 9781522509028) • US $215.00 (our price)

Handbook of Research on Intelligent Techniques and Modeling Applications in Marketing Analytics
Anil Kumar (BML Munjal University, India) Manoj Kumar Dash (ABV-Indian Institute of Information Technology and Management, India) Shrawan Kumar Trivedi (BML Munjal University, India) and Tapan Kumar Panda (BML Munjal University, India)
Business Science Reference • copyright 2017 • 428pp • H/C (ISBN: 9781522509974) • US $275.00 (our price)

Applied Big Data Analytics in Operations Management
Manish Kumar (Indian Institute of Information Technology, Allahabad, India)
Business Science Reference • copyright 2017 • 251pp • H/C (ISBN: 9781522508861) • US $160.00 (our price)

Eye-Tracking Technology Applications in Educational Research
Christopher Was (Kent State University, USA) Frank Sansosti (Kent State University, USA) and Bradley Morris (Kent State University, USA)
Information Science Reference • copyright 2017 • 370pp • H/C (ISBN: 9781522510055) • US $205.00 (our price)

Strategic IT Governance and Alignment in Business Settings
Steven De Haes (Antwerp Management School, University of Antwerp, Belgium) and Wim Van Grembergen (Antwerp Management School, University of Antwerp, Belgium)
Business Science Reference • copyright 2017 • 298pp • H/C (ISBN: 9781522508618) • US $195.00 (our price)

Organizational Productivity and Performance Measurements Using Predictive Modeling and Analytics
Madjid Tavana (La Salle University, USA) Kathryn Szabat (La Salle University, USA) and Kartikeya Puranam (La Salle University, USA)
Business Science Reference • copyright 2017 • 400pp • H/C (ISBN: 9781522506546) • US $205.00 (our price)

Data Envelopment Analysis and Effective Performance Assessment
Farhad Hossein Zadeh Lotfi (Islamic Azad University, Iran) Seyed Esmaeil Najafi (Islamic Azad University, Iran) and Hamed Nozari (Islamic Azad University, Iran)
Business Science Reference • copyright 2017 • 365pp • H/C (ISBN: 9781522505969) • US $160.00 (our price)

IGI GLOBAL
DISSEMINATOR OF KNOWLEDGE
www.igi-global.com

701 E. Chocolate Ave., Hershey, PA 17033
Order online at www.igi-global.com or call 717-533-8845 x100
To place a standing order for titles released in this series, contact: cust@igi-global.com
Mon-Fri 8:00 am - 5:00 pm (est) or fax 24 hours a day 717-533-8661

Editorial Advisory Board

Table of Contents

Detailed Table of Contents

In the last couple of decades, clustering has become a very crucial research problem in the data mining research community. Clustering refers to the partitioning of data objects such as records and documents into groups or clusters of similar characteristics. Clustering is unsupervised learning, because of unsupervised nature there is no unique solution for all problems. Most of the time complex data sets require explanation in multiple clustering sets. All the Traditional clustering approaches generate single clustering. There is more than one pattern in a dataset; each of patterns can be interesting in from different perspectives. Alternative clustering intends to find all unlike groupings of the data set such that each grouping has high quality and distinct from each other. This chapter gives you an overall view of alternative clustering; it's various approaches, related work, comparing with various confusing related terms like subspace, multi-view, and ensemble clustering, applications, issues, and challenges.

In the study, The Nomenclature of Territorial Units for Statistics (NUTS) Level 1 regions of Turkey are evaluated with MULTIMOORA Method according to banking sector using hypothetical data which are adapted from real world data. There are 12 regions as alternatives which are assessed with 6 objectives. Calculations are made by using MS Excel which is powerful spreadsheet software. This application is an example how multi criteria decision making methods can use when a manager making decision. Results are given as lists of regions ranking and commented. By this way, it is shown that how the multi criteria decision making methods can help to decision makers.

Big Data is transforming industries such as healthcare, financial services and banking, insurance, pharmacy, and telecommunication. Big Data concerns datasets that are not only big, but also high in variety and velocity, which makes them difficult to manage applying traditional tools and techniques. Big Data causes multitude benefits and advantages for industries such as marketing and selling, fraud detection, competitive advantage, risk reduction, and finally decision making and policy making. Due to the rapid growth of such data, methodologies and conceptual architectures need to be studied and provided in order to handle and extract value and knowledge from these data. The purpose of this chapter is studying Big Data benefits, characteristics, methodologies, and conceptual architectures in five different industries. Finally, according to the studies, a comprehensive methodology and architecture are proposed which might be applicable in service sector and one of the useful outcomes can be public policies.

The technology enabled service industry is emerging as the most dynamic sectors in world's economy. Various service sector industries such as financial services, banking solutions, telecommunication, investment management, etc. completely rely on using large scale software for their smooth operations. Any malwares or bugs in these software is an issue of big concern and can have serious financial consequences. This chapter addresses the problem of bug handling in service sector software. Predictive analysis is a helpful technique for keeping software systems error free. Existing research in bug handling focus on various predictive analysis techniques such as data mining, machine learning, information retrieval, optimisation, etc. for bug resolving. This chapter provides a detailed analysis of bug handling in large service sector software. The main emphasis of this chapter is to discuss research involved in applying predictive analysis for bug handling. The chapter also presents some possible future research directions in bug resolving using mathematical optimisation techniques.

Due to big data availability in markets recently, processing and making predictions with data have been becoming more difficult, and this difficulty has been affecting management decisions. As a result, competitiveness for companies are related to analyze and utilize big data in order to achieve company targets. Transforming big data into business advantage has become a vital management tool across all industries. There are many data mining techniques that are being applied to plenty of problems. One of the frequently utilized data mining technique is clustering method. Clustering techniques aim to group a set of objects in clusters that more similar objects are in the same cluster. Main utilization aim of clustering techniques is segmenting or clustering or grouping objects. Clustering techniques and their utilization within service sector by aim of clustering technique and their methodologies are presented. Energy, social media and bank sectors are found that the mostly user of clustering techniques within service sector for segmenting customers based on searched papers.

techniques. Recommendation system helps people to tackle the choice overload problem and help to select the efficient one. Even though there is lots of work have been done in the recommendation system, still there is a problem in handling various types of data and basically to handle a large amount of data. The main aim of the recommendation system is to provide the best opinion from the available large amount of data. The present chapter describes an introduction to recommender systems, its functions, types, techniques, applications, collaborative filtering, content-based filtering and evaluation of performance.

The aim of this chapter is to research and present strengths and limitations of social media analytics tools used in the financial sector. Emphasis is on the business point of view that sees the social media analytics as a collection of tools that transform semi-structured and unstructured social data into noteworthy business insight. There are two main aspects of social media analytics: the technology aspect which covers identifying, extracting, and analyzing social media data using sophisticated tools and techniques; and the business aspect which interprets the data findings and aligns them with business goals. Namely, it is simply not enough to have a social media analytics tool; the tool should be strategically aligned to support existing business goals. The chapter offers a framework for easier adoption and implementation of these tools in the financial sector.

Credit scoring is the most important and critical component conducted by the credit providers to decide whether to grant a loan to the applicant or not. Therefore credit scoring models are generally used to predict the potentiality of the loan applicant. A proper evaluation of the credit can help the service provider to determine whether to grant or to reject the credit. The objective of the study is to predict banking credit scoring assessment using a data mining technique i.e. Functional Link Artificial Neural Network (FLANN) classifier. Credit approval datasets: Australian credit and German credit have been used to do this analysis. The output of the study shows that the proposed model used for classification works better on credit dataset. Secondly, we have applied our proposed model on the two credit approval dataset to check the performance of the model for the classification accuracy. A proper evaluation of the credit using the proposed FLANN approach can help the service provider to accurately and quickly ascertain whether to grant credit or to reject.

Forecasting is the one of the important part of decision making process. It helps managers to identify short term and long term future trends in the business activities. It may help in forecasting demand in retail store, predicting customer traffic at the petrol pump, calculation of probable population in upcoming years etc. There are plenty of studies published on forecasting techniques which are just introductory or highly mathematical and lacks in providing managerial perspective of solving business problems to the students. This chapter elucidates various forecasting techniques and its application in the field of management. In addition, various examples of real life problems are solved and analyzed with multiple forecasting techniques. Through this chapter students will have a clear understanding of the various nuances of different forecasting models in one single data set. Students will be able to identify future trend and seasonality in real life data set and evaluate more appropriate forecasting technique for the decision-making process.

Preface

The complete work of this book is divided into fourteen chapters. The brief description of each chapter is as follows:

In Chapter, 1 titled "Alternative Clustering", the authors Navlani and Gupta describe that in the last couple of decades, clustering becomes very crucial research problem in data mining research community. Clustering refers to the partitioning of data objects such as records and documents into groups or clusters of similar characteristics. Clustering is unsupervised learning, because of unsupervised nature there is no unique solution for all problems. Most of the time complex data sets require explanation in multiple clustering sets. All the Traditional clustering approaches generate single clustering. There is more than one pattern in a dataset; each of patterns can be interesting in from different perspectives. Alternative clustering intends to find all unlike groupings of the data set such that each grouping has high quality and distinct from each other. This chapter gives you an overall view of alternative clustering; it's various approaches, related work, comparing with various confusing related terms like subspace, multi-view, and ensemble clustering, applications, issues, and challenges.

Chapter 2 is named "An Evaluation of Turkey's NUTS Level 1 Regions According to Banking Sector With MULTIMOORA Method". In this chapter, the author Onur önay evaluated the Nomenclature of Territorial Units for Statistics (NUTS) Level 1 regions of Turkey. For evaluation, MULTIMOORA Method has been used on banking sector data. There are 12 regions as alternatives which are assessed with 6 objectives. Calculations are made by using MS Excel which is powerful spreadsheet software. This application is an example how multi criteria decision making methods can use when a manager making decision. Results are given as lists of regions ranking and commented. By this way, it is shown that how the multi criteria decision making methods can help to decision makers.

In Chapter 3, titled "Analytics in Public Policy Related to Service Sector", the author, Maryam Ebrahimi, describes that recently, Big Data is transforming industries like healthcare, financial services and banking, insurance, pharmacy, and telecommunication. Big Data concerns datasets that are not only big, but also high in variety and velocity, which makes them difficult to manage by applying traditional tools and techniques. Big Data causes multitude benefits and advantages for industries such as marketing and selling, fraud detection, competitive advantage, risk reduction, and finally decision making and policy making. Due to the huge increase in data, there is a need to manage and take advantage of the hidden value of these data by studying and providing methodologies and conceptual architectures. The purpose of this chapter is studying Big Data benefits, characteristics, methodologies, and conceptual architectures in five different industries. Finally, according to the studies, a comprehensive methodology and architecture are proposed which might be applicable in service sector and one of the useful outcomes can be public policies

Chapter 4 is named "Bug Handling in Service Sector Software". In this chapter, the authors Goyal and Sardana explain how the technology enabled service industry is emerging as the most dynamic sectors in world's economy. Various service sector industries such as financial services, banking solutions, telecommunication, investment management, etc. completely rely on using large scale software for their smooth operations. Any malwares or bugs in these software is an issue of big concern and can have serious financial consequences. This chapter addresses the problem of bug handling in service sector software. Predictive analysis is a helpful technique for keeping software systems error free. Existing research in bug handling focus on various predictive analysis techniques such as data mining, machine learning, information retrieval, optimisation, etc. for bug resolving. This chapter provides a detailed analysis of bug handling in large service sector software. The main emphasis of this chapter is to discuss research involved in applying predictive analysis for bug handling. The chapter also presents some possible future research directions in bug resolving using mathematical optimisation techniques.

In Chapter 5, "Clustering Techniques Within Service Sector", İbrahim Yazici, Ömer Faruk Beyca and Selim Zaim from İstanbul Technical University determine that due to big data availability in markets recently, processing and making predictions with data have been becoming more difficult, and, this difficulty has been affecting management decisions. As a result, competitiveness for companies are related to analyze and utilize big data in order to achieve company targets. Transforming big data into business advantage has become a vital management tool across all industries. There are many data mining techniques that are being applied to plenty of problems. One of the frequently utilized data mining technique is clustering method. Clustering techniques aim to group a set of objects in clusters that more similar objects are in the same cluster. Main utilization aim of clustering techniques is segmenting or clustering or grouping objects. Clustering techniques and their utilization within service sector by aim of clustering technique and their methodologies are presented. Energy, social media and bank sectors are found that the mostly user of clustering techniques within service sector for segmenting customers based on searched papers.

In Chapter 6, "Descriptive Analytics", A. Sheik Abdullah, S. Selvakumar, and Ramya C explain that how data analytics has becoming one of the challenging platforms across various domains such as telecom, health care, social media and so on. The challenging and most promising task in analytics is the understanding of various patterns in the data. The mechanism of data retrieval and analysis seems to be the promising one in which the algorithms, techniques, way of processing data are in need with the ability to target upon large volumes of data. There are various types of analytical methods such as predictive analytics, descriptive analytics, text analytics, social media analytics and survival analytics. This chapter mainly focuses towards the mechanism of descriptive analytics its types, algorithms and applications. There are various forms of tools and techniques such as association rule mining, sequence rule mining, and data categorization such as hierarchical and non-hierarchical clustering methods with its variants.

In Chapter 7, "Personalized Content Recommendation Engine for Web Publishing Services Using Text Mining and Predictive Analytics", the authors Başar Öztayşi, Ahmet Tezcan Tekin, Cansu Özdikicioğlu and Kerim Caner Tümkaya describe that recommendation Systems have become very important especially for internet based business such as e-commerce and web publishing. While Content based filtering and collaborative filtering are most commonly used groups in recommendation systems there are still researches for new approaches. In this study, a personalized recommendation system based on text mining and predictive analytics is proposed for a real world web publishing company. The approach given in this chapter first preprocesses existing web contents, integrate the structured data with history of a specific user and create an extended TDM for the user. Then this data is used for prediction of the users' interest in new content. In order to reach that point, SVM, K-NN and Naïve Bayesian methods are used. Finally, the best performing method is used for determining the interest level of the user in a new content. Based on the forecasted interest levels the system recommends among the alternatives.

In Chapter 8, "Predictive Analysis of Emotions for Improving Customer Services", Jain and Kumar explain how human Emotions plays a significant role in everyday communication. Emotions are formed by the combination of indicators such as relative actions, facial expressions, and gestures and reactions. Emotions are also found in written texts like in social media, chats, customer reviews. By getting inspired by works done in the domain of sentiment analysis and opinion mining, this chapter explores advances to automatic detection of emotions in text and its application in Improving Customer Services. This chapter presents a framework for automatic detection of emotions in customer reviews based on different emotions theories. These theories deal with the fields of linguistics and psychology. This framework uses advanced Machine learning (ML) techniques with Natural Language Processing (NLP) methods for better understanding of emotion detection and recognition in customer reviews. The text under study comprises data collected from leading Indian e-commerce portals like Flipkart, Snapdeal and Amazon, which contains text rich in emotions. The advantages and application based emotion detection framework has been incorporated with suitable examples.

In Chapter 9, "Predictive Modelling and Mind-Set Segments Underlying Health Plans", Gillie Gabay, Colman, Steven Onufrey and Stephen D. Rappaport discuss that health systems are facing an austerity affecting the quality and quantity of health services delivery around the world. This chapter defines predictive analytics in health, discusses how predictive analytics may contribute to health promotion and demonstrates the identification of communication elements that can be productively used by health maintenance organizations to shape health plans in accordance to mind-sets of patients. Although predictive analytics reduces costs and shifts the focus of health systems from treating the sick to preventive medicine, the focus on the 'mind' of the person, and the possibilities of personalization based upon the way a person thinks and responds to communication elements, has not been investigated. This chapter investigates how to achieve personalization in healthcare through predictive analytics.

Chapter 10 is titled "Prioritizing and Analyzing Demand Chain Management (DCM) Processes in Indian Retailing Using AHP". In this chapter the authors Deshmukh and Ashutosh Mohan talk that the extant body of literature on demand chain management (DCM) is predominantly conceptual and unequivocal on how to implement it in real business setting. Keeping the research gap into account, the study aims to identify and prioritize the DCM processes or variables in the context of Indian retailing. The research follows an inductive ontology, objectivist epistemology and positivist paradigm. The data were collected using survey method using a structured questionnaire with Saaty (1980) scale and semi-structured interview of experts from industry as well as academic. The method employed for analyzing the collected data was analytical hierarchy process or AHP. The results of the study have interesting implications for the industry vis-à-vis literature. Some quick measures revealed that the processes which are critical to implementation of DCM in retail context, in the order of importance, comprises supplier relationship management, customer relationship management assortment planning, top-management commitment and support, marketing orientation, information management, supply chain leagility, customer service management, category management, purchasing management, inventory management, and category tactics.

Chapter 11 is named "Recommender System". In this chapter, the authors Navlani and Dadhich discuss that with the increase in user choices and rapid change in user preferences, various methods required to capture such increasing choices and changing preferences. Online systems require quick adaptability. Another issue is increasing in computational time due to the expansion in a number of users and products, computation time increases considerably. Thus system needs parallel computing platform to run newer designed recommender system techniques. Recommendation system helps people to tackle the choice overload problem and help to select the efficient one. Even though there is lots of work have been done in the recommendation system, still there is a problem in handling various types of data and basically to handle a large amount of data. The main aim of the recommendation system is to provide the best opinion from the available large amount of data. The present chapter describes an introduction to recommender systems, its functions, types, techniques, applications, collaborative based and content-based recommender system and evaluation of performance.

Chapter 12 is named "Strengths and Limitations of Social Media Analytics Tools". In this chapter, Dražena Gašpar and Mirela Mabić talk about research and present strengths and limitations of social media analytics tools used in the financial sector. Emphasis is on the business point of view that sees the social media analytics as a collection of tools that transform semi-structured and unstructured social data into noteworthy business insight. There are two main aspects of social media analytics: the technology aspect which covers identifying, extracting, and analyzing social media data using sophisticated tools and techniques; and the business aspect which interprets the data findings and aligns them with business goals. Namely, it is simply not enough to have a social media analytics tool; the tool should be strategically aligned to support existing business goals. The chapter offers a framework for easier adoption and implementation of these tools in the financial sector.

In Chapter 13, "Using Functional Link Artificial Neural Network (FLANN) for Bank Credit Risk Assessment", the authors, Jena, Dwivedy, and Kumar, discuss about credit scoring is the most important and critical component conducted by the credit providers to decide whether to grant loan to the applicant or not. Therefore credit scoring models are generally used to predict the potentiality of the loan applicant. A proper evaluation of the credit can helps the service provider to determine whether to grant or to reject the credit. The objective of the study is to predict banking credit scoring assessment using a data mining technique i.e. Functional Link Artificial Neural Network (FLANN) classifier. Credit approval datasets: Australian credit and German credit have been used to do this analysis. The output of the study shows that the proposed model used for classification works better on credit dataset. Secondly, we have applied our proposed model on the two credit approval dataset to check the performance of the model for the classification accuracy

Chapter 14 is named "Vehicular Traffic Forecasting in Filling Station". In this chapter, the authors Pandey and Sengupta describe that Forecasting is the one of the important part of decision making process. It helps managers to identify short term and long term future trends in the business activities. It may help in forecasting demand in retail store, predicting customer traffic at the petrol pump, calculation of probable population in upcoming years etc. There are plenty of studies published on forecasting techniques which are just introductory or highly mathematical and lacks in providing managerial perspective of solving business problems to the students. This chapter elucidates various forecasting techniques and its application in the field of management. In addition, various example of real life problems are solved and analyzed with multiple forecasting techniques. Through this chapter students will have a clear understanding of the various nuances of different forecasting models in one single data set. Students will be able to identify future trend and seasonality in real life data set and evaluate more appropriate forecasting technique for the decision-making process.

Acknowledgment

The editors would like to acknowledge the help of all the people involved in this project and, more specifically, to the authors and reviewers that took part in the review process. Without their support, this book would not have become a reality.

We would like to thank each one of the authors for their contributions. The editors wish to acknowledge the valuable contributions of the reviewers regarding the improvement of quality, coherence, and content presentation of chapters. Most of the authors also served as referees; we highly appreciate their double task.

We are grateful to all members of IGI publishing house for their assistance and timely motivation in producing this volume.

We hope the readers will share our excitement with this important scientific contribution the body of knowledge about various applications of predictive analytics within the service sector.

Anil Kumar
BML Munjal University, India

Manoj Kumar Dash
ABV-Indian Institute of Information Technology and Management, India

Rajendra Sahu
ABV-Indian Institute of Information Technology and Management, India

Chapter 1
Alternative Clustering

Avinash Navlani
Devi Ahilya Vishwavidyalaya, India

V. B. Gupta
Devi Ahilya Vishwavidyalaya, India

ABSTRACT

In the last couple of decades, clustering has become a very crucial research problem in the data mining research community. Clustering refers to the partitioning of data objects such as records and documents into groups or clusters of similar characteristics. Clustering is unsupervised learning, because of unsupervised nature there is no unique solution for all problems. Most of the time complex data sets require explanation in multiple clustering sets. All the Traditional clustering approaches generate single clustering. There is more than one pattern in a dataset; each of patterns can be interesting in from different perspectives. Alternative clustering intends to find all unlike groupings of the data set such that each grouping has high quality and distinct from each other. This chapter gives you an overall view of alternative clustering; it's various approaches, related work, comparing with various confusing related terms like subspace, multi-view, and ensemble clustering, applications, issues, and challenges.

INTRODUCTION

Knowledge discovery is a non-trivial process of identifying legitimate, new, practical usable and apprehensible patterns and trends in data (Fayyad, Piatetsky-Shapiro, & Smyth, 1996). Clustering is the process of bunching a set of data objects into various bunches or groups or clusters in such a manner that objects inside the cluster are very similar and objects in cluster clusters different from other clusters. Clustering is an unsupervised learning knowledge discovery approach, which is applicable in various fields such as information retrieval, bioinformatics, Information security, business analytics, and environment science (Han, Kamber, & Pei, 2011). Due to unsupervised nature clustering methods are not able to achieve consistency in its results. Therefore, some researchers have proposed the use of prior domain knowledge and to direct user towards the desired consistent results. Such semi-supervised clustering algorithms named as Constrained Clustering. Traditional clustering methods create single good clustering result. Various real datasets are high dimensional in nature and require multiple patterns in

DOI: 10.4018/978-1-5225-2148-8.ch001

the dataset, so we are interested in finding clustering from different perspectives. Alternative clustering is a variant of constrained clustering aims to find all the different groups from various perspectives of high cohesion and highly distinguish from other groups (Saha & Mitra, 2014). Most of the times users are not confident enough discover what they are searching, yet may be perfectly able to convey what they are not looking for (Gondek & Hofmann, Non-redundant clustering with conditional ensembles, 2005). Such uninterested clustering can term as negative clusterings. The main concern of alternative cluster is to generate different views of complex data sets.

This chapter is structured as follows. First, we will discuss what Alternative Clustering is. Next section explains classification of alternative clustering techniques after this; we will see related work of alternative clustering. Next part contains the difference among subspace clustering, Multiview, ensemble, constrained and alternative clustering and at last, we will see its applications, issues, and challenges.

ALTERNATIVE CLUSTERING

Clustering is a common unsupervised exploratory pattern recognition approach that partitions data objects into n regions$\{C_1,C_2,...,C_n\}$ on the basis of similarity measure (Jain & Dubes, 1988). Clustering algorithms attempt to generate a suitable bunching of the input data objects. Often you may find the clustering, which may not particularly useful and actionable and wishes to find an alternative of it. Look at a clustering problem of loan request applications to find out worse loan request applications but the clustering cannot draw a line between acceptable and non-acceptable loan request applications. We can discover various optimum alternative clusterings with good amount of accuracy. Because of high dimensional data space searching alternative clusterings is quite obvious (Davidson & Qi, 2008).

Generally, clustering algorithms are designed on the idea of grouping similar data points together and form clusters of similar features. Every criterion has its own merits and demerits, and given that, different clusterings are right for different intentions, so we cannot say any clustering is optimum for all applications (Hartigan, 1985). Traditional clustering methods present a single clustering or a single view of the dataset. In hard complicated applications, various interesting views of bunching data points can lie

Figure 1. Graphical representation of clusters

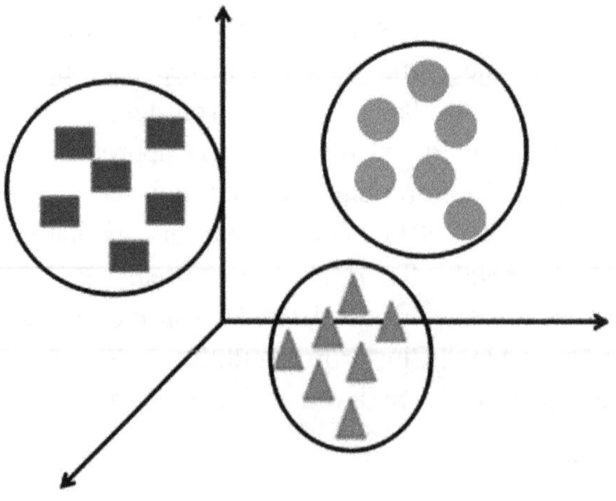

in the dataset. Consequently, user asks for alternative descriptions of data to get various views. There are various methods evolved for generating the alternative cluster sets (Truong & Battiti, 2012). Alternative clustering is a variant of constrained clustering. Its main objective is to find all the possible groups from various perspectives of quality within the cluster and isolation with other groups (Saha & Mitra, 2014).

CLASSIFICATION OF ALTERNATIVE CLUSTERING

According to Saha and Mitra (Saha & Mitra, 2014), alternative clustering can be classified in two types: objective function oriented approach and data transformation oriented approach. In objective function oriented approach, clustering is performed using objective function and in data transformation oriented approach, clustering is performed by transforming the data into alternate projections. According to Troung and Battiti (Truong & Battiti, 2012), alternative clustering can be classified in two basic groups unsupervised and supervised alternative clustering. Unsupervised approach is a set of high quality clustering is automatically generated by algorithm. In supervised approach, users already aware of undesired or negative clustering, and ask for more alternative clustering.

RELATED WORK

First algorithm for generating Alternative clustering had proposed by Gondek and Hofmann (Gondek & Hofmann, Conditional information bottleneck clustering, 2003). This supervised algorithm is extension of information bottleneck framework known as conditional information bottleneck(CIB). They consid-

Figure 2. Graphical representation of alternative clusters

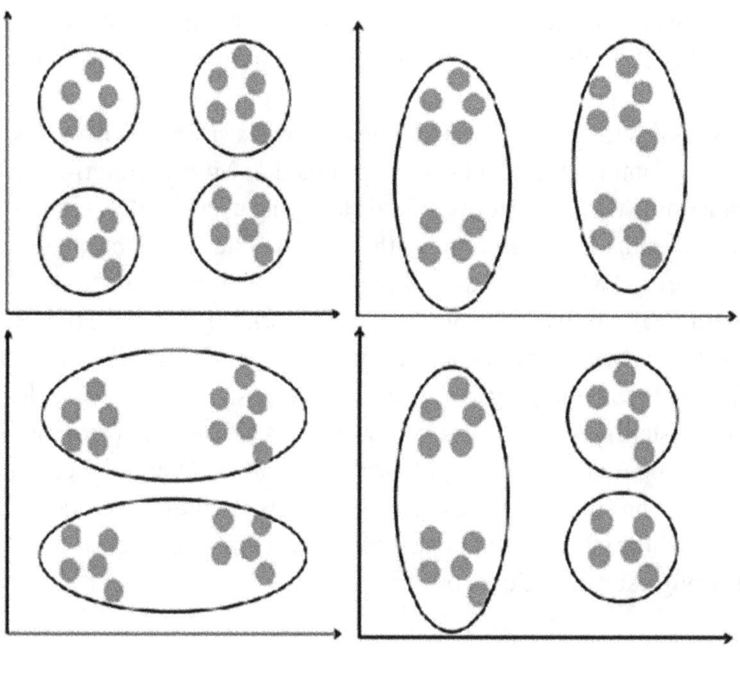

Figure 3. Classification of alternative clustering approaches

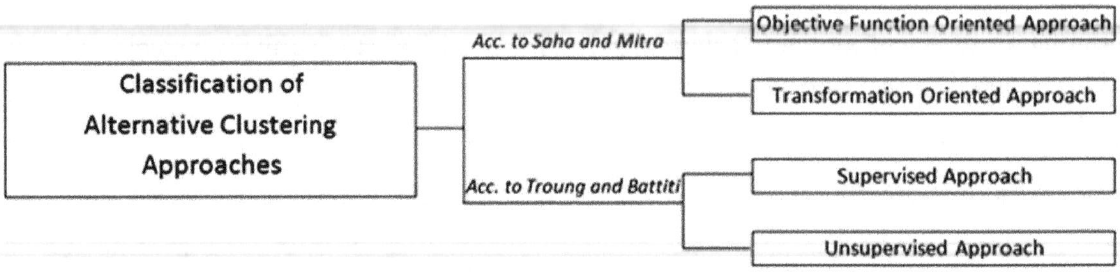

ered negative information to generate good quality cluster through maximizing the mutual information under given negative constraint. Their approach for generating non-redundant clustering is similar to data compression. Vinh and Epps (Vinh & Epps, 2010) proposed an information theoretic approach MinCEntropy++, which can accept a set of negative clustering and evaluate alternative clustering using havrda-charvat's α structural entropy. Dang and Bailey (Dang & Bailey, 2010) mainly focused on non-linear shape clusters and proposed a hierarchical information theoretic approach for finding alternative clustering quality by maximizing the mutual information between cluster labels and data, and distinctness by reducing the amount of information utilizing between different clusters. Bae and Bailey proposed COALA (Bae & Bailey, 2006), an agglomerative hierarchical clustering uses only cannot link constraints. Major drawback with COALA is as it doesn't utilize must link constraints. CIB requires the joint distribution between objects while COALA requires only similarity function between pairs of points. They also extended COALA for categorical data and proposed COALACat, which produce quite impressive results. Davidson and Qi (Davidson & Qi, 2008) proposed AFDT (Alternative Distance Function Transformation), an approach for finding alternative clustering with must-link and cannot-link constraints. These constraints transform the dataset into a different space and re-cluster the transformed data. Qi &Davidson (Qi & Davidson, 2009) proposed framework for finding alternative clusterings. This Framework uses constrained optimization problem to solve clustering problem (COP). COP decreases the Kullback-Leibler divergence between the probability distribution of the original and transformed data set. Advantage of this approach is general purpose, easy to implement and control on trade-off between alternatives and quality. Handl and Knowles (Handl & Knowles, 2007) proposed an evolutionary approach for multi-objective clustering named as MOCK (multi-objective clustering with automatic k-determination). MOCK performs initial clustering using a MOEA to optimize two clustering objectives and find no dominating clusterings with respective trade-offs between two objectives. After performing initial clustering MOCK tries to select appropriate model using trade-off curve. Truong and Battiti (Truong & Battiti, 2012) proposed multi-objective algorithm COGNAC (Cluster-Oriented GeNetic algorithm for Alternative Clusterings), which simultaneously optimizes the objectives and find Pareto solutions. COGNAC carries out merging at the cluster level instead of the object level. It also generates a series of alternative clustering set, where every clustering is unlike from previous ones. Saha and Mitra (Saha & Mitra, 2014) proposed a clustering algorithm *VLGAAC* (VariableLength Genetic Algorithm based Alternative Clustering) that optimizes quality (Davies Bouldin index) and distinctness (Jaccard and Rand index) along with finding optimal number of clusters. This algorithm generates diverse and variable length clustering using genetic algorithm.

DIFFERENCE AMONG SUBSPACE CLUSTERING, MULTIVIEW, ENSEMBLE AND ALTERNATIVE CLUSTERING

The primary objective of clustering is to discover a set of clusters in such a way that items should similar within the group while dissimilar from different groups. Recently, various improved clustering techniques were introduced, which most of the time confused with alternative clustering. Each method has been designed with different motivations still there are some similarities in them. So far in this chapter we have discussed alternative clustering now in this section we will discuss difference among ensemble clustering, multi-view clustering, and subspace clustering.

Subspace Clustering

In subspace clustering, clusters are generated using similar vectors from one of the subspace of the dataset. It is not necessary that subspaces are same for each cluster. Subspace clustering discovers multiple subspaces that represent set of points of high-dimensional space. Subspace clustering is nonstandard clustering problem in which objects are not close to each other according to previous notion of metric but rather belong to the same lower dimensional structure. Subspace clustering can be consider as a generalise form of Principle Component Analysis in which set of points represented as union of subspaces. Subspace clustering is more robust to noise, missing values, and outliers. Subspace clustering naturally fits into various applications such as recognition and classification of diseases, text classification, image and music analysis, security and privacy (Soltanolkotabi, Elhamifar, & Candès, 2014). In health informatics, patients of bird flu, have features such as patient's information, disease symptoms, environmental conditions, and family background. Now, it is difficult to discover cluster in the entire data space. Instead, we may discover clusters of same features from lower-dimensional subspace such as patients with same symptoms such as high fever, cough, and aged between 3 and 14 (Han, Kamber, & Pei, 2011).

Multi-View Clustering

Some of the real-world application domains are comprised of various representations, aspects, and views. For example, online articles can be grouped on the basis of keywords, different languages, hyperlinks, research topics, and area of concerns. Multiview clustering looks for clusterings in different subspaces of a data space. This type of approach can be considered as a specialize case of alternative clustering or subspace clustering (Kriegel & Zimek, 2010). Such multiple aspects provide compatible and complementary information. It becomes more important to integrate them together to get better results instead of depending on a single view.

Ensemble Clustering

Predictive algorithms bear from various restrictions like computational variance, statistical variance, bias, scalability, and robustness. To improve performance of supervised learning, various predicting algorithms mixed together to an ensemble method for better performance than other available base predictors or classifiers (Kriegel & Zimek, 2010). Ensemble clustering methods can improve the accuracy, scalability, robustness, diversity and exploit the complementary nature of clustering algorithms.

Figure 4. Ensemble clustering architecture

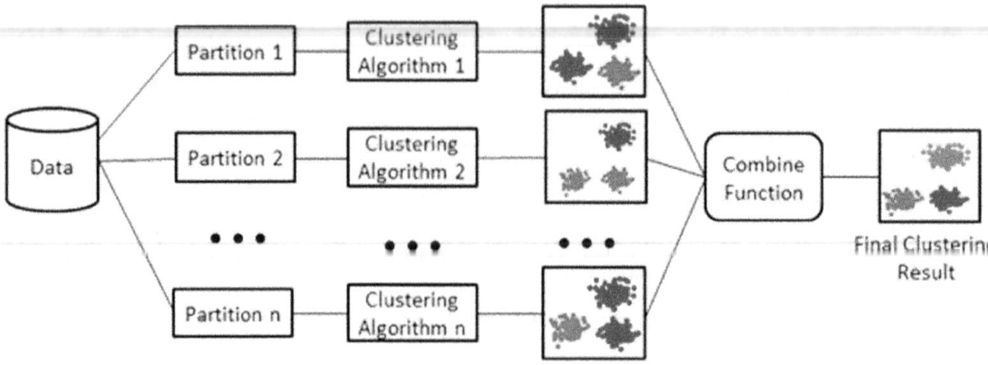

Ensemble methods used to merge both different dataset and various clustering algorithms. Ensemble methods can be utilized as in joining heterogeneous data in a distributed environment (Strehl & Ghosh, 2002). There are two basic challenges in ensemble methods: a) How to generate ensemble clustering? b) How to combine multiple partitions? Answer to the first question is clustering can be produced by partitioning method such as K-means, hierarchical clustering method such as agglomerative or divisive, fuzzy C-means, or spectral clustering. According to (Vega-Pons & Ruiz-Shulcloper, 2011), ensemble methods algorithms can be classified into two categories: Median partition based and Object co-occurrence based methods.

Constrained Clustering

Constrained Clustering concerns with three basic aspects of an object as records of clusters, cluster as a set of objects, and the closeness between objects. In this way, we can apply constraints on records, clusters and closeness metrics. Constraints on records specify how a set of records can group together. Constraints on the records can be of two sorts, Must-link constraints and Cannot-link constraints. In the first type, two objects x and y should be a group in one cluster, such type of constraints termed as must-link constraints. In the second type, two objects x and y should belong to the different group. Constraints on clusters specify the requirement of clusters. For example, k-mean c algorithm requires number of clusters as input, upper limit on number of records in a cluster, and shape of the cluster. Constraints on closeness metrics: various closeness measures like Manhattan and Euclidean metrics assess the closeness between objects. Constraints can also be classified into hard constraints and soft constrained. Hard constraints clustering can be forcefully applied in constraints clustering process. Soft constraints clustering can be viewed as an optimization problem (Han, Kamber, & Pei, 2011).

APPLICATIONS

In this chapter, we have discussed alternative clustering, its types and comparison with other similar clustering techniques. Alternative clustering is a relatively new discipline with broad and diverse applications. In this section, we look into several application domains.

Financial Analysis

Cluster analysis can be utilized for making balanced portfolios. On the basis return, volatility, and other industry and market characteristics clusters of securities generated. In target marketing, similar traits customer groups identified through alternative clustering, which helps in relate new customer with available groups. Alternative clustering can help us to detect or investigate financial crimes such as credit card fraud, insurance fraud, corporate fraud and money laundering.

Social Networks Analysis

In last few years, Social networks have gained popularity with the advent of web sites such as Facebook, Twitter, LinkedIn, and YouTube etc. such website connecting friends and relatives, students, and researchers on single platform where they can discuss their common interests. Large number of users is members in these networks and these numbers are growing day by day. These networks provide huge rich information of user's personal interest. Finding clusters or communities with common interest and dense friendship patterns. Such communities in networks help in target marketing based on similar clusters. According to existing clustering principle clusters can't overlap. Alternative clustering can overcome this problem by generating different patterns of clusters known as clusterings and also identify most optimum and important set of clustering.

Information Retrieval

World Wide Web has millions of documents, news articles, and web pages from different categories. In the response to query, the Search engine generates thousands of web pages link. Clustering can help us to create sets of similar queries into a number of clusters but some queries can be overlap in with different clusters in such case simple clustering algorithm not able to distinguish the queries. In such circumstances alternative clustering may help via generating different-different clusterings. Such clusterings can be used to improving searching algorithm.

Figure 5. Alternative clustering applications

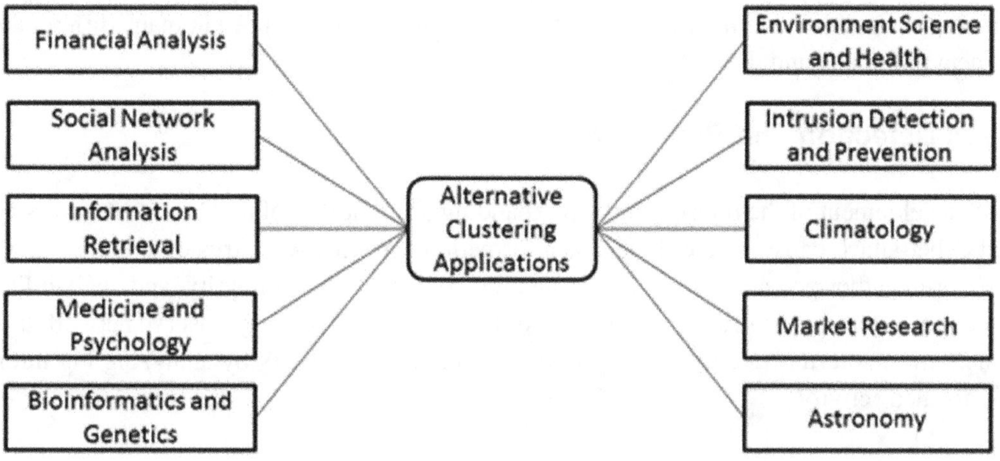

Medicine and Psychology

In medicine science, clustering can help in identification of disease hot-spots and its progress over the years and its significant year-to-year variation. Clustering results are used to study find classifying patients and similarity between various diseases. Medical image segmentation requires optimum alternative clustering of images and explains "How medical images are correlated?

Mind sickness is more slippery than other diseases of the body. Clustering can be used to identify types of depression. Psychiatrists are much interest in refine current diagnostic categories of datasets and want more interesting views of datasets. Alternative clustering finds multiple interesting patterns of patients, which can meet demand of psychiatrists and help them in prediction of depression, attempt suicide using features such as gender, age, previous suicide attempts, severe depression, impulsiveness, drug addiction and other demographic characteristics (Farmer, McGuffinb, & Spitznagelc, 1983).

Bioinformatics and Genetics

Statistics and Data mining played most crucial role in analysis of gene expression, protein sequence, protein structure prediction, and genome annotation. Proteins in similar cell forms communicate with each other. so the elements of uncharacterized proteins can be anticipated through correlation with other available known proteins (Lin, Cho, Hwang, Pei, & Zhang, 2007). Clustering can be used to organize sequences into homogenous and functionally similar groups of proteins which improve the speed, sensitivity, and readability of homology searches. Alternative clustering generates multiple patterns of protein sequences from datasets.

Clustering can solve problems such as class discovery, drug abuse treatment evaluation, and tumor tissue classification from different samples of gene expression (Yeung, Haynor, & Ruzzo, 2001) (Bandyopadhyay, Mukhopadhyay, & Maulik, 2007). Genetics have multiple coding functions and participate in different metabolic pathways. Alterative Clustering generates interesting groups of gene that have similar functions.

Environment Science and Health

Alternative clustering discovers underlying environmental factors and processes that may widely impact on health and environment. Alternative clustering can assess water and air pollutants and their effect on children, women, and premature birth rates. Alternative Clustering will present many different views of environment pollutants and there effects.

Intrusion Detection and Prevention

The rapid development of the Internet and the expanding accessibility of tools and techniques for intrusion and cyber-attack cause severe threat for information systems. An intrusion can be characterized as any set of unauthorized activities that threaten the confidentiality, Integrity, and availability. Intrusion detection systems and intrusion prevention systems both continuously observe network traffic and system activities. Alternative clusterings can identify malicious activity by analyzing log information about performed activity.

Market Research

Due to high cost of market test researcher can't conduct large survey in every city of a country. Researcher had to restrict to only a small number of cities. Alternative clustering can help them generate different clusters of cites on the basis of various features such as city size, per capita income and other attributes. Automobile manufacturer considers that purchasing a sports car is not entirely based on individual's age merely it is matter of lifestyle choice. Sports car purchasing clients have different lifestyle signature than those who do not buy sports cars. Market Researchers want to discover potential customers with a certain lifestyle which is more related with purchasing sports cars (Chakrapani, 2004). Alternative clustering helps researchers to create different clusters for focused marketing campaign.

Astronomy

Satellites generate a large amount of multivariate astronomical data of different objects of the universe. Astronomers want to identify distinct groups of these objects on the basis of some statistical criterion. Alternative clustering can provide the answer to questions such as how many different classes of astronomical objects and which astronomical objects are to be doled out to which classes? Are already obscure classes of objects present? Alternative Clustering classifies these astronomical objects from different views. Cluster set of galaxies is a helpful intermediary to detect the mass distribution of the universe.

Climatology

Alternative Clustering can analyse climate, ecological, and other environmental data sets and generate interesting clustering for environmental scientist. Stainbeach et. al (Steinbach, Tan, Kumar, Klooster, & Potter, 2003) has proposed an method for determining climate indices (climate indices are time series summarization of behaviour of region which measure the impact of the seas and environment on surface climate) using alternative clustering, In which each cluster represents regions with relatively uniform behaviour.

ISSUES AND CHALLENGES IN ALTERNATIVE CLUSTERING

With all the benefits of alternative clustering, there are some pitfalls as well that requires research attention. We briefly outline some of them.

Selection Performance Measures

Performance measures will help us in generating quality clusters. A number of measures for assess cluster quality are available. In general, these performance metrics can be grouped into two sets intrinsic and extrinsic metrics. Intrinsic metrics never uses class labels while extrinsic uses class labels or extra piece of supervised information for measuring performance.

Finding Optimal Clustering

In alternative clustering, number of clusterings is generated; now the question is *"which clustering/ clusterings is/are optimal one?"* For finding optimality of clustering we can design objective function, fitness functions, and cost function using various performance parameter. Designing such efficient function considering quality and distinctness factor is

Number of Alternative

Alternative clustering aims to find all different groupings of high quality and dissimilar from each other. But problem arises here *"How many alternatives are enough?"*. This question is very crucial because in unsupervised learning, every new clustering will have some new piece of information for domain experts.

Deciding Number of Clusters

Deciding the number of clusters in a dataset is a challenge in alternative clusterings generation. In alternative clustering, clusters can be fixed or variable for all clusterings. The number of clusters is an interesting and important statistic for variable size alternative clustering. Thus, it is worthy to figure out a number of groups or clusters for each alternative cluster set.

Alternative Clustering Visualization

Another challenge is visualization of alternative clustering because output of alternative clustering will have multiple clusterings. One way is to show all the clusterings on a grid of rows and column. In which cell of grid show single clustering. Another way is to use multi-dimensional view, in which each dimension represents single clustering.

Deploying Alternative Clustering on Large Datasets

A major question arises that *"How can we deploy the alternative clustering algorithm more on large datasets?"* Performing alternative clustering on large dataset needs high computational power to finish given task in less time. Sampling can be one of the efficient approaches to deal with large datasets. Another approach can be fit alternative clustering algorithm in distributed parallel computing environment such as Map-Reduce strategy. Map-Reduce can generate alternative cluster for large dataset in few seconds.

CONCLUSION

This chapter conducts a detailed introduction of Alternative Clustering. Conventional clustering methods results in one set of clusters. In high dimensional data set multiple patterns may exist, these patterns can be useful or cannot be useful, can be optimum and cannot be optimum. so we are interested in finding clustering from different perspectives. The main objective of Alternative clustering is to discover prominent quality clusterings from distinct perspectives and provide optimum options. Alternative clustering approaches classified as objective function oriented approach and transformation oriented approach. In objective function oriented approach, clustering is performed using objective function. In transformation oriented approach, clustering is performed by transforming the data into multiple projects in to orthogonal subspaces. Transformation-oriented approaches are more efficient than objective-oriented approach. Alternative clustering has broad and diverse application domain from finance to environment science, psychology to climatology. There are several issues that have been identified, the significant ones are optimal clusterings, number of alternatives, and scalability.

REFERENCES

Bae, E., & Bailey, J. (2006). COALA: A Novel Approach for the Extraction of an Alternate Clustering of High Quality and High Dissimilarity.*The Sixth IEEE International Conference on Data Mining* (pp. 53-62). IEEE. doi:10.1109/ICDM.2006.37

Bandyopadhyay, S., Mukhopadhyay, A., & Maulik, U. (2007). An improved algorithm for clustering gene expression data. *Bioinformatics (Oxford, England)*, *23*(21), 2859–2865. doi:10.1093/bioinformatics/btm418 PMID:17720981

Chakrapani, C. (2004). *Statistics in market research*. London: Arnold Publisher.

Dang, X. H., & Bailey, J. (2010). A hierarchical information theoretic technique for the discovery of non linear alternative clusterings.*16th ACM SIGKDD International Conference on Knowledge Discovery and Data Mining* (pp. 573-582). New York: ACM. doi:10.1145/1835804.1835878

Davidson, I., & Qi, Z. (2008). Finding alternative clusterings using constraints.*The Eightth IEEE International Conference on Data Mining* (pp. 773-778). IEEE.

Farmer, A. E., McGuffinb, P., & Spitznagelc, E. L. (1983). Heterogeneity in schizophrenia: A cluster-analytic approach. *Psychiatry Research*, *8*(1), 1–12. doi:10.1016/0165-1781(83)90132-4 PMID:6572983

Fayyad, U., Piatetsky-Shapiro, G., & Smyth, P. (1996). Knowledge discovery and data mining: Towards a unifying framework.*2nd ACM International Conference on Knowledge Discovery and Data Mining (KDD)* (pp. 82-88). Portland, OR: AAAI.

Gondek, D., & Hofmann, T. (2003). Conditional information bottleneck clustering. *Third International Conference on Data Mining, Work-shop on Clustering Large Datasets* (pp. 36-42). Citeseer.

Gondek, D., & Hofmann, T. (2005). Non-redundant clustering with conditional ensembles.*11th ACM International Conference on Knowledge Discovery and Data Mining (SIGKDD)* (pp. 70-77). Chicago: ACM.

Han, J., Kamber, M., & Pei, J. (2011). *Data mining: concepts and techniques*. San Francisco: Morgan Kaufmann.

Handl, J., & Knowles, J. (2007). An evolutionary approach to multiobjective clustering. *Evolutionary Computation IEEE Transaction*, *11*(1), 56–76. doi:10.1109/TEVC.2006.877146

Hartigan, J. (1985). Statistical theory in clustering. *Journal of Classification*, 63-76.

Jain, A. K., & Dubes, R. C. (1988). Algorithms for clustering data. Upper Saddle River, NJ: Academic Press.

Kriegel, H.-P., & Zimek, A. (2010). Subspace clustering, ensemble clustering, alternative clustering, multiview: what can we learn from each other? *MultiClust:First International Workshop on Discovering, Summarizing and Using Multiple Clusterings Held in Conjunction with KDD 2010.*

Lin, C., Cho, Y.-R., Hwang, W.-C., Pei, P., & Zhang, A. (2007). Clustering methods in a protein–protein interaction network. In X. Hu & Y. Pan (Eds.), *Knowledge Discovery in Bioinformatics: Techniques, Methods, and Applications*. Chichester, UK: John Wiley & Sons, Inc. doi:10.1002/9780470124642.ch16

Qi, Z., & Davidson, I. (2009). A principled and flexible frameworkfor finding alternative clusterings. *The15th ACM SIGKDD International Conference on Knowledge Discovery and Data Mining* (pp. 717–726). ACM.

Saha, M., & Mitra, P. (2014). VLGAAC: Variable length genetic algorithm based alternative clustering. *ICONIP*, *8835*, 194–202.

Soltanolkotabi, M., Elhamifar, E., & Candès, E. J. (2014). 05 23). Robust subspace clustering. *Annals of Statistics*, *42*(2), 669–699. doi:10.1214/13-AOS1199

Steinbach, M., Tan, P.-N., Kumar, V., Klooster, S., & Potter, C. (2003). Discovery of climate indices using clustering.*The Ninth ACM SIGKDD International Conference on Knowledge Discovery and Data Mining* (pp. 446-455). New York: ACM. doi:10.1145/956750.956801

Strehl, A., & Ghosh, J. (2002). Cluster ensembles- a knowledge reuse framework for combining multiple partition. *Journal of Machine Learning Research*, 583–617.

Truong, D. T., & Battiti, R. (2012). A cluster-oriented genetic algorithm for alternative clustering. *IEEE 12th International Conference on Data Mining (ICDM)* (pp. 1122 - 1127). Brussels: IEEE.

Vega-Pons, S., & Ruiz-Shulcloper, J. (2011). A survey of clustering ensemble algorithms. *International Journal of Pattern Recognition and Artificial Intelligence*, *25*(03), 337–372. doi:10.1142/S0218001411008683

Vinh, N. X., & Epps, J. (2010). minCEntropy: A novel information theoretic approach for the generation of alternative clusterings. *IEEE 10th International Conference on Data Mining (ICDM)* (pp. 521 - 530). Sydney: IEEE.

Yeung, K., Haynor, D., & Ruzzo, W. (2001). Validating clustering for gene expression data. *Bioinformatics (Oxford, England)*, *17*(4), 309–318. doi:10.1093/bioinformatics/17.4.309 PMID:11301299

Chapter 2
An Evaluation of Turkey's NUTS Level 1 Regions According to Banking Sector With MULTIMOORA Method

Onur Önay
Istanbul University, Turkey

ABSTRACT

In the study, The Nomenclature of Territorial Units for Statistics (NUTS) Level 1 regions of Turkey are evaluated with MULTIMOORA Method according to banking sector using hypothetical data which are adapted from real world data. There are 12 regions as alternatives which are assessed with 6 objectives. Calculations are made by using MS Excel which is powerful spreadsheet software. This application is an example how multi criteria decision making methods can use when a manager making decision. Results are given as lists of regions ranking and commented. By this way, it is shown that how the multi criteria decision making methods can help to decision makers.

INTRODUCTION

MULTIMOORA which is one of the multi criteria decision making methods. The method consists of MOORA method plus Full Multiplicative Form of Multiple Objectives. Historical development of MULTIMOORA method (Baležentis & Baležentis, 2014): Multi-objective optimization by ratio analysis (MOORA) method is offered on the "The MOORA method and its application to privatization in a transition economy" by Brauers and Zavadskas (2006). MOORA method is developed with adding full multiplicative form and it became MULTIMOORA on the study "Project management by MULTIMOORA as an instrument for transition economies" by Brauers and Zavadskas (2010). Computation steps (Baležentis & Baležentis, 2014; Brauers & Zavadskas, 2011) of the MULTIMOORA method are given at the Figure 1.

DOI: 10.4018/978-1-5225-2148-8.ch002

Figure 1. Computation steps of the MULTIMOORA method

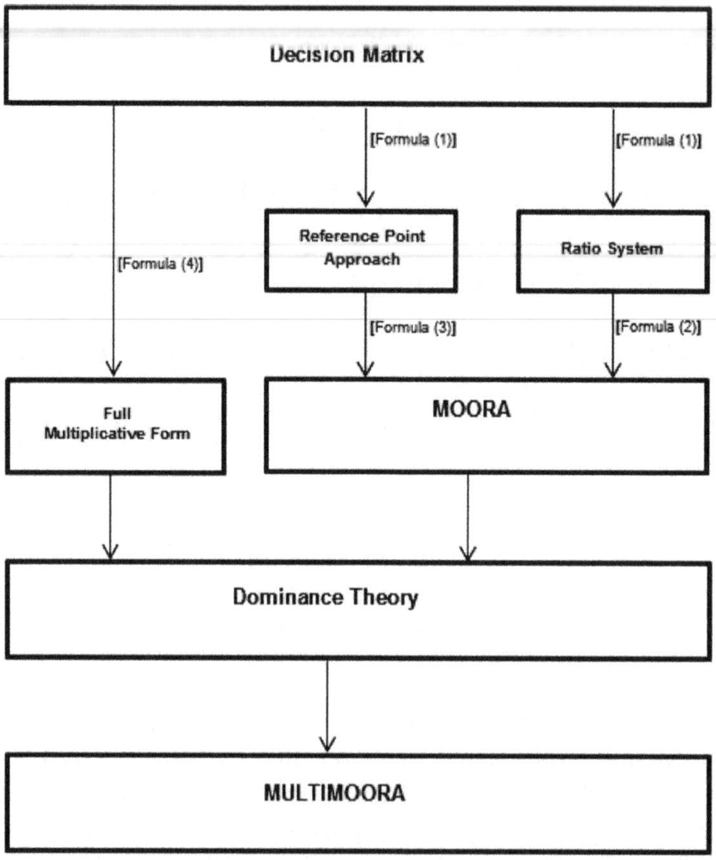

The aim of the study is introduce to MULTIMOORA method and applied it in the service sector. Application of method is given in the banking sector. There are 12 regions as alternatives and 6 objectives. They are assessed by method. Results of the application are given and commented.

In the study; general information about the method are given at the first section. Background is given after the introduction. MULTIMOORA method is given at the third section. Results are given at the solutions and recommendations section and they are discussed at the conclusion.

BACKGROUND

There are several application areas of MULTIMOORA method such as; economics, financial, banking sectors and so on. Only MOORA method is used in some applications. Some of them add the full multiplicative form to MOORA, therefore MULTIMOORA method is implemented. Performance of Lithuanian commercial banks is evaluated with using MULTIMOORA method by Brauers, Ginevicius and Podviezko (2012). MULTIMOORA method is used by Brauers and Zavadskas (2011) to decide upon a bank loan to buy property. The well–being in the European Union Member States is assessed by Balešentis, Balešentis, and Brauers (2011). The construction sector in twenty European countries during the recession 2008–2009 country are ranked with using MULTIMOORA by Brauers, Kildienė, Zavadskas, and Kaklauskas (2013). The relative farming efficiency in the European Union Member States is assessed with MULTIMOORA and data envelopment analysis by Baležentis and Baležentis (2011). The MULTIMOORA method is used for decision making problem of investment of Belgian shares by Brauers and Ginevičius (2013). MULTIMOORA method is applied to the analysis on relationship between country risk and economic sustainability in EU Baltic Sea region countries by Stankevičienė, Sviderskė, and Miečinskienė (2014). MULTIMOORA method is used to evaluate the situation of Lithuania in the European Union by Baležentis, Valkauskas, and Baležentis (2010). The MULTIMOORA method is applied to evaluation of commercial banks registered in Lithuania by Brauers, Ginevicius and Podviezko (2014a). The MULTIMOORA method is used to ranking of the Lithuanian banks during the recession of 2008-2009 by Brauers, Ginevicius and Podvezko (2014b). The TOPSIS, MOORA and VIKOR methods are applied to evaluate of NUTS Level 2 Regions of Turkey by Önay and Yıldırım (2016). The OCRA and MOORA methods are used for efficiency analysis of foreign-capital banks in Turkey by Özbek (2015). The MOORA method is implemented for bank branch location selection by Görener, Dincer and Hacioglu (2016). Fuzzy MOORA method is applied to evaluating internet branches of banks by Uygurtürk (2015).

MULTIMOORA METHOD

In this part, the computation steps of the MULTIMOORA method are given. As advert previously, MULTIMOORA method is composed with MOORA method and Full Multiplicative Form of Multiple Objectives (Brauers & Zavadskas, 2010).

Suppose that there are $i = 1, 2, \ldots, m$ alternatives and $j = 1, 2, \ldots, n$ objectives (they can call as criteria or attributes). Let A be set of alternatives and C be set of objectives which are shown as; $A = \{A_1, A_2, \ldots, A_m\}$ and $C = \{O_1, O_2, \ldots, O_n\}$. Decision matrix is composed by alternatives and objectives, $\left(x_{ij}\right)_{m \times n}$. Decision matrix can call as evaluation matrix. x_{ij} is response of alternative A_i with respect to objective O_j (Önay, 2016).

The MOORA Method

Alternatives and objectives compose the evaluation matrix and computations of the MOORA method start. The MOORA (Multi-Objective Optimization by Ratio Analysis) method consists of two parts; ratio system and reference point approach (Hafezalkotob & Hafezalkotob, 2015).

Ratio System

The square root of the sum of squares of each alternative per objective writes as the denominator on the ratio. Each response of the alternative on an objective is compared to that denominator for the ratio system as a part of MOORA. This ratio can be defined as (Brauers & Ginevičius,2013);

$$x_{ij}^{*} = \frac{x_{ij}}{\sqrt{\sum_{i=1}^{m} x_{ij}^{2}}} \tag{1}$$

x_{ij}^{*} is a dimensionless number representing the normalized response of *i-th* alternative on *j-th* objective. The normalized responses of the alternatives on the objectives belong to the interval $[0,1]$ (Brauers & Zavadskas, 2006), $x_{ij}^{*} \in [0,1]$ but sometimes the interval could be $[-1,1]$ (Brauers & Zavadskas, 2010; Brauers, Kildienė, Zavadskas & Kaklauskas, 2013).

Supposed that, there is a $\left(x_{ij}\right)_{m \times n}$ decision matrix as following;

$$\begin{array}{cccccc} & O_1 & O_2 & \cdots & O_{n-1} & O_n \\ A_1 & x_{11} & x_{12} & \cdots & x_{1(n-1)} & x_{1n} \\ A_2 & x_{21} & x_{22} & \cdots & x_{2(n-1)} & x_{2n} \\ \vdots & \vdots & \vdots & \ddots & \vdots & \vdots \\ A_{m-1} & x_{(m-1)1} & x_{(m-1)2} & \cdots & x_{(m-1)(n-1)} & x_{(m-1)n} \\ A_m & x_{m1} & x_{m2} & \cdots & x_{m(n-1)} & x_{mn} \end{array}$$

The elements of the decision matrix are normalized by using formula (1). x_{11} is normalized as following for example;

$$x_{11}^{*} = \frac{x_{11}}{\sqrt{x_{11}^{2} + x_{21}^{2} + \ldots + x_{(m-1)1}^{2} + x_{m1}^{2}}}$$

These normalized responses are subtracted in case of sum of minimization from added in case of maximization for optimization (Brauers & Zavadskas, 2006).

$$y_{i}^{*} = \sum_{j=1}^{g} x_{ij}^{*} - \sum_{j=g+1}^{n} x_{ij}^{*} \tag{2}$$

$j = 1, 2, \ldots, g$; as the objectives to be maximized,
$j = g + 1, g + 2, \ldots, n$; as the objectives to be minimized,

An ordinal ranking of the y_{i}^{*} shows the final preference (Brauers & Zavadskas, 2006). Optimal ranking of the alternatives are obtained by listing the assessment values in descending order (Hafezalkotob & Hafezalkotob, 2015; Hafezalkotob, Hafezalkotob & Sayadi, 2016).

Reference Point Approach

The reference point approach starts from equation (1) (Balešentis, Balešentis & Brauers, 2011). Reference point (r_i) is determined. As a reference point; the highest co-ordinate per objective of all the candidate alternatives is chosen for maximization. On the other hand, the lowest coordinate is chosen for minimization (Brauers & Zavadskas, 2006). The Tchebycheff Min-Max metric uses for measure the distance between the alternatives and the reference point;

$$\min_i \left\{ \max_j \left| r_j - x_{ij}^* \right| \right\} \tag{3}$$

Formula (3) applies for $i = 1,2,...,m$ alternatives and $j = 1,2,...,n$ objectives. According to equation (3), maximum distance values each alternative to the reference points are obtained (Kundakcı, 2016) and the assessment values are ranked in ascending order to produce the optimal alternative (Hafezalkotob & Hafezalkotob, 2015).

Full Multiplicative Form

The third part of MULTIMOORA method is full multiplicative form. Utility of each alternative is expressed in the formula. The objectives to be maximized are obtained by multiplication and the objectives to be minimized are denominators (Brauers & Zavadskas, 2010). Formulation of the full multiplicative form as follows (Baležentis & Baležentis, 2014; Brauers & Zavadskas, 2011; Balešentis, Balešentis & Brauers, 2011);

$$U_i = \frac{A_i}{B_i} \tag{4}$$

U_i is the utility of alternative i with objectives to be maximized and objectives to be minimized. Where,

$$A_i = \prod_{j=1}^{g} x_{ij} \tag{5}$$

A_i denotes the product of objectives to be maximized.

$j = 1,2,...,g$; the number of objectives to be maximized.

Where,

$$B_i = \prod_{j=g+1}^{n} x_{ij} \tag{6}$$

B_i denotes the product of objectives to be minimized. $j = g+1, g+2, \ldots, n$ the number of objectives to be minimized.

The number of objectives to be minimized is $n - g$ (Brauers & Ginevičius,2013). Optimal ranking of the alternatives are obtained by listing the assessment values in descending order (Kundakcı, 2016; Hafezalkotob & Hafezalkotob, 2015).

If any element of decision matrix is zero or negative values, it may cause problem for full multiplicative form. In this case, index number 100 replaces with zero for all element of related objective, in other words it is applied for entire column of the related objective on the evaluation matrix (Brauers & Ginevičius, 2013; Brauers, Kildienė, Zavadskas & Kaklauskas, 2013). By this way results become meaningful.

As a result, three ranking lists are obtained from ratio system, reference point approach and full multiplicative form. The MULTIMOORA Method calculation steps are completed with these three methods. A ranking list is composed from three lists as a result by using dominance theory (Brauers & Zavadskas, 2012; Brauers & Ginevičius, 2013).

Dominance theory is applied to obtain final ranking. Readers can find details in; Brauers and Ginevičius (2013); Brauers, Kildienė, Zavadskas and Kaklauskas (2013); Brauers and Zavadskas (2012); Brauers and Zavadskas (2011) for dominance theory and its applications in the MULTIMOORA method such as; dominance (absolute dominance, general dominance), being dominated, transitivity, equability and circular reasoning.

The Significance Coefficient

If the importance of the objectives is different, they can multiply with their significance coefficients (weights) (Önay, 2016). In that case, formula (7) uses instead of formula (2), formula (8) uses instead of formula (3) and formula (9) uses instead of formula (4). w_j is the weight of the objective j^{th}. Sum of the weights is 1 $\left(\sum_{j=1}^{n} w_j = 1\right)$. (Kundakcı, 2016; Hafezalkotob & Hafezalkotob, 2015; Brauers & Zavadskas, 2006).

$$y_i^* = \sum_{j=1}^{g} w_j x_{ij}^* - \sum_{j=g+1}^{n} w_j x_{ij}^* \tag{7}$$

$$\min_i \left\{ \max_j \left| w_j r_j - w_j x_{ij}^* \right| \right\} \tag{8}$$

$$U_i = \frac{A_i}{B_i} = \frac{\prod_{j=1}^{g} x_{ij}^{w_j}}{\prod_{j=g+1}^{n} x_{ij}^{w_j}} \tag{9}$$

SOLUTIONS AND RECOMMENDATIONS

In this section, applications of MULTIMOORA are given. The Nomenclature of Territorial Units for Statistics (NUTS) Level 1 regions of Turkey are evaluated with MULTIMOORA Method according to banking sector. Real world data of 2015 are reviewed and hypothetical data are produced according to them. Hypothetical data which are adapted from real world data are used for applications. Regions are taken as alternatives and some indicators of the banking sector are taken as objectives. There are 12 regions as alternatives which are assessed with 6 objectives. Calculations are made with using MS Excel which is powerful spreadsheet software. List of alternatives are given on the Table 1. List of objectives are given on the Table 2.

Table 1. List of alternatives

A1	İstanbul
A2	West Marmara
A3	East Marmara
A4	Aegean
A5	Mediterranean
A6	West Black Sea
A7	East Black Sea
A8	West Anatolia
A9	Northeast Anatolia
A10	Central Anatolia
A11	Middle East Anatolia
A12	Southeast Anatolia

Table 2. List of objectives

O1	The number of employees of banks
02	The number of branch
O3	Deposits (Million TL)
O4	Mean of deposits per branch (Million TL)
O5	Credit (Million TL)
O6	Mean of credit per branch (Million TL)

*TL: Turkish Liras

According to attribute of objectives, attribute of an objective can be benefit or cost, implementation of method may change. Different scenarios are handled in the applications.

Scenario 1. Scenario 1 is handled with customer's perspective. Attributes of objectives are changed according to customer's perspective. Since customers want to get more convenient service, the number of employees of banks (O1) and the number of branch (O2) are benefit objectives according to customers. Since customers want to get more money, deposits (O3) and mean of deposits per branch (O4) are benefit objectives according to customers. Since customers want to make less debt, credit (O5) and mean of credit per branch (O6) are cost objectives according to customers. Customers want to maximize their benefits and minimize their costs. Objectives and their attributes of the scenario 1 are shown on the Table 3.

Data are normalized with using formula (1) and they are written to cells (B37:G48) on the Excel spreadsheet. Formula (2) is applied and its conclusions are written to cells (H37:H48) on the spreadsheet. Values on the cells (H37:H48) are ranked on the (I37:I48) which are given on the Figure 2. Excel formulas are given on the Table 4. By this way, calculation steps of MOORA Ratio System are completed.

Calculation steps of Reference Point Approach are given on the Figure 3 and formulas are given on the Table 5. Reference points are determined on the cells (B65:G65). Deviations from reference points are obtained on the cells (B70:G81). By using formula (3), values are obtained on the cells (H70:H81) and they are ranked on the cells (I70:I81).

Full Multiplicative Form is applied to data set with using formulas (5), (6) and (4). Data are on the cells (B87:G98). Attributes of the objectives are given on the Table 3. Column B, C, D and E belong to maximization objectives; O1, O2, O3 and O4. F and G columns are minimization form, because of O5 and O6. Calculation steps are given on the Figure 4 and formulas are given on the Table 6.

Table 3. List of objectives and their attributes of the Scenario 1

O1	The number of employees of banks	Max
O2	The number of branch	Max
O3	Deposits (Million TL)	Max
O4	Mean of deposits per branch (Million TL)	Max
O5	Credit (Million TL)	Min
O6	Mean of credit per branch (Million TL)	Min

Figure 2. Calculation of Normalized Matrix and Ratio System for Scenario1

	A	B	C	D	E	F	G	H	I
35	Normalized Matrix	The Number of Employees of Banks	The Number of Branch	Deposits (Million TL)	Mean of deposits per branch (Million TL)	Credit (Million TL)	Mean of credit per branch (Million TL)	MOORA Ratio System	
36	Scenario 1	Max	Max	Max	Max	Min	Min	Formula (2)	Rank
37	Istanbul	0.90284	0.73336	0.91454	0.64285	0.88515	0.53924	1.76919	1
38	West Marmara	0.06225	0.11527	0.04608	0.20194	0.05310	0.19773	0.17471	6
39	East Marmara	0.17974	0.23868	0.10680	0.22647	0.15105	0.27620	0.32444	5
40	Aegean	0.21864	0.38782	0.19035	0.24902	0.22263	0.25003	0.57317	3
41	Mediterranean	0.17027	0.29277	0.13044	0.22538	0.19705	0.29454	0.32728	4
42	West Black Sea	0.07503	0.12708	0.04230	0.16801	0.05500	0.18554	0.17188	7
43	East Black Sea	0.04079	0.07772	0.02396	0.15623	0.02981	0.16340	0.10548	9
44	West Anatolia	0.23426	0.32191	0.30224	0.48073	0.29510	0.40525	0.63878	2
45	Northeast Anatolia	0.03057	0.04044	0.00945	0.12252	0.01723	0.18147	0.00427	11
46	Central Anatolia	0.05638	0.10398	0.04134	0.20126	0.05090	0.21083	0.14122	8
47	Middle east Anatolia	0.02900	0.05383	0.01647	0.15619	0.02468	0.19573	0.03507	10
48	Southeast Anatolia	0.06914	0.12105	0.03245	0.13501	0.08938	0.32175	-0.05348	12

Table 4. Formulas on the cells (H37:H48) and (I37:I48) for Scenario1

Formulas on the cells (H37:H48):		**Formulas on the cells (I37:I48):**	
H37:	=SUM(B37:E37)- SUM (F37:G37)	I37:	=RANK(H37;$H$37:$H$48;0)
H38:	=SUM(B38:E38)-SUM(F38.G38)	I38:	=RANK(H38;$H$37:$H$48;0)
H39:	=SUM(B39:E39)-SUM(F39:G39)	I39:	=RANK(H39;$H$37:$H$48;0)
H40:	=SUM(B40:E40)-SUM(F40:G40)	I40:	=RANK(H40;$H$37:$H$48;0)
H41:	=SUM(B41:E41)-SUM(F41:G41)	I41:	=RANK(H41;$H$37:$H$48;0)
H42:	=SUM(B42:E42)-SUM(F42:G42)	I42:	=RANK(H42;$H$37:$H$48;0)
H43:	=SUM(B43:E43)-SUM(F43:G43)	I43:	=RANK(H43;$H$37:$H$48;0)
H44:	=SUM(B44:E44)-SUM(F44:G44)	I44:	=RANK(H44;$H$37:$H$48;0)
H45:	=SUM(B45:E45)-SUM(F45:G45)	I45:	=RANK(H45;$H$37:$H$48;0)
H46:	=SUM(B46:E46)-SUM(F46:G46)	I46:	=RANK(H46;$H$37:$H$48;0)
H47:	=SUM(B47:E47)-SUM(F47:G47)	I47:	=RANK(H47;$H$37:$H$48;0)
H48:	=SUM(B48:E48)-SUM(F48:G48)	I48:	=RANK(H48;$H$37:$H$48;0)

Figure 3. Calculation of Reference Point Approach

	A	B	C	D	E	F	G
51	**Normalized Matrix**	**The Number of Employees of Banks**	**The Number of Branch**	**Deposits (Million TL)**	**Mean of deposits per branch (Million TL)**	**Credit (Million TL)**	**Mean of credit per branch (Million TL)**
52	**Scenario 1**	**Max**	**Max**	**Max**	**Max**	**Min**	**Min**
53	Istanbul	0.90284	0.73336	0.91454	0.64285	0.88515	0.53924
54	West Marmara	0.06225	0.11527	0.04608	0.20194	0.05310	0.19773
55	East Marmara	0.17974	0.23868	0.10680	0.22647	0.15105	0.27620
56	Aegean	0.21864	0.38782	0.19035	0.24902	0.22263	0.25003
57	Mediterranean	0.17027	0.29277	0.13044	0.22538	0.19705	0.29454
58	West Black Sea	0.07503	0.12708	0.04230	0.16801	0.05500	0.18554
59	East Black Sea	0.04079	0.07772	0.02396	0.15623	0.02981	0.16340
60	West Anatolia	0.23426	0.32191	0.30224	0.48073	0.29510	0.40525
61	Northeast Anatolia	0.03057	0.04044	0.00945	0.12252	0.01723	0.18147
62	Central Anatolia	0.05638	0.10398	0.04134	0.20126	0.05090	0.21083
63	Middle east Anatolia	0.02900	0.05383	0.01647	0.15619	0.02468	0.19573
64	Southeast Anatolia	0.06914	0.12105	0.03245	0.13501	0.08938	0.32175
65	**Reference Points:**	**0.90284**	**0.73336**	**0.91454**	**0.64285**	**0.01723**	**0.16340**

	A	B	C	D	E	F	G	H	I
68	**Deviations from reference points**	**The Number of Employees of Banks**	**The Number of Branch**	**Deposits (Million TL)**	**Mean of deposits per branch (Million TL)**	**Credit (Million TL)**	**Mean of credit per branch (Million TL)**	**MOORA Reference Point Approach**	
69	**Scenario 1**	**Max**	**Max**	**Max**	**Max**	**Min**	**Min**	**Formula (3)**	**Rank**
70	Istanbul	0.00000	0.00000	0.00000	0.00000	0.86792	0.37584	0.86792	5
71	West Marmara	0.84059	0.61809	0.86847	0.44091	0.03586	0.03433	0.86847	6
72	East Marmara	0.72310	0.49468	0.80774	0.41637	0.13381	0.11279	0.80774	4
73	Aegean	0.68420	0.34554	0.72419	0.39383	0.20540	0.08663	0.72419	2
74	Mediterranean	0.73257	0.44059	0.78410	0.41747	0.17981	0.13113	0.78410	3
75	West Black Sea	0.82782	0.60628	0.87224	0.47484	0.03777	0.02213	0.87224	7
76	East Black Sea	0.86205	0.65564	0.89059	0.48662	0.01258	0.00000	0.89059	10
77	West Anatolia	0.66859	0.41145	0.61230	0.16212	0.27787	0.24185	0.66859	1
78	Northeast Anatolia	0.87227	0.69292	0.90509	0.52033	0.00000	0.01806	0.90509	12
79	Central Anatolia	0.84646	0.62938	0.87320	0.44158	0.03367	0.04743	0.87320	8
80	Middle east Anatolia	0.87384	0.67953	0.89807	0.48665	0.00745	0.03233	0.89807	11
81	Southeast Anatolia	0.83370	0.61232	0.88209	0.50783	0.07214	0.15834	0.88209	9

Table 5. Formulas of the Reference Point Approach on the cells for Scenario1

Formulas on the cells (B65:G65):		**Formulas on the cells (H70:H81):**		**Formulas on the cells (I70:I81):**	
B65:	=MAX(B53:B64)	H70:	=MAX(B70:G70)	I70:	=RANK(H70;$H$70:$H$81;1)
C65:	=MAX(C53:C64)	H71:	=MAX(B71:G71)	I71:	=RANK(H71;$H$70:$H$81;1)
D65:	=MAX(D53:D64)	H72:	=MAX(B72:G72)	I72:	=RANK(H72;$H$70:$H$81;1)
E65:	=MAX(E53:E64)	H73:	=MAX(B73:G73)	I73:	=RANK(H73;$H$70:$H$81;1)
F65:	=MIN(F53:F64)	H74:	=MAX(B74:G74)	I74:	=RANK(H74;$H$70:$H$81;1)
G65:	=MIN(G53:G64)	H75:	=MAX(B75:G75)	I75:	=RANK(H75;$H$70:$H$81;1)
		H76:	=MAX(B76:G76)	I76:	=RANK(H76;$H$70:$H$81;1)
		H77:	=MAX(B77:G77)	I77:	=RANK(H77;$H$70:$H$81;1)
		H78:	=MAX(B78:G78)	I78:	=RANK(H78;$H$70:$H$81;1)
		H79:	=MAX(B79:G79)	I79:	=RANK(H79;$H$70:$H$81;1)
		H80:	=MAX(B80:G80)	I80:	=RANK(H80;$H$70:$H$81;1)
		H81:	=MAX(B81:G81)	I81:	=RANK(H81;$H$70:$H$81;1)

Figure 4. Calculation of Full Multiplicative Form

	A	H	I	J	K
85	**Full Multiplicative Form**	**Full Multiplicative Form**			
86	**Scenario 1**	**Formula (5)**	**Formula (6)**	**Formula (4)**	**Rank**
87	Istanbul	1.94181E+16	90598577.64	214331147.3	1
88	West Marmara	3.33062E+12	1992797.213	1671330.501	7
89	East Marmara	5.17613E+13	7918698.816	6536597.648	5
90	Aegean	2.00503E+14	10565640.18	18976891.12	3
91	Mediterranean	7.31074E+13	11016006.15	6636469.119	4
92	West Black Sea	3.38044E+12	1936922.78	1745263.939	6
93	East Black Sea	5.91809E+11	924630.6686	640049.3456	9
94	West Anatolia	5.46567E+14	22699391.24	24078480.35	2
95	Northeast Anatolia	71398113170	593592.6716	120281.3252	12
96	Central Anatolia	2.43313E+12	2036968.62	1194485.372	8
97	Middle east Anatolia	2.00283E+11	916918.3975	218430.0629	11
98	Southeast Anatolia	1.82893E+12	5458380.336	335067.4673	10

Finally, MULTIMOORA ranking list of alternatives could be obtained from three ranking lists; Ratio System, Reference Point Approach and Full Multiplicative Form, by dominance theory on the Table 7. Istanbul is the first region of ranking list and Northeast Anatolia is ranked at the last of the list.

Scenario 2: Scenario 2 is handled with bank's perspective. Attributes of objectives are changed according to bank's perspective. Since banks want to minimize their expenses, the number of employees of banks (O1) and the number of branch (O2) are cost objectives for banks. On the other hand, deposits

Table 6. Formulas of the Full Multiplicative Form on the cells for Scenario1

H87:	=PRODUCT(B87:E87)	I87:	=PRODUCT(F87:G87)	J87:	=H87/I87	K87:	=RANK(J87;$J$87:$J$98;0)
H88:	=PRODUCT(B88:E88)	I88:	=PRODUCT(F88:G88)	J88:	=H88/I88	K88:	=RANK(J88;$J$87:$J$98;0)
H89:	=PRODUCT(B89:E89)	I89:	=PRODUCT(F89:G89)	J89:	=H89/I89	K89:	=RANK(J89;$J$87:$J$98;0)
H90:	=PRODUCT(B90:E90)	I90:	=PRODUCT(F90:G90)	J90:	=H90/I90	K90:	=RANK(J90;$J$87:$J$98;0)
H91:	=PRODUCT(B91:E91)	I91:	=PRODUCT(F91:G91)	J91:	=H91/I91	K91:	=RANK(J91;$J$87:$J$98;0)
H92:	=PRODUCT(B92:E92)	I92:	=PRODUCT(F92:G92)	J92:	=H92/I92	K92:	=RANK(J92;$J$87:$J$98;0)
H93:	=PRODUCT(B93:E93)	I93:	=PRODUCT(F93:G93)	J93:	=H93/I93	K93:	=RANK(J93;$J$87:$J$98;0)
H94:	=PRODUCT(B94:E94)	I94:	=PRODUCT(F94:G94)	J94:	=H94/I94	K94:	=RANK(J94;$J$87:$J$98;0)
H95:	=PRODUCT(B95:E95)	I95:	=PRODUCT(F95:G95)	J95:	=H95/I95	K95:	=RANK(J95;$J$87:$J$98;0)
H96:	=PRODUCT(B96:E96)	I96:	=PRODUCT(F96:G96)	J96:	=H96/I96	K96:	=RANK(J96;$J$87:$J$98;0)
H97:	=PRODUCT(B97:E97)	I97:	=PRODUCT(F97:G97)	J97:	=H97/I97	K97:	=RANK(J97;$J$87:$J$98;0)
H98:	=PRODUCT(B98:E98)	I98:	=PRODUCT(F98:G98)	J98:	=H98/I98	K98:	=RANK(J98;$J$87:$J$98;0)

Table 7. MULTIMOORA for Scenario1

	MOORA Ratio System	MOORA Reference Point Approach	Full Multiplicative Form	MULTIMOORA
Scenario 1	**Rank**	**Rank**	**Rank**	**Rank**
Istanbul	1	5	1	**1**
West Marmara	6	6	7	**6**
East Marmara	5	4	5	**5**
Aegean	3	2	3	**3**
Mediterranean	4	3	4	**4**
West Black Sea	7	7	6	**7**
East Black Sea	9	10	9	**9**
West Anatolia	2	1	2	**2**
Northeast Anatolia	11	12	12	**12**
Central Anatolia	8	8	8	**8**
Middle East Anatolia	10	11	11	**11**
Southeast Anatolia	12	9	10	**10**

(O3), mean of deposits per branch (O4), credit (O5) and mean of credit per branch (O6) are benefit objectives according to bank's administration board. Bank's managers want to maximize their benefits and minimize their costs. Objectives and their attributes of the Scenario 2 are shown on the Table 8.

For MOORA Ratio System, data are normalized with using formula (1) and they are written to cells (B37:G48) on the Excel spreadsheet. Formula (2) is applied and its conclusions are written to cells (H37:H48) on the spreadsheet. Values on the cells (H37:H48) are ranked on the (I37:I48). Same spreadsheet formulas are used with Scenario1 application for calculations on the Figure 5.

Table 8. List of objectives and their attributes of the Scenario 2

O1	The number of employees of banks	Min
O2	The number of branch	Min
O3	Deposits (Million TL)	Max
O4	Mean of deposits per branch (Million TL)	Max
O5	Credit (Million TL)	Max
O6	Mean of credit per branch (Million TL)	Max

Figure 5. Calculation of Normalized Matrix and Ratio System for Scenario2

	A	B	C	D	E	F	G	H	I
35	Nomalized Matrix	The Number of Employees of Banks	The Number of Branch	Deposits (Million TL)	Mean of deposits per branch (Million TL)	Credit (Million TL)	Mean of credit per branch (Million TL)	MOORA Ratio System	
36	Scenario 2	Min	Min	Max	Max	Max	Max	Formula (2)	Rank
37	Istanbul	0.90284	0.73336	0.91454	0.64285	0.88515	0.53924	1.34558	1
38	West Marmara	0.06225	0.11527	0.04608	0.20194	0.05310	0.19773	0.32132	7
39	East Marmara	0.17974	0.23868	0.10680	0.22647	0.15105	0.27620	0.34210	6
40	Aegean	0.21864	0.38782	0.19035	0.24902	0.22263	0.25003	0.30557	9
41	Mediterranean	0.17027	0.29277	0.13044	0.22538	0.19705	0.29454	0.38437	4
42	West Black Sea	0.07503	0.12708	0.04230	0.16801	0.05500	0.18554	0.24874	12
43	East Black Sea	0.04079	0.07772	0.02396	0.15623	0.02981	0.16340	0.25489	11
44	West Anatolia	0.23426	0.32191	0.30224	0.48073	0.29510	0.40525	0.92715	2
45	Northeast Anatolia	0.03057	0.04044	0.00945	0.12252	0.01723	0.18147	0.25967	10
46	Central Anatolia	0.05638	0.10398	0.04134	0.20126	0.05090	0.21083	0.34399	5
47	Middle east Anatolia	0.02900	0.05383	0.01647	0.15619	0.02468	0.19573	0.31025	8
48	Southeast Anatolia	0.06914	0.12105	0.03245	0.13501	0.08938	0.32175	0.38841	3

Calculation steps of Reference Point Approach are given on the Figure 6. Reference points are determined on the cells (B65:G65). Deviations from reference points are obtained on the cells (B70:G81). By using formula (3), values are obtained on the cells (H70:H81) and they are ranked on the cells (I70:I81).

Full Multiplicative Form is applied to data set with using formulas (5), (6) and (4). Data are on the cells (B87:G98). Attributes of the objectives are given on the Table 8. Column D, E, F and G belong to maximization objectives; O3, O4, O5 and O6. B and C columns are minimization form, because of O1 and O2. Calculation steps are given on the Figure 7.

Finally, MULTIMOORA ranking list of alternatives could be obtained from three ranking lists; Ratio System, Reference Point Approach and Full Multiplicative Form, by dominance theory on the Table 9.

Istanbul is the first region of ranking list and Northeast Anatolia is ranked at the last of the list.

Scenario 3: Suppose that there are different significance levels of objectives of Scenario1. Those significance levels add to scenario as weights. Therefore Scenario3 is obtained.

For MOORA Ratio System, data are normalized with using formula (1) and normalized values are multiplied by their weights. Weighted normalized matrix is written to cells (B37:G48) on the Excel spreadsheet. Formula (7) is applied and its conclusions are written to cells (H37:H48) on the spreadsheet. Values on the cells (H37:H48) are ranked on the (I37:I48) on the Figure 8.

Calculation steps of Reference Point Approach are given on the Figure 9. Reference points are determined on the cells (B66:G66). Deviations from reference points are obtained on the cells (B71:G82). By using formula (8), values are obtained on the cells (H71:H82) and they are ranked on the cells (I71:I82).

Figure 6. Calculation of Reference Point Approach for Scenario2

	A	B	C	D	E	F	G
51	Nomalized Matrix	The Number of Employees of Banks	The Number of Branch	Deposits (Million TL)	Mean of deposits per branch (Million TL)	Credit (Million TL)	Mean of credit per branch (Million TL)
52	Scenario 2	Min	Min	Max	Max	Max	Max
53	Istanbul	0.90284	0.73336	0.91454	0.64285	0.88515	0.53924
54	West Marmara	0.06225	0.11527	0.04608	0.20194	0.05310	0.19773
55	East Marmara	0.17974	0.23868	0.10680	0.22647	0.15105	0.27620
56	Aegean	0.21864	0.38782	0.19035	0.24902	0.22263	0.25003
57	Mediterranean	0.17027	0.29277	0.13044	0.22538	0.19705	0.29454
58	West Black Sea	0.07503	0.12708	0.04230	0.16801	0.05500	0.18554
59	East Black Sea	0.04079	0.07772	0.02396	0.15623	0.02981	0.16340
60	West Anatolia	0.23426	0.32191	0.30224	0.48073	0.29510	0.40525
61	Northeast Anatolia	0.03057	0.04044	0.00945	0.12252	0.01723	0.18147
62	Central Anatolia	0.05638	0.10398	0.04134	0.20126	0.05090	0.21083
63	Middle east Anatolia	0.02900	0.05383	0.01647	0.15619	0.02468	0.19573
64	Southeast Anatolia	0.06914	0.12105	0.03245	0.13501	0.08938	0.32175
65	**Reference Points:**	**0.02900**	**0.04044**	**0.91454**	**0.64285**	**0.88515**	**0.53924**

	A	B	C	D	E	F	G	H	I
68	Deviations from reference points	The Number of Employees of Banks	The Number of Branch	Deposits (Million TL)	Mean of deposits per branch (Million TL)	Credit (Million TL)	Mean of credit per branch (Million TL)	MOORA Reference Point Approach	
69	Scenario 2	Min	Min	Max	Max	Max	Max	Formula (3)	Rank
70	Istanbul	0.87384	0.69292	0.00000	0.00000	0.00000	0.00000	0.87384	8
71	West Marmara	0.03326	0.07483	0.86847	0.44091	0.83205	0.34151	0.86847	5
72	East Marmara	0.15074	0.19824	0.80774	0.41637	0.73410	0.26305	0.80774	4
73	Aegean	0.18965	0.34738	0.72419	0.39383	0.66252	0.28921	0.72419	2
74	Mediterranean	0.14127	0.25233	0.78410	0.41747	0.68810	0.24471	0.78410	3
75	West Black Sea	0.04603	0.08665	0.87224	0.47484	0.83015	0.35371	0.87224	6
76	East Black Sea	0.01179	0.03729	0.89059	0.48662	0.85534	0.37584	0.89059	10
77	West Anatolia	0.20526	0.28148	0.61230	0.16212	0.59005	0.13399	0.61230	1
78	Northeast Anatolia	0.00157	0.00000	0.90509	0.52033	0.86792	0.35778	0.90509	12
79	Central Anatolia	0.02738	0.06354	0.87320	0.44158	0.83425	0.32841	0.87320	7
80	Middle east Anatolia	0.00000	0.01339	0.89807	0.48665	0.86047	0.34351	0.89807	11
81	Southeast Anatolia	0.04014	0.08061	0.88209	0.50783	0.79577	0.21750	0.88209	9

Figure 7. Calculation of Full Multiplicative Form for Scenario2

	A	H	I	J	K
85	Full Multiplicative Form	Full Multiplicative Form			
86	Scenario 2	Formula (5)	Formula (6)	Formula (4)	Rank
87	Istanbul	8.05637E+15	218367912	36893546.47	1
88	West Marmara	2.8045E+12	2366649	1185006.817	8
89	East Marmara	2.89699E+13	14148585	2047544.679	5
90	Aegean	7.5752E+13	27965518	2708762.711	4
91	Mediterranean	4.89853E+13	16440675	2979518.793	3
92	West Black Sea	2.08222E+12	3144548	662169.6516	10
93	East Black Sea	5.23405E+11	1045472	500639.641	11
94	West Anatolia	4.98851E+14	24870636	20057819.19	2
95	Northeast Anatolia	1.03968E+11	407638	255050.3602	12
96	Central Anatolia	2.56364E+12	1933272	1326061.271	6
97	Middle east Anatolia	3.56758E+11	514755	693062.8765	9
98	Southeast Anatolia	3.61701E+12	2760007	1310507.417	7

Full Multiplicative Form is applied to data set with using formula (9) and A_i and B_i are calculated. Data are on the cells (B88:G99). Attributes of the objectives are given on the Table 10. Column B, C, D and E belong to maximization objectives; O1, O2, O3 and O4. F and G columns are minimization form, because of O5 and O6. Calculation steps are given on the Figure 10.

Finally, MULTIMOORA ranking list of alternatives could be obtained from three ranking lists; Ratio System, Reference Point Approach and Full Multiplicative Form, by dominance theory on the Table11.

Table 9. MULTIMOORA for Scenario2

	MOORA Ratio System	MOORA Reference Point Approach	Full Multiplicative Form	MULTIMOORA
Scenario 2	**Rank**	**Rank**	**Rank**	**Rank**
Istanbul	1	8	1	**1**
West Marmara	7	5	8	**8**
East Marmara	6	4	5	**5**
Aegean	9	2	4	**4**
Mediterranean	4	3	3	**3**
West Black Sea	12	6	10	**10**
East Black Sea	11	10	11	**11**
West Anatolia	2	1	2	**2**
Northeast Anatolia	10	12	12	**12**
Central Anatolia	5	7	6	**6**
Middle East Anatolia	8	11	9	**9**
Southeast Anatolia	3	9	7	**7**

Table 10. List of objectives, their attributes and their weights for Scenario3

O1	The number of employees of banks	Max	0.30
O2	The number of branch	Max	0.25
O3	Deposits (Million TL)	Max	0.15
O4	Mean of deposits per branch (Million TL)	Max	0.15
O5	Credit (Million TL)	Min	0.1
O6	Mean of credit per branch (Million TL)	Min	0.05

Figure 8. Calculation of Weighted Normalized Matrix and Ratio System for Scenario3

	A	B	C	D	E	F	G	H	I
35	**Weighted Normalized Matrix**	**The Number of Employees of Banks**	**The Number of Branch**	**Deposits (Million TL)**	**Mean of deposits per branch (Million TL)**	**Credit (Million TL)**	**Mean of credit per branch (Million TL)**	**MOORA Ratio System**	
36	**Scenario 3**	**Max**	**Max**	**Max**	**Max**	**Min**	**Min**	**Formula (7)**	**Rank**
37	Istanbul	0.27085	0.18334	0.13718	0.09643	0.08851	0.02696	0.57232	**1**
38	West Marmara	0.01868	0.02882	0.00691	0.03029	0.00531	0.00989	0.06950	**7**
39	East Marmara	0.05392	0.05967	0.01602	0.03397	0.01510	0.01381	0.13467	**5**
40	Aegean	0.06559	0.09695	0.02855	0.03735	0.02226	0.01250	0.19369	**3**
41	Mediterranean	0.05108	0.07319	0.01957	0.03381	0.01970	0.01473	0.14321	**4**
42	West Black Sea	0.02251	0.03177	0.00635	0.02520	0.00550	0.00928	0.07105	**6**
43	East Black Sea	0.01224	0.01943	0.00359	0.02343	0.00298	0.00817	0.04754	**10**
44	West Anatolia	0.07028	0.08048	0.04534	0.07211	0.02951	0.02026	0.21843	**2**
45	Northeast Anatolia	0.00917	0.01011	0.00142	0.01838	0.00172	0.00907	0.02828	**12**
46	Central Anatolia	0.01691	0.02599	0.00620	0.03019	0.00509	0.01054	0.06367	**8**
47	Middle east Anatolia	0.00870	0.01346	0.00247	0.02343	0.00247	0.00979	0.03580	**11**
48	Southeast Anatolia	0.02074	0.03026	0.00487	0.02025	0.00894	0.01609	0.05110	**9**
49									
50	**Weights:**	**0.3**	**0.25**	**0.15**	**0.15**	**0.1**	**0.05**		

Figure 9. Calculation of Reference Point Approach for Scenario3

	A	B	C	D	E	F	G
50	Weights:	0.3	0.25	0.15	0.15	0.1	0.05
51							
52	**Weighted Normalized Matrix**	**The Number of Employees of Banks**	**The Number of Branch**	**Deposits (Million TL)**	**Mean of deposits per branch (Million TL)**	**Credit (Million TL)**	**Mean of credit per branch (Million TL)**
53	**Scenario 3**	Max	Max	Max	Max	Min	Min
54	Istanbul	0.27085	0.18334	0.13718	0.09643	0.08851	0.02696
55	West Marmara	0.01868	0.02882	0.00691	0.03029	0.00531	0.00989
56	East Marmara	0.05392	0.05967	0.01602	0.03397	0.01510	0.01381
57	Aegean	0.06559	0.09695	0.02855	0.03735	0.02226	0.01250
58	Mediterranean	0.05108	0.07319	0.01957	0.03381	0.01970	0.01473
59	West Black Sea	0.02251	0.03177	0.00635	0.02520	0.00550	0.00928
60	East Black Sea	0.01224	0.01943	0.00359	0.02343	0.00298	0.00817
61	West Anatolia	0.07028	0.08048	0.04534	0.07211	0.02951	0.02026
62	Northeast Anatolia	0.00917	0.01011	0.00142	0.01838	0.00172	0.00907
63	Central Anatolia	0.01691	0.02599	0.00620	0.03019	0.00509	0.01054
64	Middle east Anatolia	0.00870	0.01346	0.00247	0.02343	0.00247	0.00979
65	Southeast Anatolia	0.02074	0.03026	0.00487	0.02025	0.00894	0.01609
66	**Reference Points:**	**0.27085**	**0.18334**	**0.13718**	**0.09643**	**0.00172**	**0.00817**

	A	B	C	D	E	F	G	H	I
69	**Deviations from reference points**	**The Number of Employees of Banks**	**The Number of Branch**	**Deposits (Million TL)**	**Mean of deposits per branch (Million TL)**	**Credit (Million TL)**	**Mean of credit per branch (Million TL)**	**MOORA Reference Point Approach**	
70	**Scenario 3**	Max	Max	Max	Max	Min	Min	Formula (8)	Rank
71	Istanbul	0.00000	0.00000	0.00000	0.00000	0.08679	0.01879	0.08679	1
72	West Marmara	0.25218	0.15452	0.13027	0.06614	0.00359	0.00172	0.25218	8
73	East Marmara	0.21693	0.12367	0.12116	0.06246	0.01338	0.00564	0.21693	4
74	Aegean	0.20526	0.08639	0.10863	0.05907	0.02054	0.00433	0.20526	3
75	Mediterranean	0.21977	0.11015	0.11761	0.06262	0.01798	0.00656	0.21977	5
76	West Black Sea	0.24834	0.15157	0.13084	0.07123	0.00378	0.00111	0.24834	6
77	East Black Sea	0.25862	0.16391	0.13359	0.07299	0.00126	0.00000	0.25862	10
78	West Anatolia	0.20058	0.10286	0.09185	0.02432	0.02779	0.01209	0.20058	2
79	Northeast Anatolia	0.26168	0.17323	0.13576	0.07805	0.00000	0.00090	0.26168	11
80	Central Anatolia	0.25394	0.15735	0.13098	0.06624	0.00337	0.00237	0.25394	9
81	Middle east Anatolia	0.26215	0.16988	0.13471	0.07300	0.00074	0.00162	0.26215	12
82	Southeast Anatolia	0.25011	0.15308	0.13231	0.07617	0.00721	0.00792	0.25011	7

Figure 10. Calculation of Full Multiplicative Form

	A	H	I	J	K
86	**Full Multiplicative Form**	**Full Multiplicative Form**			
87	**Scenario3**	**Formula (9) Ai**	**Formula (9) Bi**	**Formula (9)**	**Rank**
88	Istanbul	3325.10816	4.83335055	687.950962	1
89	West Marmara	503.9363298	3.46950986	145.247124	7
90	East Marmara	958.9138555	3.91678596	244.821613	5
91	Aegean	1270.113516	4.051496098	313.492469	3
92	Mediterranean	1022.394231	4.035255139	253.365449	4
93	West Black Sea	524.4903227	3.470685494	151.120095	6
94	East Black Sea	350.8807464	3.243837792	108.168401	10
95	West Anatolia	1464.114369	4.269142401	342.952807	2
96	Northeast Anatolia	229.2018789	3.086984364	74.2478263	12
97	Central Anatolia	468.7960687	3.465985766	135.256201	8
98	Middle east Anatolia	273.1485237	3.211997729	85.0400737	11
99	Southeast Anatolia	470.1981215	3.745036318	125.552353	9

Table 11. MULTIMOORA for Scenario3

	MOORA Ratio System	MOORA Reference Point Approach	Full Multiplicative Form	MULTIMOORA
Scenario 3	**Rank**	**Rank**	**Rank**	**Rank**
Istanbul	1	1	1	**1**
West Marmara	7	8	7	**7**
East Marmara	5	4	5	**5**
Aegean	3	3	3	**3**
Mediterranean	4	5	4	**4**
West Black Sea	6	6	6	**6**
East Black Sea	10	10	10	**10**
West Anatolia	2	2	2	**2**
Northeast Anatolia	12	11	12	**12**
Central Anatolia	8	9	8	**8**
Middle East Anatolia	11	12	11	**11**
Southeast Anatolia	9	7	9	**9**

Istanbul is the first region of ranking list and Northeast Anatolia is ranked at the last of the list.

Scenario 4: Suppose that there are different significance levels of objectives of Scenario2. Those significance levels add to scenario as weights. Therefore Scenario4 is obtained.

For MOORA Ratio System, data are normalized with using formula (1) and normalized values are multiplied by their weights. Weighted normalized matrix is written to cells (B37:G48) on the Excel spreadsheet. Formula (7) is applied and its conclusions are written to cells (H37:H48) on the spreadsheet. Values on the cells (H37:H48) are ranked on the (I37:I48) on the Figure 11.

Calculation steps of Reference Point Approach are given on the Figure 12. Reference points are determined on the cells (B66:G66). Deviations from reference points are obtained on the cells (B71:G82). By using formula (8), values are obtained on the cells (H71:H82) and they are ranked on the cells (I71:I82).

Full Multiplicative Form is applied to data set with using formula (9). A_i and B_i are calculated. Data are on the cells (B88:G99). Attributes of the objectives are given on the Table 12. Column D, E, F and

Table 12. List of objectives, their attributes and their weights for Scenario4

O1	The number of employees of banks	Min	0.15
O2	The number of branch	Min	0.20
O3	Deposits (Million TL)	Max	0.20
O4	Mean of deposits per branch (Million TL)	Max	0.15
O5	Credit (Million TL)	Max	0.20
O6	Mean of credit per branch (Million TL)	Max	0.10

Figure 11. Calculation of Weighted Normalized Matrix and Ratio System for Scenario4

Weighted Nomalized Matrix	The Number of Employees of Banks	The Number of Branch	Deposits (Million TL)	Mean of deposits per branch (Million TL)	Credit (Million TL)	Mean of credit per branch (Million TL)	MOORA Ratio System	
Scenario 4	**Min**	**Min**	**Max**	**Max**	**Max**	**Max**	**Formula (7)**	**Rank**
Istanbul	0.13543	0.14667	0.18291	0.09643	0.17703	0.05392	0.22819	1
West Marmara	0.00934	0.02305	0.00922	0.03029	0.01062	0.01977	0.03751	7
East Marmara	0.02696	0.04774	0.02136	0.03397	0.03021	0.02762	0.03846	6
Aegean	0.03280	0.07756	0.03807	0.03735	0.04453	0.02500	0.03459	9
Mediterranean	0.02554	0.05855	0.02609	0.03381	0.03941	0.02945	0.04466	3
West Black Sea	0.01125	0.02542	0.00846	0.02520	0.01100	0.01855	0.02654	12
East Black Sea	0.00612	0.01554	0.00479	0.02343	0.00596	0.01634	0.02887	11
West Anatolia	0.03514	0.06438	0.06045	0.07211	0.05902	0.04053	0.13258	2
Northeast Anatolia	0.00458	0.00809	0.00189	0.01838	0.00345	0.01815	0.02919	10
Central Anatolia	0.00846	0.02080	0.00827	0.03019	0.01018	0.02108	0.04047	5
Middle east Anatolia	0.00435	0.01077	0.00329	0.02343	0.00494	0.01957	0.03612	8
Southeast Anatolia	0.01037	0.02421	0.00649	0.02025	0.01788	0.03217	0.04221	4
Weights:	0.15	0.2	0.2	0.15	0.2	0.1		

Figure 12. Calculation of Reference Point Approach for Scenario4

Weights:	0.15	0.2	0.2	0.15	0.2	0.1
Weighted Nomalized Matrix	**The Number of Employees of Banks**	**The Number of Branch**	**Deposits (Million TL)**	**Mean of deposits per branch (Million TL)**	**Credit (Million TL)**	**Mean of credit per branch (Million TL)**
Scenario 4	**Min**	**Min**	**Max**	**Max**	**Max**	**Max**
Istanbul	0.13543	0.14667	0.18291	0.09643	0.17703	0.05392
West Marmara	0.00934	0.02305	0.00922	0.03029	0.01062	0.01977
East Marmara	0.02696	0.04774	0.02136	0.03397	0.03021	0.02762
Aegean	0.03280	0.07756	0.03807	0.03735	0.04453	0.02500
Mediterranean	0.02554	0.05855	0.02609	0.03381	0.03941	0.02945
West Black Sea	0.01125	0.02542	0.00846	0.02520	0.01100	0.01855
East Black Sea	0.00612	0.01554	0.00479	0.02343	0.00596	0.01634
West Anatolia	0.03514	0.06438	0.06045	0.07211	0.05902	0.04053
Northeast Anatolia	0.00458	0.00809	0.00189	0.01838	0.00345	0.01815
Central Anatolia	0.00846	0.02080	0.00827	0.03019	0.01018	0.02108
Middle east Anatolia	0.00435	0.01077	0.00329	0.02343	0.00494	0.01957
Southeast Anatolia	0.01037	0.02421	0.00649	0.02025	0.01788	0.03217
Reference Points:	**0.00435**	**0.00809**	**0.18291**	**0.09643**	**0.17703**	**0.05392**

Deviations from reference points	The Number of Employees of Banks	The Number of Branch	Deposits (Million TL)	Mean of deposits per branch (Million TL)	Credit (Million TL)	Mean of credit per branch (Million TL)	MOORA Reference Point Approach	
Scenario 4	**Min**	**Min**	**Max**	**Max**	**Max**	**Max**	**Formula (8)**	**Rank**
Istanbul	0.13108	0.13858	0.00000	0.00000	0.00000	0.00000	0.13858	2
West Marmara	0.00499	0.01497	0.17369	0.06614	0.16641	0.03415	0.17369	6
East Marmara	0.02261	0.03965	0.16155	0.06246	0.14682	0.02630	0.16155	5
Aegean	0.02845	0.06948	0.14484	0.05907	0.13250	0.02892	0.14484	3
Mediterranean	0.02119	0.05047	0.15682	0.06262	0.13762	0.02447	0.15682	4
West Black Sea	0.00690	0.01733	0.17445	0.07123	0.16603	0.03537	0.17445	7
East Black Sea	0.00177	0.00746	0.17812	0.07299	0.17107	0.03758	0.17812	10
West Anatolia	0.03079	0.05630	0.12246	0.02432	0.11801	0.01340	0.12246	1
Northeast Anatolia	0.00024	0.00000	0.18102	0.07805	0.17358	0.03578	0.18102	12
Central Anatolia	0.00411	0.01271	0.17464	0.06624	0.16685	0.03284	0.17464	8
Middle east Anatolia	0.00000	0.00268	0.17961	0.07300	0.17209	0.03435	0.17961	11
Southeast Anatolia	0.00602	0.01612	0.17642	0.07617	0.15915	0.02175	0.17642	9

G belong to maximization objectives; O3, O4, O5 and O6. B and C columns are minimization form, because of O1 and O2. Calculation steps are given on the Figure 13.

Finally, MULTIMOORA ranking list of alternatives could be obtained from three ranking lists; Ratio System, Reference Point Approach and Full Multiplicative Form, by dominance theory on the Table13.

Istanbul is the first region of ranking list and Northeast Anatolia is ranked at the last of the list.

Figure 13. Calculation of Full Multiplicative Form

	A	H	I	J	K
86	**Full Multiplicative Form**	**Full Multiplicative Form**			
87	**Scenario 4**	**Formula (9) Ai**	**Formula (9) Bi**	**Formula (9)**	**Rank**
88	Istanbul	702.9311122	26.49609486	26.52961185	**1**
89	West Marmara	167.4833257	12.25302455	13.66873338	7
90	East Marmara	256.9125478	16.6163314	15.46144823	**5**
91	Aegean	312.9946001	18.85655946	16.59871202	**3**
92	Mediterranean	283.6107633	17.16926445	16.51851563	**4**
93	West Black Sea	160.2747481	12.84919744	12.47352209	**9**
94	East Black Sea	123.6009972	10.62824229	11.62948621	**11**
95	West Anatolia	420.7222648	18.35597921	22.92017549	**2**
96	Northeast Anatolia	89.6105453	8.931352604	10.0332558	**12**
97	Central Anatolia	163.4774665	11.82575027	13.82385581	**6**
98	Middle east Anatolia	112.4330828	9.382698889	11.98302153	**10**
99	Southeast Anatolia	171.2649441	12.56960337	13.62532604	**8**

Table 13. MULTIMOORA for Scenario4

	MOORA Ratio System	MOORA Reference Point Approach	Full Multiplicative Form	MULTIMOORA
Scenario 4	**Rank**	**Rank**	**Rank**	**Rank**
Istanbul	1	2	1	**1**
West Marmara	7	6	7	**7**
East Marmara	6	5	5	**5**
Aegean	9	3	3	**3**
Mediterranean	3	4	4	**4**
West Black Sea	12	7	9	**9**
East Black Sea	11	10	11	**11**
West Anatolia	2	1	2	**2**
Northeast Anatolia	10	12	12	**12**
Central Anatolia	5	8	6	**6**
Middle East Anatolia	8	11	10	**10**
Southeast Anatolia	4	9	8	**8**

FUTURE RESEARCH DIRECTIONS

Multi criteria decision making methods always help the decision maker. Objectives and/or alternatives can change, but MULTIMOORA Method may apply to different decision making problems. MULTIMOORA Method can improve with integrating to different methods such as; Analytic Hierarchy Process, Fuzzy Analytic Hierarchy Process(Yıldırım& Önay, 2013), Macbeth (Kundakcı, 2016) and so on.

MULTIMOORA method can use in fuzzy environment. Researchers can use MULTIMOORA method with different techniques and they can find solutions their problems in the future studies.

CONCLUSION

MULTIMOORA method is composed of multi-objective optimization by ratio analysis (MOORA) method and full multiplicative form. This method could apply to a lot of areas where the decision making problems are occurred.

In the study, MULTIMOORA method is applied to banking sector. There are 12 regions as alternatives and 6 objectives. Decision making problem is taken by four Scenarios. Perspective of customer is taken in the Scenario1. Customer's perspective is evaluated in the Scenario3 with using weights. Manager's perspective of a bank is assessed in the Scenario2 and in the Scenario4 with using weights.

In the Scenario1; O1, O2, O3 and O4 are benefit objectives for customer, so they are maximized objectives and O5, O6 are cost objectives, so they are minimized objectives according to customer. Under the attributes, MULTIMOORA method is applied and regions are ranked. Istanbul is the first region of ranking list. West Anatolia is second region. On the other hand, Northeast Anatolia is ranked at the last of the list; Middle East Anatolia is eleventh region, Southeast Anatolia is tenth region from twelve regions in the results of Scenario1. According to the results, Istanbul is most satisfactory region. But Northeast Anatolia need to improvement about banking services sector. Bank's managers can take into account to invest to Northeast Anatolia, Middle East Anatolia and Southeast Anatolia for customer pleasure.

In the Scenario3; objectives are given with different significance levels. Weights are given randomly, but they could determine with different techniques. Under the attributes and weights, MULTIMOORA method is applied and regions are ranked. Istanbul is the first region of ranking list. West Anatolia is the second region. On the other hand, Northeast Anatolia is ranked at the last of the list; Middle East Anatolia is eleventh region from twelve regions in the results of Scenario3. Weights cause changes at the ranking of the list of all regions.

In the Scenario2; O1 and O2 are cost objectives, so they are minimized objectives according to perspective of the bank. O3, O4, O5 and O6 are benefit objectives, so they are maximized objectives. Under the attributes, MULTIMOORA method is applied and regions are ranked. Istanbul is the first region of ranking list. West Anatolia is second region. On the other hand, Northeast Anatolia is ranked at the last of the list; East Black Sea is eleventh region, West Black Sea is tenth region from twelve regions in the results of Scenario2. According to the results, Istanbul is most satisfactory region. But Northeast Anatolia need to improvement about banking services sector. Bank's managers can take into account to invest to Northeast Anatolia, East Black Sea and West Black Sea for bank pleasure.

In the Scenario4; objectives are given with different significance levels. Weights are given randomly, but they could determine with different techniques. Under the attributes and weights, MULTIMOORA method is applied and regions are ranked. Istanbul is the first region of ranking list. West Anatolia is the second region. On the other hand, Northeast Anatolia is ranked at the last of the list; East Black Sea is eleventh region and Middle East Anatolia is tenth region from twelve regions in the results of Scenario4. Weights cause changes at the ranking of the regions.

As the seen from four applications, managers can use the multi criteria decision making methods as tool for their business. Alternatives or objectives may change but methods always help us.

REFERENCES

Baležentis, T., Baležentis, A., & Brauers, W. K. (2011). Multi Objective Optimization of Well Being in the European Union Member States. *Economic Research-Ekonomska Istraživanja*, *24*(4), 1–15. doi: 10.1080/1331677X.2011.11517485

Baležentis, A., Valkauskas, R., & Baležentis, T. (2010). Evaluating situation of Lithuania in the European Union: structural indicators and MULTIMOORA method. *Technological and Economic Development of Economy*, (4), 578-602.

Baležentis, T., & Baležentis, A. (2011). A multi-criteria assessment of relative farming efficiency in the European Union Member States. *Žemės ūkio mokslai, 18*(3), 125-135.

Baležentis, T., & Baležentis, A. (2014). A Survey on Development and Applications of the Multi-criteria Decision Making Method MULTIMOORA. *Journal of Multi-Criteria Decision Analysis*, *21*(3-4), 209–222. doi:10.1002/mcda.1501

Brauers, W. K., & Ginevičius, R. (2013). How to invest in Belgian shares by MULTIMOORA optimization. *Journal of Business Economics and management, 14*(5), 940-956.

Brauers, W. K., Ginevicius, R., & Podviezko, A. (2012). Evaluation of performance of Lithuanian commercial banks by multi-objective optimization. *The 7th International Scientific Conference Business and Management*, 1042-1049. doi:10.3846/bm.2012.133

Brauers, W. K. M., Ginevicius, R., & Podvezko, A. (2014b). Ranking of the Lithuanian Banks During the Recession of 2008-2009 by the MULTIMOORA Method. *Annals of Management Science*, *3*(1), 1–28.

Brauers, W. K. M., Ginevicius, R., & Podviezko, A. (2014a). Development of a methodology of evaluation of financial stability of commercial banks. *Panoeconomicus*, *61*(3), 349–367. doi:10.2298/PAN1403349B

Brauers, W. K. M., Kildienė, S., Zavadskas, E. K., & Kaklauskas, A. (2013). The construction sector in twenty European countries during the recession 2008–2009–country ranking by MULTIMOORA. *International Journal of Strategic Property Management*, *17*(1), 58–78. doi:10.3846/1648715X.2013.775194

Brauers, W. K. M., & Zavadskas, E. K. (2006). The MOORA method and its application to privatization in a transition economy. *Control and Cybernetics*, *35*(2), 445.

Brauers, W. K. M., & Zavadskas, E. K. (2010). Project management by MULTIMOORA as an instrument for transition economies. *Technological and Economic Development of Economy*, *16*(1), 5–24. doi:10.3846/tede.2010.01

Brauers, W. K. M., & Zavadskas, E. K. (2011). MULTIMOORA optimization used to decide on a bank loan to buy property. *Technological and Economic Development of Economy*, *17*(1), 174–188. doi:10.3846/13928619.2011.560632

Brauers, W. K. M., & Zavadskas, E. K. (2012). Robustness of MULTIMOORA: A method for multi-objective optimization. *Informatica*, *23*(1), 1–25.

Data Query System of the Banks Association of Turkey. (n.d.). Retrieved July 13, 2016, from https://www.tbb.org.tr/tr/bankacilik/banka-ve-sektor-bilgileri/veri-sorgulama-sistemi/illere-ve-bolgelere-gore-bilgiler/73

Görener, A., Dincer, H., & Hacioglu, U. (2016). Application of multi-objective optimization on the basis of ratio analysis (MOORA) method for bank branch location selection. *International Journal of Finance & Banking Studies, 2*(2), 41-52.

Hafezalkotob, A., & Hafezalkotob, A. (2015). Comprehensive MULTIMOORA method with target-based attributes and integrated significant coefficients for materials selection in biomedical applications. *Materials & Design, 87*, 949–959. doi:10.1016/j.matdes.2015.08.087

Hafezalkotob, A., Hafezalkotob, A., & Sayadi, M. K. (2016). Extension of MULTIMOORA method with interval numbers: An application in materials selection. *Applied Mathematical Modelling, 40*(2), 1372–1386. doi:10.1016/j.apm.2015.07.019

Kundakcı, N. (2016). Combined Multi-Criteria Decision Making Approach Based On Macbeth And Multi-MOORA Methods. *Alphanumeric Journal, 4*(1), 17–26. doi:10.17093/aj.2016.4.1.5000178402

Önay, O. (2016). Multi-Criteria Assessment of Better Life via TOPSIS and MOORA Methods. *International Journal of Business and Social Science, 7*(1), 225–234.

Önay, O., & Yıldırım, B. F. (2016). Evaluation of NUTS Level 2 Regions of Turkey by TOPSIS, MOORA and VIKOR. *International Journal of Humanities and Social Science, 6*(1), 212–221.

Özbek, A. (2015). Efficiency Analysis of Foreign-Capital Banks in Turkey by OCRA and MOORA. *Research Journal of Finance and Accounting, 6*(13), 2222–1697.

Report of The Banks Association of Turkey. (n.d.). *Distribution of selected indicators of banking system according to cities and regions in the Turkey*. Retrieved July 13, 2016, from https://www.tbb.org.tr/tr/bankacilik/banka-ve-sektor-bilgileri/4

Stankevičienė, J., Sviderskė, T., & Miečinskienė, A. (2014). Dependence of sustainability on country risk indicators in EU Baltic Sea region countries. *Journal of Business Economics and Management, 15*(4), 646–663. doi:10.3846/16111699.2014.965555

Uygurtürk, H. (2015). Evaluating internet branches of banks using fuzzy MOORA method. *Int.*[Turkish]. *Journal of Management Economics and Business, 11*(25), 115–128.

Yıldırım, B. F., & Önay, O. (2013). Ranking cloud storage technology firms using FUZZY AHP – MOORA method. *YÖNETİM: İstanbul Üniversitesi İşletme İktisadı Enstitüsü Dergisi, 24*(75), 59–81.

Chapter 3
Analytics in Public Policy Related to Service Sector

Maryam Ebrahimi
Azad University, Iran

ABSTRACT

Big Data is transforming industries such as healthcare, financial services and banking, insurance, pharmacy, and telecommunication. Big Data concerns datasets that are not only big, but also high in variety and velocity, which makes them difficult to manage applying traditional tools and techniques. Big Data causes multitude benefits and advantages for industries such as marketing and selling, fraud detection, competitive advantage, risk reduction, and finally decision making and policy making. Due to the rapid growth of such data, methodologies and conceptual architectures need to be studied and provided in order to handle and extract value and knowledge from these data. The purpose of this chapter is studying Big Data benefits, characteristics, methodologies, and conceptual architectures in five different industries. Finally, according to the studies, a comprehensive methodology and architecture are proposed which might be applicable in service sector and one of the useful outcomes can be public policies.

INTRODUCTION

In recent years, data is considered as a potential affecting factor that can boost growth in economic status and improve life quality in different fields through helping individuals and organizations make better decisions. Currently, both public and private sectors are using a large amount of data and getting benefit from it for diverse purposes. For instance, these data provides numerous opportunities for problem solving and decision making to make more efficient and effective systems in healthcare, financial services, insurance, pharmacy, telecommunication, transportation, and energy industries. It helps companies and industries predict their future and become more proactive.

The creation of value by use of Big Data can be possible via five ways:

1. It releases important value because data in greater quantities are more vivid and more practical;
2. Collecting, compiling, and storing data from corporate's transactions and operations make it possible for firms to have more precise and thorough information which leads to a more obvious image

DOI: 10.4018/978-1-5225-2148-8.ch003

of organizational performance to contribute decision makers to decide more accurately to improve the performance of their companies;

3. With better access to the customers' data, it can be easier to understand the customers and therefore it will be better to define strategies related to market and especially marketing strategies and market segmentation which result to meet the customers' needs and preferences through providing required products and services;
4. Big Data analysis can be performed by various methods and techniques which are complicated and basically it conducts to a higher quality decisions and results;
5. By supporting the prediction of the future, it helps companies develop new required products and services which cause the survival and growth of the companies in the future competitive market.

Using Big Data enables companies for better regulation and arrangement of main processes according to changing external conditions in favor of the creation of new services, and plausible innovative models and methods in the healthcare system. As a result, companies involving in healthcare sector can be more efficient and promote the quality of their services. Big Data analysis provides the possibility of clarification of hidden knowledge and exploring the trends enclosed by a wide range of data. For the sake of this understanding, companies are capable of improving treatment, decrease the death rate of patients, and reduce the cost. In this case, there are Big Data analytics applications which give an advantage of an outburst of data to discover concealed insight to make more enlightened decisions.

As a result of efforts to identify and perceive customers' preferences to provide essential and distinguished services, the quantity of data with high variety is increased. Thus, companies in financial services and banking sector adopt data storages and data warehouses to store data and computer-based tools to analyze the current conditions and predict the future regarding the customer behavior and their needs. This causes these companies to optimize their transactions and operations. The implementation of Big Data management systems including data gives greater advantages because it leads companies in this sector be able to more predictive and proactive. Additionally, it provides companies more insight which is useful to make decisions effectively.

Big Data management is also a big challenge for insurance companies. This issue in addition to having data in low quality makes difficulties higher. Insurers try to investigate illegal claims early in the wheel of life and prevent the related payment to control a huge amount of claims costs. Using data analysis leverages valuable data assets that were far being underutilized, and therefore it significantly improves enterprise-wide information flow. The aggregation of data is a formal recognition of the importance of different and new sources of information. Analytics can be used to effectively leverage partner data, for instance, and allow an enterprise to share processed data with them to improve operational intelligence.

Big Data provides the pharmaceutical industry an unbeatable circumstance to make the best or most effective use of research and clinical testing, forecast the universal patterns, control fraudulent behaviors, improve the consequences of treatment. To gain the ability to mix historical data for having more insight and competitive insight as well, companies in this area should invest more in data collection as well as data management. In the process of discovering drugs and their development, a mix of different computational approaches such as statistics and computer science can be used in medicine and biology. Using some methods such as data mining and artificial intelligence are common to analyze a high volume of data. These data in the area of biology and medicine are structured and unstructured which are gathered through diverse sources including hospitals, pharmacies, laboratories, and etc. These data can be categorized into different classes such as gene, drug, clinical testing, and patient records, their behavior, and data reported by patients in a social media, and the others.

Telecommunication industry like the other mentioned industries creates and stores large deal of data. These data includes call data, network data, and customer data. At first, call data refers to the data related to calls which passes through the networks. At second, network data is defined as the data relevant to the conditions of the hardware and software embedded in the network. At third, customer data shows the profile of each customer in the telecommunication industry. Big Data makes higher growth and efficiency in the value chain of telecommunication companies.

Big Data refers to datasets that have 3Vs characteristics: volume, variety, and velocity. First, volume is determined as the amount of data. Second, variety refers to the number of data types. Finally, velocity is related to the pace of data. All these features of Big Data cause difficulties in managing Big Data by using traditional tools and techniques. To promote better decision making in the mentioned industries, data analysis through different methodologies and architectures can be implemented. The purpose of this chapter is studying Big Data benefits, characteristics, methodologies, and conceptual architectures in five different industries. Finally, according to the studies, a comprehensive methodology and architecture are proposed which might be applicable in the service sector and one of the useful outcomes can be public policies.

BIG DATA IN HEALTHCARE SYSTEM

Recently Big Data has changed radically various service sectors in diverse ways. By providing more data and analyses, informatics applications prompt sudden opportunities including higher efficiencies and superior results in various functional areas. One of the systems that produce the greatest amount of data on a daily basis is the healthcare. Due to high-speed generation of these massive quantities of data, sometimes health organizations are unable to process and transform them into usable and fruitful knowledge. In general, the huge volume of data derived from functions of the healthcare system is scattered and unorganized. Access to these large amounts of data in diverse data types and their analyses in accurate and reliable ways can be a huge revolution in the healthcare and cause an unimaginable growth of the healthcare systems.

Recently, many countries were determined for processing Big Data in the healthcare. For this purpose, all organizations, public and private sectors in the healthcare attempted to organize all data consistently for having precise analyses.

A great deal of values caused by Big Data processing in healthcare system divided into the following categories:

- **True Lifestyle:** It is one of the most major medical data processing achievements. By using medical information of each patient with respect to privacy policy, it is possible to develop tools to monitor the daily health of the patient, and communicate with the patient during his/her daily activities for providing essential recommendations and warnings. Many diseases through early intervention can be prevented or ameliorated. Having that knowledge, patients can change their lifestyles to keep away possible risks. Due to change in lifestyles and subsequently possible abrupt shift in population disease patterns, there are savings in medical costs.

- **The Accuracy of Treatment:** Patients should receive timely, accurate, and complete treatment. With the correct processing of data, doctors are aware of the decisions of their colleagues and based on existing records grouped in precise and detailed ways, necessary treatment can be done in the fastest possible time.
- **The Cost- Effectiveness of Treatment:** Analysis of Big Data results in higher quality care at lower costs with the better outcome due to revealing patterns and providing more insights regarding diagnoses and treatments. In other words, it refers to achieving better consequences through various scenarios. For instance, as a result of the analysis of characteristics of the patients and costs and given advantages of the treatment, it is possible to determine the cost-effectiveness of treatment (Raghupathi and Raghupathi, 2014).
- **Select the Right Server:** It makes the judgment based on the name and job title put to an end. During illness, records of all the doctors and medical centers are available and patient according to factual and confirmed information and not based on advertising; put their lives in the hands of a physician.
- **Fraud Detection:** Medical frauds can be exemplified by providing false and deliberately misleading and deceiving declarations to patients, announcing the wrong cost of services, making changes in the patient case, untruthful regarding credentials or qualifications, unrequired medical treatment or drug prescription. For the purpose of fraud detection in the healthcare system, it is required to combine a large volume of data and use complicated methods related to mathematics, statistics, and computer science (Margret J. and Sreenivasan, 2013).
- **True Values:** Under these conditions, medical service providers and insurance companies can operate completely based on real values. For example, in an insurance company to refund the amount of treatment which is subject to the complete cure of the patient, the real-time patient status should be considered.
- **True Innovation:** Shareholders of healthcare systems for their survival requires growth in creativity and innovation. They will have their research and development organization, and try to achieve the highest point in modern medicine.

Because of all above advantages, acquiring applications, platform, and methods for the effective use of Big Data likely have a profound effect on healthcare organizations. In case of public health, Big Data analysis makes more care, faster response, and quicker development of more accurately targeted vaccines through studying trends of illness and exploring disease prevalence and transmission. Besides, it gives usable information in order to determine requirements, supply useful and required services for the patients, and forecast potential intense difficulties prior to the occurrence, particularly with a view to increasing the benefits to society (Raghupathi and Raghupathi, 2014).

BIG DATA IN BANKING AND FINANCIAL SERVICES INDUSTRY

Analysis and decision making in the financial sphere are complex due to large amounts of valuable financial data from one side, and on the other hand, ambiguities arising from new business models. With the advancement of organizations in the field of financial decision-making, accounting and auditing are not restricted to mere data collection, but the main concern of organizations is their ability to extract useful knowledge underlying the huge amount of data. In these conditions, effective methods and technologies should be adopted. Big Data approaches and techniques provide financial services in general and banking in particular with the depth and speed of insight required to be survived and also achieve growth by preparing the expected level of customer service. Particularly, since these companies provide services generally not physical products like manufacturing companies, data is viewed as the most important asset they possess. Thus, Big Data analytics can be recognized as a differentiating factor for these companies.

Big Data analysis in financial services industry has multitude benefits illustrated as follows:

- **Customer Engagement and Retention:** The financial services industry invests for providing enough ability to analyze Big Data, extract the preferences and spending habits of each individual customer and make the personalization of services. In other words, financial services industry moves from sale oriented strategy to customer-focused strategy by virtue of the use of Big Data analysis. This change causes a considerable development in these companies. In the banking sector, it is important to know how long a customer may stay with the companies in addition to their emotional triggers for decision making. Big Data analysis makes it happen to categorize customers into diverse client segments and understand their sensitivity to interest rate adjustments, credit scoring, or other conditions. By managing segmentation rules for predicting, guiding, and responding to customer actions, it can enhance profitability and customer loyalty. For the aim of retention of the existing customers and attracting new customers, companies in financial services industry should change their current business models and also traditional approaches.
- **Provide Significant Competitive Advantage:** In essence, Big Data analytics transform the business practices of the financial services industry. By using privately held data and publicly available sources (open data), it is possible to gain insights that were previously unavailable. Realization the output of these data to create the best measures then becomes the differentiator. In order to create differentiation with competitors, companies need to do a detailed study and review about their future. For this reason, they use historical data and analyze the patterns of specific data to make better and more precise decisions that are more aligned with the long-term planning of the company.
- **Fraud detection:** The success of the financial services industry in fraud detection is related to how it is able to proactively store and analyze a great deal of data. Banking operations must be monitored timely for finding unusual behaviors. Effective detection for identifying bizarre and illegal activities responds against to profitability risk and also makes an increase in the brand image of a company in a competitive environment.
- **Risk Reduction:** Linking data, structured and unstructured, makes it better to evaluate claims, customers and applicants, and it gives more ability to a firm to approve more customers for higher credit limits, without increasing default rates. It helps a firm predict which customers are at risk of leaving and identify any clues about why.

Big Data as a dramatic change in the deal of data shapes the methods of data analysis in central banks. Universities and private sectors carried out numerous Big Data projects. But it is not true to compare central banks with those companies and institutions because it has some distinct public responsibilities and legitimate authorities (Bholat, 2015). Several central banks think that they are able to make use of these developments to create a better base for their policy decisions and have altered their strategies for managing data (Hokkanen et al., 2015). Many central banks move in the direction of investment in the area of Big Data. They adopt Big Data analysis to predict the state of the economy at the macro level by using indicators such as inflation, GDP, unemployment rate, fees, sales, and production in private sectors. With the help of Big Data analysis, they can also analyze the financial stability and risk conditions of businesses (Irving Fisher Committee on Central Bank Statistics, 2015).

BIG DATA IN INSURANCE COMPANIES

Despite the challenges of today's environment of insurance companies, there are still opportunities by which they can outdo the competition. These circumstances allow them to improve their adaptability to changes in market and business environment with regard to being more economical and productive. For example, using Big Data analysis in insurance companies helps them optimize their operating costs. One of the opportunities for insurance companies is the capability of data and analytics which impact organizational performance. Insurers try to take the advantages of Big Data applications as a result of having access to a high volume of data from various internal and external sources. Despite their complexity in deployment, these applications can provide information for the support of organizational strategies.

It is easy to cite the reasons why insurance organizations consider the use of Big Data analysis, which relies especially on identifying and developing a better understanding of current conditions and forecasting the future. To find appropriate insurance solution, internal and additional external data that might be related to a potential insurance outcome are applied.

The key benefits of Big Data analysis in insurance industry are listed as follows:

- **Planning for Potential Future Crises:** Big Data analysis helps insurers be proactive instead of reactive by giving the ability to predict the possible catastrophe in future, making a reduction in a number of claims, and responding the requests quicker. In other words, it ameliorates customer service and profitability with accelerated claims processing. Prediction of the claim severity leads to assign and track the claims more efficient and faster.
- **Risk Avoidance:** Big Data analysis helps insurer assess the risks in insurance requests because it is able to combine and analyze the customer's data and related kinds of services and extract insight of customers' behavioral models. Therefore, insurance underwriters can evaluate the risk of each potential customer to determine required surcharge associated with that risk.
- **Fraud Detection:** By Big Data analysis, insurance companies are able to detect fraud better and more efficient. Collecting data help define the potential occurrence and existence of fraud. Through this, insurers are able to determine the behavioral model of customers, ordinary and skeptical, for the aim of defining the plausible insurance fraud. It saves time and money by automating and standardizing the scoring process.
- **Increase in Selling:** It builds more ability for insurers to suggest and sell further services to existing customers, given that these services touch the needs and preferences of the customer. It improves sales functionality and effectiveness, and optimizes customer service by enabling insurers to present customers the required policies at the quite competitive price. Scoring models of customer behavior based on particular statistical data such as demographics in addition to the account and health information makes it possible for insurers to provide services good enough to meet the needs and preferences of customers. Through Big Data analysis, insurers can effectively target high-value customers with the most meaningful offerings.

BIG DATA IN PHARMACY

Due to financial concerns relevant to the growth of health care expenditures, sharing data for the purpose of data analysis is considered. Nowadays, physicians have been compelled to change their methods to treatment that focuses on more evidence-based way such as reviewing all medical data and decisions systematically. Collecting and analyzing information in an easier way, technology can be a key element. By having suitable data and using diverse data mining techniques, evaluation of successful treatment in special situations, identification of trends of undesirable effect of drugs, and understanding the readmissions rate of hospitals are possible (Smith HW and Juarez DT, 2015).

Big Data analysis in pharmacy industry like the other industries caused a tremendous move to innovation, rise in productivity, and growth in captured value and ability of the competition. It brings about a discovery of new drugs, clinical trials, and portfolio management. It can also enhance business efficiencies in sales and marketing strategies. Big Data analysis is essentially required today due to increasingly changing marketplace, and competitive landscape. Insights that can be gained from data analysis can be indispensable in the sales promotion and marketing strategies, and ensuring reliable return on investment. To make certain for having a highly profit-driven strategy, pharmaceutical companies need not only to implement Big Data from the very beginning of the planning process but also use it for evaluating the success of their campaigns.

Regarding the benefits of Big Data analysis in pharmaceutical industry, the following items can be illustrated:

- **Improve in Decision Making:** The most significant benefit that Big Data can make for pharmaceutical companies is to improve decision-making. Managing a very extent of gathered data from numerous sources, Big Data helps them realize market dynamics at a more general level and as a result, make more informed, and strategic decisions.
- **Gain a Competitive Advantage:** For doing the planning process and especially deciding about the budget, real-time information is highly required and considering ever-changing world of pharmaceutical companies, using Big Data help them have insight concerning the keys to gain competitive advantage. These insights are crucial for making long-term decisions as well as responding to short-term changes in the market environment. Big Data makes a better understanding of the patients by identifying patient preferences. By having a good knowledge about the market environment, segmentation is possible to provide suitable marketing policies. Sales and marketing teams are able to create accurate profiles of their top targets, prepare the most appropriate channels and the best ways to reach them by using Big Data and its analysis. Big Data gives pharmaceutical companies the ability to react quickly to new development almost in real-time and enables them to be proactive enough to take preventative actions before serious damage takes place.

BIG DATA IN TELECOMMUNICATION INDUSTRY

Conducting Big Data analytics enables telecommunication industry to use their internal data for having more efficiency and profitability, and customer segmentation.

Benefits of Big Data analytics in telecommunication industry can be described as follows (Acker et al., 2013):

- **Management of Network Infrastructure:** It needs some functionalities such as deep packet inspection (DPI) in real-time for the purpose of finding the possibility of presence and existence of viruses, spams, and optimization of traffic routing by defining criteria to make decision whether a packet can pass or it is required to be directed to a different point. In addition, by the measurement of data traffic, the network can be prepared to provide new services to its users.
- **Access and Integration of Services:** In this case, the functionality of call data record (CDR) in real-time make it possible to analyze data in various formats generated through different tools such as a telephone to have insight about behavioral models of customer and in special cases to identify fraudulent behaviors. Companies in this industry can collect and integrate data from different sources to find illegal activities and promote the efficiency and precision of the processes of pattern recognition of fraud behavior.
- **Marketing & Sales:** Event-driven marketing (EDM) is derived from the collection of data profiles of customers though social media and enables companies to customize their responses in accordance with the needs and preferences of customers, to enhance cross and up selling to sell extra products and services to current customers and encourage customers to buy more expensive items with the aim of having more profits. Data collection and integration in diverse formats and from different sources contribute companies to create price plans and provide attractive features.
- **Innovation:** Data collection and integration provide patterns of purchases in real-time which can be useful to innovate and create new products and services.

CHARACTERISTICS OF BIG DATA

For the purpose of discussing Big Data and its related issues, it is essential to know its different dimensions that help define better Big Data. For illustration, usually 3Vs is cited as Big Data features, known as

- Volume,
- Velocity and
- Variety (Laney, 2001).

Volume is defined as the size of data such as terabytes and even higher. Variety shows that data can be in many formats. It can be structured such as data record, and also unstructured such as an image. In general, unstructured data is very complicated in the case of searching and analyzing. Velocity comes from the speed of data streams and represents that data has high frequencies. There is another V in accordance with especial needs which shows a value of the data (Zikopoulos and Eaton, 2011).

In Big Data analytics of the healthcare system, three features of Big Data, volume, velocity, and variety are generally considered (Raghupathi and Raghupathi, 2014). Over time, massive amounts of data are created in the healthcare system and consistently accumulated. The large volume of data contains data such as patient medical records, X-ray films, medical testing data, genetics, and genomic sequences. However, despite the progress made in the field of virtualization and cloud computing, data is updated and processed more quickly referring to the velocity and can be stored, manipulated and managed more effectively. In addition to the increasing volume and variety of data, there are some challenges regarding the velocity as the speed of data creation. It should be considered as an essential factor for retrieving, analyzing the data, and decision making.

In the healthcare system, most data has been static such as paper files. The increase in velocity happens due to regular monitoring, such as daily measurements of diabetic glucose. In addition, the constant data such as blood pressure and bedside heart monitoring in real time represents the life or death of the patient. Applying real-time data including detecting and distinguishing infections in the shortest possible time, and adopting appropriate treatments increases the likelihood of the patient's life and even prevents outbreaks of disease. Finding serious infections as early as possible by using data such as monitoring newborn child in the ICU would be useful to reduce patient mortality.

Health data is gathered in different formats regarding how they are structured or whether they are paper-based or electronic and it makes healthcare data more challenging in the case of variety. In general, storage, analysis, and a process of structured data by applications are easier due to their easiness of coding and management. By converting paper-based records to electronic data such as conversion of notes of doctors and nurses to electronic clinical records, structured and semi-structured data can be generated.

Data that is originating from multiple sources causes better and more rapidly health-related discoveries. Some professionals and researchers have presented another characteristic which is veracity meaning as the reliability of data. Data quality, leading to the death and life of the patient is critical. It means that physicians should have the accurate information to decide precisely, however especially unstructured data, is very uncertain and changeable. Having Big Data veracity requires different architectures and platforms, algorithms, and methodologies.

The volume of data in bank industry enhances considerably from different sources such as loans, ATM, and other. Significant growth of demand for more improved products and services, increase in the competition, and many other factors cause an increase in the volume of data. Variety can be illustrated as data on the basis of diverse formats derived from a great deal of internal and external sources such as bank's transactional records or supply chain processes, and others. Variety is defined as the complexity feature of several types of data categorized into three major classes:

1. Structured data which is grouped into a relational scheme,
2. Semi-structured data relies on some forms of relational structure or features in addition to some incomplete or irregular structures (e.g. XML files), and
3. Unstructured data such as web pages, contents of social media can be coded hard into relational tables for the aim of analysis or querying. Velocity is defined as the speed of data creation, data process, and analysis over time (Bedeley and Iyer, 2014).

In the financial industry, there is a fourth characteristic connected with the 3Vs, which is called vulnerability meaning as veracity. To have and analyze vast and rising amount of data accurately, it is required to be secure and conforming with regulatory requirements at all times (Gutierrez, 2016). Since the continuous growth of the 3 V's of Big Data, investment on this data creates an opportunity for strategic advantage. Finance firms can have a unique position by providing a new and critical service made by collecting and analyzing data, so they can convert vast amounts of information into actionable business insights.

In the case of insurance industry, the variety and veracity of the data are presented as one of the most difficult challenges. The ability to combine and use all sorts of the data in an analysis considered to be complicated. The veracity of the data especially unstructured one is taken into consideration as a challenge. Big Data's volume delivers a more precise understanding of customers and costs of growth and risk for insurers. In particular, e-insurance increased the velocity of Big Data. Having massive sorts of data from diverse data sources add more value to the data sets already in use.

One of the major sources of Big Data in healthcare is Pharmaceutical research and development data from pharmaceutical companies and academia. This high amount of data presents challenges related to technology not only for storing data in high volume but also for having a safe transfer of data and data analysis. The issue of velocity refers to the timeliness of performing analytics on the basis of the real-time requirements, especially in the case of healthcare workers who need to decide as quickly as possible. Slow analytics causes to detect the volume of data and its variety, in addition, the way how it should be adopted for the improvement of the quality of healthcare and in this case pharmaceutical industry considers that it has good value for the expenditures (Smith HW and Juarez DT, 2015). Big Data also enhances issues concerning the safety of information.

Data in pharmaceutical industry like the other industries is in different size and formats. In addition to the well-defined structured data, there is an increase in the amount of unstructured data. Unstructured data can be collected from various sources such as phones and the internet. Variety is also the most challenging facet for representing the right data types from one data source to the correct data type of another data source and matching to the actual information need. Velocity as a dimension shows the speed of creating new data and adding it to current data in addition to considering the data variation over time. In the pharmaceutical industry, another dimension should be added to these dimensions and it is called variability because its data is greatly variable. Pharmaceutical companies should be aware of the evaluation results of drug performance and variations in sales patterns and patient opinions at a fast speed as well so that they can act on them timely.

In pharmaceutical research and development, by an increase in implementation of electronic health records, a great deal of cross-sectional and long-term data is instantly becoming available. In addition, these companies can mine their own critical organizational data as well as scientific and patient-derived information available in the public domain. Genome data is exploding extremely large. Additionally, this high volume of data from different sources and in various formats can be integrated and brought together into one big holistic image of the patient in order to a better understanding and insight of disease mechanisms, determining patient populations and medical needs, and decision making.

The telecommunications industry constantly transfers petabytes of data across their networks. The number of sources of data for an organization in this industry is increasing. More data sources including large data sets enhance the amount of data, which is required to be analyzed. Other than typical structured data, Big Data contains much more unstructured and semi-structured data, which are available in many analog and digital formats. Additionally, the speed of data creation in telecommunication industry should be considered as another feature of Big Data (Jony, 2013).

BIG DATA ANALYTICS METHODOLOGY

Raghupathi and Raghupathi (2014) developed a methodology of healthcare Big Data analytics, shown as table1. The first step is called 'concept statement' which clarifies an idea or need for this project in words. It includes a description of the subject matter. There is a kind of compromise among alternative choices such as cost and scalability in healthcare organizations. After acceptance of this step, the stage of 'proposal development' should be performed. According to the first step, more details will be collected, and multitude questions will be addressed for the purpose of clarifying the problem, identifying the im-

Table 1. Healthcare big data analytics methodology (Raghupathi and Raghupathi, 2014)

Concept statement	• Declare the necessity of this project in healthcare with regard to the "4Vs".
Proposal	• What is the problem? • Why is it important? • Why the approach of Big Data analytics? • Background
Methodology	• Hypothesis • Selection of variables • Collection of data • Transmission of data • Selection of platform tool • Conceptual model • Techniques for the analysis • Outcomes and insight
Deployment	• Validation • Testing

portant items for the healthcare provider, and more others. Answering to these questions is required due to the complexity and cost of Big Data analysis. In addition, a team of the project should present their records of experience in line with the issue as well as previous works which were performed in this area.

In the phase of 'methodology', a series of propositions will be defined on the basis of the 'concept statement'. Concurrently, the independent and dependent variables or indicators will be determined. Besides, the data sources will be identified; collection, description, and transformation of data will be done for the aim of analytics. The next step is adopting the diverse techniques for Big Data analysis to the data. They are different from traditional techniques because of having large data sets. Understanding and insight will be achieved from Big Data analytics by doing several iterations and what-if analyses. In the next step, the examination of the models and their findings are performed, evaluated, and posted to shareholders. Deployment illustrates a phased approach to reduce the risk of failure at each step with feedback loops.

In the case of the banking industry, Simonson and Jain (2014) proposed a methodology which can be seen in Figure 1.

The phase of 'objective' is a perceived gap between the existing state and the desired state for making large volumes of unstructured data useful for analytical purposes. Many problems turn out to have several solutions. Thus, to solve the problems, many hypotheses can be created in addition to setting boundary conditions. However, there is a challenge of multiple competitive priorities.

Figure 1. Big data analytics methodology in banking industry (Simonson and Jain, 2014)

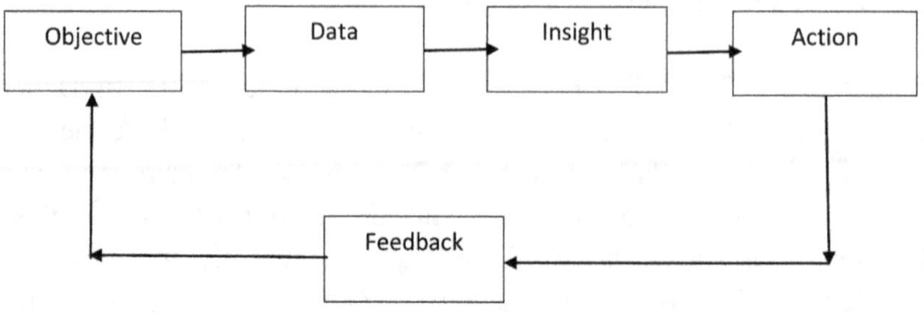

By having strong data management, the analysis of financial indicators such as the flow of money can be performed. However, the data fragmentation can be a challenge against to having an integrated and reliable internal data stream. Besides, for having a good analysis, there is a need to external data which is rapidly changing such as preferences of the customers and also the macroeconomic environment and it can be a considerable challenge in modeling and analysis. The phase of 'data' includes data extraction, data collection, storing, filtering, categorization, integration, and integrity.

They explained 'insight' by reviewing and exploring data, predictive modeling, creating an image of outputs, and dashboards which can be operationalized. There is a centralized team working on analytics across various businesses. Banks can have access to a global pool of analytics resources through using service providers as the third party. Banks are starting to realize the power of working together as a network, particularly in some areas such as fraud analytics. Additionally, collaborating with other related industries helps banks achieve more experience and resources.

'Action' refers to decision making, business rules, and business processes. Recently, banks deliver different kind of services such as asset management which are rarely integrated internally. Therefore, in order to be sure of the operationalization of insights, collaboration is essential. Through this, banks that have access to market insight and a better understanding of customer behavior can act effectively in real-time. In addition, digitalization contributes knowledge sharing of scattered business units in different geographies.

'Feedback' includes learning from actions, improving data collection sources, and refining/adjusting objective. In order to have a predictive analysis, banks should be open to learning and improving. Customer demographics, financial data, and data related to the economic and regulatory environment are used in an analytics model. Analytical and simulation models should be designed and adjusted to the further future changes.

Ernst and Young (2013) referred to the Big Data analytics methodology in insurance industry by the following components:

1. **Collection and Management of Data:** Its purpose is the maximization of the efficiency of companies and it enables companies to be sure in case of accuracy and reliability of collected data, and precision of management of data once they have been collected.
2. **Data Analysis and Modeling:** To extract insight from data of the organization, data analysis is used by a set of applications and techniques. In other words, a data warehouse of the organization should be at the access of analysts who have technical skills such as statistics to retrieve and manipulate the data. Besides, data modeling as a set of applications and techniques contributes companies to understand and analyze the way how an organization should gather, update, and store data.
3. **Business Insight:** After data analysis and modeling, it considers building new insights of conditions of business through the use of data and statistical methods.
4. **Decisions and Initiative:** As the final stage, companies can make the right decisions and initiations.

Menon and Jain (2014) explained the Big Data analytics methodology in pharmaceutical industry like bank industry proposed by Simonson and Jain, 2014. In this methodology, there is a loop of 'data-to-insight-to action'. By using data, business insight can be created which itself is used for making a decision. Results of business decisions are fed back for improving data and analysis.

'Objective' includes a problem statement, hypothesis creation, and boundary conditions. Increasing regulatory requirement is recognized as a key enabler for Big Data analysis in the pharmaceutical industry. In order to meet the regulatory requirements, organizations should build a foundation of data, people, and technology.

'Data' refers to data extraction, data collection, storing, filtering, categorization, integration, and integrity. In the case of pharmaceutical industry, data can be found from diverse sources. Data in different formats from medical testing, patients records, doctors and nurses notes, claims, reports of research projects, demographic data of patients, and sale data needs to come together for having business analysis. Data from different sources such as traditional data sources and digital ones should be integrated even from various technologies to have better analytics solutions. In addition, for reducing duplication of effort, pharmaceutical companies should collaborate and share information. It is essential for the companies to invest in data collection, data storage, and data analysis by using business intelligence applications.

'Insight' includes understanding the hidden meaning of data in special context, predictive modeling to forecast the patterns and trends, presenting an image of the outputs, and dashboards. Having high-level analytics needs experts with the expertise of medicine and analytical and statistical skills as well. However, there is a limited talent with considerable experience in this market. In addition, organizations need to invest in data analytics tools.

'Action' includes decision making, business rules, and business processes. Putting business analysis into action in the pharmaceutical industry, different business units are required to collaborate together. For instance, the collaboration among sales, operations, marketing, and even R&D is required to extract the hidden insights. Besides, the pharmaceutical firms are collaborating together in sharing data.

'Feedback' refers to learning from actions, improving data collection sources, and refining/adjusting objective. Self-learning and improvement for the aim of a continuous feedback mechanism are required for predictive analytics. Many variables in an analytics model are changing over time such as data profile of customers, procedures related to medical treatment, and the economic and regulatory environment. Having a relevant analytical model in this case is a significant challenge.

Fox et al. (2013) explained Big Data analytics methodology in telecommunication industry according to five steps of 'objective', 'data', 'analysis', 'insight', and 'feedback'. Objectives are driving Big Data initiatives. Regarding ranking top three objectives for Big Data, customer-oriented objectives such as improving the customer experience and better understanding and predicting of customer preferences and behavior can be mentioned. Providing a greater customer experience every time is essential for building customer loyalty. As stated by IBM's 2011 Global Telecom Consumer Survey, the telecommunications industry has a low level of customer loyalty. Needs and wants of customers can be understood by provided information through customers' devices and networks. Telecommunication companies must collect, store, process, and monitor the flow of incoming structured and unstructured data. The analysis of these data provides insight for telecommunication companies to define the policies of supplying services and products that meet the needs of customers. With the help of Big Data analysis, firms can define the risks immediately and perform the essential steps to be sure that it has no impact on the customer experience.

Data security in information management has always been a critical issue, but due to Big Data's size, variety and frequencies, data management becomes even more important. Not only internal data extracted from phone calls and transactions provides valuable information, but also external data extracted from social media sources enables firms to quickly detect customer issues and emotions. Both types of data sources provide insight that can cause an increase in profit and protect the brand.

ARCHITECTURAL FRAMEWORK

Raghupathi and Raghupathi (2014) explained the architectural framework for a Big Data analytics project in healthcare according to the Figure 2. The reasons why healthcare applies Big Data analytics are having access to large repositories of data which provides insights to make more reliable health-related decisions, and access to open source platforms such as Hadoop/MapReduce on the cloud.

Big Data in healthcare comes from both internal and external sources. Internal sources can be such as records of medical profiles of patients and external sources can be data from government, pharmaceutical and insurance companies, and also laboratories. These data can be found in different formats such as text, tables, and many others. They are located in diverse locations and in multiple applications.

The data in a 'raw' state should be processed or modified through several options such as middleware, extract transform load, data warehouse, and traditional formats. A service-oriented architectural approach combined with web services (middleware) is one possibility. Another approach is data warehousing wherein data from various sources is aggregated and made ready for processing. Through the steps of extract, transform, and load (ETL), data from diverse sources is cleansed and readied. Depending on whether the data is structured or unstructured, several data formats can be input to the Big Data analytics platform.

For Big Data analytics, the most significant platform is the open-source distributed data processing platform Hadoop (Apache platform). Besides, there are multiple platforms which can be adopted in the healthcare industry. Finally, on the right side of the figure, the four usual applications of Big Data analytics in healthcare are shown. These include queries, reports, OLAP, and data mining.

Feranata (2014) proposed a conceptual architecture of Big Data analytics in banking and financial services industry, as shown in Figure 3.

Big Data in bank and financial services industry is derived from multiple sources such as external and internal sources. Data transforms by data warehouse wherein data derived from various sources is

Figure 2. A conceptual architecture of big data analytics in healthcare (Raghupathi and Raghupathi, 2014)

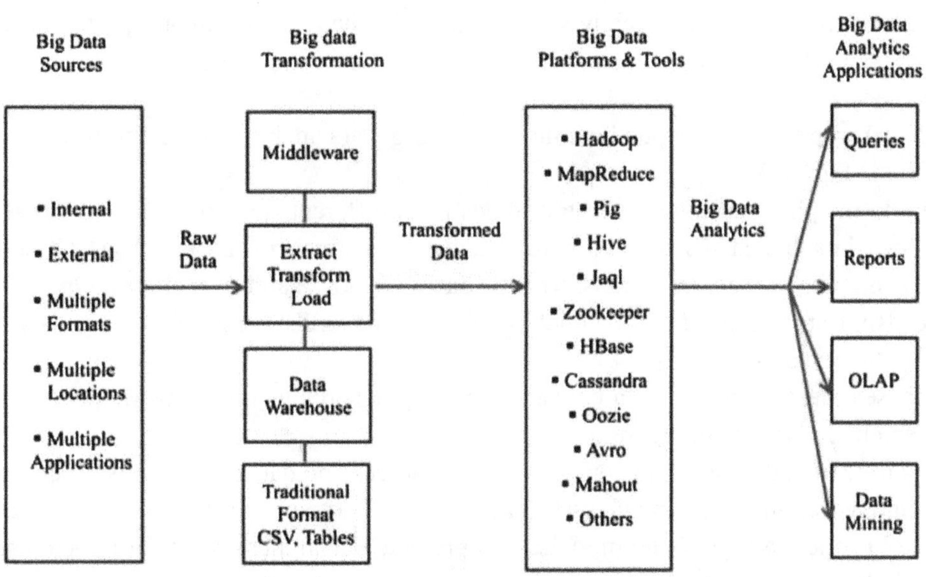

Figure 3. A conceptual architecture of Big Data analytics in financial services industry (Feranata, 2014)

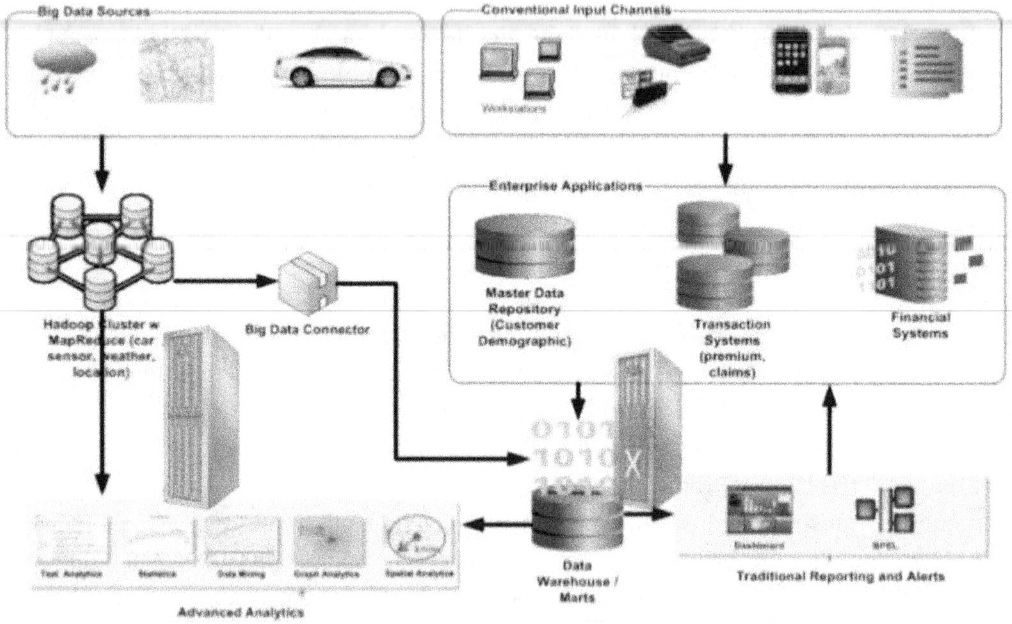

integrated and made ready for processing. The platform for Big Data analysis in this model is Hadoop which provides advanced analytics. Besides, there is also traditional reporting.

Capgemini global insurance Centre of excellence (2015) proposed the architecture of Big Data analytics in the insurance industry which is shown in Figure 4.

Big Data in insurance industry is derived from diverse sources in different formats. The data should be collected and managed. Afterward data analysis for the aim of discovery, decision making, prediction, and problem solving is performed. The foundation of data collection and management and data analysis is a secure platform on the cloud. Finally, on the right side, there are different reports such as financial performance, new business models, risk and fraud, operations, customer experience, and optimization of IT investments.

Garg (2016) proposed a conceptual architecture of Big Data analysis in the pharmaceutical industry according to the Figure 5.

Big Data in the pharmaceutical industry comes from different sources such as internal data, third party data, social media, emails, and other documents and sources in various formats. The data should be extracted and transformed. Data transforms by data warehouse and data cluster. On the basis of the platform for Big Data analysis in this model, there are some kinds of reports such as user experience, trends, and pattern analysis.

Here in case of telecommunication industry, a conceptual architecture of IBM Big Data analytics is presented which can be seen in Figure 6.

Big Data in IBM is derived from continuous feed sources and data repositories. There are different analysis including real-time scoring classification, high-performance unstructured data analysis, high-performance historical analysis, and model-based predictive analytics. Afterward, there are multitude reports and dashboards such as customer activities, campaign management, policy management, and etc.

Figure 4. A conceptual architecture of Big Data analytics in life insurance (Capgemini global insurance Centre of excellence, 2015)

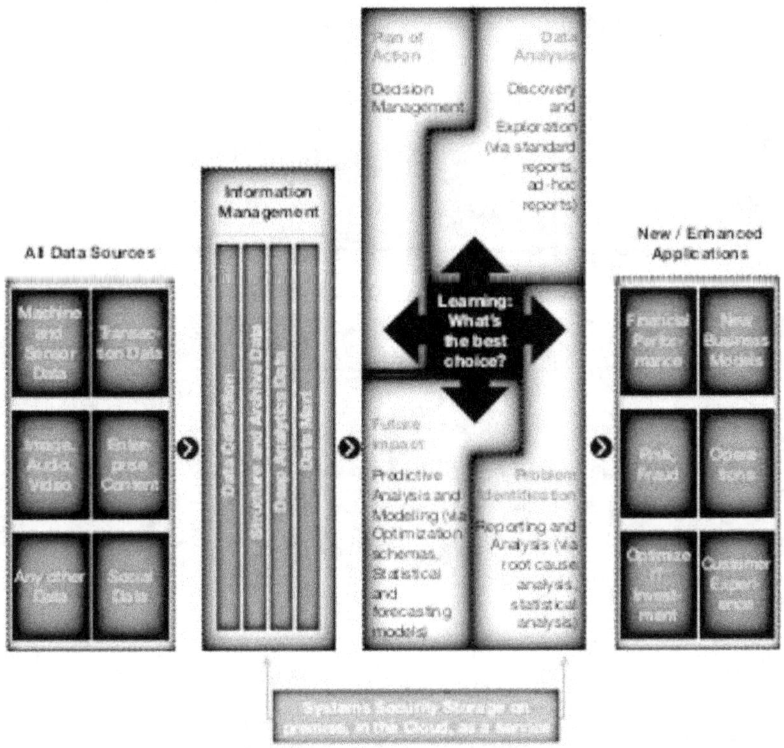

Figure 5. A conceptual architecture of Big Data analysis in pharmaceutical industry (Garg, 2016)

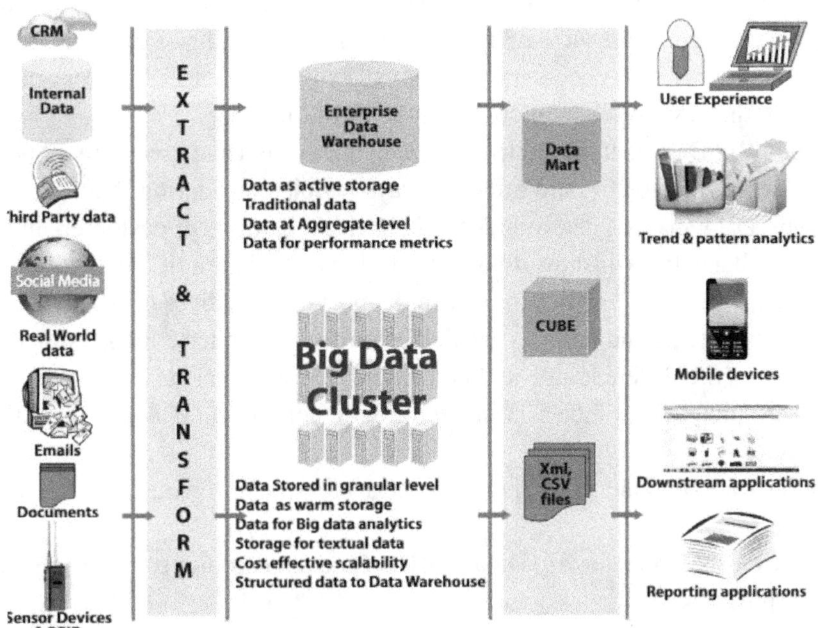

Figure 6. IBM Big Data architecture (Sathi, 2013)

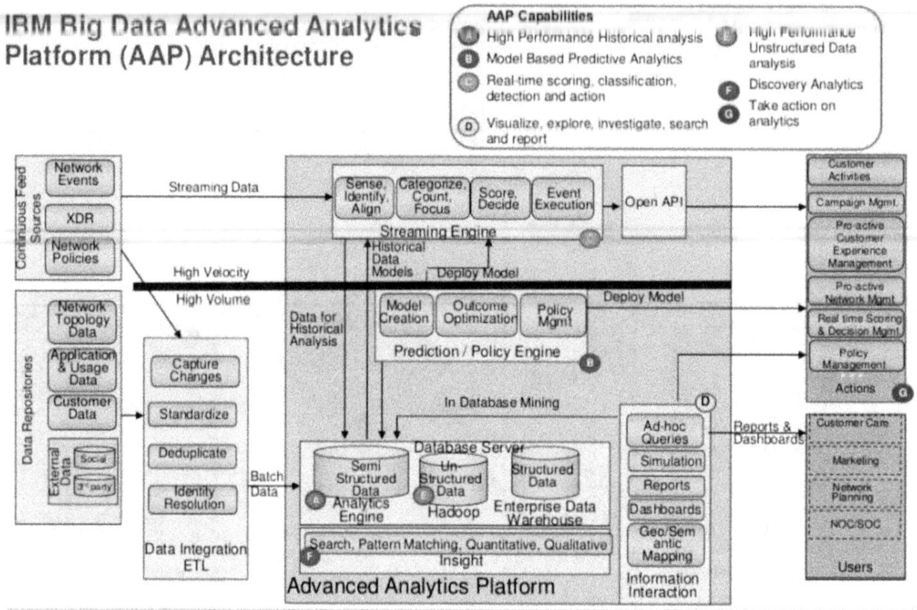

CONCLUSION

In this chapter, Big Data benefits, characteristics, methodologies, and architectures in five systems such as healthcare, financial services and banking, insurance, pharmacy, and telecommunication were explained. In a total system including all these mentioned sectors, Big Data offers common and significant benefits such as the ability to incorporating marketing and proactive customer service through having insights from all sectors. By integration of customer behavior data from all sectors, a total system like a service sector can create a single view of each customer in case of his wants, needs, and preferences. Providing high-quality services is necessary to satisfy the customers. Speed for real-time insight is very important to achieve the best possible outcomes at the right time.

In a total system, Big Data analytics helps also decision makers and especially policymaker identify fraud incidents in service sectors. Fraud affects always people considering that vast majority of fraud happens online. Big Data analysis determines the behavioral patterns of customers in case of purchasing. These models of behavior will show doubtful activities that do not fit the history of client data and behavior. In addition, Big Data analytics transform the business practices of the services sector. By using data from all five systems and publicly available sources, it can have insights that were previously unavailable to become the differentiator and contribute decision makers and policy makers to make decisions and policies that best suit the service sector in the long-term. It also reduces the risk of wrong decisions and policies.

As a methodology for Big Data analysis in service sector, the following steps can be proposed:

1. **Objective:** To define needs for Big Data analytics and also problems in the service sector, and set boundary for project,

Figure 7. A conceptual architecture of Big Data analytics in service sector

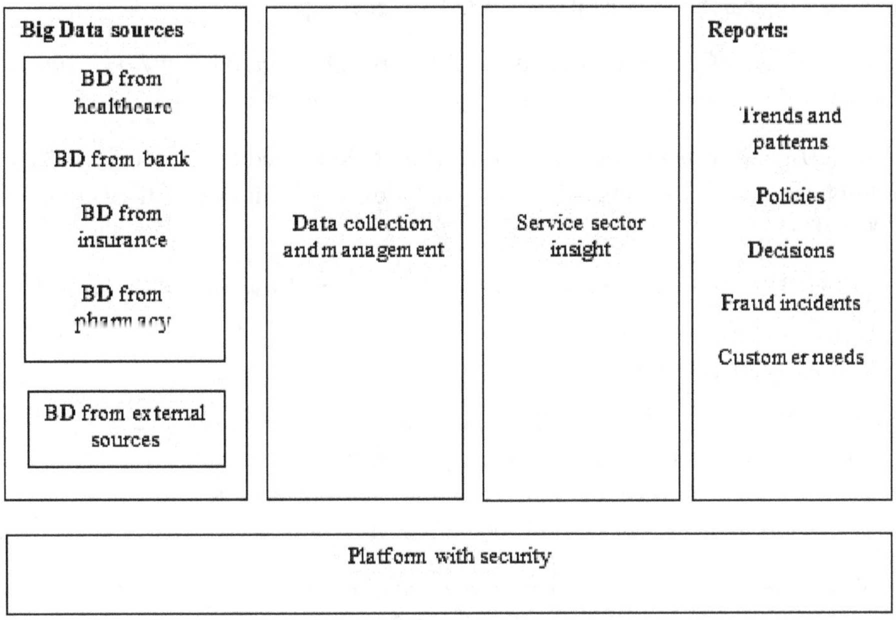

2. **Data Collection and Management:** It aims to ensure the collection and storage of precise and reliable data in service sector, and emphasize on the accurate management of data once they have been gathered.
3. **Data Analysis and Modeling:** Data analysis is a set of applications and methods to extract deep and hidden insight from the collected data.
4. **Business Insight:** It refers to developing new insights and understanding of service sector condition based on data and analysis.
5. **Decisions and Policies:** As the final stage, the total system can make the right decisions and policies more quickly.

In case of Big Data architecture in service sector Figure 7 can be proposed.

According to the Figure 7, data from all five systems in addition to other external data is collected and managed to extract service sector insight. One of the significant reports of the architecture is policies in the service sector. The infrastructure is a platform with a high degree security.

REFERENCES

Acker, O., Blockus, A., Pötscher, F. (2013). *Benefiting from Big Data: A new approach for the telecom industry.* Strategy & Formerly Booz & Company.

Bedeley, R. T., & Iyer, L. S. (2014). Big Data opportunities and challenges: the case of banking industry. *Proceedings of the Southern Association for Information Systems Conference*, 1-7.

Bholat, D. (2015). *Big Data and central banks*. Retrieved September 28, 2016, from http://www.bankofengland.co.uk/research/Documents/ccbs/bigdatawriteup.pdf

Capgemini global insurance Centre of excellence. (2015). *Big Data Analytics in Life Insurance*. Retrieved September 29, 2016, from http://www.slideshare.net/sahoodk/big-data-analytics-for-life-insurers-a

Ernst, & Young. (2013). *Advanced analytics for insurance*. Retrieved September 29, 2016, from http://www.ey.com/Publication/vwLUAssets/Advanced_analytics_for_insurance/$FILE/Adv-analytics_insurance_AUNZ00000335.pdf

Feranata, R. (2014). *Managing information explosion 'is it challenge or gold mine? How does banks response?* Retrieved September 29, 2016, from http://www.slideshare.net/RullyFeranata/bi-big-data-use-case-for-banking-by-rully-feranata

Fox, B., Dam, R. V. D., & Shockley, R. (2013). *Analytics: Real-world use of Big Data in telecommunications, How innovative communications service providers are extracting value from uncertain data.* IBM Global Business Services Business Analytics and Optimization. Retrieved September 29, 2016, from http://www-935.ibm.com/services/multimedia/Anaytics.pdf

Garg, S. (2016). *The new frontier for the Pharmaceutical and Life Sciences Industry: Real Big Value from Big Data*. TATA Consultancy Services. Retrieved September 29, 2016, from http://www.tcs.com/SiteCollectionDocuments/White%20Papers/Pharmaceutical-Industry-Big-Data-1113-2.pdf

Gutierrez, D. D. (2016). *InsideBigData guide to Big Data for finance*. Retrieved September 29, 2016, from https://www.em360tech.com/wp-content/files_mf/1427803213insideBIGDATAGuidetoBigDataforFinance.pdf

Hokkanen, J., Jacobson, T., Skingsley, C., & Tibblin, M. (2015). The risk-bank's future information supply in light of Big Data. *Economic Commentaries*, *17*, 1–5.

Irving Fisher Committee on Central Bank Statistics. (2015). *Central banks' use of and interest in "Big Data"*. Retrieved September 28, 2016, from http://www.bis.org/ifc/publ/ifc-report-bigdata.pdf

Jony, R. I. (2013). *Preprocessing solutions for telecommunication specific Big Data use cases* (Master's Dissertation). Aalto University, Finland.

Laney, D. (2001). *3D Data management: controlling data volume, velocity, and variety*. Retrieved September 29, 2016, from https://blogs.gartner.com/doug-laney/files/2012/01/ad949-3D-Data-Management-Controlling-Data-Volume-Velocity-and-Variety.pdf

Ma, C., Smith, H. W., Chu, C., & Juarez, D. T. (2015). Big Data in pharmacy practice: Current use, challenges, and the future. *Integrated Pharmacy Research and Practice*, *4*, 91–99. doi:10.2147/IPRP.S55862

Margret, J. J., & Sreenivasan, S. (2013). Implementation of Data Mining in Medical Fraud Detection. *International Journal of Computers and Applications*, *69*(5), 1–4. doi:10.5120/11835-7556

Menon, A., & Jain, A. (2014). *Analytics in Pharma and Life Sciences*. Everest Group Research. Retrieved September 29, 2016, from http://www.genpact.com/docs/default-source/resource-/analytics-in-pharma-and-life-sciences

Raghupathi, W., & Raghupathi, V. (2014). Big Data analytics in healthcare: Promise and potential. *Health Information Science and Systems*, *2*(3), 1–10. PMID:25825667

Sathi, A., Harken, R., Eunice, T., & Thomas, M. (2013). *Advanced analytics platform deep dive components, patterns, architecture decisions ISA-3637*. Retrieved September 29, 2016, from http://www.slideshare.net/arvindsathi/big-data-analytics-27981097

Zikopoulos, P., & Eaton, C. (2011). *Understanding Big Data: Analytics for Enterprise Class Hadoop and Streaming Data*. McGraw Hill Professional.

Chapter 4
Bug Handling in Service Sector Software

Anjali Goyal
JIIT, India

Neetu Sardana
JIIT, India

ABSTRACT

The technology enabled service industry is emerging as the most dynamic sectors in world's economy. Various service sector industries such as financial services, banking solutions, telecommunication, investment management, etc. completely rely on using large scale software for their smooth operations. Any malwares or bugs in these software is an issue of big concern and can have serious financial consequences. This chapter addresses the problem of bug handling in service sector software. Predictive analysis is a helpful technique for keeping software systems error free. Existing research in bug handling focus on various predictive analysis techniques such as data mining, machine learning, information retrieval, optimisation, etc. for bug resolving. This chapter provides a detailed analysis of bug handling in large service sector software. The main emphasis of this chapter is to discuss research involved in applying predictive analysis for bug handling. The chapter also presents some possible future research directions in bug resolving using mathematical optimisation techniques.

INTRODUCTION

"Prevention is better than cure" this proverb applies to the software industry significantly and since service sector industry is taking a software step nowadays, the proverb clearly applies to service sector as well. Bugs make the software system fail to meet the user requirements and make customers unhappy. Recent market studies have shown that software bugs may lead to serious financial concerns and can be dangerous for any organization. In early 2016, HSBC became the first bank to suffer a major IT outage. The bank blamed a complex technical issue for this incident. Another incident in August 2015, HSBC failed to process 275,000 individual payments which left many without any pay before the bank holiday weekend. The reason was a bug in electronic payment system. In June 2015, due to a software failure

DOI: 10.4018/978-1-5225-2148-8.ch004

600,000 payments failed to enter the accounts of The Royal Bank of Scotland (RBS) overnight. Earlier in 2012, 6.5 million customers of RBS experienced an outage due to batch scheduling software which led to a fine worth £56 million for the bank (Jee, 2016). The implications from these situations highlight the need to consider bug handling in service sector software seriously. If a bug is diagnosed efficiently it prevents the high efforts and cost incurred in the rectification of defect. Thus the software bugs need to be dealt with highest priority.

Large software development projects usually use a bug tracking systems (BTS) for gathering and organizing bugs reported by the developers and users. The use of BTS improves the software product's quality as it allows more bugs to be identified and resolved (Raymond, 1998). But the high volume of submitted bug reports makes bug handling a cumbersome task. For instance, the popular open source project Eclipse received 3426 bug reports during four-month period (01, January 2005 to 30, April 2005), averaging 29 bugs being reported daily (Anvik et al., 2006). Thus "effective resolving process of bug reports in software systems" becomes a research hotspot. (Erlikh, 2000) stated that software maintenance and evolution activities constitute 90% cost of total software development. To reduce the cost and efforts in bug handling, large scale open source software projects employ teams that utilize BTS such as Bugzilla[1], JIRA[2], FogBugz[3], etc. to keep track of the reported bugs. The users and developers of software, report all the software related issues to bug tracking repository where the bug reports are further analyzed by one of the designated team members such as bug triager, senior developer or project manager of the bug repository. The validated bugs are then assigned by the bug triager to a suitable developer who make changes in source code to successfully resolve the bug. This successful resolving leads to a robust software product.

The following sections of this chapter focuses on the development of bug handling techniques for service sector softwares. The topic of bug fixing is broad to the point of multi-disciplinarity as it requires strong background knowledge of various disciplines such as software engineering, data mining, information retrieval, text analytics, mining software repositories, optimization techniques and statistical modeling. This chapter is designed in order to present a self- contained overview of research work in bug handling process and to allow readers to quickly gather the most recent and influential developments in bug resolving. The next part of this chapter explains the preliminaries related to software development and bug fixing process. In the later sections, bug handling process has been classified into three phases and various techniques used in each phase have been described. Finally, the chapter concludes by summarizing the most popular bug handling approaches and presenting some interesting future research directions related to optimization techniques in bug fixing.

BACKGROUND

This section provides the basic information related to software development and bug handling. First the different phases of software development life cycle are described followed by basic terminology, structure and life cycle of bug. Further different special categories of bug reports are presented. These special bugs are usually software context specific and may or may not appear in each software product.

Software Development Life Cycle

A software is a collection of programs, procedures and documentation that performs a specific task when executed. Software development life cycle (SDLC) is a framework that describes the tasks performed at each step in the software development process. There are seven phases in software development life cycle as shown in Figure 1.

1. **Feasibility Analysis:** The main objective of this step is to identify whether the development of product would be financially and technically feasible.
2. **Requirement Gathering and Analysis:** This phase aims to understand and collect the exact requirements of the customer. The completion of this phase marks the creation of software requirement specification (SRS) document, which acts as a legal document between customer and company in case of any issues during later phases. This is the most crucial phase of software development.
3. **Design:** In this step the SRS document is transformed into a system architecture or software design.
4. **Implementation or Coding:** This phase translates the design documents into source code.
5. **Testing:** In this phase, the developed code is tested to ensure that the software system adheres to the requirement specifications as specified in SRS document.
6. **Delivery**: In this phase, the product is delivered / deployed to the customer for their use.

Figure 1. Software development life cycle

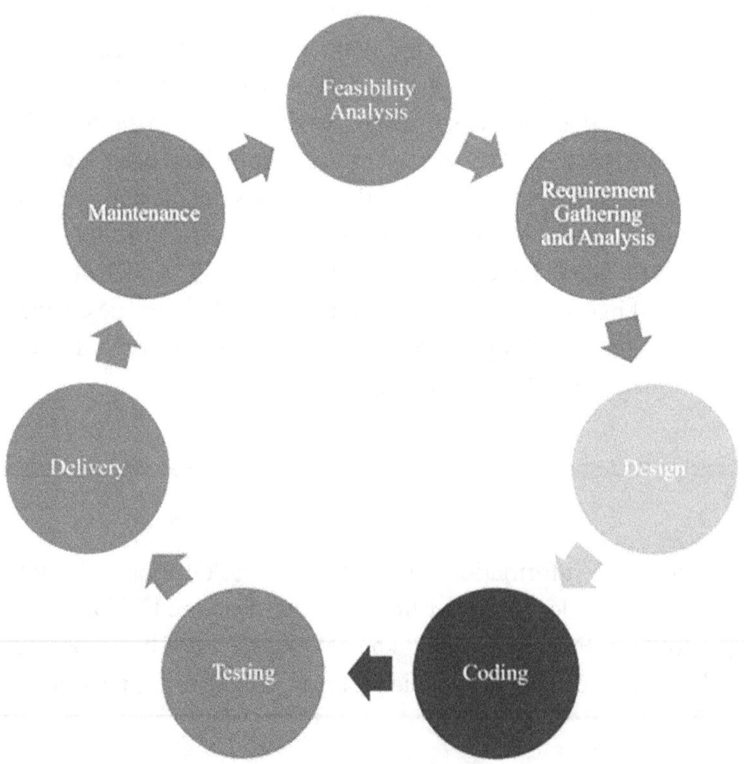

7. **Maintenance:** This phase deals with error corrections, implementation improvement, functionality enhancement or portability related activities. Maintenance is an important phase of SDLC, as this phase helps to ensure long lived project. To obtain maximum long lived projects, it is utmost important that bugs are handled efficiently. Thus, bug handling process is an integral part of the maintenance phase activities of software development and helps in making the final software product robust. This further helps in enhancing the user experience.

To do the software bug handling appropriately, we must have acquaintance with certain bug related jargons. So we hereby begin with certain terminology related to software bugs followed by the bug report structure and lifecycle of a bug.

Software Bug Related Jargons

- **Bug:** A software bug is an error, flaw, failure or fault in complete or part of a computer program that may lead to an incorrect or undesired output.
- **Bug Report:** A bug report is a document containing complete specification related to a bug. A bug report may be created by an end user, developer or beta tester of the software project. A good bug report needs to address three things:
    - Steps to reproduce the bug correctly.
    - What reporter expects to see?
    - What reporter actually observed?
- **Bug Repository:** A bug (or issue) tracking repository is an application that keeps record of all the submitted issues relating to a software project. The use of bug tracking system is considered an integral part of software development and its consistent use is examined as one of the "hallmarks of a good software project" (Spolsky, 2000). Bug repositories may be open source allowing end users to submit bug reports directly or could be used only internally in an organization. Bugzilla and JIRA are the most popular open source and proprietary BTS respectively.
- **Bug Reports types:** There are certain special categories of bug reports described as follows:
    - **Non-Reproducible Bugs**: Software developers try to reproduce the bugs with the information provided in the bug report. However, sometimes it is not possible to reproduce the reported bug with the information specified in the bug report. In such scenario, the bug is marked as Non-reproducible or worksforme. These bugs accounts for approximately 17% of all the reported bugs (Joorabchi et al., 2014).
    - **Blocking Bugs**: Blocking bugs are the software defects that prevents other bugs from being getting fixed or resolved (Garcia & Shihab, 2014). These bugs usually lead to chains of unresolved bugs thereby causing serious consequences in normal functioning of software.
    - **Concurrency Bugs**: Software systems usually perform many concurrent operations. Concurrency bugs are the synchronization problems among these concurrent tasks in concurrent programs (Lu et al., 2008). These synchronization problems often lead to inconsistent states in softwares.
    - **Dormant Bugs**: Software bugs that appear in previous versions of software (even after release of new versions of software) are known as dormant bugs (Chen et al., 2014). Although dormant bugs are usually outdated due to subsequent version releases but these bugs may work as test cases for new releases.

- **Security Bugs**: Bugs that relates to the security problems in software system are termed as security bugs (Gegick et al., 2010). These bugs generally acquire high priority values and needs experienced as well as specialized developers for fast resolving.
- **Performance Bugs**: A software bug that creates significant performance degradation in system are known as performance bugs. These bugs severely affect the software quality and performance of system (Liu et al., 2014; Nistor et al., 2013).
- **Long-Lived Bugs**: Certain bug reports take more than usual duration to get resolved. Such bugs are termed as long lived bugs. These bugs are crucial as the users may experience same failures version after version (Saha et al., 2015).

Software Bug Report Structure

A bug report constitutes various predefined meta-fields and textual contents. The predefined meta fields includes bug id, product, component, operating system, platform, milestone, severity, version, status, resolution, reporter, reported date and time, assigned to, etc. The textual contents include keywords, summary, description and comments. Figure 2 shows an instance of a bug report (Bug id: 185123) of Mozilla Firefox Product in Bugzilla repository. For instance, "Bug ID" refers to the unique sequence identification number provided to each reported bug. "Product" refers to the general area the bug belongs to. "Component" refers to the second level categorization of product. "OS" field refers

Figure 2. Instance of a bug report
Source:https://bugzilla.mozilla.org/show_bug.cgi?id=185123

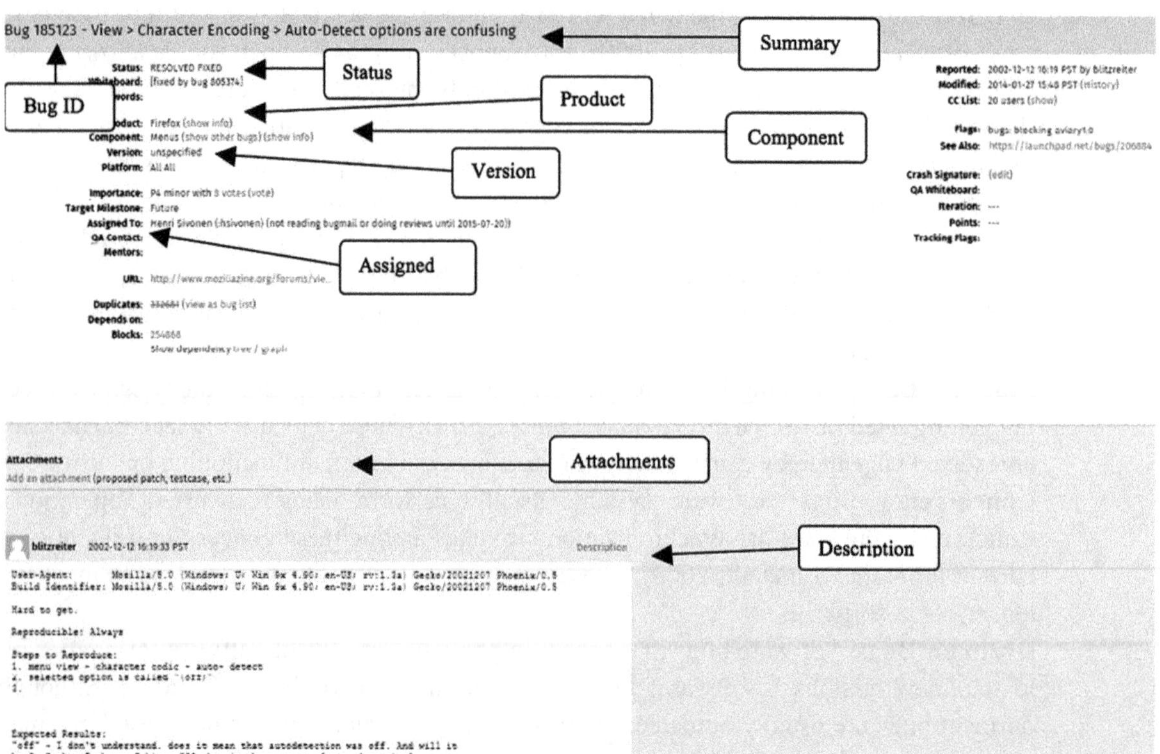

to the operating systems in which the bug occurs such as android, iOS, Windows, etc. "Severity" describes the impact or criticality of a bug. This field offers options such as severe, normal and minor (Saha et al., 2015). For example, a severe bug may lead to a series of other bugs and may even block their fixation. Such bugs are known as blocking bugs Garcia & Shihab, 2014) and their impact is high as it may prevent other bugs from considered fast. "Version" refers to the version of the software the bug was found in. Sometimes a user may report a bug in previous version of software which have already been fixed in further releases of software or are lined up to be fixed in next future releases of the project. Such bugs may be termed as dormant bugs (Chen et al., 2014). "Status" refers to the current condition of the bug.

In a bug report, free form textual contents such as summary, description and comments embodies important attributes. "Summary" refers to the one-line short definition about the bug. "Description" refers to the complete detailed specification submitted by the reporter regarding the submitted bug. It forms the main body of the bug report that generally incorporates the steps to reproduce the issue. "Comments" refers to the open discussion by a group of people to review the solutions for the reported

Figure 3. Bugzilla's mozilla bug life cycle
Source: https://www.bugzilla.org/docs/2.18/html/lifecycle.htm

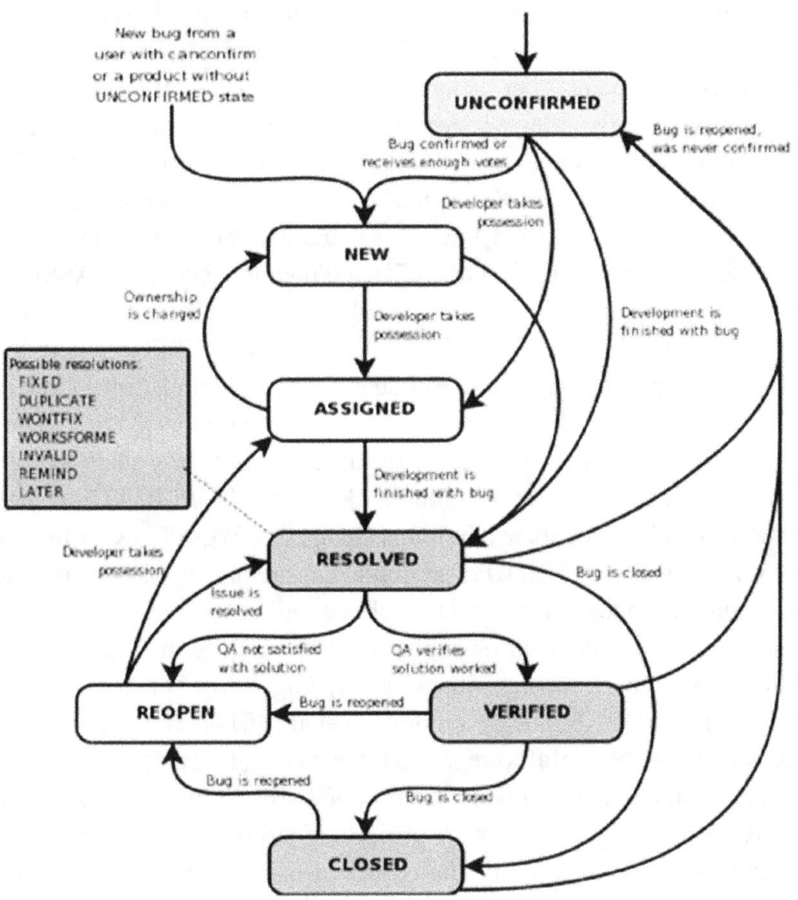

bug. This group of people generally comprehends some expertise in the related area of bug. Comments may also constitute pointers to other related bugs.

Besides the predefined meta-fields and free form textual contents, bug report may contain a set of attachments, URLs and automatically generated notes. The attachments usually provide non textual additional information in relation to the bug such as screenshot taken by the user during the abnormal behavior of the system. The URL coupled with bug report may be a pointer to a webpage where the bug is seen. Furthermore, when the developers perform an activity such as patch submission, duplicate marking or a new attachment submission, certain automatic notes or test cases get generated.

Software Bug Life Cycle

A bug goes through various stages during its lifetime. Figure 3 depicts the lifecycle of a bug of Mozilla project in Bugzilla repository. The lifecycle of bug in other projects or repositories may vary slightly but the mainstream order remains same. As a bug is reported, it is marked as UNCONFIRMED. The bug triager validates the existence of reported bug. After validation of existence or upon receiving a satisfied number of votes from the developers, the bug is marked as NEW. A bug reported by an expert may enter the NEW state directly as it is assumed to be valid and existing. Upon reaching NEW state, the bug triager assigns a suitable developer for the bug and its state is changed to ASSIGNED. The assigned developer then analyses, reproduces and makes code change in order to fix the bug. If the developer is not able to find a solution the state is again changed to NEW and a new developer is assigned to the bug by the triager. The process of designating another developer for bug is known as bug tossing.

If the developer successfully resolves the bug, its state is changed to RESOLVED. A tester, or in certain situations the original reporter, further validates the solution. If the solution is found to be valid and no further occurrence of bug is detected, the bug is marked as VERIFIED. In case the solution is not found to be appropriate, the bug may be REOPENED and then it again enters ASSIGNED state. After verification a bug is finally marked as CLOSED. At resolved status, there exist multiple resolutions that a bug report can attain such as FIXED, DUPLICATE, WONTFIX, WORKSFORME, INVALID, REMIND and LATER. If the developer makes appropriate code changes and bug is solved, the resolution of bug is changed to FIXED. Sometimes, the developer may find that the reported bug is not unique. It may be a mere duplicate of some existing or previously resolved bug or it may share the same root cause as another bug. In such situations the resolution of bug is changed to DUPLICATE. If the bug report summarizes an error that cannot be fixed its resolution is changed to WONTFIX. If the bug is found to be illegible or spam it is marked as INVALID. For example, bugs requiring changes to third party software or website, which is contrary to legal or contractual obligations.

Furthermore, many times it is difficult or impossible to reproduce the reported bug with the information provided in the bug report. In such situations, the bug report is marked with resolution NON REPRODUCIBLE (NR) or WORKSFORME (Joorabchi et al., 2014). The NR bug reopens when some patch information, which may be useful to reproduce the cause of bug, is added to the report. If a report is waiting for further input and cannot be acted upon currently it may be marked with resolution REMIND or LATER. Certain bugs in a software project are left unresolved intentionally. The possible reasons of leaving them unresolved could be the cost or efforts required for their fixation may be too high as compared to the corresponding impact they make; their rate of appearance may be very rare in the software or they may be lined up to be fixed in the future releases of the software project.

MAIN FOCUS OF THE CHAPTER

Bug handling is a crucial and time consuming process. It deals with various issues such as excess amount of available information in bug reports, incorrect fields, duplicity in bug reports, developer reassignments, etc. To address these problems various researchers and practitioners have provided a large number of solutions in the literature. This section discusses the bug resolving techniques proposed in literature. Bug handling process can be classified under three phases as shown in Figure 4.

- **Bug Report Analysis:** This phase deals with the quality optimization in bug reports. Many times bug reports are reported by customers or end users, who may not be aware of all the software related details. The information obtained from such bug reports may be incomplete or misleading. Bug report analysis deals with the manual or automated investigation of bug reports. Bug report analysis constitutes activities such as bug report summarization, duplicate detection, severity prediction and bug prioritization.
- **Bug Triaging:** This phase deals with the process of prominent developer selection for bug report who could successfully resolve the bug. This is the most important phase of bug resolving process as an incorrect assignment leads to bug tossing. Bug tossing is the activity of assigning a new developer for resolving the bug if the first assignee is unable to resolve it. Bug tossing phenomenon is critical as it leads to significant increase in time and efforts required for bug resolving. This poses a serious issue regarding the maintenance cost of project.
- **Bug Fixing:** This phase deals with the final correction in source code that leads to bug resolving. This phase constitutes activities such as bug localization and bug fix time prediction.

Figure 4. Classification scheme for bug handling process

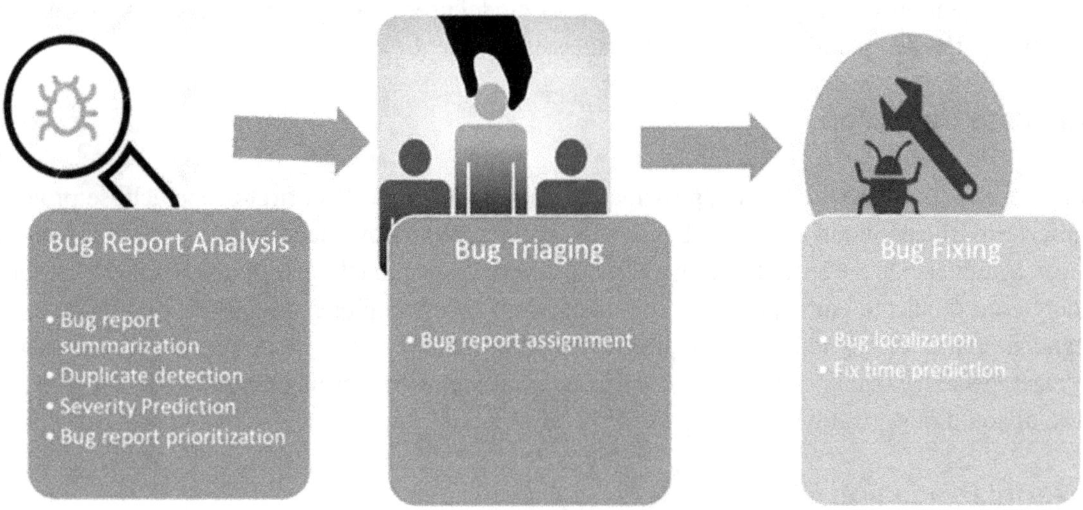

Bug Summarization

Bug reports contains a vast amount of information such as bug severity, component, platform, description, steps to reproduce, etc. Many times, this huge information becomes an overhead for the bug triager as well as for the developers. Also, in general, high quality bug reports are solved rapidly than low quality bug reports. This makes bug report quality the most important parameter in bug handling process. Bug summarization is the process to reduce the size of bug reports and extract only essential information from it. The major challenge in bug report summarization is to select most significant information from bug reports and to deal with the misclassification errors in bug reports. Approximately, 40% issue reports submitted to bug repositories are initially misclassified and 39% bug files marked as defective actually does not have bugs. To resolve such quality and misclassification issues in bug reports, supervised and unsupervised learning approaches are used.

1. **Supervised Learning Approaches:** Machine learning algorithms that uses labeled data to train the prediction classifiers are termed as supervised learning algorithms. This is the most commonly used bug summarization method. In supervised learning approaches, the classifier is trained with important set of sentences that should form the part of summary. On arrival of new bug report, all the information in the bug report is extracted and based on the classifier's previous learning, it predicts which sentences from the new bug report should be part of the bug report summary.
2. **Unsupervised Learning Approaches:** Unlike, supervised learning approaches, these approaches do not require labeled data for training of prediction model. On the other hand, it uses mathematical techniques such as centrality, page rank and similarity measures to judge the inclusion of statements in bug report summary. Since these approaches do not need manual classifier training, it helps in saving the cost incurred in training by developers.

In addition to the learning approaches, the parameter bug reporter's experience also plays an important role in measuring the misclassification errors. (Zanetti et al., 2013) conducted a case study by developing a reporter's centrality based prediction model. This model uses reporter's proficiency as a parameter for predicting if the bug parameters could be misclassified or not.

Duplicate Detection

(Anvik et al., 2005) reported that approximately 20-40% bug reports in firefox and eclipse projects are duplicates of the previously reported bugs. This creates an extra overhead for developers as well as bug triager. Natural language based techniques such as vector space modeling, n-grams, tf-idf etc. are the most widely used duplicate bug report detection methods. These techniques usually rely on calculating the textual similarity of bug reports for duplicate detection. First the topic modeling of bug reports is done to detect the semantically similar words. The final ranking of similar bug reports is done by measuring the total count of semantically similar words in bug reports.

Severity Prediction

Certain features of bug report such as priority, severity, etc. provides clear guide to the developers regarding their impact. Severity prediction is the task to predict the severity of bug report using its predefined features in order to analyze the importance of the bug. Such prediction is especially helpful in managing mission control systems. Severity prediction is often a classification task. The first automated approach for severity prediction was presented by (Menzies & Marcus, 2008). This model is based on standard text mining and machine learning techniques. (William, 1995) used Cohen's RIPPER rule learner to generate rule sets based on important tokens from the corpus. Certain approaches have also used machine learning classifiers for severity prediction. (Lamkanfi et al., 2011) studied the effect of various machine learning classifiers (i.e. Naïve Bayes, Naïve Bayes Multinomial, K-Nearest Neighbor and Support Vector Machine) for severity prediction. According to their study, Naïve Bayes is the best suited classifier foe prediction severity of bug as "severe" or "non-severe".

Bug Report Prioritization

Due to large number of incoming bug reports, it is a really difficult and time consuming process to deal with these bug reports. Among these bugs certain bugs are more impactful than others. For instance, the bugs marked as severe by the severity prediction modules often needs a quick handling process. In order to make bug handling process of severe bugs fast, they need to be prioritized. Bug report prioritization is the activity to provide special priority weights to important bug reports. This helps severe bugs to be early assigned to the developer thereby marking the early resolving. (Yu et al., 2010) proposed combination of neural networks and evolutionary training for bug report prioritization. Several other researchers also use machine learning classifiers and topic modeling to help in bug report prioritization.

Bug Report Assignment

In a bug repository, users and developers may play four different kinds of roles: reporter, triager, developer and contributor. The person who submits (or reports) the bug is termed as bug reporter. A reporter may be an end user, developer or tester of software. A senior project member known as bug triager then checks the reported bug to make sure that the reported bug is not a mere duplicate of some existing or previously resolved bug. He further analyses the bug in order to confirm the validity of bug. These two decisions made by the bug triager are known as repository oriented decisions. The purpose of these decisions is to remove the bug reports that do not need to be resolved. Remaining bug reports are analyzed for development oriented decisions. The bug triager then assigns the bug to a developer who makes the code changes to fix the bug. This is known as bug assignment. After the bug report is assigned to a developer, a group of people known as contributors, discuss the solutions for fixing the bug. Many a times, there is also a list of email addresses attached to a bug report who wants to keep them up to date about a particular bug. Such people often act as contributors. The one who finally resolves the bug and closes it is termed as resolver. The selection of suitable developer for a particular bug is often based upon various parameters such as past expertise of developer, his interest areas, current workload of developers, etc. and greatly impacts the time and cost of software maintenance.

The bug assignment approaches usually fall under one of the following seven categories of techniques: machine learning, information retrieval, auction, social network, tossing graphs, fuzzy set and operational research based techniques.

1. **Machine Learning Based Approaches:** Machine learning based approaches trains a classifier with the historically fixed bug reports and then uses the classifier for assignment of new bug reports.

(Cubranic & Murphy, 2004) proposed initial bug assignment approach based on machine learning technique. They considered the bug assignment as a text classification problem and used the description of bug reports to train the classifier. Using supervised Bayesian learning on Eclipse project, they classified 30% of bug report assignments correctly. (Xuan et al., 2010) considered the problem of deficiency of labeled bug reports. Using a combination of Naïve Bayes and Expectation Maximization algorithm, they first labeled all the unlabeled bug reports and then used the data for training purposes. Their approach increased the classification accuracy by up to 6% for top 5 recommendation list. (Anvik, 2006) proposed usage of eight information sources for recommendation in contrary to using only description of bug reports. They introduced the usage of textual description, component, operating system, hardware, version, developer who owns the code, current workload of developers and developers actively participating in the project for deciding the suitable developer. Their approach used support vector machine algorithm for classifying the bug reports and achieved a precision level of 57% for Eclipse project and 64% for Firefox project. Although, the usage of eight information sources significantly increased the efficiency of bug recommender but it is not always possible to derive all the eight parameters for each bug repository. For instance, large open source repositories do not share the data regarding the workload of their developers. Thus it is always not feasible for researchers to include all the proposed fields. (Anvik & Murphy, 2011) further extended their work to compare different machine learning algorithms namely, Naïve Bayes, Support vector machine, C4.5, Expectation Maximization, Conjunctive Rules and Nearest Neighbor algorithm. Their experimental results showed the use of Support Vector machine algorithm to be most accurate. (Bhattacharya et al., 2012) examined the impact of various dimensions on bug triaging. They considered the dimensions as classifier selection, feature selection, inclusion of tossing graphs and incremental learning. Their examination concluded Naïve Bayes algorithm for classifier, product- component pair for features and use of tossing graphs with incremental learning as best suited model for bug assignment. Their model reduced the tossing length significantly. (Xuan et al., 2015) addressed the issue of large dataset which increases the computation time and complexity of algorithms. Their approach used the combination of feature and instance selection algorithms for selecting the training data. Their results showed that scaling down the data reduces the computation complexity and also improves the classifier accuracy.

2. **Information Retrieval Based Approaches:** Information retrieval based approaches considers the bug reports as documents and often convert these documents to feature vectors which are further processed for developer assignment. These approaches work on the principle that developers with similar expertise towards a certain category of bugs are capable of solving the new bug of similar category. These techniques consider the expertise of developers towards bug reports for developer recommendation. (Moin & Neumann, 2012) proposed a string matching algorithm based on n-grams for bug assignment. Their model converted the historical bug reports of Eclipse JDT project into n gram tokens and matched the n grams of new bug report to find the most similar bug report. The developer who has fixed the historically similar bug report is assigned for the new bug report. (Matter et al., 2009) used the vocabulary found in source code contributions of developers to build a term author matrix. Each entry in the matrix represents the frequency of term with respect to developer. This frequency is regarded as expertise of developer with respect to that particular term. For a new bug report, the vocabulary found in description of bug report is compared with the vocabulary of term author matrix and the developer with highest expertise is recommended. Similarly, various other researchers used similarity computation, vector space modeling and topic or term modeling

approaches for bug assignment. (Ahsan et al., 2009) performed dimensionality reduction of the expertise matrix using feature selection and latent semantic indexing. (Somasundaram & Murphy, 2012) combined the information retrieval with machine learning technique. They studied three algorithms namely, SVM-TF-IDF (Support Vector Machine- Term Frequency- Inverse Document Frequency), SVM-LDA (Latent Dirichlet Allocation) and LDA-KL (Kullback Leibler Divergence) and concluded LDA-KL to be most appropriate for bug assignment. (Shokripur et al., 2012) extracted the information used for bug assignment from the version control repository of the project. Unlike other approaches, they did not use the information from bug tracking repositories and this allows the data to be used for new projects also as the data does not gets obsolete after a certain amount of time. (Shokripur et al., 2013) used an index of only unigram noun terms. They concluded that using only unigram noun terms simplifies the index and also maintains the accuracy. They linked the noun terms with the source code files of the project and the developers who had earlier worked on the linked files are recommended for the new bug report. (Shokripur et al., 2015) included the time based factor in the expertise computation. They emphasized that knowledge decays over time. Thus the computation of expertise of developers should also constitute time as a factor for normalization. This lowers the weight for terms that were used earlier and keeps the training data updated. This ability of information retrieval based techniques makes them popular.

3. **Auction Based Approaches:** (Hosseini et al., 2012) proposed an auction based bug assignment approach. The bug triager on receiving a new bug report auctions the bug. The developers who want to work on the bug report places their bids. The bug triager on the basis of developer's bids and their current workload assigns the bug report to the one of the bidders. Auction based approaches are useful as the chances of success is more because the developer has himself/ herself taken the responsibility of the bug and one knows what he could do better. These approaches help in moving form 'doing the job right' to 'doing the right job' trend. But it also increases the time of assignment of bug to a developer.
4. **Social Network Based Approaches:** Social network approaches utilizes the relationships between developers and bug reports for selection of suitable developer. They compute the developer expertise based on various influencing factors of network. (Wu et al., 2011) presented an approach that finds the historical similar bug reports with the help of k-nearest neighbor search and then uses indegree, outdegree, pagerank, betweeness and closeness metrics to rank the developers from a social network. Zhang et al. [49] proposed a concept profile and social network based developer selection approach. In first step, the related concept of the bug report is identified by token matching and then cooperative relationship between concepts and developers is identified from the social network.
5. **Tossing Graph Based Approaches:** Bug tossing is a major problem in bug triaging. Approximately 93% of bug reports are tossed at least once in their lifetime (Bhattacharya & Neamtiu, 2010). (Jeong et al., 2009) coined the concept of bug tossing graphs in bug assignment. They proposed a markov chain based model to address the problem of high tossing path lengths. In step one, a classifier is trained with fixed bug reports and a set of developers who had fixed similar bug reports is recommended. In step two, a tossing graph is constructed for each recommended developer which contains the information about possible re-assignees. The bug report is assigned to the developer whose probability of becoming a re-assignee is maximum. This approach reduced tossing events by upto 72%. (Bhattacharya & Neamtiu, 2010) added the developer's current activity status to the

tossing graphs. In this model, the edges of the tossing graph are labeled with current activity status and nodes are labeled with expertise of developer. This enhanced model reduced the tossing path length by up to 86%.

6. **Fuzzy Set Based Approaches:** Fuzzy set based approaches use the membership score to compute the expertise of developers with the topics. (Tamrawi et al., 2011) proposed Bugzie, which stores the membership scores of each developer with respect to each topic. For a new bug report, the membership scores of developers of all the related topics are union'ed together to rank the developers. This achieved an efficiency of 37% for top 1 recommendation. The approach is further tested on seven different projects.
7. **Operational Research Based Approaches:** Bug assignment in software systems is a NP hard problem. Thus various researchers have applied mathematical models to solve this problem. (Niknafs et al., 2013) conducted a study on personnel assignment problem and concluded the use of genetic algorithm and multi criteria decision making to be popular. (Rahman et al., 2010) used greedy optimization algorithm to solve the staffing problem.

In addition to the choice of techniques, the efficiency of bug assignment approaches is also greatly affected by the parameters used for classification. A bug report contains various predefined meta-fields and textual fields that uniquely describe each bug report. (Anvik, 2006) proposed eight information types to be used for building bug recommenders: textual description, component, operating system, hardware, version of software the bug was observed on, developer who owns the associated code, current workload of developers and list of developers actively contributing to the project. Although, the importance ranking of bug parameters are often repository specific and may even differ from project to project in the same repository, tokens generated from the textual contents of the bug report are often termed as the most important features. Recent studies are also considering non-textual feature based approaches for software engineering tasks due to limitation of text analytics methods.

Bug Localization

Bug localization deals with the process of locating final source code files that needs to be updated in order to solve the bug. For large scale system softwares, millions of files might be present making manual bug localization impossible. Information retrieval based methods are the most prominent models for bug localization. These techniques consider the new bug report as a search query and the source code files as the corpus. The source code files are ranked on the basis of similarity with search query. Various techniques for IR based bug localization includes LDA (Leukins et al., 2010), vector space model, smoothed unigram model, latent semantic analysis model. These techniques use the description of bug reports and source code files in order to calculate the similarity between search query and corpus.

Fix Time Prediction

Software bug repair time prediction allows project managers to plan the time of future releases of software. (Hewett & Kijsanayothin, 2009) presented an empirical approach to predict the software bug repair time. Various data mining approaches, namely Decision Tree Learner, Naïve Bayes Classifier, K-Nearest Neighbor, Neural Network and Support Vector Machine are used to construct the prediction models.

In order to build the training data of historical bug reports, 12 important characteristics of bug reports were identified as listed in Table 1. The training data is then classified using data mining approaches. The authors concluded that J48 algorithm achieved highest prediction accuracy of 93.44%.

Issues, Controversies and Problems

Bug handling process has gained substantial importance in the literature. Researchers and practitioners have explored each aspect of bug handling process repeatedly using various different dimensions. But there are still many open issues related to bug handling processes in system softwares. Some of these include:

1. **Cold- Start Problem**: There are various subtasks involved in bug handling process and these tasks basically use the information obtained from historically similar bugs for making any kind of predictions for the new bug report. This imposes serious problems for newer kind of bug reports. Various supervised machine learning classifiers often produce incorrect predictions for such instances.
2. **Incorrect or Misclassified Information**: Bug reports are usually submitted by customers or end users of the system who generally do not have enough technical knowledge. This leads to a large amount of incorrect or misclassified information. Handling incorrect information is a difficult, time consuming and tedious process.
3. **Heavy flow of Reported Bugs:** Large system software receives heavy amount of bug reports, especially during the initial release. Managing such high incoming flow is a challenging issue.
4. **Reliability of Information**: The dataset used for evaluation of various bug handling techniques proposed by researchers is often obtained from open source bug repositories. The reliability of information obtained from these repositories is always questionable.
5. **Lack of Benchmarks**: Despite the fact that adequate amount of literature is available for bug handling process, there is still a deficiency of proper benchmarks in evaluating the bug assignment

Table 1. List of parameters for bug fix time prediction

Attribute	Description
Testing Phase	The testing phase in which defect was found
Assessment	Assessment by the tester indicating type and action required
Component	Component of defect
State	Status of defect
Severity	Severity of defect
OriginId	Person who found the defect
OwnerId	Person assigned to fix the defect
AddDate	Date defect added to the report
AssignDate	Date assigned to be repaired
ResponseDate	Date the tester assessed the assigned defect
EndDate	Date of first repair attempt
LastUpdate	Date of last update

techniques. The researchers and practitioners often propose their novel approaches and evaluate them on variety of datasets with variable sizes and attributes. This makes it difficult to make a choice of the most appropriate approach for bug handling.

SOLUTIONS AND RECOMMENDATIONS

Although there exist various issues in bug handling process, but when software bugs in service sector softwares are concerned the above mentioned issues plays negligible effect. This is due to the reason that service sector software often involves financial data and transactions. Thus the service sector softwares usually choose self organized or proprietary bug repositories which have much more organized structure. These repositories allow only established developers to report any bugs. This reduces the heavy flow, reliability and misclassified information in incoming bugs. To tackle cold start problem, the proprietary repositories often employ senior developers and such bugs are directly assigned to them. Thus the software managers could efficiently develop a bug handling module for their projects using techniques proposed in literature.

In addition to the above issues related to bug handling process, the authors found one more interesting issue. Bug handling techniques uses bug report information for any kind of predictions but in the literature, the authors could not found work related to "how important the different bug report parameters are with respect to each other". There are relevant findings in literature that state certain bug features are more important than others. (Saha et al., 2015) reported that severity and priority fields efficiently indicate the importance of a bug but severity is more important than priority as it indicates the degree of impact of bug on proper operation of system. (Surekha et al., 2015) surveyed the industry practitioners and concluded component, severity and priority fields to be the most influential parameters for bug resolver prediction. Various other studies have also concluded component and textual contents of the bug report as the most important features of bug report. This shows that in addition to correct parameter selection the parameter prioritization is also important for effective predictive analysis. However, none of the studies in the literature consider parameter prioritization in any step of handling. We recommend to use parameter prioritization in various modules of bug handling process.

FUTURE RESEARCH DIRECTIONS

In future, the parameter prioritization in various subtasks of bug handling process could be employed. This will optimize the results of bug handling process. Various nature inspired optimization algorithms such as greedy optimization, ant colony optimization, multi criteria decision making can be used as they allow parameter prioritization. Also, ensemble based predictive analysis techniques could be employed in each stage of bug handling as it allows more optimized results.

CONCLUSION

Software bugs are inevitable and handling these bugs is a tedious and time consuming task. In relation to service sector, bug handling in softwares is really important due to involvement of financial transaction in it. Also it builds customer satisfaction. In this chapter, the authors discuss the various steps involved in bug handling process of software systems. An adequate amount of literature is available related to the various phases and sub-tasks of bug fixing. Also, bug tracking repositories have been extensively studied with respect to different features such as parameter selection, misleading information correction, report summarization, bug reopening, bug assignment, etc. The authors found that data mining and information retrieval based techniques have proved to be quite useful for controlling and rectifying the software systems error. These techniques usually consider various bug report parameters and based on historical data tries to predict the patterns for newly reported bugs. Also, the choice of parameters greatly affects the efficiency of bug handling techniques.

REFERENCES

Ahsan, S. N., Ferzund, J., & Wotawa, F. (2009, September). Automatic software bug triage system (BTS) based on Latent Semantic Indexing and Support Vector Machine. In *Software Engineering Advances, 2009. ICSEA'09. Fourth International Conference on* (pp. 216-221). IEEE.

Anvik, J. (2006, May). Automating bug report assignment. In *Proceedings of the 28th international conference on Software engineering* (pp. 937-940). ACM.

Anvik, J., Hiew, L., & Murphy, G. C. (2005, October). Coping with an open bug repository. In *Proceedings of the 2005 OOPSLA workshop on Eclipse technology eXchange* (pp. 35-39). ACM. doi:10.1145/1117696.1117704

Anvik, J., Hiew, L., & Murphy, G. C. (2006, May). Who should fix this bug? In *Proceedings of the 28th international conference on Software engineering* (pp. 361-370). ACM.

Anvik, J., & Murphy, G. C. (2011). Reducing the effort of bug report triage: Recommenders for development-oriented decisions. *ACM Transactions on Software Engineering and Methodology*, *20*(3), 10. doi:10.1145/2000791.2000794

Bettenburg, N., Just, S., Schröter, A., Weiss, C., Premraj, R., & Zimmermann, T. (2008, November). What makes a good bug report? In *Proceedings of the 16th ACM SIGSOFT International Symposium on Foundations of software engineering* (pp. 308-318). ACM. doi:10.1145/1453101.1453146

Bhattacharya, P., & Neamtiu, I. (2010, September). Fine-grained incremental learning and multi-feature tossing graphs to improve bug triaging. In *Software Maintenance (ICSM), 2010 IEEE International Conference on* (pp. 1-10). IEEE. doi:10.1109/ICSM.2010.5609736

Bhattacharya, P., Neamtiu, I., & Shelton, C. R. (2012). Automated, highly-accurate, bug assignment using machine learning and tossing graphs. *Journal of Systems and Software*, *85*(10), 2275–2292. doi:10.1016/j.jss.2012.04.053

Chen, T. H., Nagappan, M., Shihab, E., & Hassan, A. E. (2014, May). An empirical study of dormant bugs. In *Proceedings of the 11th Working Conference on Mining Software Repositories* (pp. 82-91). ACM.

Cohen, W. W. (1995, July). Fast effective rule induction.*Proceedings of the twelfth international conference on machine learning*, 115-123.

Cubranic, D., & Murphy, G. (2004). Automatic bug triage using text categorization.*Proceedings of the Sixteenth International Conference on Software Engineering & Knowledge Engineering.*

Erfani Joorabchi, M., Mirzaaghaei, M., & Mesbah, A. (2014, May). Works for me! characterizing non-reproducible bug reports. In *Proceedings of the 11th Working Conference on Mining Software Repositories* (pp. 62-71). ACM. doi:10.1145/2597073.2597098

Erlikh, L. (2000). Leveraging legacy system dollars for e-business. *IT Professional, 2*(3), 17–23. doi:10.1109/6294.846201

Gegick, M., Rotella, P., & Xie, T. (2010, May). Identifying security bug reports via text mining: An industrial case study. In *2010 7th IEEE Working Conference on Mining Software Repositories (MSR 2010)* (pp. 11-20). IEEE.

Hewett, R., & Kijsanayothin, P. (2009). On modeling software defect repair time. *Empirical Software Engineering, 14*(2), 165–186. doi:10.1007/s10664-008-9064-x

Hosseini, H., Nguyen, R., & Godfrey, M. W. (2012, March). A market-based bug allocation mechanism using predictive bug lifetimes. In *Software Maintenance and Reengineering (CSMR), 2012 16th European Conference on* (pp. 149-158). IEEE. doi:10.1109/CSMR.2012.25

Jee, C. (2016, January 18). *Top software failures 2015/2016: The worst software glitches this year*. Retrieved July 23, 2016, from http://www.computerworlduk.com/galleries/infrastructure/top-10-software-failures-of-2014-3599618/

Jeong, G., Kim, S., & Zimmermann, T. (2009, August). Improving bug triage with bug tossing graphs. In *Proceedings of the 7th joint meeting of the European software engineering conference and the ACM SIGSOFT symposium on The foundations of software engineering* (pp. 111-120). ACM. doi:10.1145/1595696.1595715

Kanwal, J., & Maqbool, O. (2012). Bug prioritization to facilitate bug report triage. *Journal of Computer Science and Technology, 27*(2), 397–412. doi:10.1007/s11390-012-1230-3

Lamkanfi, A., Demeyer, S., & Giger, E. (2010, May). Predicting the severity of a reported bug. In *Proceedings of the International working conference on mining software repositories* (pp. 1-10). ACM. doi:10.1109/MSR.2010.5463284

Lamkanfi, A., Demeyer, S., Soetens, Q. D., & Verdonck, T. (2011, March). Comparing mining algorithms for predicting the severity of a reported bug. In *Software Maintenance and Reengineering (CSMR), 2011 15th European Conference on* (pp. 249-258). IEEE. doi:10.1109/CSMR.2011.31

Liu, Y., Xu, C., & Cheung, S. C. (2014, May). Characterizing and detecting performance bugs for smartphone applications. In *Proceedings of the 36th International Conference on Software Engineering* (pp. 1013-1024). ACM. doi:10.1145/2568225.2568229

Lu, S., Park, S., Seo, E., & Zhou, Y. (2008, March). Learning from mistakes: a comprehensive study on real world concurrency bug characteristics. In ACM Sigplan Notices (Vol. 43, No. 3, pp. 329-339). ACM. doi:10.1145/1346281.1346323

Lukins, S. K., Kraft, N. A., & Etzkorn, L. H. (2010). Bug localization using latent Dirichlet allocation. *Information and Software Technology*, *52*(9), 972–990. doi:10.1016/j.infsof.2010.04.002

Matter, D., Kuhn, A., & Nierstrasz, O. (2009, May). Assigning bug reports using a vocabulary-based expertise model of developers. In *2009 6th IEEE International Working Conference on Mining Software Repositories* (pp. 131-140). IEEE doi:10.1109/MSR.2009.5069491

Menzies, T., & Marcus, A. (2008, September). Automated severity assessment of software defect reports. In *Software Maintenance, 2008. ICSM 2008. IEEE International Conference on* (pp. 346-355). IEEE. doi:10.1109/ICSM.2008.4658083

Moin, A., & Neumann, G. (2012, November). Assisting bug triage in large open source projects using approximate string matching.*Proc. 7th Int. Conf. on Software Engineering Advances*.

Niknafs, A., Denzinger, J., & Ruhe, G. (2013). A systematic literature review of the personnel assignment problem.*Proceedings of the International Multiconference of Engineers and Computer Scientists*.

Nistor, A., Jiang, T., & Tan, L. (2013, May). Discovering, reporting, and fixing performance bugs. In *Proceedings of the 10th Working Conference on Mining Software Repositories* (pp. 237-246). IEEE Press.

Rahman, M. M., Sohan, S. M., Maurer, F., & Ruhe, G. (2010, September). Evaluation of optimized staffing for feature development and bug fixing. In *Proceedings of the 2010 ACM-IEEE International Symposium on Empirical Software Engineering and Measurement* (p. 42). ACM. doi:10.1145/1852786.1852841

Rao, S., & Kak, A. (2011, May). Retrieval from software libraries for bug localization: a comparative study of generic and composite text models. In *Proceedings of the 8th Working Conference on Mining Software Repositories* (pp. 43-52). ACM. doi:10.1145/1985441.1985451

Raymond, E. S. (1998). The cathedral and the bazaar. *First Monday*, *3*(3).

Saha, R. K., Khurshid, S., & Perry, D. E. (2015). Understanding the triaging and fixing processes of long lived bugs. *Information and Software Technology*, *65*, 114–128. doi:10.1016/j.infsof.2015.03.002

Saha, R. K., Lawall, J., Khurshid, S., & Perry, D. E. (2015, May). Are these bugs really normal? In *Proceedings of the 12th Working Conference on Mining Software Repositories* (pp. 258-268). IEEE Press.

Shokripour, R., Anvik, J., Kasirun, Z. M., & Zamani, S. (2013, May). Why so complicated? simple term filtering and weighting for location-based bug report assignment recommendation. In *Proceedings of the 10th Working Conference on Mining Software Repositories* (pp. 2-11). IEEE Press. doi:10.1109/MSR.2013.6623997

Shokripour, R., Anvik, J., Kasirun, Z. M., & Zamani, S. (2015). A time-based approach to automatic bug report assignment. *Journal of Systems and Software*, *102*, 109–122. doi:10.1016/j.jss.2014.12.049

Shokripour, R., Kasirun, Z. M., Zamani, S., & Anvik, J. (2012, November). Automatic bug assignment using information extraction methods. In *Advanced Computer Science Applications and Technologies (ACSAT), 2012 International Conference on* (pp. 144-149). IEEE. doi:10.1109/ACSAT.2012.56

Somasundaram, K., & Murphy, G. C. (2012, February). Automatic categorization of bug reports using latent dirichlet allocation. In *Proceedings of the 5th India software engineering conference* (pp. 125-130). ACM. doi:10.1145/2134254.2134276

Spolsky, J. (2000). *Painless Bug Tracking*. Retrieved July 23, 2016, from http://www.joelonsoftware.com/articles/fog0000000 029.html

Sureka, A. kumar Singh, H., Bagewadi, M., Mitra, A., & Karanth, R. A Decision Support Platform for Guiding a Bug Triager for Resolver Recommendation Using Textual and Non-Textual Features. *3rd International Workshop on Quantitative Approaches to Software Quality*, 25.

Tamrawi, A., Nguyen, T. T., Al-Kofahi, J., & Nguyen, T. N. (2011, May). Fuzzy set-based automatic bug triaging: NIER track. In *2011 33rd International Conference on Software Engineering* (pp. 884-887). IEEE.

Tian, Y., Lo, D., & Sun, C. (2012, October). Information retrieval based nearest neighbor classification for fine-grained bug severity prediction. In *2012 19th Working Conference on Reverse Engineering* (pp. 215-224). IEEE. doi:10.1109/WCRE.2012.31

Valdivia Garcia, H., & Shihab, E. (2014, May). Characterizing and predicting blocking bugs in open source projects. In *Proceedings of the 11th working conference on mining software repositories* (pp. 72-81). ACM. doi:10.1145/2597073.2597099

Wu, L. L., Xie, B., Kaiser, G. E., & Passonneau, R. (2011). BugMiner: Software reliability analysis via data mining of bug reports? In *Proceedings of the International Conference on software engineering and knowledge engineering* (pp. 95-100).

Wu, W., Zhang, W., Yang, Y., & Wang, Q. (2011, December). Drex: Developer recommendation with k-nearest-neighbor search and expertise ranking. In *2011 18th Asia-Pacific Software Engineering Conference* (pp. 389-396). IEEE.

Xuan, J., Jiang, H., Hu, Y., Ren, Z., Zou, W., Luo, Z., & Wu, X. (2015). Towards effective bug triage with software data reduction techniques. *IEEE Transactions on Knowledge and Data Engineering*, *27*(1), 264–280. doi:10.1109/TKDE.2014.2324590

Xuan, J., Jiang, H., Ren, Z., Yan, J., & Luo, Z. (2010, July). Automatic Bug Triage using Semi-Supervised Text Classification. SEKE, 209-214.

Yu, L., Tsai, W. T., Zhao, W., & Wu, F. (2010, November). Predicting defect priority based on neural networks. In *International Conference on Advanced Data Mining and Applications* (pp. 356-367). Springer Berlin Heidelberg. doi:10.1007/978-3-642-17313-4_35

Yuan, T. I. A. N., David, L. O., & Chengnian, S. U. N. (2013). DRONE: Predicting Priority of Reported Bugs by Multi-factor Analysis.*29th IEEE International Conference on Software Maintenance*, 200-209.

Zanetti, M. S., Scholtes, I., Tessone, C. J., & Schweitzer, F. (2013, May). Categorizing bugs with social networks: a case study on four open source software communities. In *Proceedings of the 2013 International Conference on Software Engineering* (pp. 1032-1041). IEEE Press. doi:10.1109/ICSE.2013.6606653

Zhou, B., Neamtiu, I., & Gupta, R. (2015, April). Predicting concurrency bugs: how many, what kind and where are they? In *Proceedings of the 19th International Conference on Evaluation and Assessment in Software Engineering* (p. 6). ACM. doi:10.1145/2745802.2745807

KEY TERMS AND DEFINITIONS

Bug: An error, flaw, failure or fault in complete or part of a computer program that may lead to an incorrect or undesired output.

Bug Assignment: A process to select prominent developer for bug report who could successfully resolve the bug.

Bug Localization: A process to identify source code files to be updated in order to fix the bug.

Bug Prioritization: A process to provide high priority values to bugs in case of some necessity.

Bug Report: A document containing complete specification related to a bug.

Bug Repository: An application that keeps record of all the submitted issues relating to a software project.

Bug Tossing: A phenomenon to assign new developer for bug report if previously assigned developer is unable to fix the bug.

Chapter 5
Clustering Techniques Within Service Sector

İbrahim Yazici
İstanbul Technical University, Turkey

Ömer Faruk Beyca
İstanbul Technical University, Turkey

Selim Zaim
İstanbul Technical University, Turkey

ABSTRACT

Due to big data availability in markets recently, processing and making predictions with data have been becoming more difficult, and this difficulty has been affecting management decisions. As a result, competitiveness for companies are related to analyze and utilize big data in order to achieve company targets. Transforming big data into business advantage has become a vital management tool across all industries. There are many data mining techniques that are being applied to plenty of problems. One of the frequently utilized data mining technique is clustering method. Clustering techniques aim to group a set of objects in clusters that more similar objects are in the same cluster. Main utilization aim of clustering techniques is segmenting or clustering or grouping objects. Clustering techniques and their utilization within service sector by aim of clustering technique and their methodologies are presented. Energy, social media and bank sectors are found that the mostly user of clustering techniques within service sector for segmenting customers based on searched papers.

INTRODUCTION

Big data refers to large and complex datasets, whether they are structured or unstructured, growing in size and complexity. Big data term is often used instead of analytics term. Even the aim of both of these terms is to extract useful information from data, then, to acquire business advantages from the useful information, three distinctions are available among them. These distinctions are named as the three Vs (McAfee & Brynjolfsson (2012));

DOI: 10.4018/978-1-5225-2148-8.ch005

- **Volume:** Collections of much more information from transactions, records, tables and files. Big data are defined with terabytes even with petabytes.
- **Velocity:** Data streams or delivery from any kind of machine. Storing and processing data whether in real time or not is growing.
- **Variety:** Availability of data stream sources such as clickstreams, geo-spatial feedbacks, RFID, logs, clickstreams. And some audios and videos that are hard to be categorized (Russom (2011)).

The three Vs are illustrated in Figure 1. The figure illustrates the components of the three Vs of big data.

In addition to the three Vs, two dimensions are regarded for big data: *variability* and *complexity*. Variability means periodic or non-periodic peaks of data stream creating more unstructured data, hence, difficulty of manageability of the data. Complexity means that the availability of difficulty in data cleansing, linking, transforming across systems due to the fact that data come from various resources In today's world, not only storing and having data but also processing and transforming them into the business advantage is important for the companies. Big data management may provide efficient customer solutions, and reductions in cost, time and improvements in decision making.

Measurability and manageability is related terms in any industry. To manage a system better, the measurability of the processes or components in the system is a vital issue for companies McAfeeBrynjolfsson et al. (2012). Advances in data acquiring and storage technology provide huge amount of data to companies, and enable them to analyze and process the acquired data to manage the system more efficiently. In 2011 alone over 1.8 zettabytes (1 zettabyte = 10^{21} bytes) of information created IDC (2011). Today, over 300 users generate 500 millions of tweets every day, 200 billions of tweets every year, and 1.7 billion of Facebook users responds to 4 million of posts every minute (InternetLiveStats (2016)). Information has become profuse, and been increasing geometrically every minute. Social media providers such as Twitter, Facebook stores huge amount of daily data to the extent of 10 TB. Acquired much more

Figure 1. The three Vs in big data (Russom (2011))

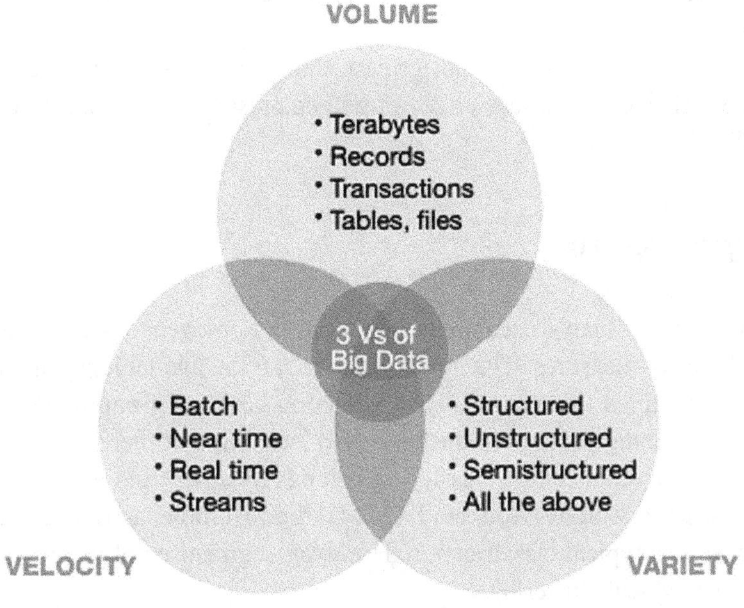

information from sensors or machine-to-machine data, or about customers such as demographic and transaction history information are valuable assets for companies to design their management strategies by storing and analyzing them. Growing data in the worldwide creates burden for companies to analyze data, and, then, make decision with obtained results to reach the specified targets. To process data and transform them into business advantage, data mining tools are utilized for companies to reach the manageability by succeeding in measurability as mentioned before. However, conventional data mining techniques are inadequate to understand and analyze big data. New technologies in big data enable us to extract useful information from abundant data which can be used in various areas such as healthcare, energy, social media, finance and banking etc.

In this chapter we will cover one of the most important tasks of big data analytics, namely, clustering. Clustering can be defined as identifying similar objects based on objects' features using particular similarity measures. Various tasks are available in cluster analysis depending on the application area. Some of the examples related with clustering task can be listed as follows (Hair et al. (2010; Kotu et al. (2014; Shmueli et al. (2007)):

- Taxonomy construction,
- Data cleansing and outlier detection,
- Identification of relationships in the observations,
- Market segmentation,
- Customer segmentation,
- Market structure analysis,
- Portfolio analysis,
- Industry analysis in finance,
- Document clustering,
- Session grouping.

Main utilization of clustering in service sector is to segments within customers or observations or discover groups within given data. The main focus of this chapter is to present clustering techniques utilization within service sector.

The rest of this chapter is as follows; clustering techniques will be introduced, then, taxonomy of clustering techniques utilized within service sector will be presented, finally, future research directions and conclusion will be presented.

CLUSTERING TECHNIQUES

Clustering is a multivariate analysis technique to discover homogeneous and meaningful groups in data by utilizing similarity measures. The aim is discovering the available group nature in data rather than predicting the predefined target class. The distinction between grouping and classifying have to be highlighted here. Grouping belongs to unsupervised learning that there is no predefined or known class in advance for observations while classifying belongs to supervised learning that has predefined or known class for the observations (Kotu et al. (2014)). For example, assigning a given bank whether it is bankrupted or not is a typical classification. However, segmenting of a company's customers into meaningful groups is a typical clustering.

In this section, clustering techniques will be presented by their utilized algorithms to form clusters Before that presentation, cluster typologies will be presented according to the data point's belonging to defined groups. In Kotu et al. (2014), clusters may be classified into 4 categories according data point's belonging to defined groups. These 4 categories are as follows:

- **Exclusive or Strict Partitioning Clusters:** Each observation in data belongs to strictly a group,
- **Overlapping Clusters:** Each observation in data may belong to more than one cluster. For example, in energy sector segmentation, a consumer may be high-volume consumer, and also be in high income consumer group. There is multiview in this type of clusters and they are called as multiview clusters.
- **Hierarchical Clusters:** There is a merging in child clusters and child clusters creates parent clusters. For example, EU countries can be merged into some different clusters according to their GDP, at the end of the clustering, there will be one cluster solution whereas homogeneity of groups are decreasing when the merging is increasing. Clusters may be formed by high GDP, low GDP and mid GDP countries. Finally, they will merge in the next steps, and it will result in forming one cluster whether meaningful or not depending on the researcher's aim.
- **Fuzzy or probabilistic clusters:** Observations' belonging to a group is not strict and they may be a member of distinct groups with membership degrees. For example, there are three customer segments for a company, and one of selected customer is a member of group 1,2 and 3 with degrees of 0.5, 0.7 and 0.8, respectively.

In Kotu et al. (2014), clustering techniques categorized into their utilized algorithms to form clusters for given data. These categories are as follows:

- **Prototype-Based Clustering:** Clusters are designed by prototypes (i.e. predefined cluster characteristics). K-means clustering is a type of prototype-based clustering. Predefined number of clusters are introduced with centroids of the clusters (prototypes) in this technique. k-means clustering is actually a kind of non-hierarchical clustering technique, and requires in procedures specification of cluster seeds (centroids) and assignment. Based on these requirements, three algorithms are the most frequently utilized ones; sequential threshold, parallel threshold and optimizing partition. The difference between these algorithms is that having different assignment procedures of objects to seeds. All of these three algorithms belongs to k-means algorithms (Hair et al. (2010)) Self-organizing map (SOM) is a type of prototype-based clustering combined with neural networks. SOM is actually a visual clustering technique, and has no labeled groups in result so that it has a drawback from this side. SOM projects objects (observations) to grid space, hence, labeling and clustering is dependent on researcher(s) aim, interpretation and experience. They are utilized by numerical variables due to the fact that SOM contains neural network algorithm in performing. SOM is utilized with some other data mining techniques such as text mining, speech recognition and graph mining (Kotu et al. (2014)).
- **Density Based Clustering:** In a given data space, data space is segregated into data concentrated and less concentrated regions in this technique. These emerged regions are analyzed, more dense area objects are defined as clusters and the other ones are regarded as noise in the data. Density Based Spatial Clustering Analysis (DBSCAN) is that kind of algorithm and discovers the groups

or clusters utilizing density distributions in n-dimensions. There is no enforcement to define number of clusters in advance in the technique. Defining threshold of data points (MinPoints) is important for the technique due to the fact that algorithm searches neighborhood by means of this threshold. This technique does not include noise or outliers to the clusters in final cluster solution, it is not as good as k-means clustering in discovering varying density patterns in data, and it may merge different and homogeneous groups into one group unlike k-means clustering. Hence, these two algorithms may be combined to get more efficient results by utilizing from advantages of both of them Kotu et al. (2014).

- **Hierarchical Clustering:** Hierarchical clustering technique aims to group objects under a hierarchy or a tree diagram based on similarity between variables. Agglomerative and divisive methods are types of this clustering technique. Agglomerative methods are commonly utilized method with respect to divisive methods. Agglomerative methods starts with number of clusters as the number of objects in given data, and iteratively merges the most similar (the most closest) clusters at a time, and one cluster solution is obtained at the end of the procedure. Divisive methods starts with single solution, all objects are in one cluster, and this single solution is successively divided until all objects forms one cluster. Hierarchical method presents a valuable visual tool called as dendogram. Dendogram is very useful tool for researchers but interpreting the dendogram may be convoluted task with large data sets.

  In hierarchical clustering there are some algorithms to define the similarities (or proximity) between multiple-member clusters. These algorithms are as follows Hair et al. (2010):
  - Single linkage method (the nearest-neighbor method),
  - Complete linkage method (the farthest-neighbor method),
  - Average linkage method,
  - Centroid method,
  - Ward's method.

  Hierarchical clustering and k-means (non-hierarchical) clustering may be seen complementary of each other. Suggested utilization of these techniques is to combine them to reach more robust solutions. Range of cluster solutions may be found by utilizing hierarchical methods, then, validation process may be performed by utilizing k-means according to obtained results by the hierarchical technique Hair et al. (2010).
- **Model-Based Clustering:** This technique is based on statistics and probability distributions. Data points are grouped into their probability distributions, clusters are identified by probability distributions. Mixture Models is one of the utilized model-based clustering techniques. Growing Gaussian Mixture Model (2G2M) is an example of mixture models Kotu et al. (2014).

Each of clustering techniques has its own advantages and disadvantages. Utilization decision of one of these techniques depends on problem, data type, and experiments of researcher(s) on the techniques.

CLUSTERING TECHNIQUES IN SERVICE SECTOR

In this section, taxonomy of clustering techniques utilized within service sector papers are presented in Table 1. We searched on Science Direct, Scopus and Web of Science Databases. We presented taxonomy of only articles, not including procedias on service sector that utilize clustering techniques. Table 1 il-

Clustering Techniques Within Service Sector

Table 1. Taxonomy of studies on utilization of clustering techniques within service sector

Study	Method(s)	Sub-sector	Aim of Clustering
Stewart et al. (2017)	k-means clustering	Trade-Off Shore	Grouping the phsique groups of UK off shore workers
Andrenacci et al. (2016)	Fuzzy k-means clustering	Energy	The optimal location zones discovery for charging infrastructure of electric vehicles
Amaro et al. (2016)	Hierarchical+k-means clustering	Tourism&Social Media	Social media users' segment identification for travel purposes, and identification of the distinctions between these segments
Daie et al. (2016)	Hierarchical clustering	Manufacturing and Service (Supply chain)	Structuring and planning supply chain network regarding precedence orders of supply chain components (suppliers and sub-assemblers)
Tokito et al. (2016)	k-means+NMF	Trade (Platinum trade network)	Analyzing the clusters of international trade networks and interdependency relationhsips in the international trade of platinum
Arias et al. (2016)	Hierarchical clustering+Relational Analysis+Decision Tree	Energy	Clustering historical traffic data into several patterns
do Carmo et al. (2016)	k-means +Regression Analysis	Energy	Discovering patterns in daily heating load profiles
Ghaemmaghami et al. (2016)	Hierarchical clustering	Telecom.	Diarization and speaker linking (Speaker clustering)
Kuo et al. (2016)	k-means +Metaheuristics+PCA	Social Media	A mobile application user's segmentation
Cerquitelli et al. (2016)	k-means clustering+DBSCAN	Telecom.	Internet user with similar internet access performance segmentation and analyze through Internet measurement collections obtained from end-users
Ormazabal et al. (2016)	PCA+Hierarchical clustering	Firm Management	Clustering the different UK companies that are in maturity state by predefined factors
Gu et al. (2016)	Hierarchical Clustering+PCE	Automotive	Analyzing and reducing the number of requirements for the automobile applications
C. Lee et al. (2016)	Hierarchical+k-means clustering	Sevice (Restaurant) Management	Segmentation of 198 businesses considering their performance level
Akhavan et al. (2016)	Hierarchical+k-means clustering	Manufacturing and Service (Supply chain)	Developing a taxonomy of sustainable sourcing and supply management profiles
Gölz et al. (2016)	Factor analysis + ANOVA + MANOVA+k-means clustering	Energy	Discovering distinct energy feedback goal profiles according to the defined goal factors
Todde et al. (2016)	PCA+k-means clustering	Farm Management	Grouping dairy farms with respect to defined criteria
Boudet et al. (2016)	k-means clustering	Energy	Clustering household energy-saving behaviours by behavioural attribute
Herp et al. (2016)	k-means clustering+Multivariate analysis+Bayesian classification	Energy	The outlier detection in the power curve of modelling of the wind turbine performance analysis
Le Cam et al. (2016)	Fuzzy C-means clustering+ANN	Energy	Partitioning of daily energy consumption profiles
Dong et al. (2016)	k-means clustering+ANN	Energy	Dividing numerical weather prediction data into groups for wind power day-ahead prediction
Herrera-Restrepo et al. (2016)	DEA+Robust PCA+k-means clustering	Banking	Discovering bank branch manegarial groups according to operating characteristics

continued on following page

Table 1. Continued

Study	Method(s)	Sub-sector	Aim of Clustering
Petrovic et al. (2016)	Hierarchical clustering+ANOVA	Healthcare	Clustering Parkinson disase patients regarding of the resemblance in neuropsychiatric problems
Schmöller et al. (2015)	PCA+LRA+k-means clustering	Car Rental	Discovering groups of days with respect to the spatial booking patterns and presenting the imbalance of the spatiotemporal distribution of vehicle supply and demand
Wong et al. (2014)	Factor Analysis+Hierarchical+k-means clustering	Human Resource Management	Discovering distinct group of employees (equivalent to market segments) among the workforce
Rid et al. (2014)	Hierarchical+k-means clustering+PCA+ANOVA	Tourism	Obtaining the heterogeneous tourist population segmentation
Abrate et al. (2016)	Hierarchical clustering+Economic Analyses	Hotel Management	Identifying the heterogeneous groups across tour operators
Agovino et al. (2016)	ESDA+Hierarchical clustering	Waste Management	Discovering groups of Italian provinces that have heterogeneous and different features
Fedoseeva et al. (2016)	Hierarchical+k-means clustering	Trade(International Exports)	Clustering exports in order to analyze existing bottlenecks and discovering opportunities for European exporters in the BRIC markets
Dardac et al. (2009)	Hierarchical Clustering	Banking	Discovering homogenous groups according to banks' attitude towards risk profile and profitability
Niyagas et al. (2006)	k-means clustering+SOM+RFM+Apriori Algorithm	Banking	Grouping customers according to their personal profiles and e-banking utilizings
Knotek (2014)	Hierarchical Clustering	Banking	Discovering the available similarity of banking sectors in European Union area and finding available clusters of them
Kumar et al. (2012)	k-means clustering+SOM+RFM+LTV	Banking	Clustering the customers according to their RFM(Recency Frequency Monetary)
Alvandi et al. (2012)	k-means clustering+CLV+LRFM	Banking	Grouping customers in order to design marketing strategies
Ghosh et al. (2016)	Density based clustering+Fuzzy Logic	Social Media	Segmenting the (social media) topics by processing their status
Pohl et al. (2016)	Growing Gaussian Mixture Model (2G2M)	Social Media	Discovering and processing the groups of sub-events using the indices obtained by online indexing on social media streams
Pereira et al. (2016)	Fuzzy subtractive clustering	Energy	Discovering the consumption pattern
Miguel et al. (2016)	Hierarchical Clustering	Energy	Obtaining the clusters of diagrams for energy types of the study
Vergados et al. (2016)	Spectral clustering+Genetic algorithm+adaptive algorithm	Energy	Classifying the energy prosumers into clusters
Mäenpää (2006)	k-means clustering	Banking	Clustering consumers according to their perceptions of the internet banking services
Croitoru et al. (2015)	DBSCAN	Social Media	Clustering social media feeds by considering the nature of temporal data stream
Han et al. (2015)	Planner(Adaptive algortihm)	Social Media	Clustering of landmarks by utilizing geo-tagged social media

continued on following page

Table 1. Continued

Study	Method(s)	Sub-sector	Aim of Clustering
Hsu (2017)	CHNN	Healthcare	Clustering a medical image to obtain homogeneous regions
Wang et al. (2016)	Density peaks-based clustering	Social Media	Discovering social circles with overlap by utilizing the user's profile
Haldar et al. (2016)	Fuzzy c-means clustering+MTS	Healthcare	Grouping the arrhytmic beats for mobile health monitoring systems
Delias et al. (2015)	k-means+spectral clustering	Healthcare	Grouping customer flows and representing effective informations
C.-H. Lee (2012)	DBSCAN	Social Media	Identitification of real world events' temporal and geo-spatial features by utilizing microblogging text streams
Ordoñez et al. (2016)	MultiModalGroup(adaptive algorithm)	Business Mng.	Classifying and searching business processes
Khoshnevisan et al. (2015)	Fuzzy c-means clustering	Energy&Farm Mng.	Clustering the farms considering energy attributes

lustrates paper names, used method(s) in the papers, application area and aim of clustering method(s) in the study. The studies are in the time span from 1990 to present.

We presented ring diagram of clustering applications on service sectors in Figure 2 in order to give some descriptive information about the table.

Figure 2. Ring diagram of clustering applications on service sectors

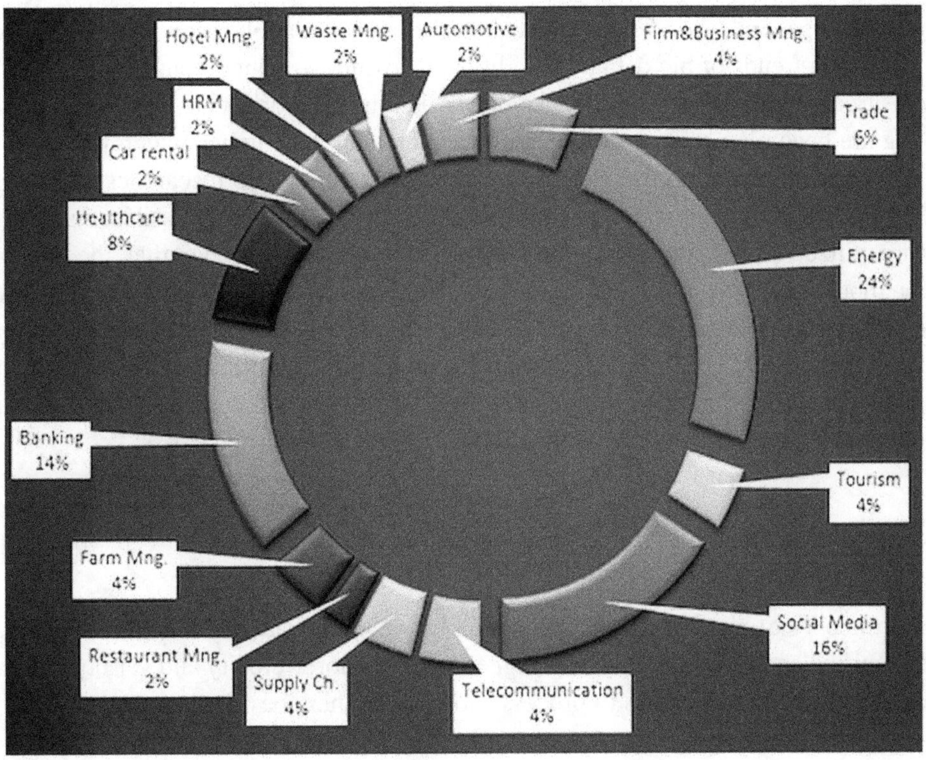

Based on reviewed papers clustering methods are mostly applied in energy sector with rate of 24%. Energy sector are followed by social media with rate of 16%, and by banking and healthcare with rate of 14% and %8, respectively. Clustering applications rate on trade is 6%, on tourism, telecommunication, supply chain, farm management is 4%. The least rate of clustering applications belongs to automotive, waste management, hotel management, HRM (Human Resources Management) and car rental with 2%.

From the result of the table, clustering techniques aim grouping or segmenting energy user's or energy usage profiles in the papers on energy sector. Clustering techniques aims segmenting social media user profiles, and grouping data streams, clickstreams and data feeds on social media in the papers about social media. Clustering techniques aims segmenting customers and highlighting managerial issues such as designing strategies or bank branch operational performance in the papers about banking. Clustering techniques were mostly preferred to segment customers, identifying user profiles and usage behaviors of customers especially in energy and social media sector.

Segmenting and grouping of customers and their service usage profiles are being vital managerial issue for companies since they design their strategies according to the results of customers' profile. As mentioned before, due to the availability and advances of big data in service sectors, clustering techniques have gained importance for companies to design their strategies and reach their targets by means of clustering, obtaining customers' profiles and/or customers' service usage profiles, in recent years. The most emerging areas in service sector which clustering techniques utilized are energy and social media, and they are followed by banking and healthcare. The main reason of these sectors' emergence may possibly be that they are rapidly growing sectors in the industry related to the three Vs of big data, especially energy and social media sectors.

FUTURE RESEARCH DIRECTION

In this chapter, most general type of clustering techniques and their applications within service sector are presented. Emerging trends of big data availability and advances in energy and social media are drawing attention of companies. With the advance of big data in the worldwide, real time data processing and analyzing are becoming crucial for companies. Clustering techniques which they will be utilized in energy and social media sector may distinctly be analyzed in future researches due to the fact that it is not only utilized clustering techniques in these areas but also some classification and regression techniques are utilized as complementary tools with clustering. In addition to that, the future researches may focus on model based clustering, more efficient technique for high dimensional data, and on fuzzy clustering within industry due to the fact that nature of data is not certain all time. Besides that, in order to increase the efficiency of clustering algorithms, some adaptive algorithms are utilized to analyze big data. Researches may focus on utilization of adaptive algorithms and their performance contributions and application areas in industry.

CONCLUSION

Emerging the three Vs of big data makes distinction between big data and business analytics. With the advance of acquiring and hoarding data with higher volume, more velocity and variety enforces companies to utilize data mining techniques to process and analyze them besides hoarding. Hence, extracting meaningful data groups or clusters from raw data is a vital issue while looking from this perspective. One of the frequently utilized data mining tool is clustering analysis in order to extract meaningful data for companies and practitioners in decision making. Clustering analysis technique has some types of algorithms in forming clusters from data to extract meaningful and homogeneous groups. These varying clustering techniques has been utilized in many industrial areas such as energy, social media, tourism, bank and finance. In this chapter, service sector utilization of clustering techniques are introduced, and the primary aim of clustering techniques utilization within service sector is segmenting customers or discovering customer profiles or identifying natural groups in data. It is concluded that this utilization aim presents that companies within service sector regard clustering analysis as a tool of segmenting and clustering customers, documents or clickstreams or web sessions for management tool. In addition to that, with the advance of social media data, model-based clustering techniques and fuzzy clustering techniques will be likely to gain importance in clustering in that area in the near future.

REFERENCES

Abrate, G., & Viglia, G. (2016). Strategic and tactical price decisions in hotel revenue management. *Tourism Management*, *55*, 123–132. doi:10.1016/j.tourman.2016.02.006

Agovino, M., Ferrara, M., & Garofalo, A. (2016). An exploratory analysis on waste management in Italy: A focus on waste disposed in landfill. *Land Use Policy*, *57*, 669–681. doi:10.1016/j.landusepol.2016.06.027

Akhavan, R. M., & Beckmann, M. (2016). A configuration of sustainable sourcing and supply management strategies. *Journal of Purchasing and Supply Management*. doi:10.1016/j.pursup.2016.07.006

Alvandi, M., Fazli, S., & Abdoli, F. S. (2012). K-Mean clustering method for analysis customer lifetime value with LRFM relationship model in banking services. *International Research Journal of Applied and Basic Sciences*, *3*(11), 2294–2302.

Amaro, S., Duarte, P., & Henriques, C. (2016). Travelers use of social media: A clustering approach. *Annals of Tourism Research*, *59*, 1–15. doi:10.1016/j.annals.2016.03.007

Andrenacci, N., Ragona, R., & Valenti, G. (2016). A demand-side approach to the optimal deployment of electric vehicle charging stations in metropolitan areas. *Applied Energy*, *182*, 39–46. doi:10.1016/j.apenergy.2016.07.137

Arias, M. B., & Bae, S. (2016). Electric vehicle charging demand forecasting model based on big data technologies. *Applied Energy*, *183*, 327–339. doi:10.1016/j.apenergy.2016.08.080

Boudet, H. S., Flora, J. A., & Armel, K. C. (2016). Clustering household energy-saving behaviours by behavioural attribute. *Energy Policy*, *92*, 444–454. doi:10.1016/j.enpol.2016.02.033

Cerquitelli, T., Servetti, A., & Masala, E. (2016). Discovering users with similar internet access performance through cluster analysis. *Expert Systems with Applications*, *64*, 536–548. doi:10.1016/j.eswa.2016.08.025

Croitoru, A., Wayant, N., Crooks, A., Radzikowski, J., & Stefanidis, A. (2015). Linking cyber and physical spaces through community detection and clustering in social media feeds. *Computers, Environment and Urban Systems*, *53*, 47–64. doi:10.1016/j.compenvurbsys.2014.11.002

Daie, P., & Li, S. (2016). Hierarchical clustering for structuring supply chain network in case of product variety. *Journal of Manufacturing Systems*, *38*, 77–86. doi:10.1016/j.jmsy.2015.10.002

Dardac, N., & Boitan, I. A. (2009). A Cluster Analysis Approach for Banks' Risk Profile: The Romanian Evidence. *European Research Studies*, *12*(1), 109.

Delias, P., Doumpos, M., Grigoroudis, E., Manolitzas, P., & Matsatsinis, N. (2015). Supporting healthcare management decisions via robust clustering of event logs. *Knowledge-Based Systems*, *84*, 203–213. doi:10.1016/j.knosys.2015.04.012

do Carmo, C. M. R., & Christensen, T. H. (2016). Cluster analysis of residential heat load profiles and the role of technical and household characteristics. *Energy and Building*, *125*, 171–180. doi:10.1016/j.enbuild.2016.04.079

Dong, L., Wang, L., Khahro, S. F., Gao, S., & Liao, X. (2016). Wind power day-ahead prediction with cluster analysis of NWP. *Renewable & Sustainable Energy Reviews*, *60*, 1206–1212. doi:10.1016/j.rser.2016.01.106

Fedoseeva, S., & Zeidan, R. (2016). A dead-end tunnel or the light at the end of it: The role of BRICs in European exports. *Economic Modelling*, *59*, 237–248. doi:10.1016/j.econmod.2016.07.016

Ghaemmaghami, H., Dean, D., Sridharan, S., & van Leeuwen, D. A. (2016). A study of speaker clustering for speaker attribution in large telephone conversation datasets. *Computer Speech & Language*, *40*, 23–45. doi:10.1016/j.csl.2016.03.005

Ghosh, G., Banerjee, S., & Yen, N. Y. (2016). State transition in communication under social network: An analysis using fuzzy logic and Density Based Clustering towards big data paradigm. *Future Generation Computer Systems*, *65*, 207–220. doi:10.1016/j.future.2016.02.017

Gölz, S., & Hahnel, U. J. (2016). What motivates people to use energy feedback systems? A multiple goal approach to predict long-term usage behaviour in daily life. *Energy Research & Social Science*, *21*, 155–166. doi:10.1016/j.erss.2016.07.006

Gu, F., Hall, P., & Miles, N. (2016). Development of composites based on recycled polypropylene for injection moulding automobile parts using hierarchical clustering analysis and principal component estimate. *Journal of Cleaner Production*, *137*, 632–643. doi:10.1016/j.jclepro.2016.07.028

Hair, J. F., Black, W. C., Babin, B. J., Anderson, R. E., & Tatham, R. (2010). *Multivariate Data Analysis*. Pearson Education.

Haldar, N. A. H., Khan, F. A., Ali, A., & Abbas, H. (2016). Arrhythmia Classification using Mahalanobis Distance based Improved Fuzzy C-Means Clustering for Mobile Health Monitoring Systems. *Neurocomputing*.

Han, J., & Lee, H. (2015). Adaptive landmark recommendations for travel planning: Personalizing and clustering landmarks using geo-tagged social media. *Pervasive and Mobile Computing*, *18*, 4–17. doi:10.1016/j.pmcj.2014.08.002

Herp, J., Pedersen, N. L., & Nadimi, E. S. (2016). Wind turbine performance analysis based on multivariate higher order moments and Bayesian classifiers. *Control Engineering Practice*, *49*, 204–211. doi:10.1016/j.conengprac.2015.12.018

Herrera-Restrepo, O., Triantis, K., Seaver, W. L., Paradi, J. C., & Zhu, H. (2016). Bank branch operational performance: A robust multivariate and clustering approach. *Expert Systems with Applications*, *50*, 107–119. doi:10.1016/j.eswa.2015.12.025

Hsu, W.-Y. (2017). Clustering-based compression connected to cloud databases in telemedicine and long-term care applications. *Telematics and Informatics*, *34*(1), 299–310. doi:10.1016/j.tele.2016.05.010

IDC. (2011). *IDC's Digital Universe study*. Retrieved from http://idcdocserv.com/1142

Internet Live Stats. (2016). Retrieved from http://www.internetlivestats.com/

Khoshnevisan, B., Rafiee, S., Omid, M., Mousazadeh, H., Shamshirband, S., & Ab Hamid, S. H. (2015). Developing a fuzzy clustering model for better energy use in farm management systems. *Renewable & Sustainable Energy Reviews*, *48*, 27–34. doi:10.1016/j.rser.2015.03.029

Knotek, P. (2014). Banking sectors in EMU-cluster analysis. *European Scientific Journal, 10*(34).

Kotu, V., & Deshpande, B. (2014). *Predictive analytics and data mining: concepts and practice with rapidminer*. Morgan Kaufmann.

Kumar, M. V., Chaitanya, M. V., & Madhavan, M. (2012). Segmenting the banking market strategy by clustering. *International Journal of Computers and Applications*, *45*, 10–15.

Kuo, R., Mei, C., Zulvia, F., & Tsai, C. (2016). An application of a metaheuristic algorithm-based clustering ensemble method to APP customer segmentation. *Neurocomputing*, *205*, 116–129. doi:10.1016/j.neucom.2016.04.017

Le Cam, M., Daoud, A., & Zmeureanu, R. (2016). Forecasting electric demand of supply fan using data mining techniques. *Energy*, *101*, 541–557. doi:10.1016/j.energy.2016.02.061

Lee, C., Hallak, R., & Sardeshmukh, S. R. (2016). Drivers of success in independent restaurants: A study of the Australian restaurant sector. *Journal of Hospitality and Tourism Management*, *29*, 99–111. doi:10.1016/j.jhtm.2016.06.003

Lee, C.-H. (2012). Mining spatio-temporal information on microblogging streams using a density-based online clustering method. *Expert Systems with Applications*, *39*(10), 9623–9641. doi:10.1016/j.eswa.2012.02.136

Mäenpää, K. (2006). Clustering the consumers on the basis of their perceptions of the Internet banking services. *Internet Research*, *16*(3), 304–322. doi:10.1108/10662240610673718

McAfee, A., & Brynjolfsson, E. (2012). Big data *The management revolution. Harvard Business Review*, *90*, 61–67. PMID:23074865

McAfee, A., Brynjolfsson, E., Davenport, T. H., Patil, D., & Barton, D. (2012). Big data. *The management revolution. Harvard Business Review*, *90*(10), 61–67. PMID:23074865

Miguel, P., Gonçalves, J., Neves, L., & Martins, A. G. (2016). *Using clustering techniques to provide simulation scenarios for the smart grid*. Sustainable Cities and Society.

Niyagas, W., Srivihok, A., & Kitisin, S. (2006). Clustering e-banking customer using data mining and marketing segmen-tation. *ECTI Transactions on Computer and Information Technology*, *2*(1), 63–69.

Ordoñez, H., Corrales, J. C., Cobos, C., Wives, L. K., Thom, L. H., & Ordoñez, A. (2016). Grouping of business processes models based on an incremental clustering algorithm using fuzzy similarity and multimodal search. *Expert Systems with Applications*.

Ormazabal, M., & Puga-Leal, R. (2016). An exploratory study of UK companies taxonomy based on environmental drivers. *Journal of Cleaner Production*, *133*, 479–486. doi:10.1016/j.jclepro.2016.06.011

Pereira, R., Fagundes, A., Melício, R., Mendes, V., Figueiredo, J., Martins, J., & Quadrado, J. (2016). A fuzzy clustering approach to a demand response model. *International Journal of Electrical Power & Energy Systems*, *81*, 184–192. doi:10.1016/j.ijepes.2016.02.032

Petrovic, M., Stefanova, E., Ziropadja, L., Stojkovic, T., & Kostic, V. S. (2016). Neuropsychiatric symptoms in Serbian patients with Parkinsons disease. *Journal of the Neurological Sciences*, *367*, 342–346. doi:10.1016/j.jns.2016.06.027 PMID:27423616

Pohl, D., Bouchachia, A., & Hellwagner, H. (2016). Online indexing and clustering of social media data for emergency management. *Neurocomputing*, *172*, 168–179. doi:10.1016/j.neucom.2015.01.084

Rid, W., Ezeuduji, I. O., & Pröbstl-Haider, U. (2014). Segmentation by motivation for rural tourism activities in The Gambia. *Tourism Management*, *40*, 102–116. doi:10.1016/j.tourman.2013.05.006

Russom, P. (2011). *Big data analytics*. TDWI Best Practices Report, Fourth Quarter.

Schmöller, S., Weikl, S., Müller, J., & Bogenberger, K. (2015). Empirical analysis of free-floating carsharing usage: The Munich and Berlin case. *Transportation Research Part C, Emerging Technologies*, *56*, 34–51. doi:10.1016/j.trc.2015.03.008

Shmueli, G., Patel, N. R., & Bruce, P. C. (2007). *Data mining for business intelligence: concepts, techniques, and applications in Microsoft Office Excel with XLMiner*. John Wiley & Sons.

Stewart, A., Ledingham, R., & Williams, H. (2017). Variability in body size and shape of UK offshore workers: A cluster analysis approach. *Applied Ergonomics*, *58*, 265–272. doi:10.1016/j.apergo.2016.07.001 PMID:27633221

Todde, G., Murgia, L., Caria, M., & Pazzona, A. (2016). A multivariate statistical analysis approach to characterize mechanization, structural and energy profile in Italian dairy farms. *Energy Reports*, *2*, 129–134. doi:10.1016/j.egyr.2016.05.006

Tokito, S., Kagawa, S., & Nansai, K. (2016). Understanding international trade network complexity of platinum: The case of Japan. *Resources Policy*, *49*, 415–421. doi:10.1016/j.resourpol.2016.07.009

Vergados, D. J., Mamounakis, I., Makris, P., & Varvarigos, E. (2016). Prosumer clustering into virtual microgrids for cost reduction in renewable energy trading markets. *Sustainable Energy. Grids and Networks*, *7*, 90–103.

Wang, M., Zuo, W., & Wang, Y. (2016). An improved density peaks-based clustering method for social circle discovery in social networks. *Neurocomputing*, *179*, 219–227. doi:10.1016/j.neucom.2015.11.091

Wong, S. C., & Huang, C. Y. (2014). A Factor– Cluster Approach to Understanding Hong Kong Hotel Employees Symptom-management-related Coping Behavior Towards Job Stress. *Asia Pacific Journal of Tourism Research*, *19*(4), 469–491. doi:10.1080/10941665.2012.749929

Chapter 6
Descriptive Analytics

Sheik Abdullah A
Thiagarajar College of Engineering, India

Selvakumar S
G. K. M. College of Engineering and Technology, India

Ramya C
Thiagarajar College of Engineering, India

ABSTRACT

Data analytics has becoming one of the challenging platforms across various domains such as telecom, health care, social media and so on. The challenging and most promising task in analytics is the understanding of various patterns in the data. The mechanism of data retrieval and analysis seems to be the promising one in which the algorithms, techniques, way of processing data are in need with the ability to target upon large volumes of data. There are various types of analytical methods such as predictive analytics, descriptive analytics, text analytics, social media analytics and survival analytics. This chapter mainly focuses towards the mechanism of descriptive analytics its types, algorithms and applications. There are various forms of tools and techniques such as association rule mining, sequence rule mining, and data categorization such as hierarchical and non-hierarchical clustering methods with its variants.

ANALYTICS

The word analytics have be utilized by several Business Intelligence (BI) software vendors to explain quite totally different functions. Data analytics is that the science of process data and changing into information that is employed to increase productivity and business profit. Data is extracted and differentiated to recognize and evaluate behavioral data and patterns, and approaches are utilized by organizations differ from one organization to another. Data analytics are employed in several organizations to permit firms to form higher trade decision and in the sciences to verify or contradict existing models. Trendy data analytics typically use information dashboards supported by real-time data streams.

DOI: 10.4018/978-1-5225-2148-8.ch006

TYPES OF ANALYTICS

There are four types of analytics. They are interpreted in the Figure 1.

Descriptive Analytics

Descriptive analytics generates a summary of past data to find useful information and that data is used for future analysis. It aims to describe the customer behavior while buying the products. Descriptive analytics has no target variable in contrast to predictive analytics. Therefore, descriptive analytics is also known as unsupervised learning. There are three types of descriptive analytics. They are as follows,

1. Association rule mining
2. Sequence rule mining
3. Clustering/Segmentation

ASSOCIATION RULE MINING

In data mining, Association rule mining is the most essential and well known technique. The main idea of this technique is towards extracting the exciting relations or common patterns among groups of items in the transactional or relational databases. The buying of individual product when an additional product is bought represents an association rule. It is commonly used in different zones such as classification, telecommunication systems, clustering, market basket analysis, cross-marketing, loss-leader, catalog design, etc. Knowledge can be gained through the rules generated by association rule mining from the various application data.

There are two steps to mine the association rule. They are,

- **Generate Frequent Itemsets in the Transactional Database:** Each and every itemsets should take place at least as often as a predefined min_ supp count.

Figure 1.

- **Construct an Association Rules using Generated Frequent Itemsets:** Association rules should met the predefined min_ supp and min_ confi.
  Where, min_ supp is the minimum support count.
  Min_ confi is the minimum confidence.

Classification of Association Rule Mining

- Based on the level of abstraction
  - **Single Level Association Rule:** It represents the attributes at exactly one level
  - **Multi-Level Association Rule:** It refers to the attributes at more than one level
- Based on the number of dimension
  - **Single-Dimensional Association Rule:** It represents the attributes at exactly one dimension
  - **Multidimensional Association Rule:** It refers to the attributes at more than two levels
- Based on kinds of values
  - **Boolean Association Rule:** It describes relationships among presence or absence of items
  - **Quantitative Association Rule:** It describes the relationships among quantitative items
- Based on the types of forms to extract
  - **Frequent Itemset Mining:** It extracts the repeated itemsets from the transactional dataset
  - **Sequence Pattern Mining:** It examines for the repeated subsequence in a sequence dataset
  - **Structured Pattern Mining:** It examines for the repeated substructures in a structure dataset
- Based on several extension to association rule mining
  - Restrictions applied
  - Causality analysis
  - Close itemsets

Different methods to mine association rule

1. Apriori algorithm
2. FP-Growth Algorithm

Apriori Algorithm

Apriori algorithm is considered as the greatest interesting crisis in data mining. This algorithm is to extract frequent item sets from the huge transactional database. It is the best algorithm for mining the hidden relations of the items. An Apriori uses a bottom up approach method.

Rule Measures

Both Support and Confidence are important to compute the strong point of the association rule. An association rules which satisfies the minimum support count and minimum confidence are known as strong association rules.

Support - It is defined as the proportion of transactions in databases which include AUB.

$$Support(A => B) = P(AUB) \tag{1}$$

Confidence- It is defined as the proportion of transactions in databases which contains A that also contains B.

$$\boldsymbol{Confidence}(A => B) = \boldsymbol{P}\left(\frac{\boldsymbol{B}}{\boldsymbol{A}}\right) = \boldsymbol{Support\ count}(\boldsymbol{AUB}) / \boldsymbol{Support\ count}(A) \tag{2}$$

Consider a sample; the database contains 9 transactions. The customer buys Butter, Bread, Cheese, Sugar and Milk. The minimum confidence required is 70% and minimum support count required is 22%. First generate the frequent itemset using apriori algorithm and then generate an association rules from the found frequent itemset using min_ supp and min_ confi. The transaction item details are described in Table 1. Assume, Bu= Butter, Br= Bread, Ch= Cheese, Su= Sugar, Mi= Milk.

Step 1: Generate 1- Frequent Itemset

Search the database and calculate count the of candidate item set as in Table 2.

Compare candidate itemset support count and minimum support count as in Table 3.

The group of 1- frequent itemsets L1 contains candidate 1- itemsets met the predefined minimum support count. All the itemset in C1 satisfies min _support count. In the very first iteration, each item is present in the candidate itemset.

Step 2: Generate 2- Frequent Itemset

Produce candidate itemset C2 from L1 as in Table 4.

Pseudo Code for Apriori Algorithm

```
Input: D, a transaction database
Output: L, Frequent itemsets in D
        C_p : Candidate itemset of range p
        L_p : Frequent itemset of range p
        For (p=1; L_p ! Ø; p++)
              do begin
              C_{p+1} = Candidate itemsets produced from L_p;
              For each transaction t in database do
              increase the count of the entire candidates in C_{p+1} at are in t
              L_{p+1} = Candidates in C_{p+1} with min_supp
              end
              return U_p L_p
```

Table 1. Transaction items

TID	List of Items
T101	Bu, Br, Mi
T102	Br, Su
T103	Br, Ch
T104	Bu, Br, Su
T105	Bu, Ch
T106	Br, Ch
T107	Bu, Ch
T108	Bu, Br, Ch, Mi
T109	Bu, Br, Ch

Min _sup = 2/ 9 = 22%
So, min_ sup count = 2

Table 2. 1-itemset generation

Itemset	Support count
Bu	6
Br	7
Ch	6
Su	2
Mi	2

C1

Table 3. Comparison of item support count with minimum support count.

Itemset	Support count
Bu	6
Br	7
Ch	6
Su	2
Mi	2

L1

Search the database and calculate count the of candidate item set as in Table 5.
Compare candidate items support count and minimum support count as in Table 6.

- To determine the 2- frequent itemset L2, the algorithm joins L1 andL1, to produce the candidate itemset of 2- frequent itemset C2.
- Then, the database transactions are searched and each candidate itemset support count is stored in C2.
- The 2- frequent itemsets L2 contains candidate 2- frequent itemsets met the predefined min_ supp count.

Step 3: Generate 3- Frequent Itemset

Generate candidate itemset C3 from L2 as in Table 7.
Search the database and calculate count the of candidate item set as in Table 8.
Compare Candidate items support count to the minimum support count as in Table 9.

Table 4. Generation of 2 frequent item sets

Itemset
{Bu, Br}
{Bu, Ch}
{Bu, Su}
{Bu, Mi}
{Br, Ch}
{Br, Su}
{Br, Mi}
{Ch, Su}
{Ch, Mi}
{Su, Mi}

C2

Table 5. Calculation of item set count

Itemset	Support count
{Bu, Br}	4
{Bu, Ch}	4
{Bu, Su}	1
{Bu, Mi}	2
{Br, Ch}	4
{Br, Su}	2
{Br, Mi}	2
{Ch, Su}	0
{Ch, Mi}	1
{Su, Mi}	0

C2

Table 6. Comparison of item support count with minimum support count

Itemset	Support count
{Bu, Br}	4
{Bu, Ch}	4
{Bu, Mi}	2
{Br, Ch}	4
{Br, Su}	2
{Br, Mi}	2

L2

Table 7. Generation of 3-frequent item set

Itemset
{Bu, Br, Ch}
{Bu, Br, Mi}
{Bu, Br, Su}
{Bu, Ch, Mi}

C3

Table 8. Count of candidate item set

Itemset	Support Count
{Bu, Br, Ch}	2
{Bu, Br, Mi}	2
{Bu, Br, Su}	1
{Bu, Ch, Mi}	1

C3

Table 9. Comparison of item support count with minimum support count

Itemset	Support Count
{Bu, Br, Ch}	2
{Bu, Br, Mi}	2

L3

- To determine the 3- frequent itemset L3, the algorithm joins L2 join L2, to generate the candidate itemset of 3- frequent itemset C3.
- Then, the database transactions are scanned for each candidate itemset and store support count of itemset in C3.
- The 3- frequent itemsets L3 contains candidate 3- frequent itemsets should met the predefined min_ supp count.

Step 4: Generate 4- Frequent Itemset

As in Table 10.

Search the database and calculate count the of candidate item set ass in table 11.

- To determine the 4- frequent itemset L4, the algorithm joins L3 join L3, to generate the candidate itemset of 4- frequent itemset C4.
- Then, the database transactions are scanned for each candidate itemset and store support count of itemset in C4.
- The 4- frequent itemsets L4 is ∅. The algorithm terminates in this step. The next step is to create the strong association rules using the generated frequent itemsets.

Step 5: Generate Strong Association Rules from Frequent Itemsets

For every frequent itemset I, Create all subsets of I except ∅. For every non empty subset S of I, the output rule S→I-S,

Support _count (I)/ support _count(S)>= min _confidence.

Let's take I= {Bu, Br, Mi}

The subsets are {Bu, Br}, {Br, Mi}, {Bu, Mi}, {Bu}, {Br}, {Mi}.

Minimum confidence= 70%

Rule 1: Bu^ Br→Mi

Confidence= support count {Bu, Br, Mi}/ Support count {Bu, Br} = 2/4 = 50%

Rule 1 is rejected.

Rule 2: Br ^ Mi→ Bu

Confidence = support count {Bu, Br, Mi}/ support count {Br, Mi} = 2/2 = 100%

Rule 2 is selected.

Rule 3: Bu ^ Mi→ Br

Confidence = support count {Bu, Br, Mi}/ Support count {Bu, Mi} = 2/2 = 100%

Rule 3 is selected.

Rule 4: Bu→Br ^ Mi

Table 10. Generation of 4-item sets

Itemset
{Bu, Br, Ch, Mi}

C4

Table 11. Count of candidate item sets

Itemset	Support Count
{Bu, Br, Ch, Mi}	1

C4

Confidence = support count {Bu, Br, Mi}/ support count {Bu} = 2/6 = 33%
Rule 4 is rejected.
Rule 5: Br→Bu^ Mi
Confidence = support count {Bu, Br, Mi}/ support count {Br} = 2/7 = 29%
Rule 5 is rejected.
Rule 6: Mi → Bu ^Br
Confidence = support count {Bu, Br, Mi}/ support count {Mi} = 2/2 = 100%
Rule 6 is selected.
Rule 2, 3, 6 are the strong association rules.
From the selected rule 2 we inferred that if the customer buys Milk and Bread then he buys Butter.
From the rule 3 we inferred that if customer buys Butter and Milk then he buys Bread.
From the rule 6 we inferred that if customer buys Milk then he buys Butter and Bread.

Steps to Generate Association Rules Using Apriori Algorithm in Weka Tool

1. Open Weka Explorer
2. Click Open file to load the dataset from the destination
3. There are many tabs in the Weka Explorer window i.e, Preprocess, Classify, Cluster, Associate, Select Attributes, and Visualize. Choose Associate.
4. Choose the Apriori algorithm and click start.
5. It takes few seconds to generate the association rules.

For example, For example, Transaction dataset is used for implementation using Weka tool. The dataset contains 267 attributes and 4627 instances. Candidate itemsets are displayed in Figure 2. Association rules are generated using Apriori algorithm is depicted in the Figure 3.

Figure 2.

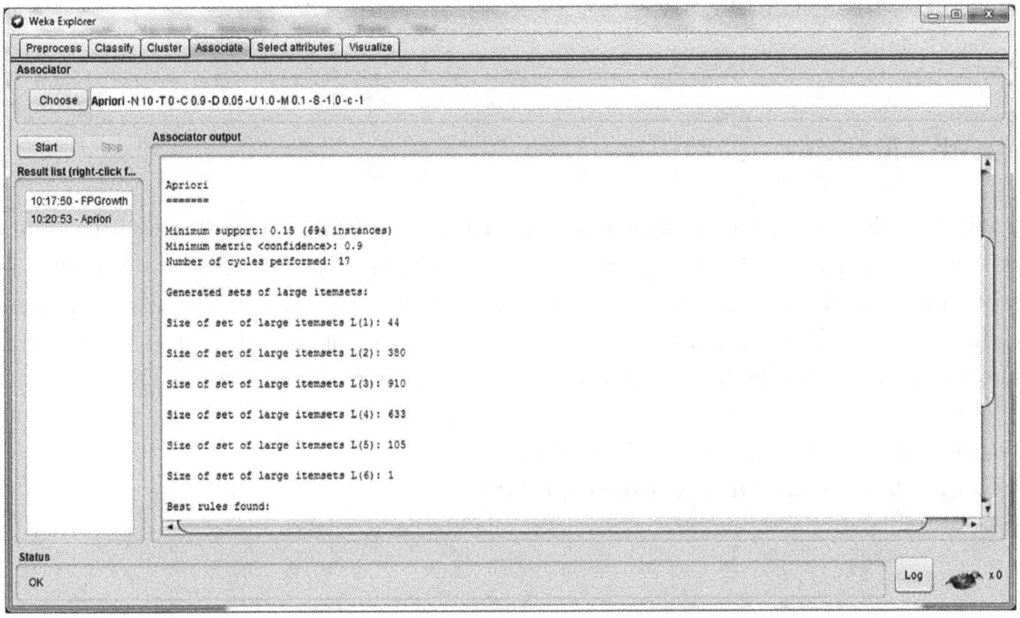

Figure 3.

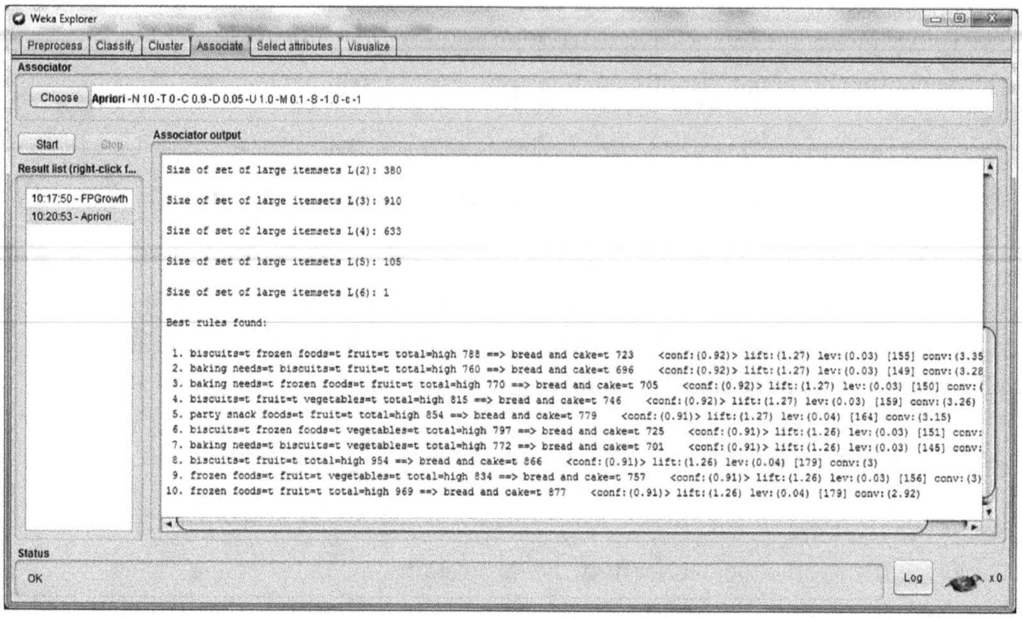

Drawbacks of Apriori

- It scans database multiple times.
- Assume transaction database is memory resident.

Different Ways to Increase Apriori's Performance

- Sampling
- Dynamic itemset counting
- Reduce the transaction
- Partitioning

FP-Growth Algorithm

FP-Growth algorithm is known as Frequent Pattern Growth algorithm. It is an additional way to find the most frequent item sets without the generation of candidate itemset. FP growth is faster than Apriori algorithm which is used to mine the association rules. It uses 2 passes over the dataset. Therefore the scan of entire database is reduced. In this algorithm, all the elements are saved in tree structure.

There are two steps to mine the association rules using FP-Growth algorithm. They are,

1. Construct a dense data structure called FP-tree.
2. Directly extract frequent itemset from the FP-tree.

Step 1: Construction of FP-Tree

Analyze whole database and find out an each items support count.

Arrange all the items in decreasing array with the use of their support count.

Discard infrequent items.

Step 2: Generate Frequent Itemset

Using FP tree, generate frequent itemsets.

Reverse process i.e, starts from the leaves and towards the root.

Splitting and merging method to extract the items.

Consider an example, finding the frequent itemsets without the candidate itemset (FP-Growth) as in Table 12.

Step 1: Scan the database transaction for the count of each candidate as in Table 13.
Step 2: Sort the items in the descending support as in Table 14.
Step 3: Construction of FP-Tree.

- Create root node of the tree as NULL.
- Scan the database D.
- Process the item in the descending support and child node is created for each transaction.

Scan T101 = Bu, Br, Mi

<Br: 1>, <Bu: 1>, <Mi: 1>. Br is the child node for the root because the support count is in the descending order. Bu is the child node for Br and Mi is the child node for Bu. Figure 4 shows the first level of FP-tree construction after the scan of T101 transaction.

Scan T102 = Br, Su

<Br: 1+1><Su: 1>

<Br: 2><Su: 1>

Figure 5 shows the next level of FP-tree construction after the scan of T102 transaction.

Pseudo Code for FP- Growth Algorithm

Input: D, transaction database
Output: Set of frequent patterns

```
Procedure FP-Growth (Tree, T)
if Tree contains a single path P then
for each combination (denoted as B) of the nodes in the path P
generate pattern B ∪ T with support _ count = minimum support count of nodes in B;
else for each a_i the header of Tree {
generate pattern B = a_i ∪ T with support _ count = a_i support_ count;
Construct B's conditional pattern base and then B's conditional FP_tree
Tree_B ; if Tree_B ≠ ∅ then
call FP_growth (Tree_B, B);
```

Table 12. Transaction item sets

TID	List of Items
T101	Bu, Br, Mi
T102	Br, Su
T103	Br, Ch
T104	Bu, Br, Su
T105	Bu, Ch
T106	Br, Ch
T107	Bu, Ch
T108	Bu, Br, Ch, Mi
T109	Bu, Br, Ch

Table 13. Count of candidate item sets

Itemset	Support Count
Bu	6
Br	7
Ch	6
Su	2
Mi	2

Table 14. Sorting of items as per support count

Itemset	Support Count
Br	7
Bu	6
Ch	6
Su	2
Mi	2

Figure 4.

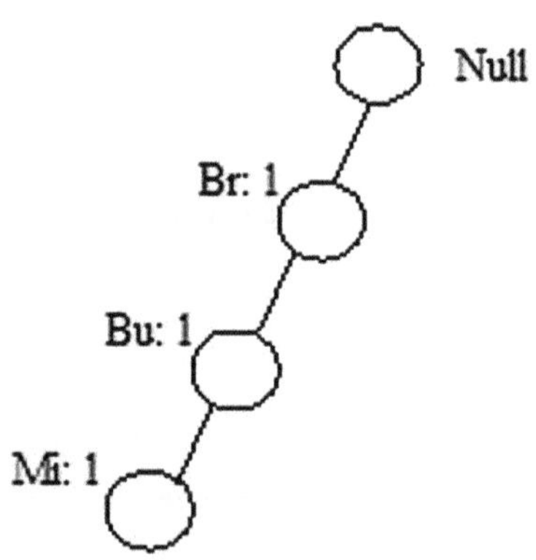

Figure 5.

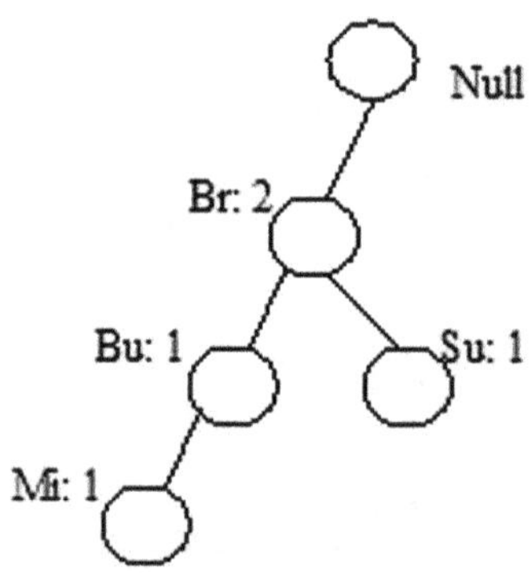

Scan T103 = Br, Ch
<Br: 2+ 1><Ch: 1>
<Br: 3><Ch: 1>
Figure 6 shows the next level of FP-tree construction after the scan of T103 transaction.
Scan T104 = Bu, Br, Su
<Br: 3+1><Bu: 1+1><Su: 1+1>
<Br: 4><Bu: 2><Su: 2>
Figure 7 shows the next level of FP-tree construction after the scan of T104 transaction.

Figure 6.

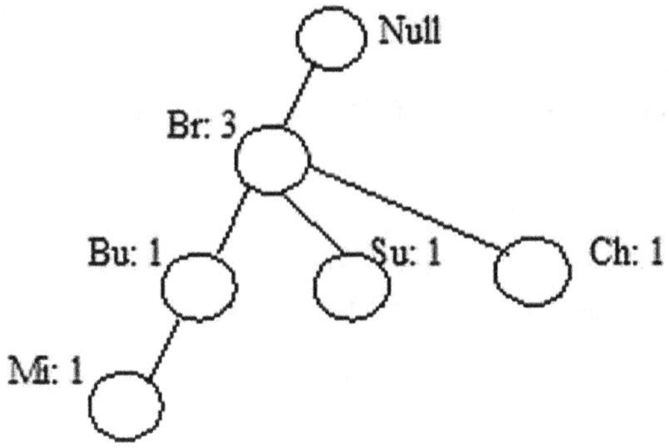

Figure 7.

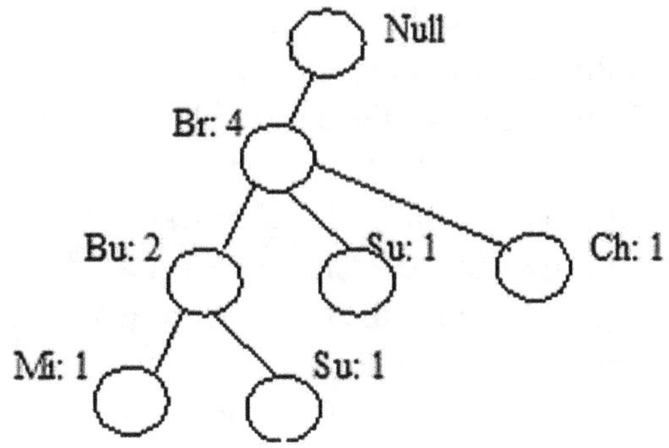

Scan T105 = Bu, Ch
Figure 8 shows the next level of FP-tree construction after the scan of T105 transaction.
Scan T106 = Br, Ch
<Br: 4+1><Ch: 1+1>
<Br: 5><Ch: 2>
Figure 9 shows the next level of FP-tree construction after the scan of T106 transaction.

Figure 8.

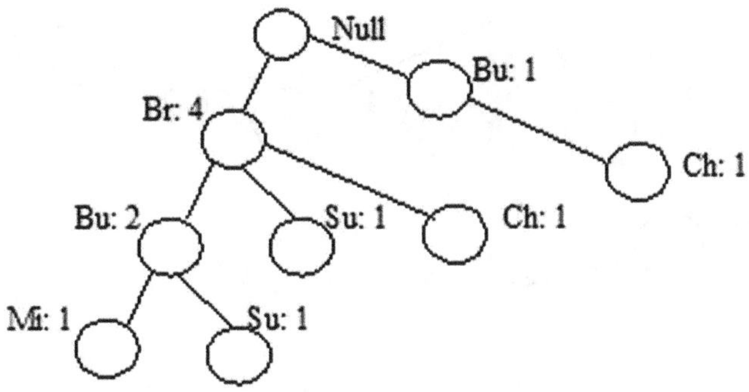

Figure 9.

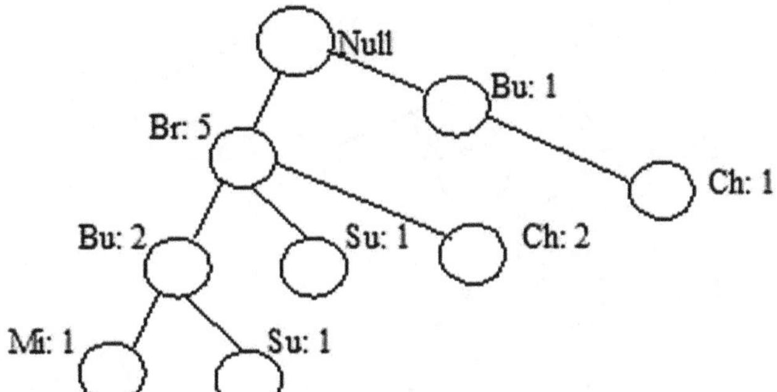

Scan T107 = Bu, Ch
<Bu: 1+1><Ch: 1+1>
<Bu: 2><Ch: 2>
Figure 10 shows the next level of FP-tree construction after the scan of T107 transaction.
Scan T108 = Bu, Br, Ch, Mi
<Br: 5+1><Bu: 2+1><Ch: 1><Mi: 1>
<Br: 6><Bu: 3><Ch: 1><Mi: 1>
Figure 11 shows the next level of FP-tree construction after the scan of T108 transaction.
Scan T109 = Bu, Br, Ch
<Br: 6+1><Bu: 3+1><Ch: 1+1>
<Br: 7><Bu: 4><Ch: 2>
Figure 12 shows the next level of FP-tree construction after the scan of T109 transaction.

Step 4: Create conditional pattern base as in table 15.

Figure 10.

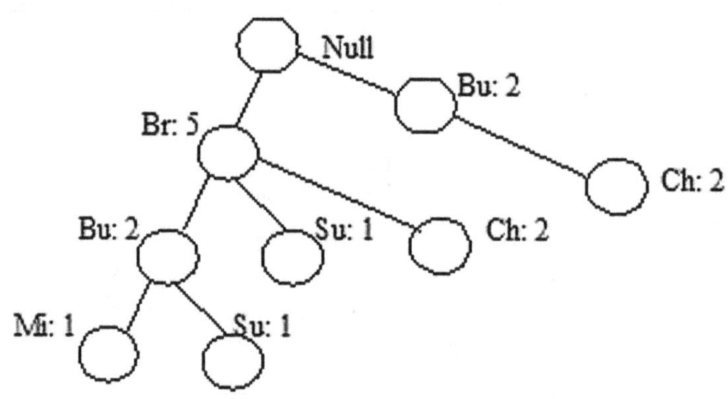

Figure 11.

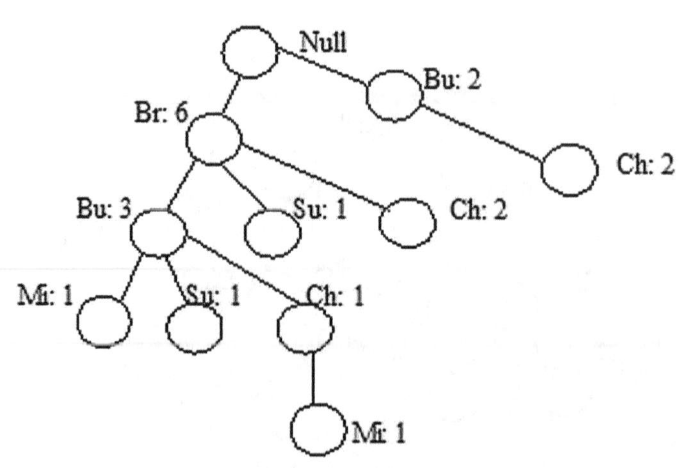

Figure 12.

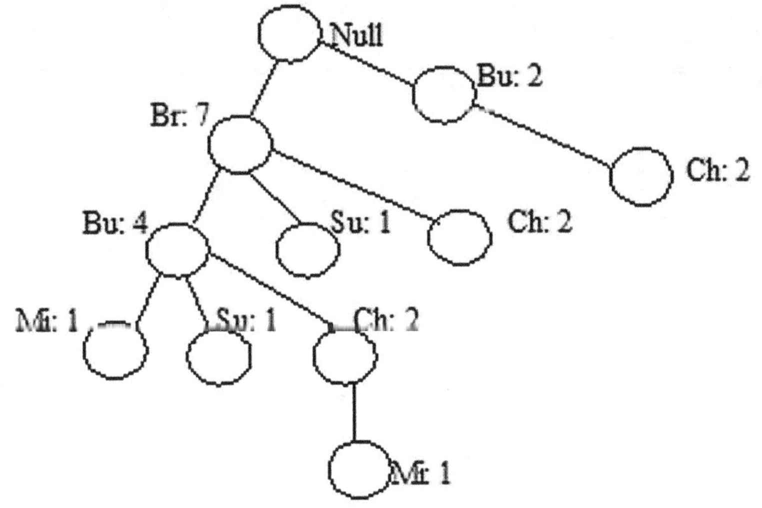

Table 15. Frequent patterns identification

Item	Conditional Pattern Base	Conditional FP-Tree	Frequent Pattern
Mi	<Br, Bu: 1> <Br, Bu, Ch: 1>	<Br: 2> <Bu: 2>	<Br, Mi: 2> <Bu, Mi: 2> <Bu, Br, Mi: 2>
Su	<Br, Bu: 1> <Br: 1>	<Br: 2>	<Br, Su: 2>
Ch	<Br, Bu: 2> <Br, Bu, Ch: 2>	<Bu: 4, Br: 4>	<Br, Ch: 4> <Bu, Ch: 4>
Bu	<Br: 4>	<Br: 4>	<Br, Bu: 4>

Steps to Generate Association Rules Using FP- Growth Algorithm in Weka Tool

1. Open Weka Explorer
2. Click Open file to load the dataset from the destination
3. There are many tabs in the Weka Explorer window i.e, Preprocess, Classify, Cluster, Associate, Select Attributes, and Visualize. Choose Associate tab.
4. Choose the FP Growth algorithm and click start.
5. It takes few seconds to generate the association rules.

For example, Transaction dataset is used for implementation using Weka tool. The dataset contains 267 attributes and 4627 instances. Figure 13 shows the association rules generated using FP-Growth algorithm.

Figure 13.

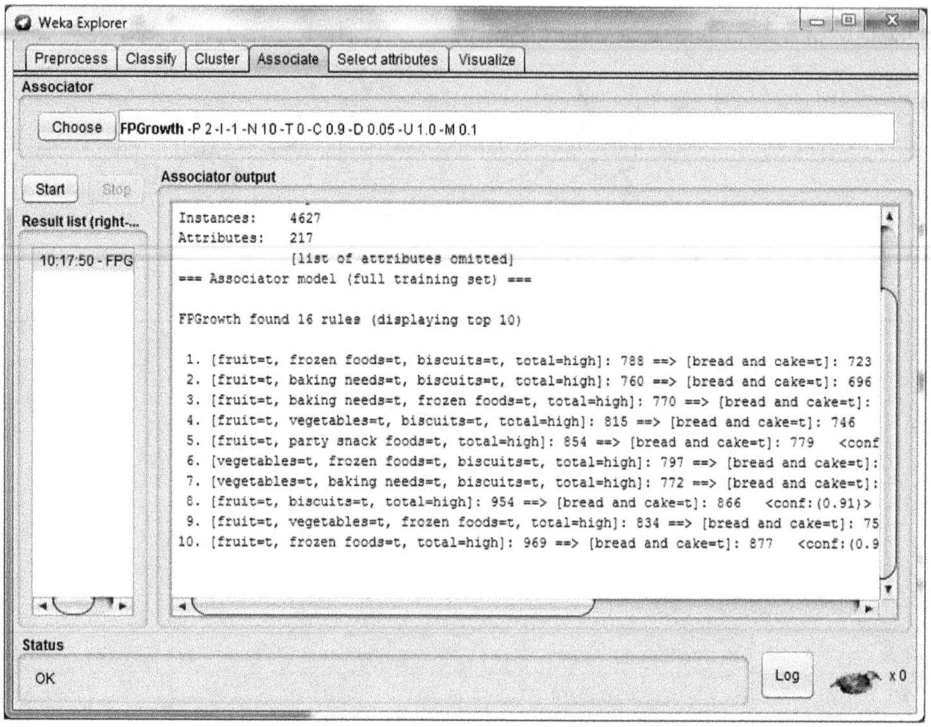

Advantages of FP- Growth

1. No Candidate key generation.
2. Reduces the multiple times database scan.
3. Use compact data structure

Disadvantages of FP- Growth

1. FP-tree might not robust for memory
2. It is exclusive to build

Applications of Association Rule Mining

1. Medical treatments
2. Weblog click streams
3. Customer shopping sequences

SEQUENCE RULES MINING

A sequential rule mining is a subsequence of several sequences of a database. It is used to know the customer has bought in supermarket, in what sequence the customer visiting the WebPages over the time, Telephone call patterns, Medical treatment for the patients, DNA sequences and so on.

Formal Definition of Sequence

A sequence is in the form of an ordered list of transactions

$s = \langle t_1, t_2, \ldots, t_n \rangle$

each transaction is a collection of items

$t_i = \{ i_1, i_2, \ldots, i_n \}$

Length of the sequence = the number of transactions of the sequence. A n-sequence is a sequence which contains n items.

- **Input:** a database consists of sequences

  a user defined minimum support

- **Output:** find all subsequences with support $\geq$ minimum support

For example, there are 4 sequences such as S1, S2, S3, and S4. Consider a, b, c, d, e, f, g, h are some webpages seen by the customer in the e-Commerce as in Table 16.

Assume

a represents as Homepage
b represents as Electronics
c represents as Mobile page
d represents as Samsung mobile
e represents as mobile cover
f represents as shopping cart
g represents order confirmation
h represents as return to shopping.

Table 16. Items with its sequences

ID	Sequences
S1	{a, c},{d},{g},{f}
S2	{a, f},{c},{e, d, f, g}
S3	{e},{a},{g},{c}
S4	{e,f, g},{a}

In S1, the customer seen a and c webpages together seen the customer but in S2 the customer seen a and f webpages together. Likewise the webpages seen by the customers are varying over a time.

Applications of Sequence Rule Mining

1. Quality control
2. Web page prefetching
3. Customer behavior analysis
4. Embedded systems
5. E-learning

CLUSTERING

Clustering is the most important unsupervised learning problem. It finds the useful structure among the items in the dataset without using the class label. Clustering aims to form a group based on their similarities. The main method used for finding the similarities or dissimilarities of the items is Manhattan distance, Euclidean distance and Minkowski distance. The term similarity is to measure how much the items are alike. If the distance is small then similarity measure is high. On the other hand, the distance is high then the similarity measure is low. Similarity is measured in the range 0 to 1. The similarity within the cluster is maximum and dissimilarity between the clusters is maximum (i.e. similarity between the clusters is minimum).

Two main criteria about similarity

s(P,Q) = 1, if P= Q (where P and Q are items)

s(P, Q)= 0, if P $\neq$ Q

Types of Clusters

There are different types of based on the visualization of the clusters. They are as follows.

Well-Separated Cluster

A cluster is simply a group of items where each item is nearer to every other item in the cluster than the other items not in the cluster. Some threshold value is specified that all the items in the cluster should closely relate than the other cluster items. The distance between two items in the different cluster is large when compared to the distance between the two different items in the cluster.

Prototype-Based Cluster

A cluster is a group of items where each item is nearer to the prototype that defines every other item in the cluster than to the prototype that defines the other items in the cluster. For the continuous data attribute, prototype of the cluster is mean of all the items in the cluster. For the categorical data attribute, prototype of the cluster is medoids of all the items in the cluster. Prototype based clusters are commonly referred to as center- based clusters.

Graph-Based Cluster

All the data are represented in the graph. Items are represented in the nodes and links are represented as the connection among the items. A group of items are connected to each other; there is no connection to the items of the other groups. An example for graph- based is contiguity based cluster, the two items are linked only if the items are in the stated distance to each other. One common approach for the graph-based cluster is clique. In clique, all the nodes are completely connected with each other.

Density-Based Cluster

A cluster is a crowded area of items is enclosed by an area of small density. This type of cluster is frequently employed when the clusters are unbalanced, noise and outliers are present. But in the contiguity based cluster will not work well for this type of data.

Shared- Property Cluster

Actually, cluster is a group of item that has same property. An item having the same property belongs to the one cluster. Items in the different cluster have different properties. For example, center- based cluster have the same property that they are all closet to the same centroid. Even if the different clusters are very close to each other means then it is not the problem, using the exact property or concept of the cluster we can detect the clusters.

Clustering can be classified into hierarchical and non-hierarchical clustering. Figure 14 shows the classification of clustering.

Hierarchical Clustering

Divisive Hierarchical Clustering

Divisive clustering is a top-down approach. Initially, complete dataset is considered as a cluster, and in further iteration clusters are recursively divide into small clusters.

Figure 14.

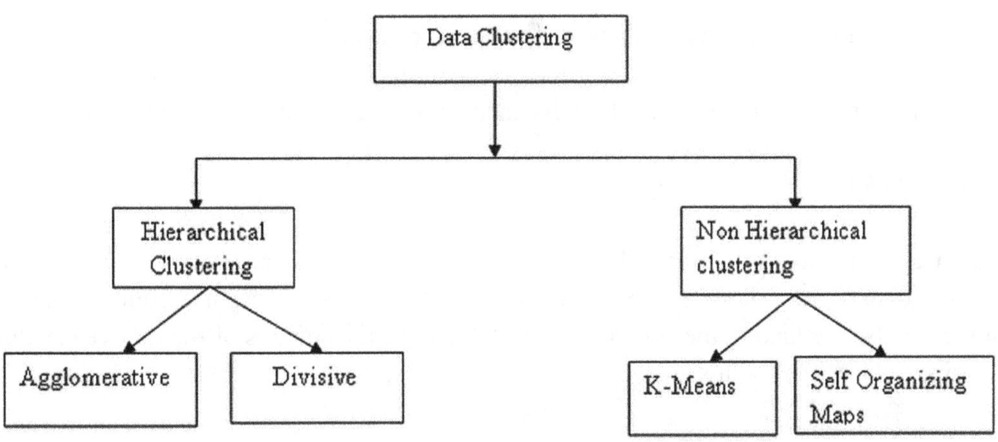

Steps:

Initially all items $A_1, A_2, \ldots\ldots, A_n$ one cluster C.

Split the cluster C, say C_x and C_y.

Repeat the steps until each data items have separate clusters.

Agglomerative Hierarchical Clustering

Agglomerative clustering is a reverse approach. Every data item is considered as a cluster, and in further iteration the clusters are recursively combined to yield a large and good cluster.

Steps:

Initially each item namely $A_1, A_2, \ldots\ldots, A_n$ in their corresponding cluster named as $C_1, C_2, \ldots\ldots, C_n$.

Merge the nearby clusters, say C_x and C_y.

Repeat the steps until there is only one cluster left.

Manhattan Distance

Manhattan distance computes the distance between the data points. It is defined as the summation of the absolute difference of the corresponding components. It is also known as City block distance, L1-norm, rectilinear distance. Consider two points a and b,

$$a = \left(a_1, a_2, \ldots\ldots, a_n\right).$$

$$b = (b_1, b_2, \ldots\ldots, b_n)$$

$$\boldsymbol{d}\left(\boldsymbol{a}, \boldsymbol{b}\right) = \sum_{i=1}^{n} \left|\boldsymbol{a}_{i\_}\boldsymbol{b}_i\right| \quad (3)$$

where,

n = number of attributes.

a_i and b_i = values of a & b attributes at i^{th} records respectively.

Consider an example, find the Manhattan distance between two points P and Q as in Table 17.

Euclidean Distance

Euclidean distance is the most commonly used distance measure. It is also known as simply distance. Whenever the data is dense it is the most suitable method. Euclidean Distance computes the distance between the points, calculating the square root of the sum of the squares of the difference along with corresponding values. Two points are

Table 17. Points determining speed cost and performance

Points	Cost	Speed	Performance
P	3	2	5
Q	6	3	4

d(P, Q) = |3- 6| + | 2- 3| + |5- 4|
= 3+ 1 + 1
= 5

$$a = \left(a_1, a_2, \ldots.., a_n\right).$$

$$b = (b_1, b_2, \ldots.., b_n).$$

$$d\left(\boldsymbol{a}, \boldsymbol{b}\right) = \sqrt{\sum_{i=1}^{n}\left(\boldsymbol{a}_i - \boldsymbol{b}_i\right)^2} \tag{4}$$

where,

n = number of attributes
a_i and b_i = values of a & b attributes at i^{th} records respectively.

Consider an example, compute Euclidean distance between two points (2, -3) & (-1, 1)

P= (2, -3) Q= (-1, 1)

$$\text{dist (P, Q)} = \sqrt{\left((2-\left(-1\right)\right)^2 + ((-3)-1))^2} \,.\, \sqrt{\left((2-\left(-1\right)\right)^2 + ((-3)-1))^2}$$

$$= \sqrt{(2+1)^2 + (-3-1)^2} \,.\, \sqrt{(2+1)^2 + (-3-1)^2}$$

$$= \sqrt{3^2 + \left(-4\right)^2} \,.\, \sqrt{3^2 + \left(-4\right)^2}$$

$$= \sqrt{9+16} \,.\, \sqrt{9+16}$$

$$= \sqrt{25} \,.\, \sqrt{25}$$

$$= 5$$

The horizontal distance between the points is 3 and the vertical distance between the points is 4. The main basis of the Euclidean distance is the Pythagoras theorem.

Minkowski Distance

Minkowski is the combination of both Manhattan and Euclidean distance. Consider two points,

$a = \left(a_1, a_2, \ldots.., a_n\right).$

$b = (b_1, b_2, \ldots.., b_n)$

$$\boldsymbol{d}\left(\boldsymbol{a}, \boldsymbol{b}\right) = \left(\sum_{i=1}^{n} \mid \boldsymbol{a}_i - \boldsymbol{b}_i \mid^{c}\right)^{1/c} \tag{5}$$

where,

n = number of attributes

a_i and b_i = values of a & b attributes at i^{th} records respectively.

C is the degree of the distance.
When c= 1, Minkowski becomes Manhattan distance.
When c= 2, Minkowski becomes Euclidean distance.
When c= $\propto$. Minkowski becomes the Chebyshev distance.

Non Hierarchical Clustering

K-Means

K-Means clustering is very simple. First choose k parameter which is an user defined parameter. It decides the number of clusters to form. Each item is then assigned to the nearby centroid (mean).A group of items are assigned to a centroid (mean) is called as a cluster. Assigning an item to the cluster those centroid is the nearby to that item. Recalculate the centroid for receiving the new item and for losing irrelevant item in the cluster. Repeat the step until the items in the cluster remains same. In the given example transaction data set is used and K=5, so therefore 5 clusters are formed namely Cluster 0, Cluster 1, Cluster 2, Cluster 3, Cluster 4.

Consider an example, Transaction dataset is used for implementation. The dataset contains 217 attributes and 4267 instances. Figure 15 shows that the dataset is loaded in the rapid miner. The clusters are formed and depicted in Figure 16. Number of items in each cluster is displayed in Figure 17.

Figure 15.

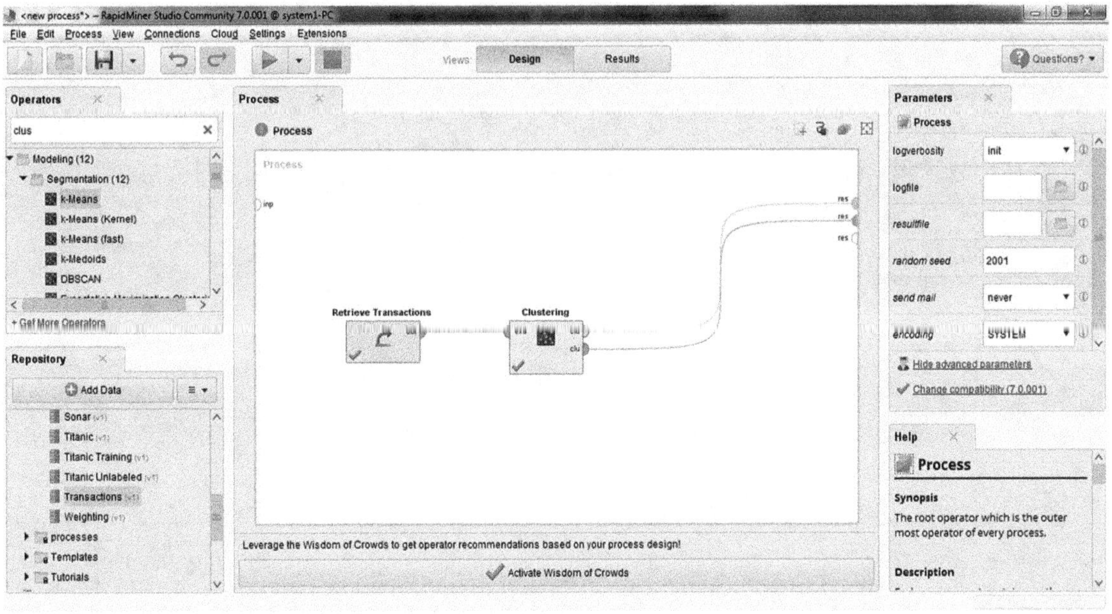

Figure 16.

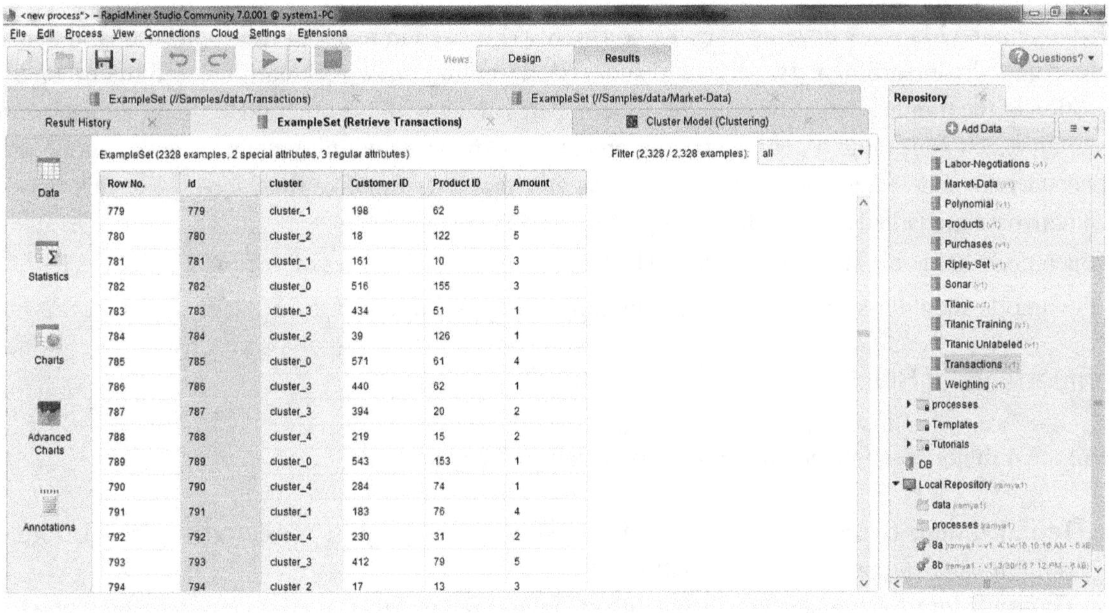

Figure 17.

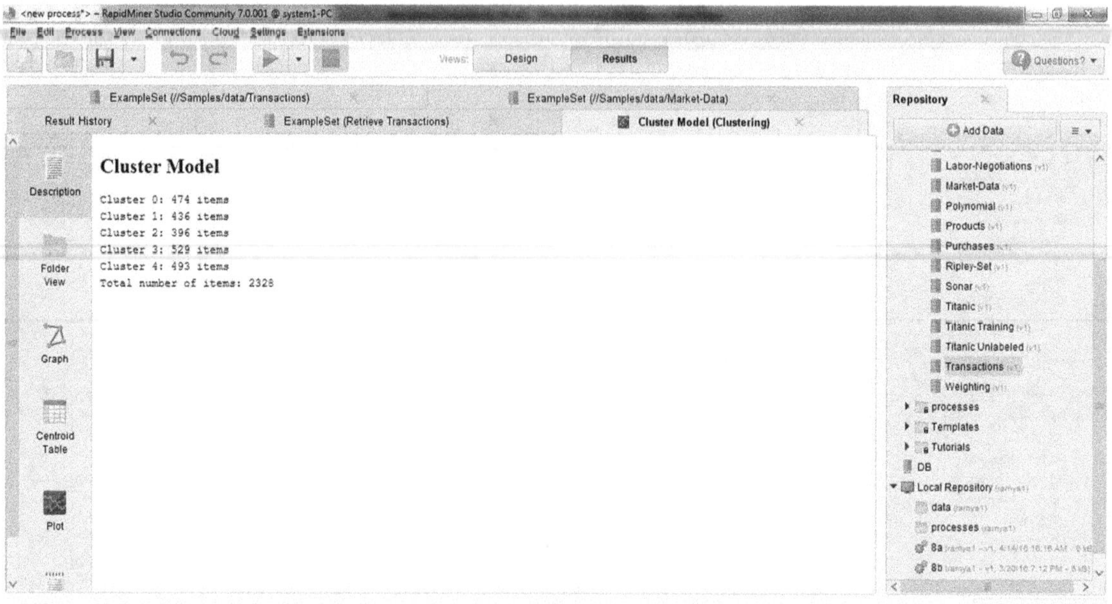

Self Organizing Maps (SOM)

Self-Organizing Maps are developed by Kohonen. SOM is used in many of the applications. It belongs to the competitive learning networks. In unsupervised training, networks learn to form their own classification of the training data. The output node competes along with the other nodes to be activated, after the result exactly one node is activated at a moment. It is known as winning node. There is a connection between every node. The result is that the nodes are forced to organize themselves. For this reasons, such networks are called as Self Organizing Map (SOM).

Each node has some specific position. The training data contains set of vectors $V_1, V_2, \ldots, V_n$.

Each node should assign with the corresponding weights namely $W_1, W_2, \ldots, W_n$.

Components of SOM

There are 4 major components in the self-organization. They are,

1. **Initialization:** Every node should be assigned with the weights. A vector is selected from the training data and presented to the lattice.
2. **Competition:** Each node is analyzed and calculates the weights of all nodes and which one most likes the input vector. That is considered as the winning node.
3. **Cooperation:** Radius of the neighborhood of the winning node is computed.
4. **Adaptation:** Every neighborhood node is adjusted the weights to the input vector

Several stages in SOM algorithm are given below,

i. **Initialization:** Chooses arbitrary values for the initial weight vectors W_i.
ii. **Sampling:** Take an example training input vector x from the input space.
iii. **Similarity:** Locates the winning node with weight vector nearby to input vector.
iv. **Updating:** Update the weight of the node.
v. **Extension:** Continues from step 2 till the feature map stops changing.

REFERENCES

Agrawal, R., Imielinski, T., & Swami, A. (1993), Mining Association Rules Between Sets Of Items In Large Databases. *Proceedings of the ACM SIGMOD International Conference on Management of data*, 207-216. doi:10.1145/170035.170072

Agrawal, R., & Shafer, J. C. (1996). Parallel Mining of Association Rules. *IEEE Transactions on Knowledge and Data Engineering*, *8*(6), 962–969. doi:10.1109/69.553164

Al-Maolegi, M., & Arkok, B. (2014). An Improved Apriori Algorithm for Association Rules. *International Journal on Natural Language Computing*, *3*(1), 21–29. doi:10.5121/ijnlc.2014.3103

Bouguessa, M. (2013). Clustering categorical data in projected spaces. *Data Mining & Knowledge Discovery, Springer*, *1*(29), 3–38.

Cios K.J., Pedrycz, W., Swiniarski, R.W., & Kurgan, L.A. (2012). *Data mining: A knowledge discovery approach.* Springer.

Hall, M., Frank, E., Holmes, G., Pfahringer, B., Reutemann, P., & Witten, I. H. (2009). The WEKA Data Mining Software: An Update. *SIGKDD Explorations*, *11*(1), 10–17. doi:10.1145/1656274.1656278

Han, J., Pei, J., & Yin, Y. (2003). Mining Frequent Patterns without Candidate Generation.*ACM SIGMOD Intl. Conference on Management of Data*, 54-87.

Hunyadi. (n.d.). Performance comparison of Apriori and FPGrowth algorithms in generating association rules. *Proceedings of the European Computing Conference*, 376-381.

Kouser & Sunita. (2013). A comparative study of K Means Algorithm by Different Distance Measures. *International Journal of Innovative Research in Computer and Communication Engineering,* 2443-2447.

Mythili, M. S., & Mohamed Shanavas, A. R. (2013). Performance Evaluation of Apriori and FP-Growth Algorithms. *International Journal of Computers and Applications*, *79*(10), 34–37. doi:10.5120/13779-1650

Pei, J., & Han, J. (2004). Mining Sequential Patterns by Pattern Growth: The Prefix Span Approach. *IEEE Transactions on Knowledge and Data Engineering*, *16*(10), 1–17.

Rao, S., & Gupta. R. (2012). Implementing Improved Algorithm Over APRIORI Data Mining Association Rule Algorithm. *International Journal of Computer Science And Technology,* 489-493.

Shah, Khandakar & Abu. (2008). Reverse Apriori Algorithm for Frequent Pattern Mining. *Asian Journal of Information Technology*, 524-530.

Singh, A., Yadav, A., & Rana, A. (2013). K-means with Three different Distance Metrics. *International Journal of Computers and Applications*, *67*(10), 13–17. doi:10.5120/11430-6785

Sinwar & Kaushik. (2014). Study of Euclidean and Manhattan Distance Metrics using Simple K- Means Clustering. *International Journal for Research in Applied Science and Engineering Technology,* 270-274.

Suresh & Ramanjaneyulu. (2013). Mining Frequent Itemsets Using Apriori Algorithm. *International Journal of Computer Trends and Technology, 4*(4), 760-764.

Tan, P.-N., Kumar, V., & Srivastava, J. (2004). Selecting the right objective measure for association analysis. *Information Systems*, *29*(4), 293–313. doi:10.1016/S0306-4379(03)00072-3

Yabing, J. (2013). Research of an Improved Apriori Algorithm in Data Mining Association Rules. *International Journal of Computer and Communication Engineering*, *2*(1), 25–27. doi:10.7763/IJCCE.2013.V2.128

Zaki, M. J. (2000). Scalable algorithms for association mining. *IEEE Transactions on Knowledge and Data Engineering*, *1*(2), 372–390. doi:10.1109/69.846291

Chapter 7
Personalized Content Recommendation Engine for Web Publishing Services Using Textmining and Predictive Analytics

Başar Öztayşi
Istanbul Technical University, Turkey

Cansu Özdikicioğlu
Kontra Digital, Turkey

Ahmet Tezcan Tekin
Kontra Digital, Turkey

Kerim Caner Tümkaya
Kontra Digital, Turkey

ABSTRACT

Recommendation systems have become very important especially for internet based business such as e-commerce and web publishing. While content based filtering and collaborative filtering are most commonly used groups in recommendation systems there are still researches for new approaches. In this study, a personalized recommendation system based on text mining and predictive analytics is proposed for a real world web publishing company. The approach given in this chapter first preprocesses existing web contents, integrate the structured data with history of a specific user and create an extended TDM for the user. Then this data is used for prediction of the users interest in new content. In order to reach that point, SVM, K-NN and Naïve Bayesian methods are used. Finally, the best performing method is used for determining the interest level of the user in a new content. Based on the forecasted interest levels the system recommends among the alternatives.

INTRODUCTION

Web publishing service includes building and uploading websites, updating the associated webpages, and posting contents to these webpages online. The content meant for web publishing is composed of mainly text, videos, and digital images. Web publishing service providers must hold a web server, a web publishing software, and an Internet connection to carry out publishing process.

DOI: 10.4018/978-1-5225-2148-8.ch007

The main revenue model of web publishers is the advertisement-based model which means providing contents with advertisements and getting fees from advertisers. In this model, advertisers are charged for the number of times readers view or click on the advertisements. The first one is known as "Cost for impression" and the second one is known as "Cost Per Click". Thus, for publishes the total amount of time the readers spend on the website is the key point to increase the revenues. If the readers spend more time in website, this situation affects the revenue in directly proportional.

As a result, web publishers search for new ways to keep the visitors in the web site. Especially content based websites are making efficient content recommendations to increase current visitors. The most common way for content recommendation is to provide a web part on the page and listing the titles of most popular contents. The basic assumption behind the idea is; the content that have attracted high attention from all visitors will probably get the attention of the current visitor. However, it is obvious that the visitors may have different interests. Thus, systems can be modeled for better recommendations.

The study is conducted in association with Kontra Digital Services (KDS) which is established in 2012 and works as value added services provider for GSM carriers and web publisher since it was founded. The study is conducted for a web portal entitled Gazetemsi, which is a comprehensive web publishing service. Gazetemsi is involved with news on sustainable living, physical and mental health, sports, arts and crafts, culture, entertainment, technology, gaming, automotive, fashion, food, travel and daily news. KDS brings unique news to the readers in order to help them live more fulfilling lives, and feed their sense of wonder, instead of using the internet just for killing time. KDS is differentiated from its competitors by providing "beneficial content with entertaining aspects". To achieve this, KDS crawls the popular web sites, makes additional researches, merges the information with editors' knowledge and creativity, and offers contents worth reading or watching. In a nutshell, KDS is in the systematical process of publishing original contents on the website to unique users.

The aim of this study is to search for an efficient content recommendation systems in the web publishing content. The presented approach integrated text mining and predictive analytics to construct a personalized recommendation engine. The paper also provides a real world example for Turkey containing predictive modeling technique such as K-NN, Support Vector Machine and Naïve Bayesian. The rest of the chapter is as follows: in the second section a brief overview of recommendation systems are given. In the third section, after introducing the basics of text mining and predictive analytics the personalized recommendation system is resented with a real world example. After giving, results and recommendations in forth section, future research suggestions are listed. Finally, in the last section the conclusion takes place.

BACKGROUND

Recommendation Systems have been widely investigated in industrial, academic, and educational fields. There are many approaches in literature. In the literature, the best known approaches are content based filtering and collaborative filtering (CBF). In CBF, items are grouped in specific properties. When users register a system firstly user profile is created for each of them. The profile is defined by items which are examined, liked or bought by users before. Based on this user profile, list of item recommendation is defined. Schein & Popescul (2002) underline that content based filtering ignore the preferences of the other users. Each recommendation engine has its own advantages and disadvantages when compared with others. In previous decades hybrid approaches are proposed in order to eliminate their disadvantages (Resnick et al.,1997). Recommendation systems can be classified in five main categories. These categories can be given as:

1. Content based filtering (Pazzani & Billsus, 2007; Barranco & Martínez, 2010; Chen et al., 2011).
2. Collaborative filtering (Herlocker et al. 1999; Gong, 2010.
3. Knowledge based systems (Burke, 2000; Felfernig et al. 2006)
4. Hybrid systems (Burke, 2002; Salter & Antonopoulos, 2006).
5. Semantic recommendation (Ruotsalo, 2010; Pukkhem, 2013).

Content-based approaches are mainly based on information retrieval and information filtering research (Baeza & Ribeiro, 1999). In this approach, text based applications as documents, websites, news contents and messages are taken into account. Content based systems only use active users' preferences, instead of using preferences of all users (Balabanović & Shoham, 1997). Content Based filtering systems utilize past ratings of a user for determining the interest level of that user to different contents and make a recommendation based on this interest level. A profile is created for each user in the system. This profile is based on product evaluations, previous preferences or demographics. This system works by comparing the user profile vector and the item properties vector with each other. In the result of this process, similar item of user profile is recommended to the user. As an example, in a movie recommendation system, specifications of the movie which is watched in the past are being compared with other movies that user did not watch. As a result, the characteristics that the user is interested in is determined and the recommendations are done based on these characteristics.

Collaborative Filtering is a filtering type in which, to find how a user will rate an item which is never seen before, by comparing previously given rates of that user with other users' rates. This technique is based on; similar users have similar tastes. Users, who rate items similar to the rates of active user, have similar tastes with active user. A user is similar to active user based on how much rates of the user in the system is close to rates of active user. In guessing stage, the users which are most similar to active user, will have active role when deciding what items active user could like.

In Collaborative filtering systems, rates of users about items are stored in a single matrix. Since the systems can serve many users, there can be many users and products registered to the system. As a result, the size of these matrices become larger as the number of users and products increase. Let's assume there are m items and n users in a system, in this case total user rating of this system will be m x n. Most probably, it is impossible for every user to have a rating about every product. So, a huge amount of this matrix may be empty which leads to sparsity problem.

In Collaborative Filtering, the main input is above mentioned item-user matrix in which rows are items and columns are users. The main approach is to make the recommendation based on similarities between users, which is also called user based (user-user) Collaborative filtering. On the other hand, another approach is item based (item-item) which is based on similarities between products. When reviewing similarities between items, each rate of items from each user is calculated as distinct column vectors. In other words, when calculating similarities, considering only columns vector.

Collaborative filtering algorithms are based on product rates which users give. But, there can be situations where there may not be sufficient information. For example, in the case of buying a house or buying a house, it is not easy to form an item user matrix. Both Collaborative filtering and content based filtering does not produce decent results where there are small number of ratings. Moreover, time is very important in recommendation systems. The evaluations or interests of people may change as the time passes. As time passed, accuracy and validity of the recommendation could decrease. For example, in a recommendation system for a computer, rating from 5 years before, may not be efficient using content based algorithms (Jannach, 2004). Generally in these situation knowledge based recommendation systems is the best perform than other approaches. This group of recommendation systems can be conversational recommendation (McCarthy et al., 2010), search based recommendation (Felfernig and Burke, 2008) or navigation based recommendation (Chen and Pu, 2010).

Hybrid recommendation systems are produced by combining two or more recommendation approach. These systems are mostly created by combining content based filtering collaborative and knowledge filtering. Hybrid systems are produced to solve disadvantages of other approaches such as cold start, data sparsity, limited content analysis (Miranda et al., 1999).

The last group is semantic recommendation approach. Semantic web systems create important data model not only for web based systems but also for other information systems. In semantic recommendation approach the recommendation process is generally based on concept diagram or an ontology describing acknowledge based and uses semantic web technologies. For knowledge representation ontologies are used to show concepts in a domain and relation between them. In the field of recommendation systems, ontologies are used to handle cold start and data sparsity problems of CF system (Wang and Kong, 2007).

PERSONALIZED CONTENT RECOMMENDATION APPLICATION

Text Mining

This section includes the steps of the Text Mining methodology which are designated with a plot summary. There are three main processes that are separated sequentially in text mining level (Figure 1). Each of them has particular contributions to create certain outputs. (Turban et al. 2011).

The first step is to constitute the repository. The repository is included a huge and the specific unstructured data which are collected from the analysis. The main aim of this process is to crawl all contents to prepare them for the next step. In projects of text mining area, the repository should be classified and gathered by software programs. The software programs ramble the sources which are HTML files, email, content based documents, blogs and collect data from these sources. Therefore, several type of documents are collected and prepared for the second step.

Figure 1. Three process of Text mining

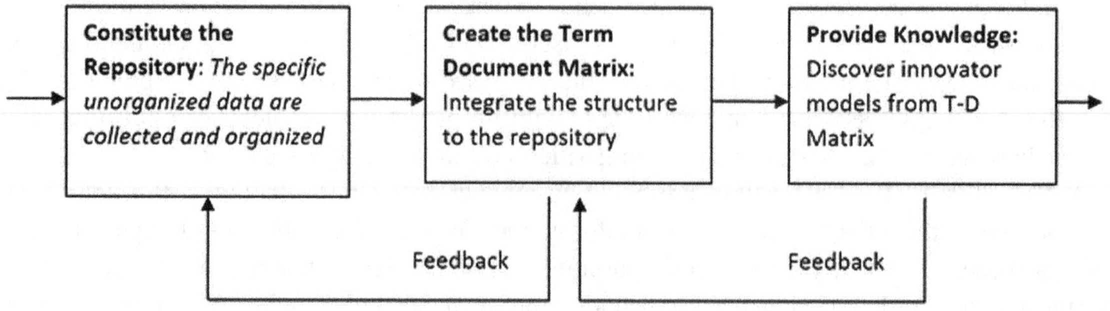

The second step of the process is to create the term-document matrix (TDM). When the TDM is completed the unorganized data is converted into the organized data. The columns of the TDM corresponded by terms and the rows of the TDM corresponded by documents. A sample TDM is shown in Table 1.

The TDM matrix represents the frequency of terms in documents. (Miner et al. 2012). When the relational matrix is created there is a critical point that should be completed. The documents not include the terms which have an equally importance to count. Some conjunctions, auxiliary verbs and prepositions which are called as "stop words" should be identified and excluded from the document before the second step completed. Also the specific type of terms and synonyms terms should be considered and identified when the TDF matrix is created. As a result, the TDF matrix is completed with the remaining significant words.

In the first table, the frequencies are in the raw form. Nevertheless, they should be in consistent form for more analysis. When the TDM matrix is normalized, it transformed in the Term Frequency – Inverse Document Frequency matrix. This transformation model is created to combine term frequency and inverse document frequency therefore the TF – IDF weighting scheme is occurred. The TF – IDF matrix assigns to term "t" a weight in document "d" which is in the following formula:

$$tf - idf_{t,d} = \left(1 + \log tf_{t,d}\right) * \log\left(N / df_t\right) \quad (1)$$

If the number of times the term occurs in a document is high and the number of a document is small, the TF – IDF values become higher values. If the term is counted in all documents, the value of TF – IDF gets lower values. On the other hand, if the number of terms occurs fewer times in a document, or occurs in many documents, the TF – IDF values become medium.

The last step is run when the second step dealing with the possible problems. In the last step the innovator models and beneficial patterns are provided from the TDM. The new form of TDM can be utilized or matched kind of matrixes which include different data to provide varied knowledge in the field of text mining. There are four extraction methods that can be used in this field; classification, clustering, association and trend analysis.

Predictive Analytics

Predictive analytics incorporates with a variety of statistical techniques, machine learning, and data mining with the purpose of analyzing current and historical facts to make predictions about future or

Table 1. Sample term-document matrix

Document \ Term	Hungry	Area	Gold	Nature
Text1	1	0	1	0
Text2	1	0	1	1
Text3	1	1	0	0
Text4	1	1	0	0
Text5	1	1	0	1
Text6	1	1	0	1

otherwise unknown events (Siegel and Davenport, 2013). In this approach the methods use the existing data to learn the nature of the situation and apply the model to new observations. The existing data set is called training set and is composed of coupled input variables "X" and output variable "Y", The overall aim is to find a function h(X) to predict of output values using the input variables (Jin et al. 2006). In the domain of recommendation systems and web publishing, the unknown event can be defined as users' interest on the proposed content. In other words, the use of predictive analytics in this domain is to find the web content which will capture users' interest so that he/she clicks on the content for details. This problem is also called as a binary classification problem which deals with classifying the observed items into two groups. In the case of web publishing the observed items are new web pages and the groups are either the user will read it or not.

Although there are various techniques that can be used for classification, we only underline some of the most popular techniques which are used in the study.

- **KNN:** One of the popular algorithms for content classification which is based on the machine learning. After the preprocessing and content preparation is completed, the machine learning algorithm is used to categorized documents. The main purpose of the algorithm is to assigned determined new unclassified documents to the class which the majority of its K nearest neighbors belongs. In other words, the algorithm checks the documents to compare with each new document and categorized them that are most similar to it.
  The distance calculation of this algorithm based on the Euclidean space as points to classify documents. The distance between two point in Euclidean space is known as Euclidean distance. The following formula (1) is used to calculate the distance between two points in the plane with coordinates. (Su, 2011)

$$d(p,q) = d(p,q) = \sqrt{(x-a)^2 + (y-b)^2} \quad (2)$$

- Naïve Bayesian is the other popular machine learning algorithm which is the probabilistic model to classified the texts. The key idea of the algorithm is to compute a probability for each class based on the probability distribution in the training data. The model of a Naïve Bayesian has not complicated iterative parameter estimation. The following formula is to calculate the prediction of class.

$$p(C_k \mid x) = \frac{p(C_k)\, p(x \mid) C_k}{p(x)} \quad (3)$$

  The result of the calculation gives the predictable values about the class of texts in text mining area.
- Support Vector Machine which is another popular machine learning algorithm used for binary classification. The main idea is to find a hyperplane to divide d-dimensional data into two classes. One of the Kernel – based techniques of SVM is used to predict various properties in areas of chemical, physical, biological, especially text mining (Chen et al., 2011). In the area of text mining, it is applied to classification or regression.

Personalized Recommendation Application

After presenting the main techniques used, in this section the proposed flow of the system is given.

Step 1: All current web content is selected from the database.
Step 2: Each web content is pre processed so that the stop words are deleted and stemming is finalized. In the application of this step Zemberek, a special software developed for Turkish language, is used.
Step 3: A term document matrix is formed composed of unique terms, contents and TF-IDF values. A part of the TDM is given in Table 2.
Step 4: For a specific user, the user's historical preferences are listed. These preferences can be either a rating or a binary variable showing the user has read the content or not.
Step 5: The user preferences are integrated with TDM formed in Step 3 in order to construct extended personalized TDM (EP-TDM) matrix. In the application instead of content rating, which is very hard to capture, binary reading data is used. However, in order to get more accurate results the content that the user is not aware are eliminated from the list. In other words, the content that user has read is represented as 1 and the content that has recommended to the user but the user has no interest on are represented with zeros. As a result, Table 3 which show EP-TDM do not have the some rows (i.e Content 3, 5,6..) since it is not recommended to him/her before.
Step 6: Using EP-TDM and predictive analytics techniques different predictive models are formed and tested. The methods namely, K-NN, Naïve Bayesian and Support Vector Machine are used to form the predictive models. In order to test the performance of the methods the sample data splits into two parts. The first 70% is used as training set and the other 30% is used for testing. The test results are shown in Table 4. As a result Support Vector Machine has shown the best performance.
Step 7: The method which shows the highest performance in test data is selected and the new content used as an input to this model to find weather the user will show an interest on the content or not.
Step 8: The contents with the highest interest level are recommended to the user.

The steps of the methodology is represented in Figure 2.

Table 2. A sample from the TDM

	erkek	basamak	nasil	kadro	hizli	panik	Gri	eylül	saban
Content1	0	0	0	0	0	0	0	0	0
Content2	0.128	0	0	0	0	0	0	0	0
Content3	0	0.118	0	0	0	0	0	0	0
Content4	0	0	0	0	0	0	0	0	0
Content5	0	0	0.011	0.024	0	0	0	0	0
Content6	0	0	0.038	0	0	0	0	0	0
Content7	0	0	0.044	0	0	0	0	0	0
Content8	0	0	0	0	0.12	0.126	0	0	0
Content9	0	0	0.014	0	0	0	0	0	0
Content10	0	0	0	0	0	0	0	0	0

Table 3. A sample from the EP-TDM

	erkek	basamak	Nasil	kadro	hizli	panik	gri	eylül	saban	Level of Interest
Content1	0	0	0	0	0	0	0	0	0	**1**
Content2	0.128	0	0	0	0	0	0	0	0	**1**
Content4	0	0	0	0	0	0	0	0	0	**0**
Content7	0	0	0.044	0	0	0	0	0	0	**1**
Content8	0	0	0	0	0.12	0.126	0	0	0	**0**
Content10	0	0	0	0	0	0	0	0	0	**0**
Content11	0	0	0.041	0	0.04	0	0	0	0	**1**
Content13	0	0	0.149	0	0	0	0	0	0	**1**
Content14	0	0	0	0	0	0	0	0	0	**0**
Content15	0	0	0	0	0	0	0	0	0	**1**

Table 4. Best classifier models for the sample data

	Percentage Split			Cross Validation		
	55 Read – 45 Unread – %70 Split			55 Read – 45 Unread – 3 Fold		
Algorithm	**Read Accuracy**	**Unread Accuracy**	**Accuracy**	**Read Accuracy**	**Unread Accuracy**	**Accuracy**
KNN (K=1)	61.54%	25%	56.67%	56%	54.55%	56.18%
KNN (K=3)	60.71%	0%	56.67%	56.18%	54.55%	56%
KNN (K=5)	67.67%	38.10%	45.67%	55.81%	50%	55%
NAÏVE BAYES	73.47%	53.85%	66.67%	57.47%	54.29%	58%
SVM	76.68%	54.55%	67.67%	60.00%	61.54%	58.8%

SOLUTIONS AND RECOMMENDATIONS

In this chapter a personal recommendation system for web publishing services is presented. The real world example shows that SVM method has the best performance when compared with other methods. However, the generalizability of the results are low since the modeling is done for a selected user. On the other hand, real effectiveness of the system can be better observed when the system goes online and actual user behaviors are traced.

One of the limitations of the study is that in order to run a predictive model a certain level of data is required. In other words, the presented model can not work well if a totally new user enters to the system. As the user does not have any previous data in the system, EP-TDM can not be formed and the models cannot be run. So, in order to handle this cold start problem, it is recommended that the approach can be used with some other methods.

The presented approach may perform well especially if most of the tasks are done before the user comes to the website. As the number of contents, users and concurrent online users increase the computations may not be carried out effectively and cause delay in web publishing.

Figure 2. The steps of personalized content recommendation

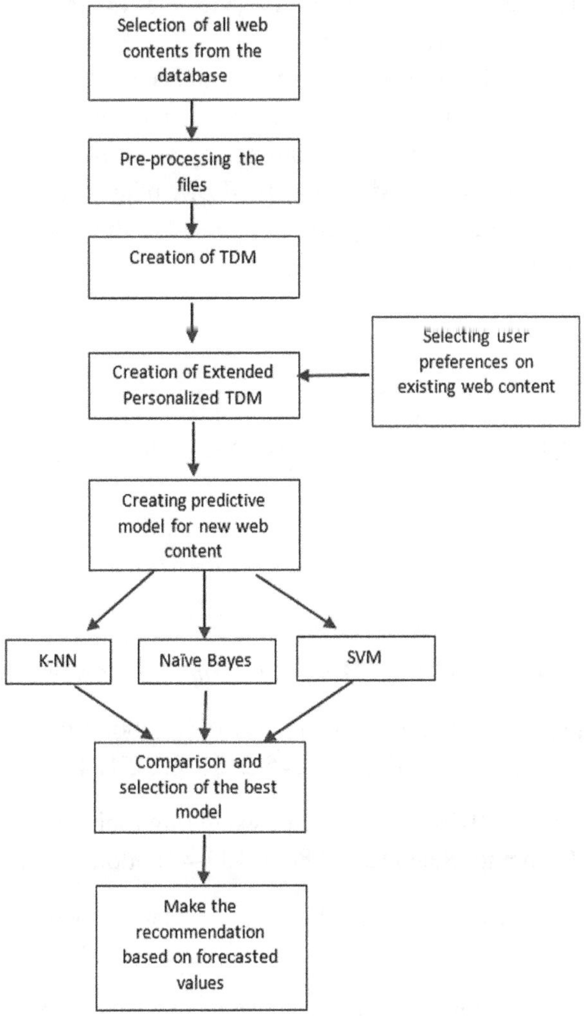

FUTURE RESEARCH DIRECTIONS

As further research, the same approach can be extended using different techniques such as decision tree and artificial neural networks. Another research direction can focus on finding generalizable results. To this end same approach can be used in a larger data set and the results are compared.

CONCLUSION

With the rapid advancement of the Internet and Information Technologies, we could reach the people all around the world. At the same time, we could use websites to reach unique information, e-mail, e-journals systems. On the internet finding information which are about peoples' interests may be hard.

The recommendation system provides a bridge between users and information. Users' interest can be captured and next actions can be estimated with the assistance of the recommendation engine and help them to find the contents they are interested in.

In this paper after reviewing different recommendation system approaches a personalized recommendation system which combine text mining and predictive analytics are represented. In the real world application, the recommendation system for web publishing is given. After preprocessing the content with Zemberek, EP-TDM matrix is formed. Using EP-TDM matrix three algorithms, namely KNN, Naïve Bayesian and SVM are used to build predictive models. The test phase showed that SVM has outperform than other methods.

ACKNOWLEDGMENT

This work is supported by Scientific and Technological Research Council of Turkey (TÜBİTAK), TEYDEB 1507, Grant No:7160551.

REFERENCES

Baeza-Yates, R., & Ribeiro-Neto, B. (1999). *Modern information retrieval* (1st ed.). New York Press.

Balabanović, M., & Shoham, Y. (1997). Fab: Content-based, collaborative recommendation. *Association for Computing Machinery*, *40*(3), 66–72. doi:10.1145/245108.245124

Barranco, M. J., & Martínez, L. (2010). A method for weighting multi-valued features in content-based filtering.Lecture Notes in Computer Science, 6098(3), 409–418. doi:10.1007/978-3-642-13033-5_42

Burke, R. (2000). Knowledge-based recommender systems. Encyclopedia of Library and Information Systems, 69, 175–186.

Burke, R. (2002). Hybrid recommender systems: Survey and experiments. User Modeling and User-Adapted Interaction, 12, 331-370.

Chen, L., & Pu, P. (2010). Critiquing-based recommenders: Survey and emerging trends. *User Modeling and User-Adapted Interaction Journal*, *22*(1-2), 125–150. doi:10.1007/s11257-011-9108-6

Chen, Z. S., Jang, J. S. R., & Lee, C. H. (2011). A kernel framework for content based artist recommendation system in music. *IEEE Transactions on Multimedia*, *13*(6), 1371–1380. doi:10.1109/TMM.2011.2166380

Felfernig, A., & Burke, R. (2008), Constraint-based Recommender Systems: Technologies and Research Issues. *ACM International Conference on Electronic Commerce*, 17-26. doi:10.1145/1409540.1409544

Felfernig, A., Friedrich, G., Jannach, D., & Zanker, M. (2006). An integrated environment for the development of knowledge-based recommender applications. *International Journal of Electronic Commerce*, *11*(2), 11–34. doi:10.2753/JEC1086-4415110201

Gong, S. (2010). A collaborative filtering recommendation algorithm based on user clustering and item clustering. *Journal of Software*, *5*(7), 745–752. doi:10.4304/jsw.5.7.745-752

Herlocker, J. L., Konstan, J. A., Borchers, A., & Riedl, J. (1999). An algorithmic framework for performing collaborative filtering. In *Proceedings of the 22nd Annual International ACM SIGIR Conference on Research and Development in Information Retrieval - SIGIR '99* (pp. 230–237). New York: ACM Press. doi:10.1145/312624.312682

Jannach, D. (2004). Preference-based treatment of empty result sets in product finders and knowledge-based recommenders. *Proceedings of the 27th Annual German Conference on Artificial Intelligence*, 145–159.

Jin, H., Huang, J., Xie, X., & Zhang, Q. (2006). Using Classification Techniques to Improve Replica Selection in Data Grid. On the Move to Meaningful Internet Systems 2006: CoopIS.DOA.GADA. and ODBASE. *Lecture Notes in Computer Science*, *4276*, 1376–1387. doi:10.1007/11914952_24

McCarthy, K., Salem, Y., & Smyth, B. (2010). Experience-Based Critiquing. *Reusing Critiquing Experiences to Improve Conversational Recommendation, ICCBR*, *10*, 480–494.

Miner, G., Elder, I. V. J., Fast, A., Hill, T., Nisbet, R., & Delen, D. (2012). *Practical Text Mining and Statistical Analysis for Non-structured Text Data Applications*. Academic Press.

Miranda, T., Claypool, M., Gokhale, A., & Sartin, M. (1999). Combining contentbased and collaborative filters in an online newspaper.*Proceedings of ACM SIGIR Workshop on Recommender Systems.*

Pazzani, M. J., & Billsus, D. (2007). Content-based recommendation systems. *The Adaptive Web, LNCS*, *4321*, 325–341. doi:10.1007/978-3-540-72079-9_10

Pukkhem, N. (2013). Ontology-based semantic approach for learning object recommendation. *ACEEE International Journal on Information Retrieval, 3*(4). Retrieved from http://hal.archives-ouvertes.fr/hal-00942526/

Resnick, P., Varian, H. R., & Editors, G. (1997). Recommender systems mende tems. *Communications of the ACM*, *40*(3), 56–58. doi:10.1145/245108.245121

Ruotsalo, T. (2010). *Methods and applications for ontology-based recommender systems. science and technology*. Retrieved December 12, 2015, from http://lib.tkk.fi/Diss/2010/isbn9789526031514/

Salter, J., & Antonopoulos, N. (2006). Recommender agent: Collaborative and content-based filtering. *Analysis*, *21*(February), 35–41.

Siegel, E., & Davenport, T. H. (2013). *Predictive Analytics: The Power to Predict Who Will Click, Buy, Lie, or Die Hardcover*. Wiley.

Su, Y. M. (2011). Real-time anomaly detection systems for Denial-of-Service attacks by weighted k-nearestneighbour classifiers. *Expert Systems with Applications*, *38*(4), 3492–3498. doi:10.1016/j.eswa.2010.08.137

Turban, E., Sharda, R., & Delen, D. (2011). Decision Support and Business Intelligence Systems (9th ed.). Upper Saddle River, NJ: Prentice hall.

Wang, R.-Q., & Kong, F.-S. (2007). Semantic-enhanced personalized recommender system. *Sixth International Conference on Machine Learning and Cybernetics*, 19–22. doi:10.1109/ICMLC.2007.4370858

KEY TERMS AND DEFINITIONS

Classification: The machine learning method which is used to categorize the data.

Clustering: An allocation or mapping of data according to the various criterion.

Collaborative Filtering: The algorithm which is a well-known algorithm in recommendation systems makes recommendations according to users' demographic information.

Content Based Filtering: The algorithm makes recommendations according to contents' information.

Predictive Analytics: The method is used to estimate users' future actions according to users' historical actions.

Recommendation Engine: Atomized software which is making suggestions for something to website users might be interested in such as a jewelry, a food, a video, a film, a content or a job.

Text Mining: The method is used to create a relationship between group of texts.

Trend Analysis: Collect information using spot trends or patterns.

Chapter 8
Predictive Analysis of Emotions for Improving Customer Services

Vinay Kumar Jain
Jaypee University of Engineering and Technology, India

Shishir Kumar
Jaypee University of Engineering and Technology, India

ABSTRACT

Human emotions plays an important role in everyday communication. Emotions are formed by the combination of cues such as relative actions, facial expressions, and gestures and reactions. Emotions are also present in written texts like in social media, chats, customer reviews. By getting inspired by works done in the domain of sentiment analysis, this chapter explores advances to automatic detection of emotions in text which help in Improving Customer Services. This chapter presents a framework for automatic detection of emotions in customer reviews based on different emotions theories in the fields of psychology and linguistics. This framework uses advanced Machine Learning (ML) techniques with Natural Language Processing (NLP) methods for better understanding of emotion detection and recognition in customer reviews. The text under study comprises data collected from leading Indian e-commerce portals like Flipkart, Snapdeal and Amazon, which contains text rich in emotions. The advantages and application based emotion detection framework has been incorporated with suitable examples.

INTRODUCTION

Language is the most important tool for communication and help to convey information in a society. Language provides suitable means to express emotions in several forms. Natural Language Processing techniques are used to identify meaningful inferences content in text. Multiple applications related to information retrievals such as topic-based modeling, text categorization, question-answering systems, has been focused on the information contained in the data (Jain & Kumar, 2015).

DOI: 10.4018/978-1-5225-2148-8.ch008

During the last few decades around the world, the growth of the internet has increased the communication levels and internet users widely used multiple platforms to post their opinions online. In current scenario, people increasingly use micro-blogging platforms and social networking sites, to share and retrieve relevant information in real-time which contains opinions and sentiments (Chesley et al.,2006). Intelligent computational tools have been used to extract meaningful inferences and help companies to utilize this information for their productivity.

The e-shopping websites provides the feature where a customer can give feedback in the form of review to the product he purchased. There are massive amount of reviews available for every product in multiple e-commerce portals. A simple example related to customer review related to smart phone has been presented in Figure 1. Most of the users view the rating given to the product and read some of the reviews before decision making. The ratings are not enough to decide whether a product is feasible to buy or not. Therefore getting a conclusion from reviews is manually a tough task.

Much of the current work for analysis of customer reviews has been focused on polarity orientation of textual data. Limited work has been done in the direction of type of emotions present in written text by the customers. Recognizing emotions that has been expressed by customer reviews could provide the general intention of customer towards products and services. This chapter presented an emotion detection based system to provide benefit to the customer in decision making before the purchase of product or services. The Emotions categories in customer reviews definitely help companies to enhance their marketing strategy in a better way. .

The methods related to automatic emotion detection can be useful in many real-time applications with the help of human psychological techniques (Dung and Cao,2012). In recent years, the growth of e-commerce has brought a boom in the business market. The concept of online shopping has become one of the biggest successful businesses. With the availability of products on the websites, the interest of public has grown towards online shopping. Whenever any user is interested in purchasing a product online, the user completely depends on the reviews that have been given for a particular product. This review can be oral or written. On internet most of the emphasis is given on written review that a product receives, and this helps the user to make a decision whether to buy a product or not. So, it is necessary to build a system that finds out the emotions present every review by users so that they can but the product It also helps the company owners to determine whether the product they launched in the market is been accepted by users or not. In concern of social media or the customer reviews data it has more complications due different geographical location. A wide variety of work has been carried out in the field of sentiment analysis and opinion mining but limited work has been carried out in the field emotion detection and recognition. This chapter presents a framework for automatic detection of emotions in customer reviews using different emotions theories in the fields of linguistics and psychology. This framework uses Machine Learning methods and Natural Language Processing (NLP) and for better understanding of emotions present in customer reviews. A simple example of customer reviews which contains emotion bearing words has been presented in Figure 1.

BACKGROUND

Emotional states have multiple cognitive bases which are formed by number of factors. The scope of this chapter is limited to provide important features relevant to recognize emotion and the process of determining the emotional orientation of customer reviews. Emotion present in multiple languages or

Figure 1. A sample of reviews collected from E-commerce website

Very nice phone in terms of looks, weight, but the Flyme OS is little tricky and not at all user friendly, If you can bear the same you may go for it rest of all is fine..

Nice phone. camera, battery backup, look etc all are perfect at this price range.

hangs, touch is too bad at end of screen...never trust this model... above all where is the support...amazon just washed it by hands return policy over so can't make replacement !! Who will repair or replace !!

Ultimate mobile phone,have used HTC, SAMSUNG, APPLE and MOTOROLA but this one is not behind them in any way.

This is very fast and all mobile future very different then other mobile I love miezu

All features is gud in this phone but i have only one problem that i can't use 2g network only 3g and wifi is working

I have also a k3 and a mi 4i.performance wise k3 is best.but in camera look sound mi is best meizu is gd in performance touch experience design.........thanks

simply in a language can be expressed in several ways and understanding of this expression can be interpreted differently by different readers.

During the last few decades, Computational techniques such as Natural language processing, Artificial Intelligence (AI), Machine learning has been used to develop intelligent systems that interpreted human emotions (Jain et al., 2016). Several real-time processes have been modeled to develop effective intelligent systems by providing learning, perception and reasoning. Development of affective interfaces is an important research area in emotions. Affective interfaces are the system which provides emotional inputs; emotional responses using this facilitate online communication with the help of animated affective agents. These affective interfaces provide better user experience in following areas such as Computer-Mediated Communication (CMC) and Human-Computer Interaction (HCI). Text-to-Speech (TTS) synthesis systems are also used these interface for developing real-time systems.

Recognizing the polarity of sentiment present in written text such as in social media posts, blogs and forums is the most popular in sentiment and opinion mining domain (Pang and Lee, 2008) .Among the less paying attention area related to sentiment is the identification of emotions present in customer reviews and social media data. Computational techniques related to emotion analysis present in text mainly deals with their emotion modalities and emotion-annotated data (Jain et al., 2016).However, only limited work has been done in developing automatic emotion recognition system which benefits customer and e-commerce companies in decision-making. The focus of this chapter is to give advantages of recognizing emotions present in customer reviews which provide an insight related to customer's intentions.

THEORIES OF EMOTION

Theories of emotion mainly categorized in terms of the context within which the explanation is developed. There are different emotion theories are used in physiology and other relevant fields (Cowie et al.,2011).Recently, researchers have investigated a number of aspects related to human emotions in multiple domains. Authors categorized emotions terms in multiple emotion classes based on emotion-bearing words which are accepted across the world (Picard, et al [4]).

Multiple milestone work has been carried out by researchers to provide right judgment related to emotion categories (Tomkins 1962; Plutchik 1980; Izard 1977; Ortony et. al., 1988; Raghavan, 2007 and Ekman, 1992). Emotion categories recognized by the different researchers has been presented in Table 1.

According to the popular emotion theory (Rasa theory) given by Bharta Muni, emotions are the primary gastric juices which represent every part of the world into the sentiments (Raghavan,2007). Rasa emotional theory is based on the Natyashastra (the Textbook on Drama) and given by Bharata Muni. According to Natyashastra(Raghavan,2007)., there are eight rasas corresponding to Bhava (mood). Ekman(Ekman,1992) has defined six basic emotions on the basis of distinctive facial expressions which are universally accepted has been presented in Table 1.

Watson and Tellegen in 1985 has presented a compressive theory i.e The Circumplex Theory of Affect which identifies two main classes as positive and negative affects which range from high to low(Watson and Tellegen, 1985). Osgood's in 1957 has proposed theory of Semantic Differentiation. (Osgood et al., 1957).In this theory words are assigned by emotive meanings using three factors such as activity factor, evaluative factor and potency factor.

Clore et al., proposed number of words which convey emotion explicitly, while other are depending on the context (Clore et al.1987). The classification of affective words into two classes 'indirect affective words' (implicit) and 'direct affective words' (explicit) has been performed by Strapparava and Valitutti (Strapparava and Valitutti, 2006).The chapter has utilized both these types of words given by Strapparava and Valitutti (Strapparava and Valitutti,2006).

EMOTION RECOGNITION

Emotion recognition in text is just one the numerous dimensions of the task of making the computers make sense of and respond to emotions. Emotion represents a complex, subjective experience which involves thinking, excitement, feeling and activation. This can be seen using native languages, physiological changes, and behavioral changes. The word "affect" is often used alternatively with "emotion" in the literature. Human emotion can be sensed from such cues as facial expression, gestures, speech and text. Research in emotion has focused on all these aspects (Cowie et al.,2011).

Emotion detection has been focused on the sentence-level analysis or document level analysis for learning emotions in customer reviews. Emotional words are used as keywords to identifying emotion in

Table 1. Emotion categories or classes identified by authors

Muni (Raghavan,2007).,	Tomkins (1962)	Izard (1977)	Plutchik (1980)	Ortony et.al. (1988)	Ekman (1992)
Hasya (Mirth) Krodha (Anger) Rati (Love) Bhaya (Terror) Jugupsa (Disgust) Soka (Sorrow) Vismaya (Astonishment) Utsaha (Energy)	Joy Anguish Shame Fear Anger Disgust Surprise Interest	Disgust Enjoyment Sadness Fear Anger Surprise Shame Shyness Guilt Interest	Joy Sorrow Anger Fear Disgust Surprise Acceptance Anticipation	Joy Sadness Fear Anger Disgust Surprise	Fear Anger Happiness Sadness Surprise Disgust

input sentences. Osgood used multidimensional scaling to visualize the affective words for calculating similarity ratings between them. Three dimensions were used by Osgood which includes "evaluation", "potency" and "activity", where evaluation can be used to measure how much a word can refer to a pleasant or an unpleasant event (Osgood et al., 1957).

Read et al. have carried out appraisal annotation of a corpus of book reviews; a genre that provides ample instances of the various kinds of appraisal classes (Read et al.2007). They found that out of the three subsystems of the Appraisal Framework, the attitude subsystem's instances (which include emotion expressions) were the easiest to identify. Mihalcea and Strapparava present results in favor of automatic recognition of humor in texts (Mihalcea and Strapparava, 2005). They perform experiments to identify humorous one-liners, which are one-line sentences generally characterized by simple syntax and use of rhetoric which gives them a humorous connotation. Neviarouskaya et al. propose a system for augmenting online conversations with a graphical representation of the user, which displays emotions and social behavior in accordance with the text (Neviarouskaya et al,2007). This system performs automatic estimation of affect in text on the basis of symbolic cues such as emoticons, popularly used IM (Instant Messaging) abbreviations, as well as word, phrase, and sentence-level analysis of text.

Ghazi et al. proposed a multiple levels of hierarchy classification to classify emotions words (Ghazi et al., 2010). Strapparava et al. has developed a linguistic resource to lexically represent affective knowledge named WordNet – Affect (Strapparava et al., 2006). The WorldNet-Affect contains affective words and available freely as open-source lexical recourses. Wang et al [63] proposed a novel approach to detect emotion from Chinese language. The algorithm proposed was segment based fine grained emotion detection model that is a supervised learning approach.

Lie Dey proposed a system for extracting emotions from the data collected from chat messenger (Dey et al.,2014). The author built a lexicon of emotion conveying words to extract emotions from the data sets. Shaheen et al. had proposed a framework for classification of emotions based on generalized concepts extracted from the English sentences (Shaheen et al.,2014). Perikos and Hatzilygeroudis developed a system that can automatically recognize emotions in natural languages (Perikos and Hatzilygeroudis, 2013). They used Tree tagger and Stanford Parser. They also used WordNet Affect lexical resource in order to spot the emotional words. They then analyzed emotional words dependencies in order to specify the strength of emotional word's strength and also determined overall sentence emotional statues that are based on dependency graph of sentence.

EMOTIONS DETECTION FRAMEWORK

The objective of this framework is to provide an insight to the process of automatically recognize emotions from customer reviews. Experimental study using appropriate corpus of text (customer reviews) has been presented using this framework for emotion recognition. Research in automatic text-based emotion analysis is limited due to unavailability emotion-annotated data for written text. To solve this problem, data has been collected from the top Indian online e-commerce websites like Snapdeal, Flipkart and Amazon under multiple categories such as LED television, smart phones, laptops, tablets, cameras.

Emotion detection in text is referring to as a classification problem. In this process multiple nominal labels are assigned to a text or sentence from a group of emotion labels. Figure 2 presents an overview of emotion detection framework for customer reviews data analysis. Presented framework for emotion detection for customer reviews has followed the methodology given as:

Figure 2. An overview of emotion detection framework

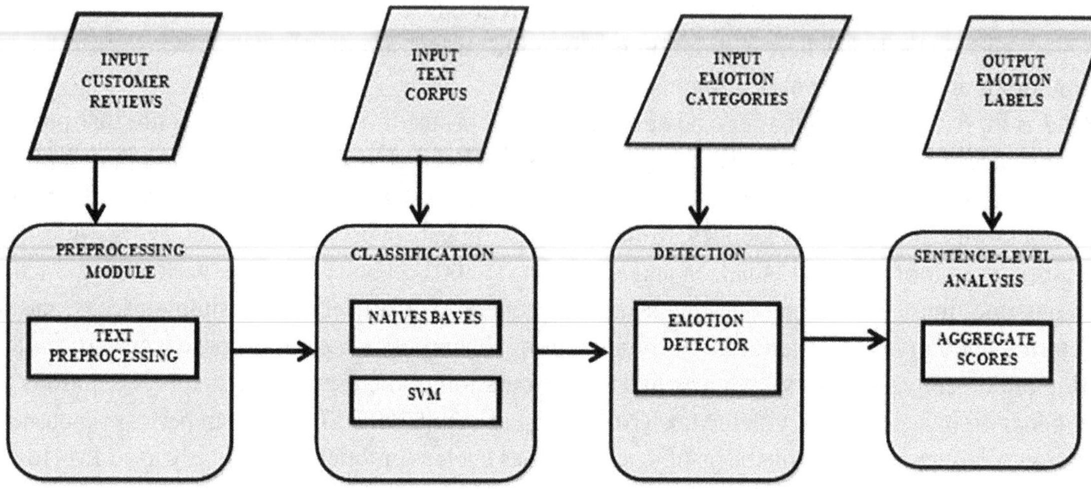

Let ***c*** is a customer review corresponding to a product or services and ***k*** is an emotion label. Let ***e*** be a set of ***n*** probable emotion categories where $e = \{e_1, e_2, e_3 \ldots\ldots\ldots e_n\}$. The classification process has been used to label ***c*** with the finest promising emotion label ***k***, where $k \in \{e_1, e_2, e_3 \ldots\ldots e_n, \text{neutral}\}$.

The framework of emotion detection is divided into four modules:

Pre-Processing Module

In this module customer's reviews data has been pre-processed to remove unwanted noise present in the data. Segmentation and Tokenization has been applied in first step. Sentence segmentation has been applied to form sentence chunks. Tokenization is has been applied to break stream of text up into multiple forms such as phrases, symbols, words, or other meaningful elements called tokens..In second step stop words removal process has been applied to filter out unnecessary words. Stemming is done on tokenized input.

Classification Module

Automatic classification of emotional sentences need a feature sets. The most appropriate features that distinguish emotional expressions from non-emotional ones are the emotion words. To recognize these words in the sentences or customer reviews, publicly available lexical resources are available such as – WorldNet-Affect (Strapparava and Valitutti, et al., 2006).Researchers have identified various categories of basic and secondary emotions. Ekman six basic emotions is one of the most popular models in various domains (Ekamn, 1992). Detection of emotional orientation of text has been performed naïve approach by determining emotion words, such as "happy", "terrified", and "amazed" in customer reviews. The clear advantage of this approach is that it requires no training data.

Table 2. Description of emotion word list that has been extracted from WordNet affect

Emotion Category	#synsets	Sample Words
Happiness	227	joy, love, rejoicing, glee, happiness, euphoria, enthusiasm, admiration, cheerful, content, happy, merrily
Sadness	123	sorrow, misery, woe, gloom, grief, depression, heartbreak, mournful, hapless, guilty, sadly, remorsefully, repent, bored
Anger	127	wrath, fury, rage, angry, annoyed, pissed, mad, sore, livid, displeasingly, aggressive, hateful, hostile, malice, spite, resentfully
Disgust	19	repulsion, nauseous, foul, abhorrent, fed_up, abominably, revolt, sicken
Surprise	28	wonder, fantastic, marvelous, baffle, bewilder, astonishing, awestruck, stupefy, dumbfound, staggering
Fear	82	scary, fright, panic, terror, chilling, frightful, terrible, intimidate, dread, anxiously, apprehension

Emotion Detection Module

After the classification of emotional words from the customer reviews a baseline system called as emotion detector has been used to counts the number of emotion words of each category in a sentence, and then assigns the category with the largest number of words to the sentence. Ties were resolved by choosing the emotion label based on a random predefined ordering of emotion classes. A sentence containing no emotion word of any type was assigned the *no-emotion* category. Emotion detector gives an insight of overall category present in Table 2 of a particular customer review of a product.

Sentence-Level Analysis

Sentence-level analysis provides aggregate score of emotion present in all the product categories with emotion levels of customer review. This provides emotion related to specific brand and categories.

IMPORTANCE OF EMOTIONS DETECTION

Emotion Detection in customer reviews is important for e-commerce industries because it identifies meaningful ways to improve their operations and marketing strategy for their products and services. This can be accounted by measuring the public's emotions on products, services, and advertisements. E-commerce companies can use emotion detection framework for prediction of their services based on diffusion of innovation theories. This framework is also helpful in new product launch in the market by examine public emotion towards the product or services. According to marketing survey agencies, customer reviews provides new battleground for brands. E-commerce companies focused to build loyalty with product buyers, which help to grow and expand their business. New emerging platforms based on social media provide rich source of information about the product or services. Emotion detection framework can help companies in measuring public feeling related to products and services.

ADVANTAGES OF EMOTION DETECTION

E-commerce companies always focused to build long term relation with their customers. Customer services such as product delivery timing, response to their query etc are mainly focused by e-commerce companies. The e-commerce should always aware their customer response about product or services they sale on their portal. Emotion detection framework can easily give real-time information about customer's mood and feelings. Emotion detection play an important role to gain advantages over other techniques or policies and helps companies in improving their market strategy. Following are the key benefits provided by emotion detection framework:

1. **Accessibility:** Emotion detection framework provides real-time emotions 24X7.
2. **Gain Business Intelligence:** This framework provides meaningful inference which help business to take rapid decisions.
3. **Quickly Identify the Tonality:** Framework provides real-time trends related to products and services with emotion spikes based on emotion models.
4. **Easily Built Engagement Platform:** Measurement of effectiveness of promotional offers and viral advertisements can easily be understood with the help of this emotion detection. This will help in better engagement with customer to build up long relationship.
5. **Beat Competition:** Track competitor responses help in improvement of action plan over time.
6. **Alerts Service:** Alerts can be set up for the brands to be notified of specific emotion labels and rapid decision cans be easily taken out.
7. **Improve Customer Service:** The major advantages of this framework help in improving customer services which is the major challenge for e-commerce companies in current scenario.

CONCLUSION

This chapter describes the potential of real –time emotion detection system based on customer reviews present in e-commerce portals. This framework can help in providing solutions to number of problems related to businesses and marketing. This chapter present an emotion detection framework based on Ekman emotion model. Methods and technique are presented help in knowing customers emotions with help of product reviews. This framework gives important and valuable knowledge towards improvement in departments such as customer management, customer relations & marketing, product management and corporate management.

The emotion detection framework presented in this chapter can be pursued further in several domains. One of the tasks is to consider emotion intensity for classification. Explore the relation between emotion classes and emotion intensity.

REFERENCES

Chesley, P., Vincent, B., Xu, L., & Srihari, R. (2006). Using Verbs and Adjectives to Automatically Classify Blog Sentiment.*Proceedings of the AAAI-2006 Spring Symposium on Computational Approaches to Analyzing Weblogs.*

Clore, G. L., Ortony, A., & Foss, M. A. (1987). The psychological foundations of the affective lexicon. *Journal of Personality and Social Psychology*, *53*(4), 751–766. doi:10.1037/0022-3514.53.4.751

Cowie, R., Douglas-Cowie, E., Tsapatsoulis, N., Votsis, G., Kollias, S., Fellenz, W., & Taylor, J. (2011). Emotion recognition in human-computer interaction. *IEEE Signal Processing Magazine*, *18*(1), 32–80. doi:10.1109/79.911197

Dey, L., Afroz, N., & Nath, R. P. D. (2014) Emotion extraction from real time chat messenger. *Proceedings of 3rd International Conference on Informatics, Electronics & Vision*, 1-5. doi:10.1109/ICIEV.2014.6850785

Dung & Cao. (2012). *A high order hidden Markov model for emotion detection from textual data* Springer Berlin Heidelberg.

Ekman, P. (1992). An argument for basic emotions. *Cognition and Emotion*, *6*(1), 169–200. doi:10.1080/02699939208411068

Ghazi, D., Inkpen, D., & Szpakowicz, S. (2010). Hierarchical versus flat classification of emotions in text.*Proceedings of the NAACL HLT 2010 workshop on computational approaches to analysis and generation of emotion in text*, 140-146.

Izard, C. E. (1977). *Human emotions*. New York: Plenum Press. doi:10.1007/978-1-4899-2209-0

Jain, V. K., & Kumar, S. (2015). An Effective Approach to Track Levels of Influenza-A (H1N1) Pandemic in India Using Twitter. *Procedia Computer Science*, *70*(1), 801–807. doi:10.1016/j.procs.2015.10.120

Jain, V. K., Kumar, S., Jain, N., & Verma, P. (2016). A novel Approach to Track Levels public emotions related to epidemics in multilingual data. *2nd International conference and Youth School Information technology and Nanotechnology,* 883-889.

Mihalcea, R., & Strapparava, C. (2005). Making Computers Laugh: Investigations in Automatic Humor Recognition. *Proceedings of the Joint Conference on Human Language Technology/Empirical Methods in Natural Language Processing*, 531-538.

Neviarouskaya, A., Prendinger, H., & Ishizuka, M. (2007). Analysis of affect expressed through the evolving language of online communication.*Proceedings of the 12th International Conference on Intelligent User Interfaces,* 278-281. doi:10.1145/1216295.1216346

Ortony, A., Clore, G. L., & Collins, A. (1988). *The Cognitive Structure of Emotions*. Cambridge University Press. doi:10.1017/CBO9780511571299

Osgood, C. E., Succi, G. J., & Tannenbaum, P. H. (1957). *The Measurement of Meaning*. Urbana, IL: University of Illinois Press.

Pang, B., & Lee, L. (2008). Opinion mining and sentiment analysis. *Foundations and Trends in Information Retrieval*, *2*(1), 1–135. doi:10.1561/1500000011

Perikos, I., & Hatzilygeroudis, I. (2013). *Recognizing emotions present in Natural Language Sentences*. University of Patras.

Plutchik, R. (1980). A General Psycho evolutionary Theory of Emotion. In Emotion: Theory, Research and Experience: Theories of Emotions (vol. 1). New York: Academic.

Raghavan, V. (1967). *The Number of Rasa-S*. Theosophical Publishing House.

Read, J., Hope, D., & Carroll, J. (2007). Annotating expressions of Appraisal in English.*Proceedings of the ACL-2007 Linguistic Annotation Workshop*, 93-100.

Shaheen, S., El-Hajj, W., Hajj, H., & Elbassuoni, S. (2014). Emotion Recognition from Text Based on Automatically Generated Rules. *2014 IEEE International Conference on Data Mining Workshop*, 383-382. doi:10.1109/ICDMW.2014.80

Strapparava, C., Valitutti, A., & Stock, O. (2006). The affective weight of lexicon.*Proceedings of the Fifth International Conference on Language Resources and Evaluation,* 423–426.

Tomkins, S. S. (1962). *Affect, imagery, consciousness. In The positive affects* (pp. 20–31). New York: Springer.

Watson, D., & Tellegen, A. (1985). Towards a consensual structure of mood. *Psychological Bulletin, 98*(2), 219–235. doi:10.1037/0033-2909.98.2.219 PMID:3901060

KEY TERMS AND DEFINITIONS

Machine Learning: It is a science of getting computers to act without being explicitly programmed.

Natural Language Processing: It uses methods of computer science, artificial intelligence, and computational linguistics to understand interactions between computers and human languages.

Opinion Mining: Categorization of opinions.

Text Classification: Classification of documents into a fixed number of predefined categories.

Chapter 9
Predictive Modelling and Mind-Set Segments Underlying Health Plans

Gillie Gabay
College of Management (COLMAN), Israel

Howard Moskowitz
Mind Genomics Advisors, USA

Steven Onufrey
Mind Genomics Advisors, USA

Stephen Rappaport
Stephen D. Rappaport Consulting LLC, USA

ABSTRACT

Health systems are facing austerity negatively affecting the delivery of services around the world. This chapter defines predictive analytics in health, discusses how predictive analytics may contribute to health promotion and demonstrates the identification of specific communication elements to be used by health maintenance organizations and insurers to shape health plans in accordance to mind-set segments of patients. Although the application of predictive analytics to health plans may reduce costs and shift the focus of health systems from treating the sick to preventive medicine, it has not been investigated and is the topic of this chapter.

INTRODUCTION

Predictive analytics (PA) is the branch of data mining concerned with the prediction of future probabilities and trends. The central element of PA is the *predictor*, a variable that can be measured for an individual or other entity to predict future behavior. For example, an insurance company is likely to take into account potential driving safety predictors such as *age*, *gender*, and *driving record* when issuing car insurance policies. When multiple predictors are at issue they are combined into a predictive model,

DOI: 10.4018/978-1-5225-2148-8.ch009

which, when subjected to analysis, can be used to forecast future probabilities with an acceptable level of reliability. In predictive modeling, data is collected, a statistical model is formulated, predictions are made and the model is validated (or revised) as additional data becomes available. PA is applied to many research areas, including meteorology, security, genetics, economics, marketing and recently to health. This chapter focuses on PA and health and more specifically on PA analysis and delivery of health care services.

BACKGROUND

Historically, medicine has been consumed by care of the sick rather than with preventive healthcare. Physicians often wait until illness surfaces and then try their best to treat that person. PA can be used to avoid illness and learn what will promote health. PA may revolutionize the way medicine is practiced today for better health, higher disease reduction and customized health plans (Kohane, Drazen & Campion, 2012). PA posits the potential to promote public health by predicting outcomes for individual patients. Even if physicians had access to the massive amounts of data needed to compare treatment outcomes for all the diseases they encounter, they would still need time and expertise to analyze the information and integrate it with the patient's own medical profile. This in-depth research and statistical analysis is beyond the scope of a physician's work, particularly facing today's global shortage in physicians and austerity in health systems (Crisp & Chen, 2014).

PA may include data from past treatment outcomes as well as from the latest medical research published in peer-reviewed journals and databases. PA not only helps with predictions, but may also reveal surprising associations in data. Predictions can range from responses to medications to hospital readmission rates. For example, predicting infections from methods of suturing, determining the likelihood of disease, helping a physician with a diagnosis, and even predicting future wellness. PA differs from traditional statistics and from evidence-based medicine. First, predictions are made for individuals and not for groups, with the ability to predict behaviors (McEachan, Conner, Taylor et al., 2011). Second, PA does not rely upon a normal (bell-shaped) curve as what may work best for people in the middle of a normal distribution may not work best for an individual patient seeking treatment. PA can help physicians decide the exact treatments for those individuals as it is wasteful and potentially dangerous to provide treatments that are not needed or that will not work for a certain individual. Better diagnoses and more targeted treatments will naturally lead to increases in good outcomes and less depletion of resources, including time of physicians.

Hospitals will need predictive models to accurately assess when a patient can safely be released. PA also increases the accuracy of diagnoses. For example, when patients come to the ER with chest pain, it is often difficult to know whether the patient should be hospitalized. If physicians were able to answer questions about the patient and his condition using a system with a tested and accurate predictive algorithm, the likelihood that the patient could be sent home safely may be assessed. The prediction would not replace their judgments but rather would assist it (Miner, Bolding, Hilbe et al, 2014).

PA will also promote preventive medicine and public health. With early intervention, many diseases can be prevented or ameliorated. PA may allow primary care physicians to identify at-risk patients within their practice. With that knowledge, patients can make lifestyle and behavioral changes to avoid risks (Armstrong, Garrett-Mayer, Yang, et al., 2007; Rise, Kovac, Kraft et al., 2008). As lifestyles change, population disease patterns may dramatically change resulting in savings in medical costs (Chin, Sipe, Elder, et al., 2012). Also, future medications might be designed just for a certain person as PA methods will sort out what works for people with similar subtypes and molecular pathways.

There will be many benefits in quality of life to patients as the use of PA increase. The patient role will change as patients become more informed. Patients who will collaborate work with their physicians, are expected to achieve better outcomes. Patients will become aware of possible personal health risks sooner due to: Alerts from their genome analysis, predictive models relayed by their physicians, the increasing use of apps and medical devices (i.e., wearable devices and monitoring systems), and due to better accuracy of the information needed for accurate predictions. Patients will make decisions about their life styles and future wellbeing (Rise, Kovac, Kraft et al., 2008). Thus, PA is the next big idea in medicine supported by the next evolution in statistics. PA will result in patients who will become better informed and have to assume more responsibility for their own care (Gabay, 2016b). Physician may adopt a consultant role rather than a decision maker role, inspiring patients to take control of their health and acknowledge higher quality of care (Gabay, 2015: Gabay & Moskowitz, 2012).

We demonstrate the ability of health maintenance organizations to customize health plans by mind-sets resulting. The role of the insurer will be to promote health by stressing and investing in preventive medicine rather than in care for the sick. The relationship between PA and health plans has not been investigated and is the focus of this chapter. Using communication elements, health maintenance organizations can understand attitudes, perceptions, needs and behaviors and shape plans accordingly saving costs and shifting to prevention and health promotion. This is the next step beyond PA requiring a different type of approach- an experiment approach to identify specific communication elements to which a person will respond.

In this chapter we demonstrate how the spirit of PA can infuse the role of the health maintenance organization in understanding the mind of the patient regarding health plans.

We compare responses to communication elements from groups of people defined in standard ways versus responses to communication elements defined by patterns of responses in the experiment. The use of PA to determine WHO and WHEN, with communication elements experiment to determine WHAT represents the next frontier of knowledge development. To restate rationale of this chapter, we assume that for any aspect of daily life we can identify communication elements, and that big data will not identify, in a systematic repeatable way, the particular communication elements to which a specific individual will positively respond.

We conducted the experiment using Mind Genomics which is a new science that studies the pattern of people's responses to communication elements about everyday life. (Gabay & Moskowitz, 2016, Forthcoming; Gabay, Moskowitz & Kochman, In Prince & Priporas, C., 2016; Gabay & Moskowitz, 2015)

The objective of Mind Genomics is to create a database showing the different communication elements about aspects of daily life, the responses to those communication elements, and the nature of the inter-personal variability in those responses. Mind Genomics grew out of the recognition that people may not act entirely rationally when presented with communication elements about the aspects of their lives. The accretion of knowledge about how people respond to these communication elements reveals new patterns of the mind allowing PA. Mind Genomics is based on statistics of conjoint analysis which has gained much reputation in the academic world and outside it (Anderson and Narus, 1998; Green, Krieger & Wind, 2001; Green & Srinivasan, 1978; Moskowitz & Gofman, 2007).

METHODOLOGY

Mind Genomics uses experimentally designed combinations of communication elements in the form of a simple vignette. The respondent sees the vignette, and rates the combination. By showing one respondent many different such vignettes, with the same elements tested in different combinations, it becomes possible to identify which particular elements 'drive' the respondent, i.e., which interest the respondent and which drive the respondent away. A systematic exploration of different communication elements done this way generates deep knowledge about how an individual makes decisions.

Up to now the notion of Mind Genomics is a simple experiment, in which the respondent is presented with systematically varied combinations of communication elements for any topic, goes through the experiment rating these combinations, with the result that afterwards statistical analysis (usually OLS, ordinary least-squares regression) generates a model or equation showing how the components of the combination, the communication elements, separately drive the overall response.

In the empirical studies, the data reveal again and again that the pattern of element contributions to the response cannot be easily predicted by knowing who the respondents ARE, or how they behave. Differences in the pattern of behavior as measured by so-called BIG DATA do not easily pass to similar differences in the pattern of responses to the elements. People who look the 'same' in terms of exogenous variables may respond quite differently to the communication elements. And, the corollary holds. People who look quite different in terms of their metrics and patterns in Big Data may show remarkably similar patterns.

There is a further complication relevant to PA. For the same person, same combination, asking the person one question (e.g., how much do you like what you read) will generate one set of patterns. Asking the same person, reading the same set of combinations another question (e.g., how much will you pay for what you just read) will generate another set of patterns. Just because we know the pattern of responses of a person when answering one question does not predict how that person will answer another question.

Running the Experiment

The demonstration of the 'incompleteness of knowledge about a person' will come from showing that the same person can belong to two different 'mind-sets,' even for the same test stimuli, simply by varying the question asked when the person evaluates the test stimuli. Even when you think you know the person's mind for a topic through the responses to a set of stimuli, all you need to do is change the question, keep the stimuli the same, and people are segmented into new and perhaps unexpected groups.

The process of demonstrating this new hypothesis about what we might call BIG MIND emerges from a simple experiment. Next, we summarize the experiment and then move on to a relevant demonstration of health plans. Here are the 10 steps to running the experiment and analyzing the data, along with demonstration.

Analysis

1. The focus of the experiment was the healthcare plan provided by a health maintenance organization. The specific study was run using the information provided by Excellus, a health maintenance organization in the U.S All the data belong to the authors, however, and represent an independent analysis of communication elements available on the Internet.

2. Based on the literature, we identified different aspects or categories of the experience (Gabay, 2016b; Gabay & Moore, 2015). These are called silos. A silo may be 'how a person is approached by the physician' or 'the key benefits of a health plan.' The study comprises four silos. Silo A: Mission, History, Emotions. Silo B: Coverage, expectations, services. Silo C: Fees and Silo D: Reward for wellness.
3. **Elements (Table 1):** The elements are the particulars. Each silo or aspect of the experience should have a certain number of communication elements. These are different features of the experience, what is, what was, what could be. Each silo comprises the same number of elements. For this study each silo comprises six elements. Thus there are a total of 24 elements. Table 1 presents the 24 elements. Note that the elements are presented as simple declarative statements rather than as questions. By presenting these declarative statements in combination, we allow the respondent to evaluate a possible 'test concept,' presented by a combination of communication elements.

Table 1. Elements used in the Excellus study on health plans

A1	We've grown with you… 25 years of one healthy community
A2	Health plans that fit your life plans… we have you covered for whatever you need
A3	Dedicated to making a difference
A4	Take on life and live well
A5	Giving back to the places we live and work
A6	It's not just healthcare…it's your care
B1	Enjoy the freedom of in-network and out-of-network… anywhere in the country
B2	New national doctor network - access to more than 500,000 doctors, specialists & hospitals
B3	On-line Personal Health Manager … powered by WebMD®
B4	Coverage wherever you go
B5	Flexible options to meet your needs
B6	Regular checkups… immunizations … routine dental and eye care, prescriptions… hospital and emergency care …and more
C1	Free preventive health checkups
C2	$0 co-pay for preventative services
C3	Enjoy the comfort and convenience of predictable co-pays
C4	A tax-free Health Savings Account (HSA) ….offers you a 15 – 40% discount on paying for current health care expenses
C5	Preventive care always covered… no out of pocket expenses
C6	Easily see whether there is a lower cost prescription drug for a medication you are taking
D1	Resources to help balance wellness and lifestyle
D2	We've partnered with community organizations…. to provide a range of valuable wellness discounts
D3	Earn up to $300 in Rewards for a range of healthy activities
D4	Up to $1,000 per year per family… for doing healthy stuff
D5	The care you and your baby get now will make a difference in the health of your child
D6	An incredible variety of resources to help you achieve your optimal health

4. **Experimental Design (Table 2):** The experimental design comprises a specified number of combinations of elements. Each respondent evaluates 40 different elements for this particular array of 24 elements, i.e., four silos with six elements each. The experimental design ensures that the 24 elements appear in a format which makes them statistically independent of each other. The elements are created according to the precise structure dictated by the experimental design. The first five vignettes for one respondent appear in Table 2. Each respondent evaluates a UNIQUE set of 40 vignettes. The basic structure of the 40 vignettes is the same, but the vignettes are slightly

Table 2. Example of an experiment design generated 40 vignettes. The table shows the structure of vignettes 01-05. The design comprises four silos, each of six elements.

	Vig01	Vig02	Vig03	Vig04	Vig05
Silo A	0	6	3	4	6
Silo B	1	0	1	0	0
Silo C	2	6	0	4	4
Silo D	1	0	0	6	6
A1	0	0	0	0	0
A2	0	0	0	0	0
A3	0	0	1	0	0
A4	0	0	0	1	0
A5	0	0	0	0	0
A6	0	1	0	0	1
B1	1	0	1	0	0
B2	0	0	0	0	0
B3	0	0	0	0	0
B4	0	0	0	0	0
B5	0	0	0	0	0
B6	0	0	0	0	0
C1	0	0	0	0	0
C2	1	0	0	0	0
C3	0	0	0	0	0
C4	0	0	0	1	1
C5	0	0	0	0	0
C6	0	1	0	0	0
D1	1	0	0	0	0
D2	0	0	0	0	0
D3	0	0	0	0	0
D4	0	0	0	0	0
D5	0	0	0	0	0
D6	0	0	0	1	1

changed, permuted, to be modest variants of each other. In that way the project covers a wide range of combinations. It does not really end up mattering what specific combinations are selecting. With 100 respondents and 40 vignettes per respondent, as an example, the study will generate 100 different, unique sets of 40 combinations

5. **Test Vignette**: Recognize at the outset that the 'experiment' comprises the presentation of a certain number of combinations (vignettes). The vignettes combine the elements according to a master plan, an experimental design. For the study presented here, with four silos, each silo having six elements, there are 24 elements, combined into a total of 40 vignettes. The same element appears several times in the 40 vignettes. Figure 1: Exhibit 1 shows an example of a vignette.
6. **Rating Questions**: The rating question is the means by which the experimenter measures the response to the test stimuli these test stimuli being the vignettes. For this particular study on responses to offers by Excellus, we looked at to different rating questions. The first instructed the respondent to rate degree of interest (how likely are you to choose this health plan). The second focused on how much the respondent would spend per month for this health plan compared to her or his existing plan? There are five numerical answers from $70 less to $70 more, and two non-numerical answers. The first of these non-numerical answers is the person who does not know the current monthly cost. The second is that the person does not currently have a health plan.
   There are many different types of questions one can ask. In these experiments the research focuses on the pattern of responses to many stimuli, stimuli systematically varied. The discovery lies in the pattern of responses, which is why there are only one or two rating questions. This is called within-

Figure 1. Exhibit 1: Example of a vignette

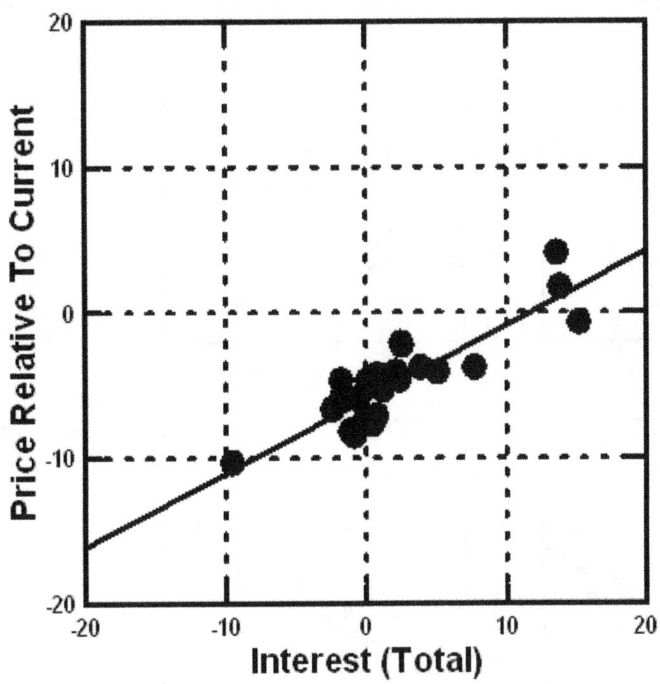

subjects designs, or longitudinal research. In contrast, most survey research use many questions, without test stimuli. The learning from surveys is the pattern of responses across individuals, or so-called cross-sectional data.

7. **Running the Study**: The study itself is run on a computer, so it is technically 'self-administered.' The respondents are selected from a pool of individuals who agree to participate. The respondent is sent a link in an email. Clicking the link brings the respondent to a website, which begins with an orientation screen (See Figure 2: Exhibit 2). The screen introduces the study, but does not provide any information other than the screen contains a description of 2-4 components of a health plan,
8. **Learning More about the Respondent**: The elements in the study, the 24 communication elements in Table 1, pertain only to one small aspect of the experience, the features and benefits of the health insurance plan. We want to learn a lot more about the respondent. One way to do it is

Figure 2. Exhibit 2: The orientation screen for the study

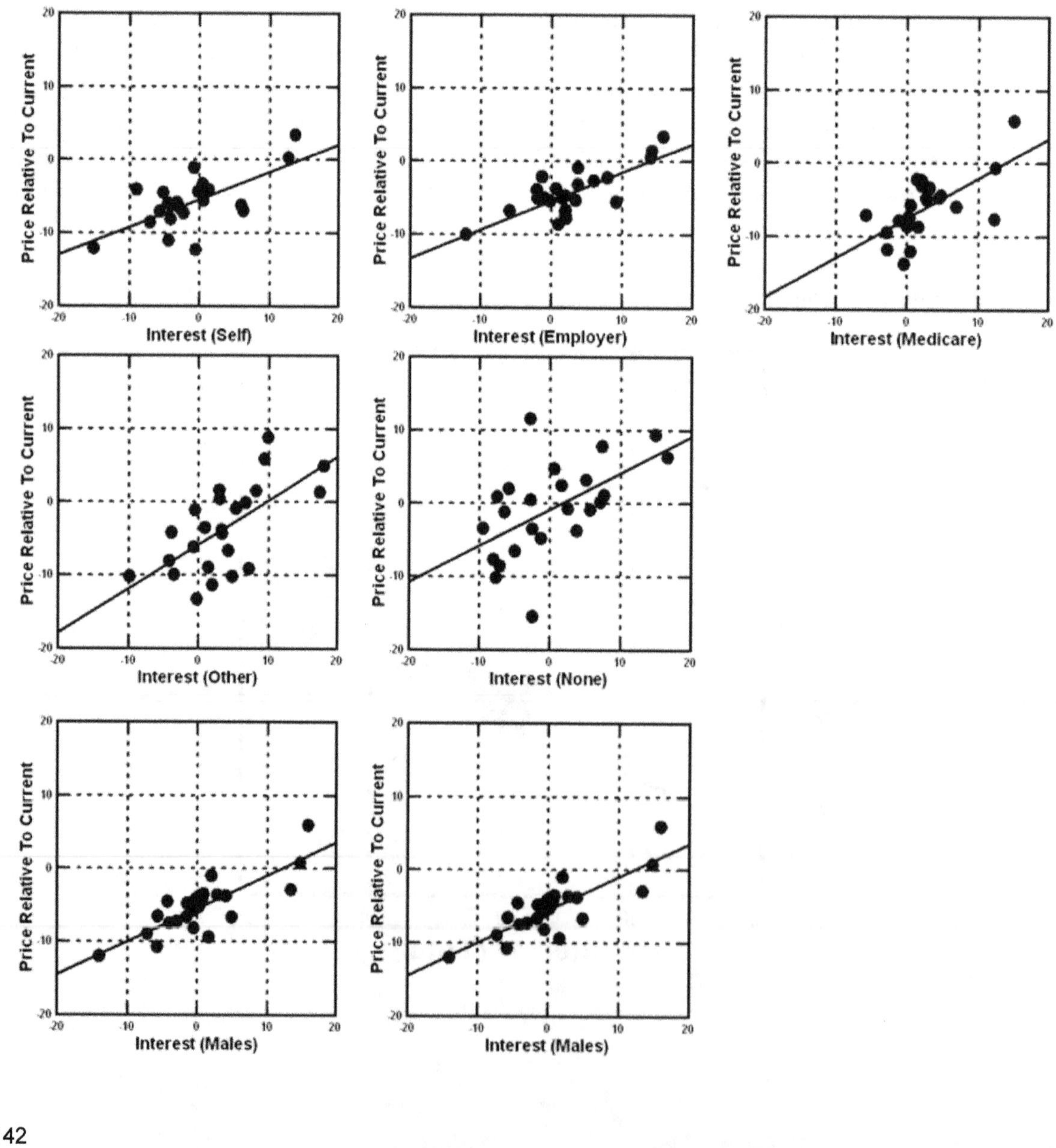

through a classical questionnaire, run AFTER the evaluation for the 40 vignettes. That is, the respondent agrees to participate, evaluates the 40 vignettes on the two attributes, and then completes a modest-size classification questionnaire dealing with general aspects. (See Table 3: Exhibit 3).

9. **Transforming the Ratings from the 9-Point Scale to the Binary Interest Scale:** The respondents rated each vignette on a 9-point scale, also called a category scale or a Likert scale. The ends of the scale are anchored, but the scale points are not anchored. Although the 9-point scale provides granularity of results in terms of degree of interest in buying the insurance, the reality is that managers do not work with these gradations, and prefer yes/no answers, i.e., does the respondent SAY he or she will buy the insurance based on the communication elements. To get to this binary response requires that we re-scale the nine rating points, transforming ratings 1-6 to 0, and ratings 7-9 to 100. The transformation certainly reduces some of the granularity of the basic information, but the benefit comes in the simplicity of understanding. The actual results become easier to interpret, as conditional probabilities of a person likely to buy an insurance policy when the elements are present in the vignette. The results discussed below will further elaborate on this interpretation.
10. Transforming the second question into dollars, with the rating replaced by the monthly amount. For example, when a respondent chooses answer 1 ($70 less), that answer is coded -70. When the respondent chooses answer 5 ($70 more), that answer is coded +70. The data was removed from analysis for respondents who did not know the amount of money they spent (answers 6 and 7). The study began with 200+ respondents, but only 148 respondents felt sufficiently comfortable answering question #2 on amount of money they would pay. It is only their data that will be presented here.

Table 3. Exhibit 3: The classification questionnaire

Q01: What is your gender?
Q10: What best describes the type of health insurance plan you are current on?
Q11: How much do you spend in health insurance premiums per month?
Q12: How satisfied are you with your present insurance plan/Company?
Q13: How much do you trust your insurance company?
Q14: Do you fear your insurance company might drop you in event of a major illness or overlooked pre-existing condition?
Q15: Would you feel safer with a plan managed by the government?
Q16: What is the single most important factor in choosing your insurance company?
Q17: Please enter your email address to be part of the sweepstakes for cash prizes.
Q02: What is your age?
Q03: What is the highest level of education that you have completed?
Q04: What is your annual household income?
Q05: For demographic purposes only, which ethnicity describes you best?
Q06: What is the number of members in your household?
Q07: Do you own or rent your home?
Q08: Which of the following best describes where you live?
Q09: Which best describes your health insurance plan?

Once the transformations are done, the data can be analyzed by standard curve-fitting methods, known as ordinary linear, least-squares regression analysis (OLS). The independent variables are the 20 elements, coded either 0 when absent or 1 when present. The dependent variables are either the binary transformed values for Interest (0 or 100), or the actual dollar values selected. Table 4 shows the regression run on the full data set. The regression analysis computes an additive constant for the Interest Model, based upon question 1, using the rationale that even in the absence of elements there is some residual level of interest in buying health insurance. The regression analysis does not compute the additive constant when creating the model for question 2, price. The rationale is that in the absence of elements no one can estimate a fair price, and thus the answer is not meaningful.

RESULTS

Table 4 shows that when all the data are combined, the additive constant to emerge is +17, meaning about one person in six is interested in a health plan in the absence of elements. It is the elements which must do the work. As a rule of thumb we should focus on the strongest performing elements. Strong is defined as coefficient of +8 or higher.

Four of the 20 elements perform well, as listed below.

- *No co-pay for preventative services*
- *Preventive care always covered... no out of pocket expenses*
- *Regular checkups... immunizations ... routine dental and eye care, prescriptions... hospital and emergency care ...and more*
- *Free preventive health checkups*

It is important to note that the elements chosen for this project are elements used in 2009-2010 by different health groups to advertise their offerings. It often comes as a surprise that so few elements really score well, here only four. The reason for the poor performance may either be that the elements are mediocre, or more typically that there might be different mind-sets operating, especially with regard to the elements which are 'emotionally tinged,' rather than elements which are more 'rational.' The elements in Table 4 which perform most strongly are those which are rational, which promise free or very low benefits for commonly used services.

The price model, shown as the second column of data in Table 4, suggest that on average the respondents feel that they would not pay more money for 18 of the 20 services, and indeed would pay less. The only element for which the respondent would pay extra, and only $4/month extra is for regular checkups: *Regular checkups... immunizations ... routine dental and eye care, prescriptions... hospital and emergency care ...and more.* There is one other element for which the respondent would pay very slightly more, $2/month: *Preventive care always covered ... no out of pocket expense*

When we plot the coefficients for price as the dependent variable versus the coefficients for interest as the independent variable we end up with an upwards trending straight line. We interpret this to mean that, on the average, as an offering is more interesting, the respondent says that he will pay more. Figure 3 shows this pattern for the total panel. The same pattern reveals itself for various subgroups, shown in Figure 4, such as males versus females, and the division of respondents by who pays the insurance. As will see, however, this well-behaved pattern may be an artifact of sampling many poor performing elements.

Table 4. Parameters of the 'grand models' relating all the ratings of either Interest (binary, question 1) or price (question 2) to the presence/absence of the 24 elements

		Interest	Price
	Total Panel (n=148 respondents)	148	148
	Additive constant	17	NA
C2	$0 co-pay for preventative services	**15**	-1
C5	Preventive care always covered… no out of pocket expenses	**14**	**2**
B6	Regular checkups… immunizations … routine dental and eye care, prescriptions… hospital and emergency care …and more	**14**	**4**
C1	Free preventive health checkups	8	-4
C6	Easily see whether there is a lower cost prescription drug for a medication you are taking	5	-4
A2	Health plans that fit your life plans… we have you covered for whatever your life has in store	4	-4
B2	New national doctor network - access to more than 500,000 doctors, specialists and hospitals	3	-2
B1	Enjoy the freedom of in-network and out-of-network… anywhere in the country	3	-2
D4	Up to $1,000 per year per family… for doing healthy stuff	2	-5
B4	Coverage wherever you go	2	-4
A1	We've grown with you… 25 years of one healthy community	1	-5
D3	Earn up to $300 in Rewards for a range of healthy activities	1	-4
A6	It's not just healthcare…it's your care	1	-7
A4	Take on life and live well	1	-8
A5	Giving back to the places we live and work	1	-8
C3	Enjoy the comfort and convenience of predictable co-pays	0	-5
A3	Dedicated to making a difference	0	-7
B5	Flexible options to meet your needs	0	-6
C4	A tax-free Health Savings Account (HSA) ….offers you a 15 – 40% discount on paying for current health care expenses	-1	-9
B3	On-line Personal Health Manager … powered by WebMD®	-1	-8
D6	An incredible variety of resources to help you achieve your optimal health	-2	-6
D2	We've partnered with community organizations…. to provide a range of valuable wellness discounts	-2	-5
D1	Resources to help balance wellness and lifestyle	-2	-7
D5	The care you and your baby get now will make a difference in the health of your child	-9	-10

Dividing Respondents into Like-Minded Groups

One of the key features of Mind Genomics is its focus on the responses of the individual to a set of different communication elements, to understand the patient's 'mind' with respect to the health plan. With 148 respondents, we want to identify different mind-sets. These mind-sets are simple heuristics, ways of looking at differences among people which lead to deeper understanding, and more effective interactions with people as prospective patients. For each patient we created two individual-level models. The first is for question1, the relation between the binary value of interest (0 vs 100) and the 24 elements. The second is for quesion2, the relation between the dollar value per month for the plan one would pay and the 24 elements.

Figure 3. How price (ordinate) co-varies with interest (abscissa), for the Total Panel. Each point corresponds to one of the 24 elements. The values come from the grand model relating the presence/absence of elements to either the interest (Grand Interest Model) or relating the presence/absence of elements to the price (Grand Price Model).

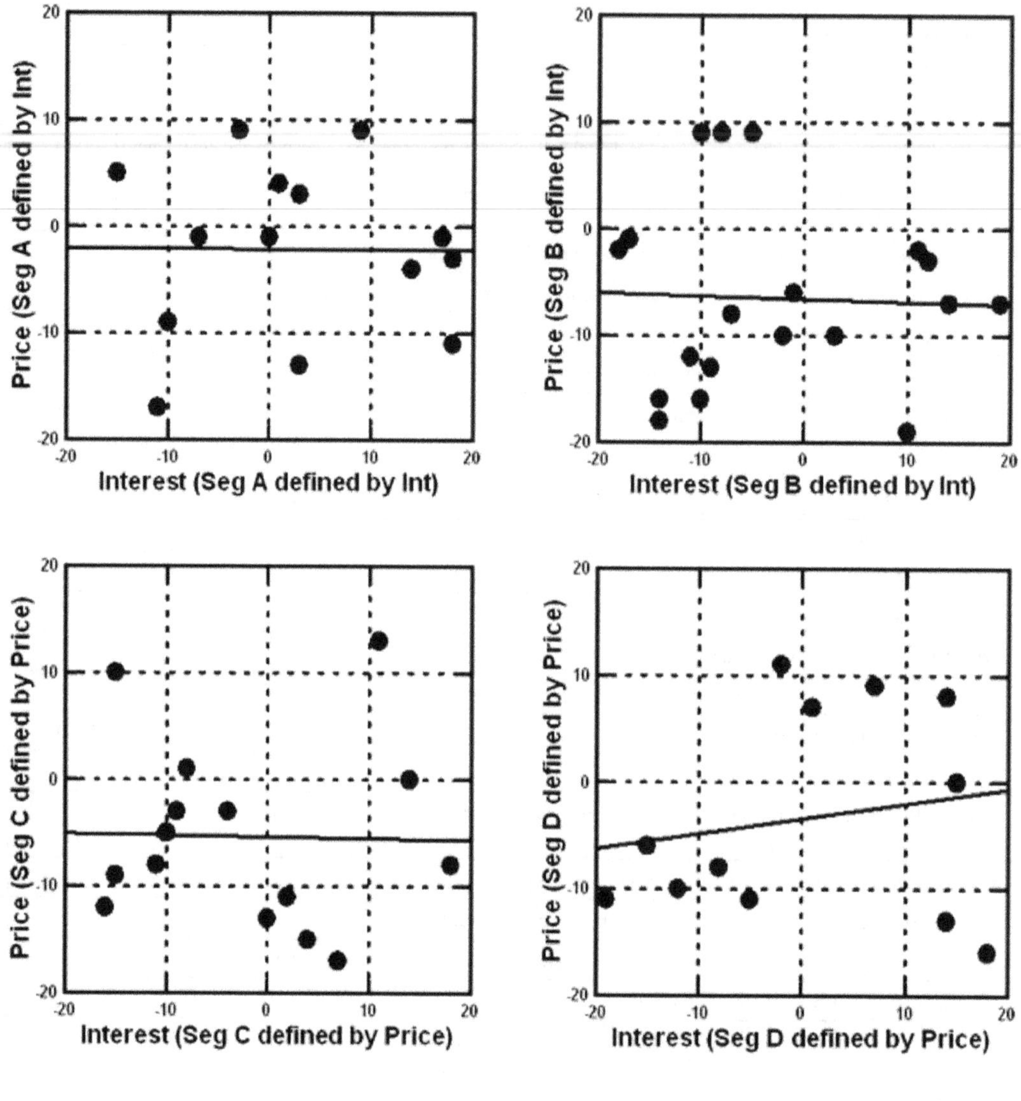

1. Using OLS ordinary least-squares regression, we estimated the coefficients. For the Binary Interest Model, OLS estimated the additive constant. For the Price Model, OLS ran the regression without the additive model, i.e., forcing the model through 0.
2. We used k-mean clustering, with the measure of distance being the value (1-Pearson R). This measure of distance is 0 when the correlation between two patterns of coefficients is +1, i.e., both are similar. When the correlation is 0, no linear relation, the measure is 1. When the correlation is -1, a perfect inverse relation, the measure is 2.
3. For the Interest model, we used the 24 coefficients, to generate a parsimonious set of clusters which can be interpreted. The first clustering was based on the 24 Interest coefficients across the 148

Figure 4. How price (ordinate) co-varies with interest (abscissa), by gender, and by who pays for the health insurance, respectively. Each point corresponds to one of the 24 elements. The values come from the grand model relating the presence/absence of elements to either the interest (Grand Interest Model) or relating the presence/absence of elements to the price (Grand Price Model). 'None' means that the respondent is uninsured.

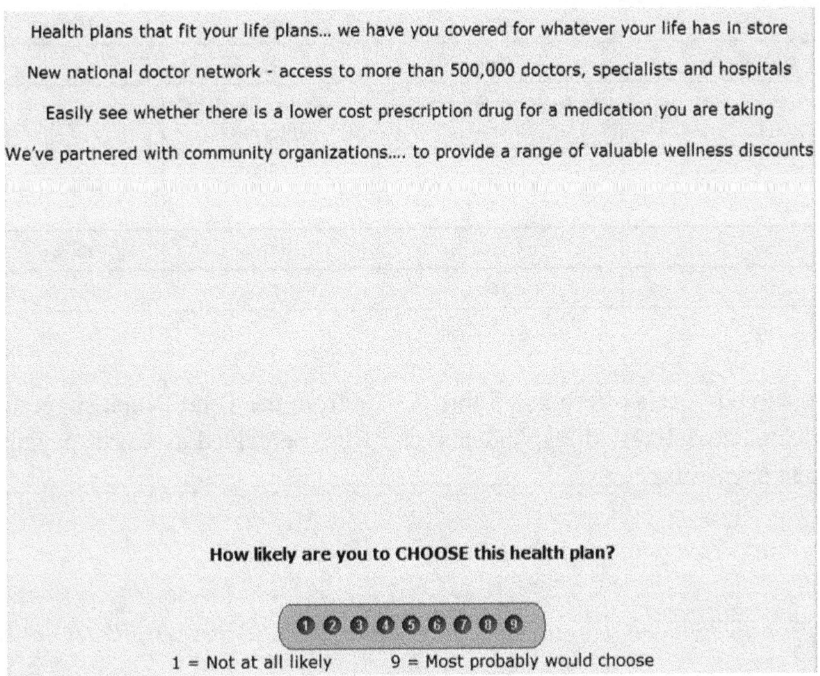

respondents. It generated two clusters or mindset segments. This clustering allocated 71 respondents to Segment 2A, and 77 respondents to segment 2B.

4. We repeated the clustering exercise using the 24 price values, with a single dollar value per element per respondent. This created Segments 2C and 2D, respectively. This second clustering also generated groups or mind-set segments, Segment 2C comprising 82 respondents, Segment 2D comprising 66 respondents.
5. A cross tabulation of the responses showed that the two segmentation schemes generated different patterns (Table 4). Simply changing the rating scale, i.e., the dimension on which the offer is considered changed the structure of the mind-set. This is of major importance to understand people. Just knowing who a person is, and how she or he behaved, does not suffice to predict how the person will react to a new test stimulus. Data suggest, that the same person, faced with the same stimuli, may fall into two unrelated mind-sets, depending upon the criteria for judgment asked of the respondent.

Practical Application: Segments Reveal New Opportunities for Health Plans

The objectives of these Mind Genomics studies are both theory (how the mind is constructed with respect to a particular topic) and application (what specific communication elements 'work' in terms of

Table 5. Cross tabulation of segment membership

	Member Seg 2A (Interest)	Member Seg 2B (Interest)	Total	Number
Member Seg2C (Price)	55%	45%	100%	82
Member Seg2D (Price)	39%	61%	100%	66
Total	48%	52	100%	148
Number	71	77		
	Member Seg 2A (Interest)	**Member Seg 2B (Interest)**	**Total**	**Number**
Member Seg2C (Price)	64%	48%	55%	82
Member Seg2D (Price)	36%	52%	45%	66
Total	100%	100%	100%	148
Number	71	77		

convincing people to buy one's offerings). Table 4, data from the Total Panel, suggested that only two communication elements interested respondents, and were perceived as worth paying for, above and beyond the current payments:

Preventive care always covered... no out of pocket expenses

Regular checkups... immunizations ... routine dental and eye care, prescriptions... hospital and emergency care ...and more

It may be that the data from the Total Panel results from the combination of different groups of people, different mind-sets, with each mind-set wanting a unique set of offerings, and rejecting other offerings. The data from each mind-set would show positive impact or coefficient values for the preferred communication elements or offerings. The complementary mind-sets might end up rejecting the same communication elements or offerings.

We see some examples of these differences when we segment the respondents either by interest (Segments 2A vs 2B; Table 5), or by price (Segment 2C vs 2D; Table 6).

1. When we segmented the respondents by the pattern of their Interest values, excluding the additive constant which is only a baseline, we see at least two radically different groups, of approximately equal size but radically different patterns of elements which are impactful
2. Segment 2A comprises individuals who respond to communication elements about 'Manage your life easily, and enjoy the good feelings you get by selecting us.' They are not interested in the insurance offerings (additive constant -1), unless the offering hits an emotional hot button, such as 'giving back to the places we live and work.).
3. Just because respondents in Segment 2A are 'interested in an offering' from the message does not mean that they will pay for offering. Some high scoring elements for interest are simply emotional statements. But there are others, that are both very interesting and can command additional premiums One example of such an element is C1, '*free preventive health checkups.*' The element interests

Table 6. Performance of elements for two segments, created by clustering respondents based upon the pattern of Interest coefficients (Question 1)

	Segmentation by Interest (Segments 2A, 2B)	Interest	Interest
		Seg2A	Seg2B
	Base size	**71**	77
	Additive constant:	**-1**	54
	Winners – Segment 2A: Manage your life easily, and enjoy the good feelings you get by selecting us		
A5	Giving back to the places we live and work	**54**	-31
A4	Take on life and live well	**38**	-18
C4	A tax-free Health Savings Account (HSA) ….offers you a 15 – 40% discount on paying for current health care expenses	**35**	-7
C1	Free preventive health checkups	**29**	**14**
A1	We've grown with you… 25 years of one healthy community	**28**	-56
C3	Enjoy the comfort and convenience of predictable co-pays	**24**	-33
D2	We've partnered with community organizations…. to provide a range of valuable wellness discounts	**18**	-17
D4	Up to $1,000 per year per family… for doing healthy stuff	**18**	-8
D1	Resources to help balance wellness and lifestyle	**17**	-2
D6	An incredible variety of resources to help you achieve your optimal health	**14**	-10
A6	It's not just healthcare…it's your care	**13**	-10
B6	Regular checkups… immunizations … routine dental and eye care, prescriptions… hospital and emergency care …and more	**9**	-30
C2	$0 co-pay for preventative services	**3**	-14
	Winners – Segment 2B – You are in charge, you make he decision, we are at your disposal		
C5	Preventive care always covered… no out of pocket expenses	-27	**19**
A3	Dedicated to making a difference	3	**12**
B2	New national doctor network - access to more than 500,000 doctors, specialists and hospitals	-15	**11**
B5	Flexible options to meet your needs	-3	**10**
	Remaining elements which do not generate any strong positive interest from the respondent		
D5	The care you and your baby get now will make a difference in the health of your child	-30	3
B1	Enjoy the freedom of in-network and out-of-network… anywhere in the country	-11	-1
B3	On-line Personal Health Manager … powered by WebMD®	-7	-5
B4	Coverage wherever you go	-37	-9
D3	Earn up to $300 in Rewards for a range of healthy activities	0	-11
A2	Health plans that fit your life plans… we have you covered for whatever your life has in store	1	-14
C6	Easily see whether there is a lower cost prescription drug for a medication you are taking	-10	-22

respondents in Segment 2A (interest value = 29 meaning an additional 29% of the respondents will rate the vignette 7-9 when this element is included), and can be sold at an additional charge (price = 14, meaning that the respondent in Segment 2A says that he or she will pay an additional $14 per month for this offering).

4. A second clustering, this time on the pattern of dollar values, generates a new pair of mindsets, groups of individuals who feel differently about what they will pay for. Table 7 shows the two emergent mind-sets based upon price, upon the pattern of dollar values for the 24 elements.
5. Segment 2C comprised individuals who will pay extra for an organization which helps them to maintain their health. The respondents in Segment 2C respond to general statements about capabili-

Table 7. Performance of elements for two segments, created by clustering respondents based upon the pattern of Interest coefficients (Question 1)

	Segmentation by Price (Segments 2C, 2D)	Seg2C	Seg2D
	Winners – Segment 2C: Will pay extra for an organization which helps them to maintain health		
A4	Take on life and live well	**13**	-11
D6	An incredible variety of resources to help you achieve your optimal health	**10**	**11**
D2	We've partnered with community organizations…. to provide a range of valuable wellness discounts	**7**	-8
B2	New national doctor network - access to more than 500,000 doctors, specialists and hospitals	**5**	-32
D4	Up to $1,000 per year per family… for doing healthy stuff	**1**	-6
	Winners – Segment 2D: Will pay for an organization which makes it financially easier, and the expensive more predictable		
A1	We've grown with you… 25 years of one healthy community	-8	**22**
C3	Enjoy the comfort and convenience of predictable co-pays	-15	**10**
C2	$0 co-pay for preventative services	-31	**10**
B6	Regular checkups… immunizations … routine dental and eye care, prescriptions… hospital and emergency care …and more	-3	**9**
A3	Dedicated to making a difference	-3	**8**
C5	Preventive care always covered… no out of pocket expenses	-5	**7**
	Remaining elements which do not command additional revenue from the respondent		
D5	The care you and your baby get now will make a difference in the health of your child	-15	0
C6	Easily see whether there is a lower cost prescription drug for a medication you are taking	-11	-4
B3	On-line Personal Health Manager … powered by WebMD®	-8	-5
C4	A tax-free Health Savings Account (HSA) ….offers you a 15 – 40% discount on paying for current health care expenses	-13	-6
D1	Resources to help balance wellness and lifestyle	-7	-8
A2	Health plans that fit your life plans… we have you covered for whatever your life has in store	-7	-10
C1	Free preventive health checkups	-9	-11
B1	Enjoy the freedom of in-network and out-of-network… anywhere in the country	-17	-11
B4	Coverage wherever you go	-12	-13
A5	Giving back to the places we live and work	0	-14
D3	Earn up to $300 in Rewards for a range of healthy activities	-10	-16
B5	Flexible options to meet your needs	-9	-28
A6	It's not just healthcare…it's your care	-12	-46

ties of the organization. They are not particularly interested in the details of the benefits to them, individually, as much as they are interested in the big picture.

6. Segment 2D comprised individuals who focus on organizations which are cost-conscious and fee-conscious. Segment 2D comprises individuals who appear to read the fine print, to know what they can expect. However, they too respond to statements about history and capability, as well as statements about customer focus. It's not just practicalities with Segment 2D.
7. One surprising results from segmentation is the disappearance of the formerly very clear relation between the interest coefficient, plotted on the abscissa, and the dollar value, plotted on the ordinate. Whether coefficients came from the equations developed for the Total Panel (Figure 1), or for genders or payers of premiums (Figure 2), the functional relation looked the same, upwards sloping with uncannily similar slopes, almost as if there were an underlying 'law' or a least an underlying 'regularity' governing the relation. That regularity disappears dramatically when we look at the data from the two pairs of mind-set segments, those created by segmenting the respondents based upon the pattern of interest (Segments 2A and 2B), or segmenting the respondents based upon the pattern of dollar value (Segments 2C and 2D). Creating the within-segment plot shows that the interest-price disappears (Figure 5).

Discovering These Different Mind-Sets in the Population

When it comes to selling 'health protection' our data suggest to use two ways to divide the population in order to create more targeted, more effective communication elements. One way divides the population according to what they say 'interests' them. The second way divides the population according to what they will 'pay for.' The data also reveals that there is no single offering which interests the respondents

Figure 5. How price fails to co-vary with interest when the respondents are segmented either by the pattern of interest towards elements (Seg A vs Seg B), or by the pattern of dollar values that the elements can command (Seg C vs Seg D)

Thank you for participating in this important and timely health insurance survey.
As you know, the topic of Health Insurance is at the center of public attention

This survey is designed to scientifically understand what you, the consumer want in an insurance plan.
The survey will take 10 - 15 minutes to take.

You will be presented 40 screens that contain a description of a health plan that has 2 - 4 components of a plan on each screen.
Although screens may appear similar and repetitive, you will not see identical screens.

PLEASE RATE YOUR REACTION TO EACH SCREEN AS A WHOLE

You will be asked two questions about each screen

Question 1: How likely are you to CHOOSE this health plan?

(answer on a 9 point scale) 1 = Not at all likely ... 9 = Most probably would

Question 2: How much would you spend PER MONTH for this health plan compared to your existing plan?

1 = $70 less 2 = $35 less 3 = SAME 4 = $35 more 5 = $70 more 6 = Don't know my current monthly cost 7 = Don't have a health plan now

You must complete the survey to be eligible for the gifts offered in the drawing.

Click the ">>" below to begin the survey

very much, and for which they say they will pay a lot more money, versus what they or others are paying currently or would pay for their health coverage.

From a managerial viewpoint it is necessary to segment the population, choose a segment, and then pursue the people in that segment with the appropriate communication elements. When one can identify a person as a member of a segment 'immediately,' it becomes possibly to change the communication to be appropriate for that person, or at least change the message to be appropriate for the segment to which one believes that person belongs.

Assignment of new people into existing groups, clusters or segments in the language of this chapter, has become increasingly popular during the past decades. When added to the basic information about gender, age, income, and other relatively static and purchasable information, the health insurer can identify a person's likely behavior in terms of being ready to choose a health plan. Big Data, mined with the appropriate algorithms, provides the power to predict a person's likely behavior for known situations.

The simple information about a respondent, however, does not necessarily predict the mind-set segment to which a person will be assigned. Table 7 shows that the membership in a mind-set segment cannot be easily predicted from knowing the typical type of information that one might have in a data base, such as age, education, income, household size, home ownership, and so forth. Furthermore, Table 4 showed us that membership in one of the two mind-set segments based upon the pattern of what interests a person cannot predict membership in one of the other two mind-set segments based upon what the respondent will pay for additional services. The problem of assigning a new person to one of the segments cannot be solved by algorithms designed to pore through Big Data when the nature of a person Mind-Set varies as a function of the stimuli, the person, AND the criterion according to which the person is responding. Today's algorithms for Big Data can pore through dynamic behavioral and static information about a person, but cannot as yet, or perhaps ever, take into account the person's momentary motives and judgment criteria. Other methods must be used.

The approach we use is called DFA, discriminant function analysis. DFA is only one of the many methods used to assign people with patterns to predefined groups, or in our case respondents to mind-set segments. The DFA approach is described by steps and summarized in Table 8:

1. Recode the individual elements of the Interest Model for each respondent. Elements generating a positive coefficient are assigned the value '2.' When the respondent rates a vignette, these elements drive the rating of interest to 7-9 on the original scale 9-point scale. Elements generating a negative coefficient or a coefficient of '0' are assigned the value '1.'
2. DFA identifies those specific elements which *in concert* best separate the two minds-segments. The degree to which the elements perform is shown by the F ratio. Table 9 (Section A) shows these five elements and their F ratios. The higher the F ratio the more the element differentiates between the two clusters, once the previous element has been incorporated. We could add other elements, with each element just added in turn being less powerful than the elements added before. We do not know ahead of time which five elements will be chosen by the DFA system. It's a sequential addition, each element adding the most predictability AFTER the other elements, previously added, have been taken in to account.
3. DFA creates a pair of classification functions. Each classification function allows us to estimate a value for any pattern of five responses. Section B shows the two classification functions.

Table 8. Composition of the two mind-set segments based upon interest in the individual elements (left side) and the price the respondent would pay for each element (right side)

AGE (rows	Seg2A	Seg2 B	Total	AGE (rows) by	Seg2C	Seg2D	Total
Over50	69	73	71	Over50	74	67	71
UnderOver500	31	27	29	UnderOver500	26	33	29
Total	100	100	100	Total	100	100	100
EDUCATION (rows)	Seg2A	Seg2 B	Total	EDUCATION (rows) s)	Seg2C	Seg2D	Total
Basic	33	37	35	Basic	42	27	35
Higher	67	63	65	Higher	58	73	65
Total	100	100	100	Total	100	100	100
INCOME (rows	Seg2A	Seg2 B	Total			Seg2D	Total
OverOver50k0k	31	27	29	OverOver50k0k	26	33	29
Refused	35	36	35	Refused	32	39	35
UnderOver50k0k	33	37	35	UnderOver50k0k	42	27	35
Total	100	100	100	Total	100	100	100
HOUSEHOLD (rows)	Seg2A	Seg2 B	Total	HOUSEHOLD (rows)	Seg2C	Seg2D	Total
Two or fewer	69	73	71	Two or fewer	74	67	71
Three or more	31	27	29	Three of more	26	33	29
Total	100	100	100	Total	100	100	100
OWN HOME (rows	Seg2A	Seg2 B	Total	OWN HOME	Seg2C	Seg2D	Total
Own	65	64	65	Own	68	61	65
Rent	35	36	35	Rent	32	39	35
Total	100	100	100	Total	100	100	100

4. Each pattern of responses (Section C) generates two estimated values, one for each classification function (Section D). The higher, positive value corresponds to the mind-set of cluster to which that pattern is assigned.

DISCUSSION

The assignment of people to a group is a topic of growing interest to data miners, and has been of interest to the medical professional and to health and applied psychologists. Data miners focusing on databases are interested in 'scoring' people in the database as likely candidates for health plans. With the growing availability of data the attractiveness of PA is growing as well as the accuracy of the assignment of a person to a group.

In the spirit of such interest we presented a way to assign a person to a mind-set, recognizing that the person's assignment to the mind-set may vary by person, by specific topic, and even by the criterion used by the person when making an evaluation. We saw these differences when we clustered respondents based upon their pattern of interest in a health plan versus the pattern of amount of money willing

Table 9. Discriminant function analysis (DFA) applied to the data from the Interest Model, to assign a new person, or pattern of responses, to one of the two mind-sets

	Section A: Variable	F Ratio
INTD4	Up to $1,000 per year per family… for doing healthy stuff Very interested =2 Moderately or not interested =1	35.55
INTB2	New national doctor network - access to more than 500,000 doctors, specialists and hospitals Very interested =2 Moderately or not interested =1	28.96
INTB4	Coverage wherever you go Very interested =2 Moderately or not interested =1	27.25
INTB6	Regular checkups… immunizations … routine dental and eye care, prescriptions… hospital and emergency care …and more Very interested =2 Moderately or not interested =1	13.40
INTC1	Free preventive health checkups Very interested =2 Moderately or not interested =1	11.11

Section B: Classification Functions			**Section C: Four response patterns, estimated values for the two classification functions and segment assignment (shaded cell) 2=definitely interested, 1=may or may not be interested, or not interested**			
	Seg A	**Seg B**	**P1**	**P2**	**P3**	**P4**
CONSTANT	-1.52	-1.16				
INTB2	0.99	-0.36	1	2	1	2
INTB4	0.51	-0.76	1	1	1	2
INTB6	0.99	0.02	1	2	1	2
INTC1	-0.15	0.66	1	2	2	2
INTD4	-0.77	0.65	1	2	2	2
		SegA	0	**1.11**	-0.9	**1.62**
	Section D:	SegB	**0.41**	-0.95	**0.02**	0.36

Classification Matrix (Cases in row categories classified into columns)			
	Assigned To Seg A	**Assigned to Seg B**	**% correct**
Seg A Actual	66	5	93
Seg B Actual	16	61	79
Total	82	66	86

to pay for the plan. The clusters or mind-set segments were radically different, even though the people were identical, the time was identical, and the stimuli were identical. All that differed was the criterion.

The objective of this chapter was to demonstrate the need to understand the 'mind' of the customer as to PA with healthcare plans. We provided a working tool which incorporated both the psychological attitudes about a health with the emotional attitude and behavioral spending about health plans.

REFERENCES

Anderson, J. C., & Narus, J. A. (1998). Business marketing: Understand what customers value. *Harvard Business Review, 76*, 53–67. PMID:10187246

Armstrong, A. J., Garrett-Mayer, E. S., Yang, Y. C. O., de Wit, R., Tannock, I. F., & Eisenberger, M. (2007). A contemporary prognostic nomogram for men with hormone-refractory metastatic prostate cancer: A TAX327 study analysis. *Clinical Cancer Research, 13*(21), 6396–6403. doi:10.1158/1078-0432.CCR-07-1036 PMID:17975152

Chin, H. B., Sipe, T. A., Elder, R., Mercer, S. L., Chattopadhyay, S. K., Jacob, V., & Chuke, S. O. et al. (2012). The effectiveness of group-based comprehensive risk-reduction and abstinence education interventions to prevent or reduce the risk of adolescent pregnancy, human immunodeficiency virus, and sexually transmitted infections: Two systematic reviews for the Guide to Community Preventive Services. *American Journal of Preventive Medicine, 42*(3), 272–294. doi:10.1016/j.amepre.2011.11.006 PMID:22341164

Crisp, M. A., & Chen, L. (2014). Global supply of health professionals. *The New England Journal of Medicine, 370*(10), 950–957. doi:10.1056/NEJMra1111610 PMID:24597868

Gabay, G. (2015). Perceived control over health, communication and patient-physician trust. *PEC, 98*(12), 1550–1557. PMID:26187177

Gabay, G. (2016a). Exploring perceived control and self-rated health in re-admissions among younger adults: A retrospective Study. *Patient Education and Counseling, 99*(5), 800–806. doi:10.1016/j.pec.2015.11.011 PMID:26626068

Gabay, G. (2016b). Does loyalty of patients to their physicians predict loyalty to the healthcare insurer? *Health Marketing Quarterly, 33*(2).

Gabay, G. & Moore, D. (2015). Antecedents of patient trust in health-care insurers. S*ervices Marketing Quarterly, 36*(1), 77-93.

Gabay, G., & Moskowitz, H. R. (2015a). Extending Psychophysics Methods to Evaluating Potential Social Anxiety Factors in Face of Terrorism. *Jahrbuch für Psychologie und Psychotherapie, 4*(6), 167–176.

Gabay, G., & Moskowitz, H. R. (2016). Reducing congestive heart failure patient re-admissions. In M. Prince & C. V. Priporas (Eds.), Market Sensing and Marketing Research. Academic Press.

Gabay, G., & Moskowitz, R. H. (2015b). Mind Genomics: What profesisonal conduct enhances the emotional wellbeing of teens at the hospital. *Journal of Psychological Abnormalities in Children, 4*(3). doi:10.4172/2329-9525.1000147

Green, P. E., Krieger, A. M., & Wind, Y. (2001). Thirty years of conjoint analysis: Reflections and prospects. *Interfaces, 31*(3), S56-S73.

Green, P. E., & Srinivasan, V. (1978). Conjoint analysis in consumer research: Issues and outlook. *The Journal of Consumer Research, 5*(2), 103–123. doi:10.1086/208721

Kohane, I. S., Drazen, J. M., & Campion, E. W. (2012). A glimpse of the next 100 years in medicine. *The New England Journal of Medicine*, *367*(26), 2538–2539. doi:10.1056/NEJMe1213371 PMID:23268669

McEachan, R. R. C., Conner, M., Taylor, N. J., & Lawton, R. J. (2011). Prospective prediction of health-related behaviors with the theory of planned behaviour: A meta-analysis. *Health Psychology Review*, *5*(2), 97-144.

Miner, L., Bolding, P., Hilbe, J., Goldstein, M., Hill, T., Nisbet, R., & Miner, G. (2014). *Practical Predictive Analytics and Decision Systems for Medicine: Informatics Accuracy and Cost-Effectiveness for Healthcare Administration and Delivery Including Medical Research*. Academic Press.

Rise, J., Kovac, V., Kraft, P., & Moan, I. S. (2008). Predicting the intention to quit smoking and quitting behaviour: Extending the theory of planned behaviour. *British Journal of Health Psychology*, *13*(2), 291–310. doi:10.1348/135910707X187245 PMID:17535498

Chapter 10
Prioritizing and Analyzing Demand Chain Management (DCM) Processes in Indian Retailing Using AHP

Arun Kumar Deshmukh
Banaras Hindu University (BHU), India

Ashutosh Mohan
Banaras Hindu University (BHU), India

ABSTRACT

The extant body of literature on demand chain management (DCM) is predominantly conceptual and unequivocal on how to implement it in a real business setting. Keeping the research gap into account, the study aims to identify and prioritize the DCM processes or variables in the context of Indian retailing. The data were collected using survey method using a structured questionnaire with Saaty (1980) scale. The method employed for analyzing the collected data was analytical hierarchy process or AHP. The results of the study have interesting implications for the industry vis-à-vis literature. Some quick measures revealed that the processes which are critical to implementation of DCM in retail context, in the order of importance, comprises supplier relationship management, customer relationship management assortment planning, top-management commitment and support, marketing orientation, information management, supply chain leagility, customer service management, category management, purchasing management, inventory management, and category tactics.

INTRODUCTION

Supply chain management (SCM) has come forward as an unassailable strategic business weapon for attaining competitive advantage during the previous decades as it has been asserted that supply chains are gradually becoming the bases of competition, as a result the real competition is between the supply chain of the firms and instead of between the companies themselves (Christopher & Ryals, 2014). Thus,

DOI: 10.4018/978-1-5225-2148-8.ch010

the practitioners'vis-à-vis the academics started speaking in one voice to transform the hyper efficiency led SCM process into customer responsive or marketing oriented demand chain.If the specialities of the two are to be discussed, it can be observed that SCM on the one hand is effective in moving products from focal firm to the end user efficiently. However, this hyper-efficiency focussed thinking caused a lopsided thinking of the business operations. And, the efficiency can not be over-emphasized at the cost of effectiveness as the successful businesses were found growing with their co-existence.

In the later stage, the scholars began realizing the overarching need for such co-existence and customer-centric corporate philosophy became the new order contemporaneous with the development of marketing concept from sales orientation to marketing orientation and more recently the societal marketing orientation. This paradigm shift in marketing philosophy not only influenced the marketing function of business but the back-end functions such as operations and supply chain too could not remain unperturbed. Under such unprecedented pressure from the marketplace, firms confronted radical philosophical transition in the way they manage their business functions (typically isolated), and the discussion began among the practitioners to break down the functional silos and promote integration in order for their business to not only satisfy their customers but to gain the differential advantage.

The integration based thinking in the context of supply chain and marketing gave birth to a relatively new concept of 'demand chain management' or DCM (Agrawal, 2012 and Juttner et al., 2007) which synthesizes the 'demand creation' and 'demand fulfillment' dimensions of market and supply chain respectively. The academic literature of recent past gave much space to the concept and simultaneously the industry freaks also realized it as the new business world order of the 21st century. However, due to lack of clarity on its definition, ways of implementation, and lack limiting demarcation boundaries to the concept could not properly demystify it. The studies so far believe that the demand chain management commands wider scope when compared with its counterpart supply chain because of its capability in sensing real-time customer demand and developing an offering to meet the changing market tastes and preferences (Agrawal, 2012 and Santos & D'Antone, 2014).

Taking cognizance of the shift in organizational philosophy about SCM and emergence of DCM with much to be researched around,the aforesaid study was conducted. The present study aimed to meet two key objectives- a) to explore various key processes that constitute demand chain and enable its implementation, and b) to analyze DCM processes or enablers through prioritization. The context of study was Indian apparel retailing.

THEORETICAL BACKGROUND

Demand Chain Management

The concept of 'demand chain' originated from it's superset i.e. 'value chain'. The primary activities of the value chain comprise'supply chain' and 'demand chain'. They together forms the value chain in the sense that upstream activities are catered by the supply chain whereas the downstream activities from marketing by retailers to end-user is taken care of by DCM. In other words, it can be termed as amalgamation of demand fulfillment and creation aspects of supply chain and demand chain respectively (Hilletofth and Ericsson, 2007; Rainbird, 2004; Heikkila, 2002, Wend & Song, 2015). In other words, the emphasis of demand chain management lies on sensing the real time customers' demand followed by devising a mechanism for rapid respond to it (Agrawal, 2012, 2010, Ericsson, 2007). Some scholars posited it as a mechanism to comprehend as the customer's demand and the transformation of such comprehension of demand into working strategies and plans for the whole group of firms involved in the chain (Langabeer & Rose, 2001; Wend & Song, 2015). In this context, DCM is seen as a function that integrates the supply chain and marketing (Jüttner, et al., 2007). However, the research in the domain is scarce; especially, the literature that can shape the future research proposing an agenda. The concept of demand chain holds great promise even though the present state of research on the concept and its application in the industry is in despair.

The present study moves a step further as it identified the variables from the existing literature survey and expert consultation and then arranged them under the three heads which were assigned according to the level of management hierarchy. These variables along with the researcher base are presented in the *table 1*.All variables under study are classified according to their nature and based on which level of management performs them.

DCM being an integrative function comprises several processes and sub-processes linking the two aspects of value chain. On the one hand, supply chain deals with the back-end operations whereas the demand chain represents the front-end or customer facing interface (Deshmukh and Mohan, 2016). The processes that facilitates effective execution of DCM in an organization are- information management, customer service management, supplier relationship management, top-management commitment and support, category management, supply chain Leagility, marketing orientation, assortment planning, customer relationship management, sourcing efficiency, inventory holding, and category tactics. These

Table 1. Variable-wise literature base (Authors' creation)

SN		Variables	Authors
1	**Strategic Variables**	Information Management	Chander, Jain & Shankar (2013); Langabeer & Rose, (2002); Vollmann, Cordon,& Heikkila, (2000), and De Treville, Shapiro,& Hamei, (2004)
		Customer Service Management	Mentzer, (2001); Parvatiyar and Sheth, (2001), and Deshmukh & Mohanty (2008)
		Supplier Relationship Management	Deshmukh & Mohan, (2012); Agariya and Singh, (2011), Parvatiyar & Sheth, (2001); and Spekman, Kamauff,& Myh, (1998)
		Top Management Commitment & Support	Mentzer, (2001), and Charan, Shankar,& Baisya, (2008)
		Category Management	Sinha and Uniyal, (2008); Jacobs, (2006), andNewman & Cullen, (2002)
2	**Tactical Variables**	Supply Chain Leagility	Deshmukh & Mohanty, (2010) and Mentzer, (2001).
		Marketing Orientation	Narver and Slater, (1990); Jaworski & Kohli (1993); Deshmukh and Mohan, (2012), Jacobs (2006), and Selen & Soliman (2002)
		Assortment Planning	Syam& Bhatnagar, (2015); Jacobs, (2006); Agrawal, (2012); Sinha & Uniyal, (2008); Newman & Cullen, (2002).
		Customer Relationship Management	Parvatiyar and Sheth, (2001),, Mentzer, (2001); and Deshmukh & Mohanty (2008)
3	**Operational Variables**	Purchasing Management	Jacobs, (2006); Agrawal, (2012), and Agrawal, (2003)
		Inventory Management	Jacobs, (2006); Christopher & Ryals, (2014); Ryals, & Holt, (2007); Agrawal, Agrawal,& Deshmukh, (2007), and Agrawal, (2012)
		Category Tactics	Sinha & Uniyal, (2008); Jacobs, (2006);

enablers of demand chain have been further classified according to the levels of management at which they are operated. These variables were classified as strategic variables, tactical variables and operational variables. A precise classification report is shown with literature support in *table 5*A precise operational definitions of variables are also presented in *table 2*.

The review of literature on demand chain management reveals that numerous studies were done to describe the concept and its application in the industry using qualitative methods such as case study that too in western context. Therefore, the need for exploring the phenomena in Indian context was felt, and for this purpose, a research base has to be developed. The present study attempted to fill the research gap mentioned above by analyzing various processes of DCM in retailing through multi-object modelling (analytical hierarchy process / AHP). The context of the study is apparel retailing.

Based on extant literature review all demand chain management (DCM) processes were classified into two parts, first, the supply chain related processes and the second was marketing related processes at theoretical and conceptual level. The SCM processes contributing to demand chain include information management, supplier relationship management, supply chain leagility, purchasing management, and

Table 2. Definition of variables of DCM (Authors' creation)

S. N.	Variables	Definition
1	**Information Management**	A process of acquiring, sharing, analyzing and responding to demand information obtained through ICT tools and techniques in an ecosystem of mutual trust.
2	**Customer Service Management**	"It is referred to as the ability of a firm to provide value added benefits to the customers by meeting customer demand and information needs (Christopher, 2002)."
3	**Supplier Relationship Management**	An interface between the focal firm and its suppliers with focus on upstream trust based long term relations.
4	**Top Management Commitment & Support**	"An assurance from the senior managers for the implementation of demand chain philosophy across the company operations Mentzer, 2000)."
5	**Category Management**	A process of managing categories as strategic business units (SBUs). This produces enhanced business results by achieving a robust bottom line for each category.
6	**Supply Chain Leagility**	An ability of an organization to respondrapidly and efficiently to changes in customer demand both in terms of variety and volume while minimizing the process waste (especially the time).
7	**Marketing Orientation**	"An organizational culture in which all employees are committed to the continuous creation of values for customer through three behavioural components: customer orientation, competitor orientation, and inter-functional coordination (Narver and Slater, 1990)."
8	**Assortment Planning**	It is the process of making available at one point of purchase, products that are inter-related and therefore, bought together.
9	**Customer Relationship Management**	"It refers to practices, strategies and technologies that companies use to manage and analyze customer interactions and data throughout the customer lifecycle, with the goal of improving business relationships with customers, assisting in customer retention and driving sales growth (Sheth and Parvatuyar, 2002."
10	**Purchasing Management**	An operational decision encompassing planning, classifying, and controlling the flow of goods (raw, semi finished and finished).
11	**Inventory Management**	A operational decision encompassing planning, classifying, and controlling the flow of goods (raw, semi finished and finished).
12	**Category Tactics**	It refers to a set of store variables that the retailer uses to keep the store and its offer relevant to its target customers through assortment, pricing, promotions and store's overall presentation.

inventory management while the marketing processes comprises customer relationship management, category management, assortment planning, marketing orientation, and customer service management. Also, in the same questionnaire these processes were presented under three decision level classifications- strategic, tactical and operational ones for two purposes, first, to ensure the aptness from experts' opinion and other was for triangulation. The strategic decision level processes are- information management, customer service management, supplier relationship management, top-management commitment & support, and category management. The tactical processes include- supply chain leagility, marketing orientation, and customer relationship management, and assortment planning. Finally, the operational processes encompass purchasing management, inventory management, and category tactics. The pictorial representation of the same can be seen in *figure 3*.

About Indian Apparel Retail

The retail sector in India is one of the most attractive destinations as far as employment and income generation are concerned. India ranks high among the top ten most favourable retail destinations (EY, 2015). Retail remains one of the numero uno sectors if India the economic contribution of which in terms of GDP accounts for more than 10 percent. It also provides employment to its 8 percent of total population. Despite this very fact it can not be denied that it is still in its infancy (Garg, 2010). The recent market research report by PwC Report (2015) and KPMG (2014) revealed that the Indian retail market has shown the growth in CAGR of 12.47 percent during the period 2007–2012 and is projected to grow at the rate of 13.23 per cent from 2012 to 2018. In 2015, food & grocery accounted for nearly 69 per cent of total revenues in the retail sector, followed by apparel (8.0 per cent). The demand for the Western outfits and readymade garments has been growing at the annaul rate of 40–45 per cent; apparel penetration was projected to increase 30-35 per cent by 2015; however, it hovered around 17-20 percent which is highest among all other categories (IBEF, 2015).

Figure 1. Indian retail sector and its subsectors (Source: ibef, 2015)

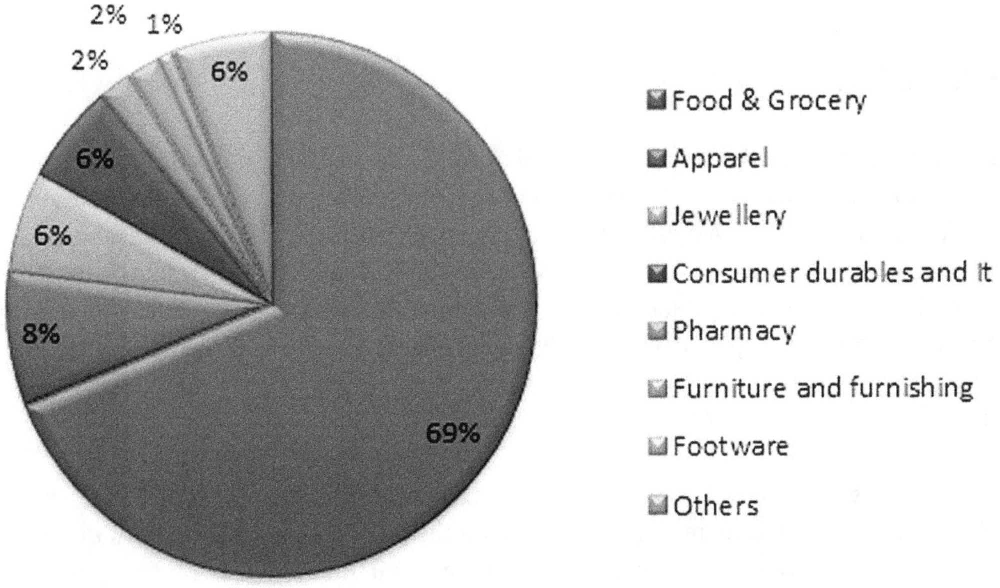

The Indian retail industry has experienced a phenomenal growth of 10.6% between 2010 and 2012 and is likely to increase to US$ 750-850 billion by the end of 2016. Food and grocery is the largest category within the retail sector with 69 per cent share followed by apparel and jewellery and consumer durable segment (IBEF, 2015).

After food and groceries (F&G), apparel is the second largest category which contributes around 8 percent of the total merchandise ratail market of India. As per IBEF (2015) report, apparels would be the largest retail segment, accounting for 22 per cent of total retail space by 2014–15. The apparel retailing is undergoing a radical transformation where the focus of retailers has been shifting from traditional physical store concept to multi-channel or omni-channel retailing (IBFR, 2015). In order to propel the growth engine in the category, the brands and apparel retailers are leveraging their know-how of the local market and regional factors, which direct the consumer psyche. While the international retailers and brands are able to capitalize upon their impeccable brand image and ability to produce unparallel products with innovative designs and to exploit the prospective market opportunities.

As a category, apparel has demonstrated higher propensity towards corporatization or modern retailing (IBFR, 2015). The share of modern retail in apparel segment is around 20 percent. Besides apparel the other two competing merchandise categories are footwear and consumer durables with a higher penetration in modern retailing.

India's apparel market accounted for INR 2,48,250 crore in 2014 which is estimated to grow at a CAGR of 9.9 percent, to reach INR 3,94, 450 crore in 2019, and 6,40,800 crore in 2024. Of the entire apparel market, the lion's share is held by menswear category (42%), followed by women's wear (38%) and kids-wear (20%). With a CAGR of 10.4 percent between 2014-2024, women's wear was observed as the fastest growing category which is also likely to grab 39 percent of the apparel market share by 2024. Thus, it is emerging as another promising category. Despite fast growth in kids-wear, it will remain the smallest category with a 22 percent share of the total apparel market by 2024. However, the readiness of apparel retailers to cater and harness the huge customer base with higher efficiency and enhanced effectiveness seems half hearted. The changes in the assortment are not in sync with the changing trends and preferences of the customer, this calls for an altogether innovative way of reaching and serving customers. The scholars see DCM as an approach to offer such solutions.

METHODOLOGY

The study aimed to analyze the key variables and / or processes of demand chain management (DCM) through prioritization, which senior management of a typical retail firm should ideally focus upon. These strategies are keys to accomplish higher organizational performance and differential advantage through enhanced supply chain practices. These variables or processes were explored primarily through a review of literature. Keeping this into consideration, a group of retail experts, practitioners and academicians were empanelled to act as respondents for analyzing the same.

Data and Sample

The paper makes use of both secondary vis-à-vis primary data. Secondary data were collection process involved the access to literature, reports, and books on the topic under study whereas the primary data were collected through expert choice method. As per the requirement of AHP modeling the sample was selected from among the academic and industry experts. In totality,30 experts were consulted; of them 22 responded to the survey. From the 22 response sheets 18 were found suitable for the AHP analysis. The sample of 18 expertsconsists of 11 from retail industry and 7 academicians from SCM and Retail area who provided their inputs in prioritizing the variables through a structured AHP questionnaire with Saaty scale(*vide Table 3*).The sole criterion behind selection of experts as respondents was their rich experiencein the respective industry and seniority in the hierarchy.

Measures and AHP Process

Since, the principal objective of the present study is to prioritize various processes of DCM apparel retailing context, the Multi-Criteria Decision Making (MCDM) tool was found to be useful. The data was collected and analyzed through Analytical Hierarchy Process (AHP) approach for prioritizing the various DCM strategies using MS-Excel package.

Keeping the objective of prioritizing various DCM variables in the context of apparel retailing into consideration, one of the Multi-Criteria Decision Making (MCDM) tools- Analytical Hierarchy Process (AHP)was found helpful and effective in solving such complex decision problems with multiple choices. The underlying assumption for using AHP is that it produces solution based on multi-criteria (Cheng et al., 2005) and thus, can be applied to both qualitative and quantitative kinds of research (Saad, 2001).

Primarily developed by Saaty (1980), Analytical Hierarchy Process (AHP) has become a useful and significant technique for solving complex decision problems that involve uncertainty and complexity (Zahedi, 1986; Madu*et al.,*1991; Saaty,1980; Yang and Huang, 2000; Wu et al, 2008). It helps in decomposing the complex problem into simple hierarchy and prioritizes the variables that influence a particular behaviour . Decision making has evolved to be a complex task as it consists of several criteria that should be taken into account in decision making. AHP has been systematic multi-criteria decision making technique available for such problem with multi-criteria. A brief description of the step-by-step procedure (Goyal, Rehman and Kazmi, 2015) along the pictorial presentation (*videFigure 2*) is described below;

- **Step1**: Define the objectives of the multifaceted and vague problem in an unambiguous way.
- **Step 2**: The problem is developed in the form of a hierarchy. The top-level of the hierarchy refers to the goal or objective of the given problem. The goal is further divided into various criteria at the next level. These criteria are additionally divided into the sub-criteria on the level three. A researcher has to continue this practice until the decomposition of all sub-criteria is taken place/.

Table 3. AHP Scale of Relative Importance (Adopted from Saaty1977; 1980)

Scale value	Importance
1	Equal importance
3	Moderate importance of one over the other
5	Essential or strong importance
7	Very strong or demonstrated importance
9	Extreme or absolute importance
2,4,6,8	Intermediate values between the two adjacent judgments

- **Step 3**: In this step, pair-wise comparison of a criterion over another with the help of respective decision matrix is performed. Considering the responses of the experts, the decision matrix is prepared using 9-point Saaty (1994)scale, the description of which is illustrated precisely in *table 3*. In this pair-wise comparison, factors that fall under a dimension are compared with the other factors under the same. For example, if there are "n" elements under a dimension, then n (n-1)/2 comparisons will take place in that paticular dimension
For example, there are "n" criteria B1, B2, B3 […] […], ...Bn with the corresponding weights W1, W2, W3 […]. The pair-wise comparison matrix of these matrices according to their relative weights is shown below:

$$Z = \begin{array}{c} \\ B_1 \\ B_2 \\ B_3 \\ \vdots \\ B_n \end{array} \begin{array}{c} \begin{array}{ccccc} B_1 & B_2 & B_3 & \cdots & B_n \end{array} \\ \begin{bmatrix} W_1/W_1 & W_1/W_2 & W_1/W_3 & \cdots & W_1/W_n \\ W_2/W_1 & W_2/W_2 & W_2/W_3 & \cdots & W_2/W_n \\ W_3/W_1 & W_3/W_2 & W_3/W_3 & \cdots & W_3/W_n \\ \vdots & \vdots & \vdots & \vdots & \vdots \\ W_n/W_1 & W_n/W_2 & W_n/W_3 & \cdots & W_n/W_n \end{bmatrix} \end{array}$$

$$Z = \begin{array}{c} \\ B_1 \\ B_2 \\ B_3 \\ \vdots \\ B_n \end{array} \begin{array}{c} \begin{array}{ccccc} B_1 & B_2 & B_3 & \cdots & B_n \end{array} \\ \begin{bmatrix} a_{11} & a_{12} & a_{13} & \cdots & a_{1n} \\ a_{21} & a_{22} & a_{23} & \cdots & a_{2n} \\ a_{31} & a_{32} & a_{33} & \cdots & a_{3n} \\ \vdots & \vdots & \vdots & \cdots & \vdots \\ a_{n1} & a_{n2} & a_{n3} & \cdots & a_{nn} \end{bmatrix} \end{array}$$

Here, aij stands for wi/wj (i, j = 1,2,3 […]. n). It presents the comparative judgment among the pair of elements Bi and Bj. In case of i = j, aij = 1 and aij = 1/ aji for aij>0.

- **Step 4:** After the comparative matrix is prepared, the next step is to compute the priority vector (PV) of the factors with the help of eigen value or vector (EV).For detailer calculations *appendices 1-4* may be referred.

$$\sum_{j=1}^{n} a_{ij} \frac{W_j}{W_i}$$

- **Step 5:** At this step, the consistency check is performed. The consistency assessment in the pair-wise comparison is one of the key issues in AHP technique. Any sort of negligence and at any level may lead to inconsistency. An inconsistency in an assessment may result in misleading results. The AHP method provides a method called a consistency ratio (CR) to assess the consistency of every judgment provided by experts (Atthirawong and MacCarthy, 2001). The CR provides vital information on validity if a criterion.for decision-making. The CR value may range from 0.0 (means 0 per cent inconsistency) to 1.0 (means 100 per cent inconsistency). In the words of Saaty (1980), acceptable upper limit of CR is0.1. In case, CR is greater than 0.1, then decision-maker needs to re-evaluate the judgment of pair-wise comparison. CR is usually calculated with the help of an equation- CR = CI/RI. Then the researcher computes the consistency index (CI) using the equation given below:

Figure 2. Steps involved in the AHP method (Source: Authors' creation)

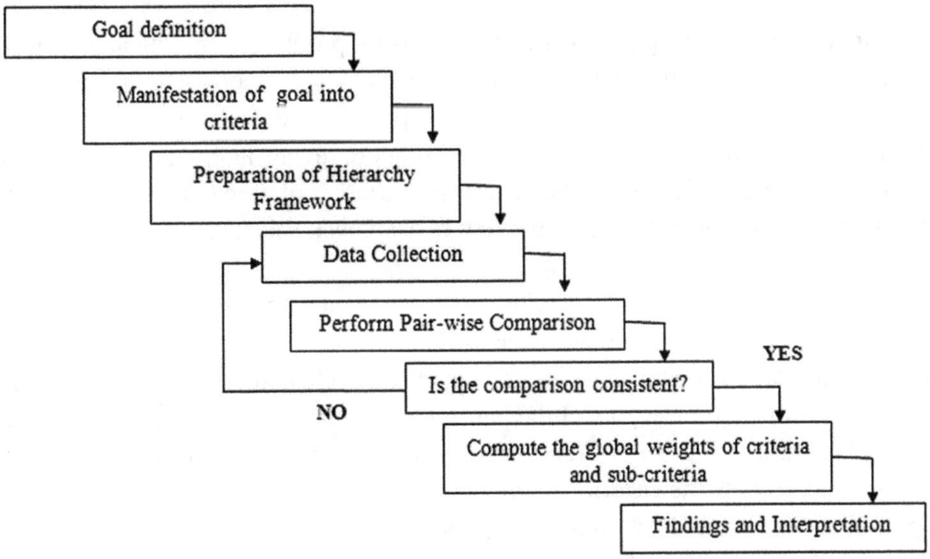

$CI = (\lambda_{max} - n) / n - 1$

where:

n = number of criteria or sub-criteria at each level; and
λ_{max} = Maximum calculated in matrix z.

The number of factors (criteria or sub-criteria) decides the RI value. The *table 4* given below informs the researcher that for instance there are three criteria or sub-criteria then the value of RI will be 0.58. Then, λ can be calculated by following steps:

- **Step 6:** After the priority weight aka local weights for each factor is computed, the global weight of each element is calculated with relation to the goal described at the top-level of AHP model (*videTable 5*).
- **Step 7:** the priority weights so computed are then organized in accordance with their weight the criteria are ranked by arranging either in ascending or descending order.

Table 4. Random index (Source: RI by Saaty & Vergas, 1991)

N	1	2	3	4	5	6	7	8	9	10	.
RI	0	0	0.58	0.9	1.12	1.24	1.32	1.41	1.45	1.49	CRrandomnumber Index index

Development of AHP Model for DCM

In the AHP approach, the first step is to structure a decision problem hierarchically at different levels wherein each level comprises a finite number of decision elements. It consists of purpose, criteria, sub-criteria and alternatives. The overall goal is represented by the upper level of hierarchy, whereas all the possible alternatives are depicted in lower level. The literature review along the opinions of experts has been used for developing an AHP model to evaluate the variables of demand chain management. Based on this criterion, the following factors and sub-factors have been selected for the problem under study as shown in *figure 3*.

In the second step, the pair-wise comparison of the same elements of the hierarchy at each level is performed by applying a Saaty scale. Saaty scale is a 9-point scale that indicates the importance of one element over the other element with regard to the higher-level element as shown in *figure 4*.

In the step 3, to compute the weights of the pair-wise comparison, adaptive matrices are formed on the basis of the data collected in step 2. The relative priority or weights of the factors is the result of scaling process with regard to the criterion or element at the top level of the hierarchy. The elements so judged are placed in the rows and columns of adaptive matrix in such a fashion that if i-th row criterion is superior to j-th column criterion, the intersection number of these two criteria will be greater than 1, else, it will be smaller than 1. One should take a note that in AHP method, the criterion rAB is an inverse of rBA and this way the adaptive matrix is formed using this principal..

Figure 3. AHP hierarchy of DCM variables (Source: Authors' Creation)

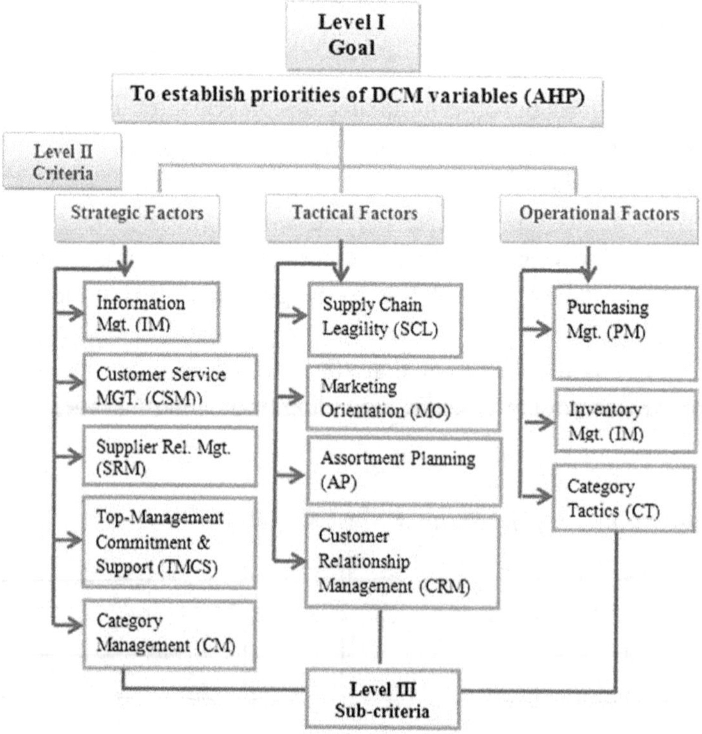

In the next step, the adaptive matrix obtained in step 3 is normalized applying Saaty (1980) norms. The mean of the elements of each row expresses the weight of the corresponding alternative. When the comparison is done, it is expected to obtain certain inconsistencies. For this reason, Saaty demonstrated a consistency index, popularly termed as CI. As per the acceptable norm, CI $\leq$0.10 should be upheld so that the matrix remains consistent. If the matrix is not consistent, the reliability and validity of the paired-wise comparisons and the results can be challenged.

The comparisons are done for all criteria in a level with respect to all the criteria in the level mentioned above. The final and global weights of the elements at the lowest level of the hierarchy are calculated by adding all the contributions of the criteria in a level with regard to all elements at the top of the hierarchy.

SOLUTIONS AND RECOMMENDATIONS

The aforesaid study attempted to explore and analyze the DCM processes using one of the multi-criteria decision modelling (MCDM) techniques i.e., AHP where the same DCM processes (main decision criterion) were put under different sub-criteria. The first classification of sub-criteria was based on the functional divide (SCM & Marketing) in an organization while the second classification was based on levels of decision making (Strategic, Tactical and Operational). The global ranking of decision levels sub-criteria through AHP indicates an obvious ranking sequence of all is strategic, tactical, and operational. Whereas, the ranking of functional divide sub-criteria indicates that for demand chain implementation marketing processes are more critical over the SCM processes this approves the existing theory and literature on DCM.

The processes that are critical to implementation of DCM in retail context, in the order of importance, comprises supplier relationship management, customer relationship management assortment planning, top-management commitment and support, marketing orientation, information management, supply chain leagility, customer service management, category management, purchasing management, inventory management, and category tactics. The sequence or order of these processes revealed an apparent fact that the core processes of supply chain domain such as supplier relationship management, supply chain leagility, and customer service management should be given equal importance along with the front-end marketing processes i.e., customer relationship management and assortment planning. Some processes which but naturally requires cross-functional interface such as information management (Korhonen et al, 1998), marketing orientation (Narver and Slater, 1990), and factors such as top management support (Mentzer, 2001) also hold place among the prima facie aspects according the experts. Even though at the level of execution the situation seems altogether different which gives a clear sign of silo based thinking and doing. The DCM processes put together can enable the firms transcend its position in the market with an integrative philosophy (Wend and Song, 2014). However, in practice, these aspects are easier said than done.

Another aspect of discussion crops-up from the triadic classification of the DCM processes i.e., strategic, tactical and operational. This classification was based on the extant literature survey and deliberation with the academic and industry experts. The twelve DCM processes or variables were subdivided under these three heads according to their level of operation or who or which level of management performs or / and influences it more. The priority ranking of the sub-criteria under the strategic factor shows that supplier relationship management (SRM) is of utmost importance. It clearly indicates that in order for

Table 5. AHP global and local ranking of criteria and sub-criteria. (Source:Authors' creation)

Hierar-chy Level	Sub-Factors	Priority Vectors (PV) of Sub-factor	Priority Vectors (PV) of Main Factor	Global Weight	Ranking
Level 2	**Pair-wise comparison of three categories or criteria w.r.t. DCM**				
	Strategic Factors	0.48656		0.48656	1
	Tactical Factors	0.43528		0.43528	2
	Operational Factors	0.07817		0.07817	3
Level 3	**Pair-wise comparison of sub-criteria(among 12 factors) or w.r.t. DCM**				
Strategic Factors	**Information Management (IM)**	0.10582	0.48656	0.05149	6
	Customer Service Mgt. (CSM)	0.09507		0.04626	8
	Supplier Relationship Management (SSP)	0.40590		0.19749	1
	Top-Management Commitment & support (TMCS)	0.21026		0.10230	4
	Category Management (CM)	0.18295		0.03063	9
Tactical Factors	**Supply Chain Leagility (SCL)**	0.06684	0.43528	0.04807	7
	Marketing Orientation (MO)	0.07036		0.08902	5
	Assortment Planning (AP)	0.41801		0.18195	3
	Customer Relationship Management (CRM)	0.44479		0.19361	2
Operational Factors	**Purchasing Management (PM)**	0.61502	0.07817	0.02910	10
	Inventory Management (IM)	0.29236		0.02285	11
	Category Tactics (CT)	0.09262		0.00724	12

management to implement DCM in practice, a firm must consciously focus on having a well chalked out plan for developing strategic alliance or partnership with its key suppliers. Also, such relationship must be long term based and not just transactional one. This argument is supported by and deeply grounded in the transaction cost economics (TCE) theory which propounded that long term partnering relationship with suppliers reduces the searching and switching cost in the long run. The second significant sub-criterion is top-management commitment and support. Though it is obvious to pinpoint the very fact that without constant support from the senior management for implementing even a any business decision, no practice can be sustained for the long term. Especially when it is a breakthrough change such as implementing DCM in practice which not only requires a long term plan but also th requisite resources have to be mobilized for smooth function at all levels. The resource based view (RBV) and strategic choice theory (SCT) provide evidence to this.

The other key variables under strategic factor include information management (IM), customer service management, and category management. Information being a linking pin among various functional areas in an organization plays a crucial role in integrating them in cohesive whole to minimize the uncertainty by obtaining and sharing timely, accurate, adequate, reliable and complete information within and outside the organization. While the customer service management (CSM) ensures a congenial pre-transactional, transactional, and post-transactional service to the customers.It in turn endows a firm with a pool ofdelighted customers and higher retention rate. Category management (CM) deals with

Figure 4. Global ranking for various sub-criteria (Source: Authors' creation)

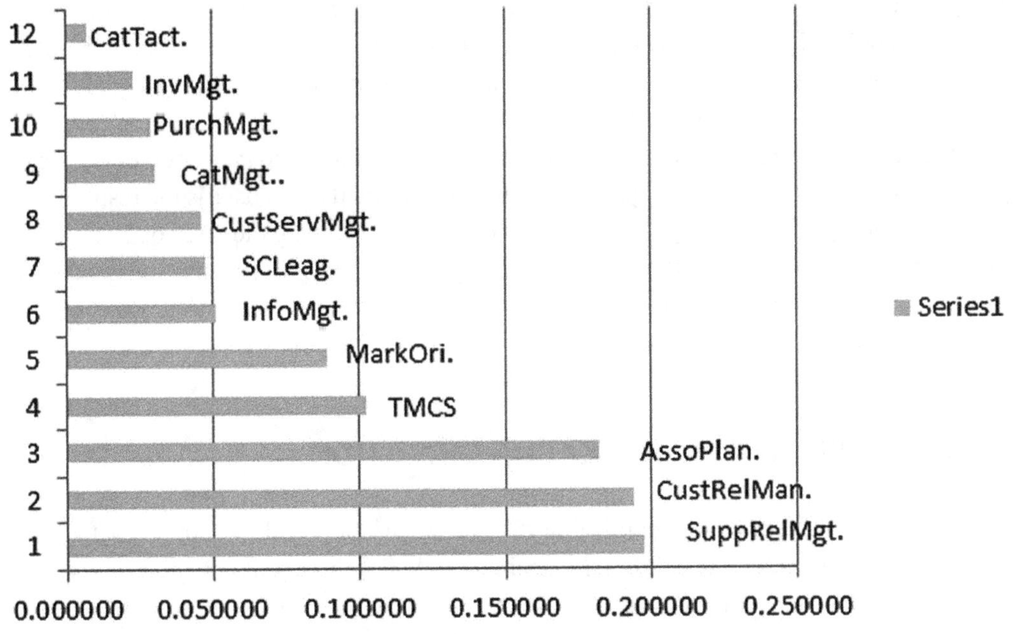

whether a firm manages its various product lines as strategic business units (SBUs)? Thus, the retail firms managing their categories in traditional ways confront lesser acceptance from their customers and inapt periodic evaluation.

The tactical factors on the other hand comprisesub-criteria in the order of importance are-customer relationship management (CRM), assortment planning (AP), marketing orientation (MO), and supply chain leagility (SCL). CRM emerged as key tactical factor to influence as DCM practice. It deals with the getting, keeping, growing the customer base so as to attain higher profitability, enhanced customer lifetime value, and reduced customer acquisition cost. TCE also operates here with a view that the acquisition cost for a new customer is ten times higher than keeping the existing customers. Hence, it primarily emphasizes on the customer retention strategies. The second in the order is assortment planning (AP) which refers to a firm-wide plan to manage the point-of-purchase of apparels in a store in such a manner that the apparels usually bought together are kept together and so on, for instance, Zara complete men range displays all possible apparel that a male customer can think of buying together . This not only offers convenience to the customers and sales team but also facilitates cross-selling and up-selling which fetches more revenues to the firm with rising customer satisfaction.

Third in the order is marketing orientation (MO) which as a term was initially propounded by Narver and Slater (1990) and Jowarsky& Kohli (1993). It incorporates three component customer orientation, competitor orientation and inter-functional coordination though not included in the prioritization due to the methodological limitations. The research reveals that the firms with higher marketing orientation perform better in terms of customer satisfaction as well as the bottom-line when compared to their non-conforming industry counterparts. Finally, the supply chain leagiity (SCL) refers to the degree to which a firm is able to simultaneously reduce the process-wide waste (especially time) and provide the volume and variety to the dynamically changing customer demand. Thus, the processes are supposed to be the leagile in firm's supply chain. The ranking of the different elements of sub-criteria suggests that retailers should primarily focus on them to ensure the effective execution of demand creation aspect i.e., demand chain management. This in turn, will fetch a higher organizational performance and differential advantage.

Lastly, the operational variable encompasses purchasing management (PM), inventory management (InvM), and category tactics (CT). Although some scholars treat purchasing as a strategic function (Mentzer, 2001, Kraljic, 1973) in different contexts, some other believe it to be an operational construct (Jacob, 2006, Raibbird, 2004) in the context of DCM. The present study classified it as operational variable, still it hold greater significance because the quality product desired by the end user is the result of the quality of input received through the sourcing. Thus, it holds the first rank among the three operational variables. The next variable in the sequence is the inventory management. The effective inventory management in a firm reduces the cost, uncertainty and risk of going out-of-order. The category tactics is situated as last sub-criterion that refers to the overall store-wide presentation of apparels relevant to the target market.

CONCLUSION AND FUTURE RESEARCH DIRECTION

The study met the two objectives of identifying the DCM variables and thereby prioritizing them using multi-criteria decision technique (MCDM) technique-AHP. The results of the study will have two key outcomes; one that relates to the contribution to the body of knowledge on demand chain while the other is the implications for practitioners. The study attempted to enrich the existing theoretical base on DCM which was majorly conceptual. This study will pave the way for further exploration of the concept in different context. The context specific analyses delimited the scope of the study which was though ideallynecessary, future studies may extend the same in cross-context analysis to ensure its generalizability. Moreover, mere identification and prioritization of DCM variables in Indian retail context is the half work done and a lot is yet to be done such as development of relational and causal models from it for exploring and describing the phenomena so as to posit the relevance of the DCM concept in literature vis-à-vis in practice. Future studies may also consider studyingthe concept with a mix methodology which combines the multi-criteria decision tools and statistical modelling for better results and validity of the results.

REFERENCES

Agrawal, Agrawal, & Singh. (2010). *Demand Chain Management.* Macmillan.

Agrawal, D. K. (2012). Demand chain management: Factors enhancing market responsiveness capabilities. *Journal of Marketing Channels*, *19*(2), 101–119. doi:10.1080/1046669X.2012.667760

Cheng, E. W., Li, H., & Yu, L. (2005). The analytic network process (ANP) approach to location selection: A shopping mall illustration. *Construction Innovation*, *5*(2), 83–97. doi:10.1108/14714170510815195

Christopher, M., & Ryals, L. J. (2014). The supply chain becomes the demand chain. *Journal of Business Logistics*, *35*(1), 29–35. doi:10.1111/jbl.12037

De Treville, S., Shapiro, R. D., & Hameri, A. P. (2004). From supply chain to demand chain: The role of lead time reduction in improving demand chain performance. *Journal of Operations Management*, *21*(6), 613–627. doi:10.1016/j.jom.2003.10.001

Deshmukh, A. K., & Mohan, A. (2012). Role of relationship marketing in demand chain collaboration. In Exploring Consumer Dynamics: A Relationship and Behavioral Approach. New Delhi: Himalaya Publishing House.

Deshmukh, A. K., & Mohan, A. (2016). Demand Chain Management (DCM): The Marketing and Supply Chain Interface Redefined. *The IUP's Journal of Supply Chain Management, 13*(1), 20–36.

Garg, P. (2010). Critical success factors for enterprise resource planning implementation in Indian retail industry: An exploratory study. *Int. J. Comput. Sci. Inf. Secur, 8*(2), 358–363.

Goyal, P., Rahman, Z., & Kazmi, A. A. (2015). Identification and prioritization of corporate sustainability practices using analytical hierarchy process. *Journal of Modelling in Management, 10*(1), 23–49. doi:10.1108/JM2-09-2012-0030

Heikkilä, J. (2002). From supply to demand chain management: Efficiency and customer satisfaction. *Journal of Operations Management, 20*(6), 747–767. doi:10.1016/S0272-6963(02)00038-4

Hilletofth, P., & Ericsson, D. (2007). Demand chain management: Next generation of logistics management. *Conradi Research Review, 4*(2), 1–18.

Hua Lu, M., Madu, C. N., Kuei, C. H., & Winokur, D. (1994). Integrating QFD, AHP and benchmarking in strategic marketing. *Journal of Business and Industrial Marketing, 9*(1), 41–50. doi:10.1108/08858629410053470

Jacobs, D. (2006). The promise of demand chain management in fashion The promise of demand chain management in fashion. *Journal of Fashion Marketing and Management, 10*(1), 84–96. doi:10.1108/13612020610651141

Jüttner, U., Christopher, M., & Baker, S. (2007). Demand chain management-integrating marketing and supply chain management. *Industrial Marketing Management, 36*(3), 377–392. doi:10.1016/j.indmarman.2005.10.003

Jüttner, U., Peck, H., & Christopher, M. (2003). Supply chain risk management: Outlining an agenda for future research. *International Journal of Logistics: Research and Applications, 6*(4), 197–210. doi: 10.1080/13675560310001627016

Korhonen, P., Huttunen, K., & Eloranta, E. (1998). Demand chain management in a global enterprise-information management view. *Production Planning and Control, 9*(6), 526–531. doi:10.1080/095372898233777

KPMG Report. (2014). *Indian Retail: The next growth story.* Available at: https://www.kpmg.com/IN/en/IssuesAndInsights/ArticlesPublications/Documents/BBG-Retail.pdf

Langabeer, J., & Rose, J. (2002). Is the supply chain still relevant? *Logistics Manager*, (March), 11-13.

Madu, C., Kuei, C., & Madu, A. (1991). Establishing priorities for the information technology industry in Taiwan: A Delphi approach. *Long Range Planning, 24*(5), 105–118. doi:10.1016/0024-6301(91)90256-N

Mentzer, J.T. (2001). *Supply Chain Management: Strategy, Planning & Operation.* New Delhi: Response Books/ Sage India.

Narver, J. C., & Slater, S. F. (1990). The effect of a market orientation on business profitability. *Journal of Marketing*, *54*(4), 20–35. doi:10.2307/1251757

Newman, A. J., & Cullen, P. (2002). *Retailing: environment & operations*. Cengage Learning EMEA.

Parvatiyar, A., & Sheth, J. N. (2001). Customer relationship management: Emerging practice, process, and discipline. *Journal of Economic and Social Research*, *3*(2), 1–34.

PwC Report. (2015). *Total Retail 2015: Retailers and the age of disruption*. Available at: https://www.pwc.in/assets/pdfs/publications/2015/retailers-and-the-age-disruption.pdf

Rainbird, M. (2004). Demand and supply chains : The value catalyst. *International Journal of Physical Distribution & Logistics Management*, *34*(3), 230–250. doi:10.1108/09600030410533565

Report, E. Y. (2015). *India — pulse of retail and consumer markets What does a changing consumer mean for the sector?* Available at: http://www.ey.com/Publication/vwLUAssets/EY-india-a-pulse-on-the-consumer-products-market-march-2015.pdf/$FILE/EY-india-a-pulse-on-the-consumer-products-market-march-2015.pdf

Saad, G. H. (2001). Strategic performance evaluation: Descriptive and prescriptive analysis. *Industrial Management & Data Systems*, *101*(8), 390–399. doi:10.1108/EUM0000000006169

Saaty, T. L. (1977). A scaling method for priorities in hierarchical structures. *Journal of Mathematical Psychology*, *15*(3), 234–281. doi:10.1016/0022-2496(77)90033-5

Saaty, T. L. (1980). *The Analytic Hierarchy Process*. New York, NY: McGraw-Hill.

Santos, J. B., & DAntone, S. (2014). Reinventing the wheel? A critical view of demand-chain management. *Industrial Marketing Management*, *43*(6), 1012–1025. doi:10.1016/j.indmarman.2014.05.014

Selen, W., & Soliman, F. (2002). Operations in todays demand chain management framework. *Journal of Operations Management*, *20*(6), 667–673. doi:10.1016/S0272-6963(02)00032-3

Shapiro, B. P. (1977). Can marketing and manufacturing co-exist. *Harvard Business Review*, *55*(5), 104.

Sinha, P. K., & Uniyal, D. P. (2008). *Managing Retailing*. Oxford University Press.

Soliman, F., & Youssef, M. (2001). The impact of some recent developments in e-business on the management of next generation manufacturing. *International Journal of Operations & Production Management*, *21*(5/6), 538–564. doi:10.1108/01443570110390327

Udo, G. G. (2000). Using analytic hierarchy process to analyze the information technology outsourcing decision. *Industrial Management & Data Systems*, *100*(9), 421–429. doi:10.1108/02635570010358348

Vollmann, T. E., & Cordon, C. (1998). Building Successful Customer Supplier Alliances. *Long Range Planning*, *31*(5), 684–694. doi:10.1016/S0024-6301(98)00073-9

Walters, D. W., & Rainbird, M. (2007). *Strategic Operations Management: A Value Chain Approach*. Basingstoke, UK: Palgrave.

Wen, H., & Song, L. (2015). A demand chain design for Chinese oatmeal companies. *Journal of Industrial Engineering and Management*, *8*(2), 335–348. doi:10.3926/jiem.1316

Wu, C. R., Chang, H. Y., & Wu, L. S. (2008). A framework of assessable mutual fund performance. *Journal of Modelling in Management*, *3*(2), 125–139. doi:10.1108/17465660810890117

Yang, C., & Huang, J. B. (2000). A decision model for IS outsourcing. *International Journal of Information Management*, *20*(3), 225–239. doi:10.1016/S0268-4012(00)00007-4

Zahedi, F. (1986). The analytic hierarchy process-a survey of the method and its applications. *Interfaces*, *16*(4), 96-108.

Zeithaml, V. A. (1988). Consumer perceptions of price, quality, and value: A means-end model and synthesis of evidence. *Journal of Marketing*, *52*(3), 2–22. doi:10.2307/1251446

ADDITIONAL READING

Ericsson, D. (2011a). Demand chain management-The implementation. *Orion*, *27*(2), 119–145. doi:10.5784/27-2-111

Ericsson, D. (2011b). Demand chain management-The evolution. *Orion*, *27*(1), 45–81. Retrieved from http://www.orssa.org.za

Mohan, A., & Deshmukh, A. K. (2013). Conceptualization and Development of a Supply Chain-Customer Relationship Management (SC^{2}RM) Synergy Mode. *Journal of Supply Chain Management and Systems*, *2*(3), 9–25.

APPENDIX 1

Table 6. AHP calculation for criteria or main variables

	SV	TV	OV	PV	WV	EV	CI	R1	CR
SV	1	1	7	0.486	1.469	3.019	0.006	0.58	0.010
TV	1	1	5	0.435	1.312	3.015			
OV	0.142	0.2	1	0.078	0.234	3.002			
	2.142	2.2	13			3.012			

SV=Strategic Variables, TV=Tactical Variables, OV=Operational Variables
***PV=Priority Vectors, WV=Weighted Vectors, EV=Eigen Vectors, CI=Consistency Index**
RI=, CR=Consistency Ration. *here on the notations will have same expansion in the upcoming tables.

APPENDIX 2

Table 7. AHP calculation for sub-criterion-strategic variables

	IM	CSM	SRM	TMCS	CM	PV	WV	EV	CI	RI	CR
IM	1	1	0.2	1	0.5	0.105	0.583	5.516	0.106	1.12	0.095
CSM	1	1	0.333	0.5	0.333	0.095	0.502	5.283			
SRM	5	3	1	3	2.000	0.405	2.216	5.461			
TMCS	1	2	0.333	1	3.000	0.210	1.190	5.661			
CM	2	3	0.5	0.333	1.000	0.182	0.952	5.208			
	10	10	2.366	5.833	6.833			5.426			

IM=Information Management, CSM=Customer Service Management, SRM=Supplier Relationship Management, TMCS=Top-management Commitment and Support, CM=Category Management.

APPENDIX 3

Table 8. AHP calculation for sub-criterion-tactical variables

	SCL	MO	AP	CRM	PV	WV	EV	CI	RI	CR
SCL	1	1	0.2	0.111	0.066	0.270	4.042	0.019	0.9	0.021
MO	1	1	0.142	0.2	0.070	0.285	4.063			
AP	5	7	1	1	0.418	1.689	4.041			
CRM	9	5	1	1	0.444	1.816	4.083			
	16	14	2.342	2.311			4.057			

SCL=Supply Chain Leagility, MO=Marketing Orientation, AP=Assortment Planning,, CRM=Customer Relationship Management

APPENDIX 4

Table 9. AHP calculation for sub-criterion-operational variables

	PM	InvM	CT	PV	WV	EV	CI	R1	CR
PM	1	2	7	0.615	1.84809	3.00493	0.00132	0.58	0.00228
InvM	0.5	1	3	0.2924	0.87773	3.00225			
CT	0.14286	0.33333	1	0.0926	0.27793	3.00075			
	1.64286	3.33333	11			3.00264			
PM=Purchasing Management, InvM=Inventory Management, CT=Category Tactics									

Chapter 11
Recommender System

Avinash Navlani
Devi Ahilya Vishwavidyalaya, India

Nidhi Dadhich
Devi Ahilya Vishwavidyalaya, India

ABSTRACT

With the increase in user choices and rapid change in user preferences, various methods required to capture such increasing choices and changing preferences. Online systems require quick adaptability. Another aspect is that with the increase in a number of items and users, computation time increases considerably. Thus system needs parallel computing platform to run newer designed recommender system techniques. Recommendation system helps people to tackle the choice overload problem and help to select the efficient one. Even though there is lots of work have been done in the recommendation system, still there is a problem in handling various types of data and basically to handle a large amount of data. The main aim of the recommendation system is to provide the best opinion from the available large amount of data. The present chapter describes an introduction to recommender systems, its functions, types, techniques, applications, collaborative filtering, content-based filtering and evaluation of performance.

INTRODUCTION

Recommendation system changes its suggestions in a manner individual search products, information or even another person on the internet. Recommendation system studies the pattern of user surfing to identify what someone will like from the big volume of data. Recommendation system technology has evolved over twenty years using various advanced programming and statistical tools that help the developer in design and implement of efficient recommendation system. It is an information filtering system which will provide relevant and useful suggestions to users. Recommendation system works as a guide, an advisor to people for selecting relevant and useful thing. The goal of Recommender System is to provide the best option in omnipresent alternatives. Recommender System is automatic suggestion system which substitutes the natural process of recommendation like asking to your friends, relatives or through word of mouth. Recommender system begins with our daily life like someone needs a recommendation which is the best newspaper? Which article to read? Which movie to watch? Traditionally,

DOI: 10.4018/978-1-5225-2148-8.ch011

Folks have a tendency to listen, watch and read reviews appeared on Television, radio or newspaper. But now a day's people get the review from the internet using social websites. With the dawn of the internet, resources to use the information have become pervasive in nature but information grows exponentially. The problem arises here is that how to find the right information which meets customer's need. The user was finding it very difficult to arrive at right choice with this flood of information. The rapid development of e-business domain leads to increase the amount of available information. The increasing number of alternative for items (e.g. movies, books, music, food, and news) makes harder for the user to decide which item to choose. Alternatives, instead of raising gain, it started to fall user satisfaction level. The choices are very helpful for decision making but it is not necessary more choices are always better. The main problem arises in today's information world: overloaded and not related answers. To, solve this problem Recommender System came into the picture. Recommender system provides avenues to predict rating and preferences given by the user for an item, i.e., it will contract the choices, discover the options and find the things that are fascinating to the users.

In this chapter, we shall attempt to answer such question. We will discuss what Recommender system is? and how it will deal with information overload? What are the functions of the Recommender System after this, we will learn about different types and techniques for Recommender System. Next part contains the applications for Recommender System, and we will learn how to give recommendation using collaborative filtering and content-based approach. At last, we shall also discuss the evaluation of Recommender System.

RECOMMENDER SYSTEM

With the dawn of the internet, a resource to recover and utilize the information has become pervasive but information is growing exponentially. The problem arises here, how to find the right information which meets customer needs. In this context, Recommender System can save us from going through such huge information. The rapid development of e-business market leads to increase the amount of information available. Customers were finding it very hard to achieve the right decision from this overloaded information. This flood of information creates a problem in decision making.

E-business ventures are instead of producing benefits, started losing users' due to high load of information. The choices are always good but more choices are not always better. The recommendation is generated based upon the data about user, types of knowledge, previous transactions then the following step is implicit/ explicit feedback input. Each user action and feedback kept in a dataset and utilized in next recommendation. A recommender system is new research area as compared to other information tools and technique.

A recommender system is appealing and increased user interest which helps in engaging customer on the website. A recommender system is software tools and technique providing suggestions, advice for products that is useful to the user (liebowitz, 2010) (Park & Jang, 2013). This suggestion helps in decision-making processes such as purchasing items finding best holiday destination, listen to music albums, finding best hotel deals, and interesting articles and much more. In Recommender system, products or items are something that is recommended to the user. Recommendations provided by the system must be efficient and useful. Recommender System provides the best options from available alternatives.

Figure 1. Recommender System

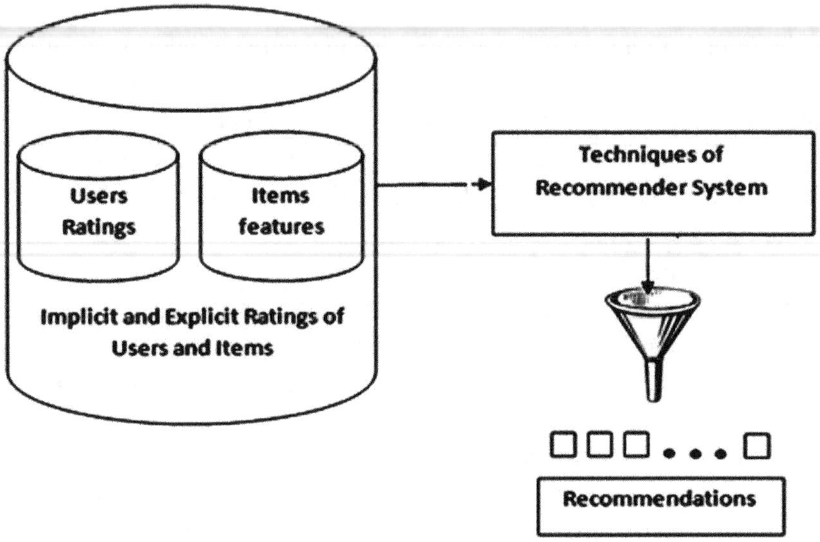

Recommender system fills the gap between customer, alternative, and providers. Recommender is very helpful from both perspective consumer, and supplier. From a consumer side, it will contract the choices, discover the options, and find the things that are fascinating to a consumer. From this, it will increase good customer relationship management, trust, loyalty and increase profit.

FUNCTIONS OF RECOMMENDER SYSTEM

From Service Provider Perspective (Ricci, Rokach, & Shapira, 2010)

Increases the Number of Sold Items

This is the most significant function of a business recommender system. It says that Recommender System is capable of increase sale of those items which are given recommendations using any recommender system technique, as compared to those items which are sold without recommendation. This will be achieved as recommending most suitable items to the user. From the supplier's perspective, the key objective is to introduce Recommender System, which raises the number of transactions, i.e. the more

Figure 2. Solution of information overload

customers acknowledge the recommendations, the more items will consume. Recommender System increases the quantity of items sold via suggesting items to users which are previously rated or visited by the user himself or other users.

Increases the Selling of Diverse/Unpopular Items

Another function of Recommender System is to increase the selling of such items which are less popular and are not in the list of user's interest. Such items don't provide any recommendation and are not very much visited by users. As it is hard for any service provider to advertise such items which are not likely to suit user's interest, Recommender System is beneficial here because it advertises unpopular and diverse items to users.

Increases the User's Satisfaction

While using recommender system with/on any application or website users will find it interesting. Well, designed recommender system gives a better experience to the users. It is relevant from a user-computer interaction perspective and users will enjoy working with such system. This will enhance the system practices and the probability to keep the recommendations conventional.

Increases User's Reliability

When the user is regular on any website and loyal to it, that website identifies the previous customer and take them as valuable customers. Thus, the longer the user will spend time on the site, a more efficient the prediction model, which implies that system represents the user's perspective.

Understands the User's Need

Recommender System predicts exact user's needs on the basis of user's tastes and previous browsing history. Recommender system acts as user's requirement brain which identifies user need and suggests required accessory items on the basis of other user purchasing habits.

Some Other Functions of Recommender System

Herlocker et al. (Herlocker, Konstan, Terveen, & Riedl, 2004) identified ten popular tasks of Recommender System that can assist in the implementation of Recommender System.

Recommending the Best Items

Recommend all best items that fulfill the customer's desire or wants. It is useful in medical and financial products. Financial products such as new insurance policy, health insurance, and tax saving schemes which will beneficial for every working consumer can be recommended to all working customers.

Footnote in Context

In this long-term preference of the user is important. For example online movie and TV shows can be recommended on the footnote of the movies and TV shows. Such footnote will keep engaging the customer in the long run.

Recommend in a Queue/Sequence

Recommender Systems not only a single item but also a queue or sequence of items (e.g. music track, books, TV programs) as a whole is pretty good idea.

Recommend in a Bundle

Recommender system suggests not only one item, but it will suggest a group of items. These alternative suggestions can be considered as available and suggested options on the basis of likes dislikes of other people and users own previous browsing history.

Just Searching/Surfing

In this user don't have an intention of buying or purchasing, they just browse the catalog. Recommender system assists the user to browse the items (what is likely to like). In such a way user will get the item or product information, which will help him to make decisions and maybe in future user find the product useful. This will increase chances of purchasing item.

Finding Trustworthy Recommendations

Some customers don't trust on recommendations provided by a recommender system. So recommender system is design or implemented in such a way that it provide trustworthy or credible recommendations. How good the recommender system is estimated by user experience or user preference.

Improve the Profile

It is related to a user what the user like or dislike. It is helpful in providing the personalized recommendation. It is a very important task in recommendation system. The user behavior or user profile helpful in providing good recommendation otherwise same or average recommendations are given.

Utter Self

Some users are interested in giving their opinions, rating, and belief. They don't care about any recommendation at all. They express their behavior what he likes or dislikes. It is important to take in account user experience. Such active user's feedback helps in increasing the profit and holds the user on that application.

Lend a Hand to Other

Some users are willing to contribute by giving information. They assess the items, gives feedback so that society gets advantage from their contribution. In this way, recommender system gets information regularly to updates its perception according user's need. For example, a user purchases a new product and gives their feedback and rating. He knows that his feedback will help the other user who will buy the product.

Influence Other

There is a user whose main goals are to influence other users in buying a product. So this will help in the recommendation. In this, there are two side good recommendation and bad recommendation. The following point indicates the role of a recommender system. From the above point, we conclude that the role of a recommender system is diverse. Diversity leads to a range of application of recommender system. In various domains, recommender systems are used like movie, TV, book coffee, tourism, retail, finance, automobile and much more.

TYPES OF RECOMMENDER SYSTEM

Non-Personalized Recommender System

Non-personalized Recommender Systems essentially do not take in account user's model to provide recommendations; thus, non-personalized Recommender Systems recommend the same items for every user. For example, they can present to users unseen items sorted out by popularity (e.g. the Top Pop algorithm) or by average rating (e.g. Movie average algorithm). It is commonly seen in newspapers and magazine. For example, top ten best places to visit India, best seller, most popular. Non-personalization is not so trending research issue.

Personalized Recommender System

Personalized Recommender Systems build a specific user's model to provide individual recommendations. The goal of this type of recommender systems is to offer recommendations by utilizing available

Figure 3. Non–Personalized Recommender System

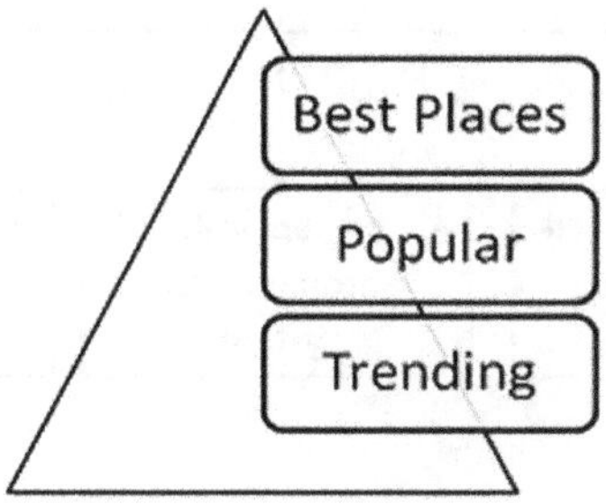

user previous browsing history and profile. Output recommendations were arranged in ordered lists of items. It dynamically filters the available information sources on the basis of personal user information and build personalized user information base, and offers assistance to the user according to their interest (Ricci, Rokach, & Shapira, 2010).

TECHNIQUES OF RECOMMENDER SYSTEM

The main goal of Recommender System is to predict the product's utility and link with this utility to customer need and profile. There are two approaches achieve this goal. First one is based on similar user taste and preferences named as collaborative based recommender system and second one based on past behavior of an individual. These recommendations must be fruitful and interesting to the user. Bruke (Burke R., 2007) (Burke R., 2002) had given detailed overview and classification of recommender system techniques. They classified techniques into five different classes of recommendation approaches.

Content-Based Recommender System

Content-based recommender system generates recommendations on the basis of ratings given by the user in the past. In such recommender system, final suggested items are the ones that were the user preferred in the previous visit. Similarity among items computed on the basis of a feature associated with items. Suppose, if the user liked a TV series in the past and the feature of the TV series is the genre, liked TV series is comedy one then Recommender System will recommend the next on the basis of genre, next recommendation is a comedy TV series. From the above example, the system learns the behavior of the user and gives the recommendation on the basis of that behavior. It plays a diverse role in individual advertising. According to (Gorakala & Michele, 2015) for building such type of recommender system two important points are:

1. How to find the similarity between items?
2. How to create and update user profiles continuously?

Figure 4. Techniques of Recommender System

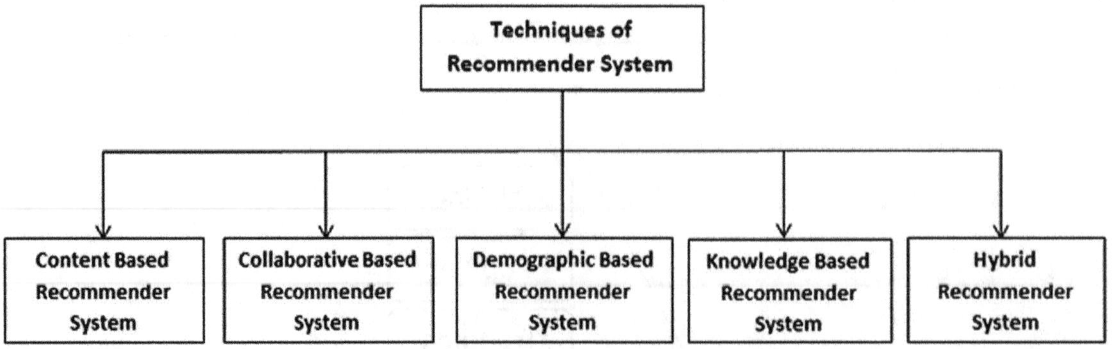

This system does not require a large amount of data for better recommendation accuracy; it only considers users past likes and properties of the items.

Collaborative-Based Recommender System

Collaborative based recommendation system or collaborative filtering technique is based on finding similarities between like-minded people i.e. this technique is basically compared different users having similar likes and recommends accordingly. So the algorithm depends on similar user or items. Collaborative based recommender systems can categorize in two parts first one is item based collaborative recommender systems and the second one is user-based collaborative recommender systems.

Item-Based Collaborative Recommender System

Such systems suggest items, which are most similar with items purchased by the user. It computes the similarity between items.

User-Based Collaborative Recommender System

Such systems suggest items, which are most preferred by the similar user. It computes the similarity between users.

Basic intuition behind this technique is that if two users share the same likes in the past that are they like the same movie then they may have same preferences in future. The movie recommendation in Netflix is good recommendation example of this type of recommendation.

For this type of filtering, it is required a large set of data from its filtered data collaboratively on the basis of user preferences and likes. According to (Gorakala & Michele, 2015) for building such type of recommender system three important points are:

1. How to calculate the similarity between users?
2. How to calculate the similarity between items?
3. How to deal with new items and the new user whose data is not known?

One important thing related to collaborative filtering is that it only works on user interest does not work on the property or content of the item to recommend that means it matches features with respect to the user only and it requires a large set of data for more accurate result.

Demographic-Based Recommender System

In the demographic recommendation system, the recommendations are basically done on the basis of demographic features such as age, occupation, salary, and qualification etc. of the particular user. Basically, this type of recommendation system is used to avoid cold start problem. Demographic recommendation system finds similarity according to demographic attributes for example In marketing domain we say it select age attribute and try to find the group of same age group people for targeting customer for a new product.

Knowledge-Based Recommender System

In knowledge-based recommender system, given recommendations depends on the domain knowledge, how the certain feature meets user needs and preference. The best example of the knowledge-based recommender system is case-based recommender system. Another type of knowledge-based recommender system is constraint-based recommender system. Case-based recommender system determines suggestions using similarity metrics whereas Constraint-based recommender system utilizes explicit rules contained in predefined knowledge-bases. Such explicit rules associate customer need with item features. According to (Gorakala & Michele, 2015) for building such type of recommender system two important points are:

1. Which type of knowledge about the items is taken into the model?
2. How is user information collected explicitly?

Hybrid Recommender System

In hybrid based recommender system recommendation are given on combining on any two or three technique that's why it is called a hybrid. The hybrid recommender system is the blend of the at least two or may have more than two techniques that mean use the advantage of the first technique to overcome the disadvantage of other technique. For example, collaborative recommender system suffers from new item problem, whereas in the content based recommender system there is no such problem. Content-based recommender system predicts using feature description of items, so on the basis of that, it can recommend items more accurately and efficiently. According to (Gorakala & Michele, 2015), important points for building hybrid based recommendation system are:

1. What technique should be combined to achieve the business solution?
2. How should we combine various techniques and their result for better predictions?

APPLICATIONS OF RECOMMENDER SYSTEM

In this section, we will discuss several application domains of Recommender System. Applications of Recommender System are as follows:

E-Governance Recommender Systems

Electronic governance stands for the utilization of the information, internet and technologies to perform government operations in order to provide superior services to its citizens and business people. With the increase number users and shift of governance operations on the internet causes the problem of information overload. The increase in information overloading obstructs the efficiency of services offered by e-governance portals and various problems in providing correct information to the correct user. This problem can be solved using recommender system within the E-governance services. This will help citizens to adapt and access services supplied by public administrations of government system provided to citizens through e-government service, but after using recommendation it lowers the problems of citizens regarding the government work and administration work. In the recommendation, the multi-agent system was proposed. This proposed recommender system searches and offers more concerning services for users according to their need and profile. In government to business services, most of the services offered from a business perception. A Recommender System named STEF (Smart Trade Exhibition Finder) offers appropriate trade fair to whom their business has been urbanized.

Online Business Recommender System

Dozens of recommender systems have been created for online business applications. Generally, most of the systems emphasize on suggestions produced for the individual user. Such systems offer business-to-consumer (B2C) and business-to-business (B2B) services, which intend to provide suggestions about goods and services to customers as well as business users. In short, online business recommender system works to improve the growth of the business and generates more profit to the business. It provides customers interesting products and attractive deals so that customers can show their interest towards it and pay for the product so that business deals can be cracked successfully. To improve keyword directory administrators in B2B marketplaces preserve updated product records and use ontology and knowledge in recommender systems for producing keyword-based recommendations.

Online Shopping Recommender System

In last two decades, a large number of exclusive online shopping portals such as Amazon, eBay and many more local and global portals were introduced in the marketplace. Most of them have been developed

Figure 5. Applications of Recommender System

recommender systems to offer products to visited customers. Online shopping is a highly dedicated and acceptable field of business and computer world. Portals utilize the product or item rating given by the user who purchased products. For example, on Amazon portal customer are capable of giving feedback and ratings. These feedbacks and ratings will be the foundation for generating recommendations. Tag features are one more way to associate user-item data. Collaborative Filtering and social tag analysis both are most successful approaches. Hybrid environment system will utilize independently or cooperatively both ratings and tags to improve recommendations. Major online shopping portals suggest products by analyzing demographic characteristics of customer and seller, and past purchasing behaviors. In short, online shopping recommender systems can execute on the online platform. Developer interacts with product researcher and tries to discover more features and try to quantify features to improve the user experience.

Online Library Recommender System

Online libraries are the collection of e-Books, articles, journals, and case studies with related services offered to its member. Online libraries use recommender system to provide users ability to search and select knowledgeable and useful information and services. Generally, online library recommender system adopts hybrid recommendation approach. Hybrid recommender system takes the advantages of all the other recommendation techniques and that's why it is mostly used here. The Stanford University Digital Library Project (Porcel & Herrera-Viedma, 2010) is hybrid a recommender system which is a combination of content and collaborative filtering approaches. CYLADES were introduced to give improved personalized digital library services (Renda & Straccia, 2005). CYCLADES gives an incorporated space for library users, college communities, and other communities in extremely individualized and supple way. Recommendation algorithms can work previous and modified information.

E-Learning Recommender System

Since the early 2000s, E-learning has become more popular amongst the new generation for the purpose of institutional knowledge and study knowledge based on the growth of conventional classroom teaching system. E-Learning recommender systems provide the learner's facility to choose study/learning material, subjects and courses of their interest area, in the form of study portal where students can search and select their related options. In Last couple of years various e-learning recommender systems have been evolved. Zaiane (Zaiane, 2002) developed autonomous software known as an agent that uses association rule mining to build a recommendation model that captures learners searching patterns and use the model to suggest courses according to the area of interest of learners. The recommended suggestions improve learner's experience. A Personalized e-learning recommender system (PLRS) was introduced in the work of Chen et al. (Lu, 2004). In the PLRS system once all the databases for learning material or activities is being created and the learner registers themselves and their information is created by system in the form of the database, the PLRS uses an additional study model to identify user's requirement for learning and later uses the corresponding set of rules for recommending study material. The collection of leaner's preferences initially performed by Fuzzy item response theory (FIRT) (Chen, Duh, & Liu, 2004) on the basis of preferences generated via user click behavior patterns. In FIRT learners give a fuzzy response in the form of the percentage of what they have understood while learning courseware. In an additional e-learning recommender system, Courseware Agent, produced by Farzan and Brusilovsky (Farzan &

Brusilovsky, 2006), students can give their response in ambiguous and unambiguous form. Students can select difficulty level of offered courses with respect to their career objective. When students register for any course, they can give their implicit feedback about it. The main advantage of this system is to provide the suggestion for the courses selected by students to overcome their difficulties and also provide facility to take advice about the courses they have opted, taking help of the advisor. Recently various MOOC (massive open online courses) platforms such as Coursera, edx, Udacity also uses e-learning recommendation for joining new courses. The study of E-learning recommender system inculcates that designing personalized course recommendation should take a count learners' requirements.

Online Tourism Recommender System

Many government websites, tourism websites and other personal blogs over the internet and the web provide plenty of information on tourism for tourists and give many opportunities to find tourist places according to their interests. Mobile devices are also very useful to search places to visit through different applications on tourism. Tourist places and locations can be easily accessed by tourists but due to a large number of tourism options makes it difficult for tourists to decide which alternative they choose. Online tourism recommender System is implemented to give recommendations to tourists on the basis of their previous traveling plans and personal information. On the other hand, some sources offer only attractive and popular locations and some systems provide tour packages/plans that also include all the accommodations, transportation, and restaurants information.

COLLABORATIVE FILTERING

A recommender system is modern research area applications that work as a filter in the world of information overload. Recommender systems suggest the user list of recommended items on the basis of their likes or preference. Generally, such kinds of systems reduce user's effort and time in searching information. One of the great examples is 'Netflix'. Netflix is USA based company provides DVD on rent. It uses collaborative filtering to predict ratings for movies and recommend the user list of movies which customer can rent. Similarly Pandora similarly provides a rating for music. All such systems can classified as recommender systems.

Collecting Opinions

This is the first step, in which response of the users were collected. User assigns rating between 1 and 5 as shown in Table 1. Here empty cell indicates a missing value i.e. user did not rate the place.

Similarity Measures

Manhattan Distance

Manhattan distance is defined as the absolute distance between two points or absolute difference between two points x and y (Ricci, Rokach, & Shapira, 2010) . Manhattan distance is easiest distance measure. In two dimension case, each person is represented by (x, y) points. It is calculated as

Table 1. User – Item Ratings

	Yuvam	Surbhi	Namrata	Pragya	Vikas	Kuldeep	Aman	Bhavna
P1	3.5	2	5	3	-	-	5	3
P2	2	3.5	1	4	4	4.5	2	-
P3	-	4	1	4.5	1	4	-	-
P4	4.5	4	3	-	4	5	3	5
P5	5	2	5	3	-	5	5	4
P6	1.5	3.5	1	4.5	-	4.5	4	2.5
P7	2.5	-	-	4	4	4	5	3
P8	2	3	-	2	1	4	-	-

$$d(x,y) = \sum_{k=1}^{n} \left| x_k - y_k \right| \quad (1)$$

Euclidean Distance

Euclidean distance defined as distance between items. It is the square root of the sum of the squares of the differences of the data points. Whenever distance between two points *d* is less, it means two data points are same. When distance *d* is large, it means the two data points are not same. it means two points are similar. Euclidean distance mathematically can be defined as:

$$d(x,y) = \sqrt{\sum_{k=1}^{n} \left(x_k - y_k \right)^2} \quad (2)$$

Where n stands for number of features or dimensions and x_k and y_k are the kth features (Components) of data objects x and y, respectively (Ricci, Rokach, & Shapira, 2010). These two distance measures are helpful to measure similarity. It is not suitable when there is a missing value.

Minkowski Distance

Minkowski distance is the more generalized form of Euclidean distance and Manhattan distance and it is expressed as

$$d(x,y) = \left(\sum_{k=1}^{n} \left| x_k - y_k \right|^r \right)^{\frac{1}{r}} \quad (3)$$

Where, r is the degree of distance. On the basis of value of r, Minkowski distance is recognized with particular distance measures:

r = 1, represents Manhattan distance;
r = 2, represents Euclidean distance;

Pearson Correlation Coefficient

Suppose we have two people, first person rating is between middle i.e.2 and 3 and second person rating is between 4 and 5. Some person likes everything whereas other is in the middle. This variability creates a problem and this problem is fixing by Pearson correlation coefficient. Pearson correlation coefficient was given by Karl Pearson its value is lie between -1 to +1. -1 indicates that he is not satisfied or agreed whereas +1 indicates that he is satisfied or strongly agreed. The formula for Pearson is as follows

$$r = \frac{\sum_{i=1}^{n}\left(X_i - \bar{X}\right)\left(Y_i - \bar{Y}\right)}{\sum_{i=1}^{n}(X_i - \bar{X})^2 \sum_{i=1}^{n}(Y_i - \bar{Y})^2} \tag{4}$$

Cosine Similarity

Cosine similarity measures angle between two vectors. Cosine similarity can be used to compare two documents using term- frequency vector. Cosine value 0 means that there is no match. Cosine values closer to 1, the greater the match between two vectors. Cosine similarity can be represented as

$$\cos(x, y) = \frac{x.y}{\|x\| \times \|y\|} \tag{5}$$

Here (.) represent dot product and x represents the length of vector X and it is given by

$$\|x\| = \sqrt{\sum_{i=1}^{n} x_i^2} \tag{6}$$

Now the question arises here how to decide which distance measure is used? Pearson correlation coefficient used when user rate an item on scale 1-5 in decimals or grade-inflation (means different users are using different scales) Euclidean and Manhattan distance is used when data is dense or all feature values are non –zero. In this magnitude of attribute is important. Cosine similarity used when user data is sparse.

Weighted Scoring Method

Weighted scoring method generates a list of superior items against the given priority or weights. This weight ranks the reviewers. In tourist recommender system, we view the profile of a person who has most similar preferences (or destination likes whish are not visited by user) to user we are going to rec-

Figure 6. Steps for Implementing Collaborative-Based Recommender System

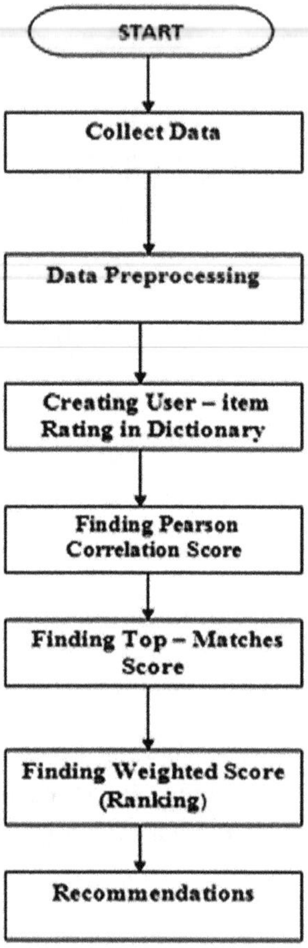

ommend. In this scenario may be in some cases reviewer's ratings are not available that user will like or may be like destinations which were got poor reviews from reviewer. In order to resolve such issues, researcher or developer need to assign a score to destination by using weighted score. This score helps in order the reviewrs response.

$$x = \frac{\sum_{i=1}^{n} \left(x_i * w_i\right)}{\sum_{i=1}^{n} w_i} \tag{7}$$

User ratings given in Table 1 are in grade-inflation (or in assigned different scale 1-5) so Pearson correlation coefficient can be used to calculate similarity and after that weighted score used to generate recommendations. The final score for Table 1 missing ratings or score calculated via multiplying each item with similarity and then all products are summed up together. Finally, the scores were normalized by dividing sum by the sum of similarity. Calculated predicted ratings for collaborative filtering shown bow in Table 2.

Table 2. Predicted Ratings

	Yuvam	Surbhi	Namrata	Pragya	Vikas	Kuldeep	Aman	Bhavna
P1	3.5	2	5	3	3.9	3.85	5	3
P2	2	3.5	1	4	4	4.5	2	2.8
P3	2.5	4	1	4.5	1	4	1	3.1
P4	4.5	4	3	4.0	4	5	3	5
P5	5	2	5	3	4.5	5	5	4
P6	1.5	3.5	1	4.5	2.9	4.5	4	2.5
P7	2.5	4	3.7	4	4	4	5	3
P8	2	3	2.5	2	1	4	2.0	2.96

CONTENT BASED FILTERING

Content based Filtering is a technique which recommends items to the user according item's properties and also by analyzing the profile of the user that is their past likes and dislike. This recommendation system may use in various domains from news articles to recommending different items such as sales, movies, serial, songs etc. The details and structure of various systems differ. Content based filtering works on similarity that is similarity in purchased or visited items. Common items were recommended means for describing the items that may be recommended, the basic object is to create a user profile which explains the item types liked by user. In tourism recommender suppose a person like historic places like forts and museums then our next recommend will be a historic place. Similarly movie recommender recommends movie on the basis of previous liked movie's actors, director, and genre.

Now, calculate the similarity between features of places using nearest neighbor. Here in Table 3, P1, P2…P5 are products or items and F1, F2 ….F5 are features of product. Cell value 0 represents dislike and 1 represents like. Another way of representing likes and dislikes are shown in Table 4. In Table 4, L represents like and D represents dislike. With the help of above given Tables 3 and 4, we need to find out the nearest neighbor of this P6 (0, 0, 1, 0, 1) or (D, D, L, D, L) product. P5 is most nearest neighbor of product P5.

Table 3. Item- feature Ratings

	Feature (F1)	Feature (F2)	Feature (F3)	Feature (F4)	Feature (F5)
P1	1	0	1	0	0
P2	1	0	0	1	0
P3	1	0	1	0	0
P4	0	1	0	0	1
P5	0	0	1	0	1

K-Nearest Neighbor Algorithm

K-Nearest Neighbor can be used for classification as well as regression prediction problems. This algorithm is also known as a lazy learner because it stores all of its data, like preferences, rating, like, dislike, purchasing history of user, features of item or item description in memory and using similarity measure classifies a new item (attraction) by matching it to the previously rated item and find the k nearest neighbors. In other words, K-nearest neighbor finds a set of similar places that attracts user. For regression, this algorithm computes average of their opinions and figures out an approximate value at what rating or like or dislike for particular item. For classification, KNN algorithm find K nearest neighbors to take vote for predict class of given object.

After that classification is done, classifier perform mapping among attributes of objects for classify known as features and classes known as tags. Recommender system can be consider recommend item or not as classification problem. Classification problem uses number of features for predicting list of items. Classification problem can be of two types supervised and unsupervised classification. In supervised classification, class label is known in advance .In unsupervised classification, the class labels or categories are not available.

EVALUATION OF RECOMMENDER SYSTEM

In this section, we evaluate the performance of a recommender system. For evaluation process, we can use several metrics such as prediction accuracy and decision-based metrics.

Prediction Accuracy

Predictive metrics objective is to weigh against the predicted labels to the actual labels. Overall results generated via average of the dispersion. Prediction accuracy is widely accepted feature in the evaluation of recommender system. Recommender engine predicts user views about items or evaluate the chances of next purchase. So the engineers and statistician from all over the world are developing recommender algorithms for better prediction results. Measuring accuracy of any recommender algorithm is not affected by design of user interface, so most of the performance evaluation experiments performed offline.

Table 4. User -Ratings

	Feature (F1)	Feature (F2)	Feature (F3)	Feature (F4)	Feature (F5)
P1	L	D	L	D	D
P2	L	D	D	L	D
P3	L	D	L	D	D
P4	D	L	D	D	L
P5	D	D	L	D	L

Figure 7. Content-based recommender system

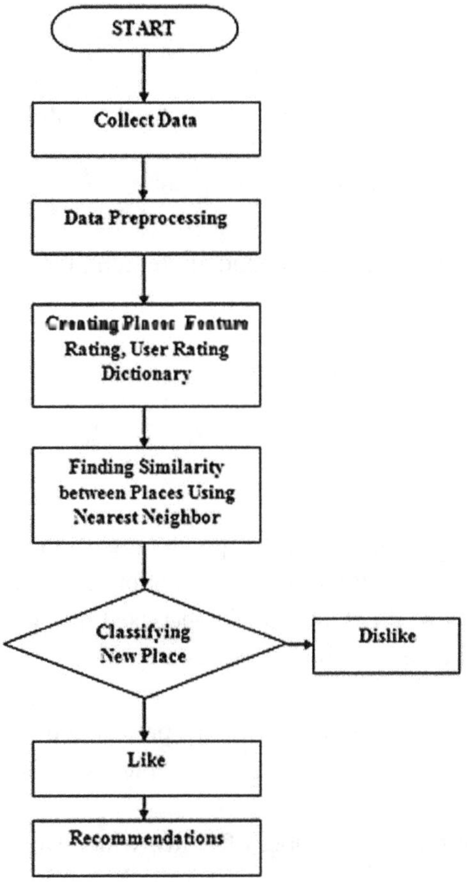

Mean Absolute Error

Mean Absolute Error (MAE) determines the absolute difference between the expected and the actual value. It is also known as absolute.

$$MAE = \frac{1}{n}\sum_{i=1}^{n}\left|x_i - \hat{x}_i\right| \tag{8}$$

Where x_i is actual value and $\hat{x}_i$ is estimated or forecasted value.

Mean Squared Error (MSE)

Mean Squared Error (MSE) determines the squared difference between the expected and the actual value:

$$MSE = \frac{1}{T} \sum_{(u,i)\in T} (\hat{r}_{ui} - r_{ui})^2 \tag{9}$$

Where $\hat{r}_{ui}$ is expected value and r_{ui} is actual value for user u and item i.

Root Mean Squared Error (RMSE)

RMSE is the most widely accepted and recommended prediction accuracy metric. It offers more consistent results in various applications.

$$RMSE = \sqrt{MSE} \tag{10}$$

Decision-Based Metrics

Such type of metrics assesses the top-N or most popular suggestions offered to a user. Generally, suggestions are an order of items, items ordered in descending priority. But, results of these metrics do not consider the ordering or ranking of the items. Decision-Based metrics uses four basic building blocks for measuring performance. Four basic building blocks are:

- **True Positive (TP):** It represents number of items preferred by users from recommended Items.
- **False Positive (FP):** It represents number of items which were not preferred by users from recommended Items.
- **True Negative (TN):** It represents number of items, which were not recommended and not preferred by users.
- **False Negative (FN):** It represents number of items, which were not recommended but preferred by users.

These four building blocks were arranged in a square matrix known as confusion matrix. With the help of confusion matrix various evaluation measures such as accuracy, error, recall, precision and F-measures can be computed. In evaluation of recommender, if an item has not been visited or purchased by user it means doesn't like the item. In short, we can say that accuracy measure fits to those problems, where resultant class labels uniformly distributed and remaining metrics such as precision and recall are suitable for problems, where resultant class labels are rare for example in cancer or HIV prediction models. Core metrics used for recommender systems are precision and recall.

Table 5. Confusion- Matrix

	Relevant	**Not relevant**
Recommended	TP	FP
Not recommended	FN	TN

Precision

Precision represents measure of exactness. Exactness is number of items actually preferred or liked by user out of all the recommended items. Precision computes the portion of appropriate items to the recommended items.

$$precision = \frac{TP}{TP + FN} \tag{11}$$

Recall

Recall measures the completeness or coverage. Completeness is number of items actually preferred by user out of all relevant items like by user (it consist recommended and non-recommended item like by user). Recall is also known as Sensitivity or True positive rate. Recall measure can be com $recall = \frac{TP}{TP + FN}$

(12)

F-Measure

F-measure is a combination of *Precision* and *Recall* measures results. It is the weighted harmonic means of both precision and recall measures. Here, β is a no-n negative weight to recall as to precision. When the value of β is 1, it means precision and recall is equally weighted and β is 0.5, it means precision is twice as much as recall.

$$F_\beta = \frac{\left(1 + \beta^2\right).\left(precision.recall\right)}{\left(\beta^2.precision\right).recall} \tag{13}$$

CONCLUSION

During last few decades, the use of recommendation system is increasing to that point so as many well-known successful business ventures depend on it. Recommender system provides the best solution for information overload problem provides the best alternatives from available all the alternatives. Recommendation system in nowadays is an essential requirement, we need options suggestions in every field of life whether we want to purchase a mobile phone, dress or daily household thing our human mind needs various suggestions so that it can select best suited from all this large number of products. Recommendation system helps to select right thing from a large number of suggestions by analyzing various attributes of that particular item feature and user profile. Content-based approach suggests products that were previously preferred by the customer. It relies on item features while collaborative filtering approach recommends items on basis of likes and dislikes of other customers i.e. it compares preference of customer with other customers. In the future, we look forward to seeing an increasing amount of recommender systems, its applications in several fields to connect users and solve an information overload problem. Some of these challenges go beyond the current trends of scalability and data sparsity.

REFERENCES

Burke, R. (2002). Hybrid recommender systems: Survey and experiments. *User Modeling and User-Adapted Interaction*, *12*(4), 331–370. doi:10.1023/A:1021240730564

Burke, R. (2007). Hybrid web recommender systems. In *The AdaptiveWeb*. Springer.

Chen, C., Duh, L., & Liu, C. (2004). A personalized courseware recommendation system based on fuzzy item response theory.*IEEE International Conference on e-Technology, e-Commerce and e-Service* (pp. 305–308.). IEEE. doi:10.1109/EEE.2004.1287327

Cornelis, C., Guo, X., Lu, J., & Zhang, G. (2005). A fuzzy relational approach to event recommendation. *Proceedings of 2nd Indian International Conference on Artificial Intelligence*, 2231–2242.

Farzan, R., & Brusilovsky, P. (2006). Social navigation support in a course recommendation system. Springer. doi:10.1007/11768012_11

Gorakala, S. K., & Michele, U. (2015). *Building a recommendation system with R*. Packt Publishing.

Guo, X., & Lu, J. (2007). Intelligent e-government services with personalized recommendation techniques. *International Journal of Intelligent Systems*, *22*(5), 401–417. doi:10.1002/int.20206

Herlocker, J. L., Konstan, J. A., Terveen, L. G., & Riedl, J. T. (2004). Evaluating collaborative filtering. *ACM Transactions on Information Systems*, *22*(1), 5–53. doi:10.1145/963770.963772

Lu, J. (2004). Personalized e-learning material recommender system.*Proc. of the International Conf. on Information Technology for Application*, 374-379.

Park, J.-Y., & Jang, S. (2013). Confused by too many choices? Choice overload in tourism. *Tourism Management, 35*, 1-12. doi:10.1016/j.tourman.2012.05.004

Porcel, C., & Herrera-Viedma, E. (2010). Dealing with incomplete information in a fuzzy linguistic recommender system to disseminate information in university digital libraries. *Journal Knowledge-Based Systems, 23*(1), 32–39.

Liebowitz, J. (2010). *Business Analytics An Introduction.* Boca Raton, FL: PressCRC

Renda, M., & Straccia, U. (2005). A personalized collaborative digital library environment: A model and an application. *Information Processing & Management*, *41*(1), 5–21. doi:10.1016/j.ipm.2004.04.007

Ricci, F., Rokach, L., & Shapira, B. (2010). *Recommender systems handbook.* New York: Springer-Verlag New York, Inc.

Zaiane, O. (2002). Building a recommender agent for e-learning systems. *Proceedings of the International Conference on Computers in Education* (vol. 51, pp. 55–59). Washington, DC: IEEE Computer Society. doi:10.1109/CIE.2002.1185862

Chapter 12
Strengths and Limitations of Social Media Analytics Tools

Dražena Gašpar
University of Mostar, Bosnia and Herzegovina

Mirela Mabić
University of Mostar, Bosnia and Herzegovina

ABSTRACT

The aim of this chapter is to research and present strengths and limitations of social media analytics tools used in the financial sector. Emphasis is on the business point of view that sees the social media analytics as a collection of tools that transform semi-structured and unstructured social data into noteworthy business insight. There are two main aspects of social media analytics: the technology aspect which covers identifying, extracting, and analyzing social media data using sophisticated tools and techniques; and the business aspect which interprets the data findings and aligns them with business goals. Namely, it is simply not enough to have a social media analytics tool; the tool should be strategically aligned to support existing business goals. The chapter offers a framework for easier adoption and implementation of these tools in the financial sector.

INTRODUCTION

Social media analytics is a relatively new, but fast-growing, field. The term appeared in 2009, and since then it has become a buzz word used to describe the practice of gathering data from social networks and blogs to analyze them and make business decisions. Businesses view the chance to use the vast amounts of data produced by social media users to increase brand loyalty, generate leads, drive traffic, and more. Very soon, social media analytics has become successful in finding:Which customers use social media to comment about brand or a new product launch; which posted contents on social media resonate better with customers; which social media conversations about company, product, or services are positive, negative, or neutral; who are the most influential social media followers, fans, or friends; which social media nodesare influential; which social media platforms are generating the most traffic; which keywords and terms are trending.

DOI: 10.4018/978-1-5225-2148-8.ch012

The early implementations of social media analytics were related to marketing and brand management. Namely, consumer and brand discussions became the basis that enabled marketers and brand managers to create value from social media analytics.

The financial sector did not stay immune to the explosive growth of social media. Whether financial institutions like it or not, their customers have discussed their reputations and brands within social networks. However, as a highly regulated industry, the financial sector was slower in the implementation of social media analytics. The first adopters of social media analytics in finance were small private hedge funds. The growth of discussion around capital markets, equities, macroeconomic indicators, and breaking news was the basis that enabled the creation of value by social analytics for financial services. Since 2013, the implementation of social media analytics in the financial sector has evolved significantly regarding structure, depth, and breadth.

The massive use of social media analytics could not be possible without different software tools that support it. The early software tools enabled companies to monitor, listen, and measure their social media efforts. Nevertheless, the market for social media analytics tools has grown rapidly. Indeed, since 2012 it had started to consolidate when large IT providers entered the market with significant acquisitions of smaller, independent companies.

Social media analytics tools are becoming a huge business and can be divided into two broad categories: comprehensive platforms and specific solutions focused on one particular feature, like social monitoring, sentiment analysis, community responsiveness, content analysis, competitive benchmarking, and similar.

The financial sector started with social media monitoring, slowly changing focus on applying advanced social media analytics to create scores, signals, and other derived data from social media. Now, the implementation of social media analytics tools in the finance sector is oriented to the integration of social data, calculation of sentiment index, and use of text analysis as a part of risk assessment. Through intelligent use of social media analytics tools, the financial institutions can ensure enormous values for themselves. Applying these tools to the social data (tweets, blogs, posts, etc.) enable financial institutions to derive customer intelligence, understand the need for specific services or products, develop adequate marketing strategies, and transform customer relationship management into social customer relationship management.

However, besides huge potential benefits offered by social media analytics, some challenges remain. One of the big issues is a lack of standards and methods for mining social data, especially non-Cashtag data. Despite all social media potential, organizations that have implemented social media analytics tools still state complexity and lack of tangible return on investment (ROI) as a big challenge. The main question is how to make effective use of collected social media data. Also, as highly regulated organizations, financial institutions have to ensure that their implementation of social media analytics is in compliance with existing regulations and guidance.

The practical implementation shows that just using of social media analytics software is not enough, that organizations have to consider individuals in the process of analysis and interpretation of collected data. Since software tools are still in the process of maturing, organizations need to understand the limitations and risk that come with investing in these tools.

Financial organizations need to evaluate different software tools to find solutions that fit with their business goals. The concerns that can successfully implement social media analytics tools and integrate them with their business will stand to reap advantage, information, and returns. It is simply not enough to have a social media analytics tool; the tool should be strategically aligned to support existing business goals.

Most of the financial institutions are discovering the challenges of social media analytics, and many are not sure how to proceed. The purpose of this chapter is to provide a clear analysis of the social media analytics tools used in the financial sector, to research their strengths and limitations, and to offer a framework for easier adoption and implementation of these tools in the financial sector.

BACKGROUND

Social media analytics is a relatively new and fast-developing discipline. The Merriam-Webster Collegiate Dictionary added the term *social media* in its dictionary in 2011and stated that this phrase was first used in 2004. The dictionary defines social media as "forms of electronic communication (as Web sites for social networking and microblogging) through which users create online communities to share information, ideas, personal messages, and other content (as videos)" (Merriam-Webster, 2016). Social media offer completely new and different possibilities for organizations that seek two-way communication with their customers. Social media promise real engagement where organizations also see a new way of binding their customers, new revenue opportunities, and lower costs. Nonetheless, if organizations want to achieve these benefits, in order to manage and understand customer interactions they need different methods when engaging in social media; in addition, entities have to change and adapt more quickly (Petrocelli, 2013). In order to ensure quick adaptability, today's organizations need adequate IT support, e.g. platforms that can help both of them to design, publish, and manage social media campaigns and to perform social media analytics for a deeper understanding of customers. According to Gartner (2016), the terms "social media analytics comprise monitoring, analyzing, measuring and interpreting digital interactions and relationships of people, subjects, concepts and content" (p. 1).

Based on an analysis of 27 research papers on social media analytics in the period 2008-2013, Holsapple, Hsiao, and Pakath (2014) proposed an integrated definition of business social media analytics:

Business social media analytics refers to all activities related to gathering relevant social media data, analyzing the gathered data, and disseminating findings as appropriate to support business activities such as intelligence gathering, insight generation, sense making, problem recognition/opportunity detection, problem solution/opportunity exploitation, and/or decision making undertaken in response to sensed business needs. (p. 3706)

This definition is a good starting point for further research related to social media analytics for the following reasons: first, it clearly motivates why a business should choose to apply social media analytics; second, it supports evidence-based decision making; third, it includes both external and internal environments.

Brand awareness and image are the main drivers that force organizations to start using social media. Namely, an organization's engagement in social media can improve a brand name in many ways: by providing customer education, positioning its own business as a source of expertise, giving information about the organization's philanthropic and activities in community, and providing location-specific updates that affect service availability to customers, including closings and changes in opening hours due to weather conditions (Hansche & Chen, 2014).It is not surprising that companies operating in retail and consumer goods sectors are those that are most active on social media. Facebook lists (Facebook,

2016) the following brands with the most fans: Coca-Cola, YouTube, Red Bull, Nike Football, Oreo, PlayStation, Converse All Stars, Starbucks Cofee, and Pepsi.

Social media analytics has come into the limelight of the wide area of analytics as a result of the application of appropriate analytics capabilities to social media (and, as such, user-generated) content, in order to achieve specific goals (Holsapple, Hsiao, & Pakath, 2014). The development of effective and efficient social media analytics techniques appears important in collecting, monitoring, and analyzing social media data and in extracting useful patterns and intelligence from them (He, Wu, Yan, Akula & Shen, 2015). Recent social media analytics researchesare oriented towards sentiment analysis, insight mining, trend analysis, topic modeling, influence analysis and visual analytics. They are more oriented towards *listening* of available user-generated content, and acting upon it (Holsapple, Hsiao, & Pakath, 2014).

Although the Facebook fans' top ten list does not include any financial institution, it does not mean that financial institutions are not present on social media. Table 1 shows the first 10 of 100 banks listed according to Facebook fans (Financial Brand, 2015).

In the financial sector, social data analytics were initially adopted by a small band of hedge funds and high-frequency traders (HFTs)–mostly private (Greenfield, 2014). However, social media have become more attractive to financial institutions after their regulators published official guidelines on the subject, requiring that financial institutions include these guidelines in their risk management programs. The Federal Financial Institutions Examination Council (FFIEC) Guidance came into force in December 2013; it applies to all financial institutions that are regulated by the federal banking agencies. Since when this document was issued, the FFIEC has urged state banking regulators to adopt it for the financial institutions they oversee (Hansche & Chen, 2014).

The second crucial factor that makes it possible for financial discussions to take place on social media is the adoption of the *Cashtag*. Cashtagging is when a discussion is associated with tradable equities by attaching a "$TICKER(s)" tag to content. StockTwits started with this practice in 2008, but it was formally adopted by Twitter in July 2012. There has been an immense increase of Cashtagged discussions in the last years. In comparison with periods from 2011 to 2014, Cashtagged conversations

Table 1. The first ten banks according to Facebook fans (Financial Brand, 2015)

No.	Name	Country	Facebook likes	New likes in the third quarter of 2015
1	ICICI	India	4,016,863	376,091
2	State Bank of India	India	3,851,046	988,811
3	Capital One	USA	3,701,221	201,324
4	GT Bank	Nigeria	3,432,842	399,577
5	Axis	India	3,132,153	44,663
6	Chase	USA	2,917,989	206,060
7	BofA	USA	2,274,439	85,800
8	HDFC	India	2,269,837	12,646
9	Yes	India	2,248,226	97,595
10	CIMB	Malaysia	1,342,010	37,694

on Twitter about Russell 1000 securities increased over 550%, reaching million of messages per quarter (Greenfield, 2014).

The research shows that the financial sector was slower in the adoption of social media (Greenfield, 2014). Although many financial professionals resorted to their own Twitter accounts to follow breaking news or to share articles, real data analytics use cases were still rare.

Nevertheless, as consumer and brand discussions were the breaking point for adoption of social media analytics by marketers and brand managers, the growing discussion about capital markets, macroeconomic indicators, the foreign exchange market, and financial news are the breaking point for higher adoption of social media in the financial sector.

Recent research related to the *large bank content analysis* reviewed and analyzed every Facebook post and Tweet during the first quarter of 2016 (Golesworthy, 2016). The results of content posted on social platforms by financial institutions show that the highest ranked content list is held by sponsorship news –events, teams, and activities sponsored by bank, whilenews on bank philanthropic activitiesand advice (i.e., content related to customer education) are at the third and fourth place respectively (Golesworthy, 2016).

Although essential, content creation is only one element of social media adoption. There have been two schools of thought on the best social-media based financial market evaluation methodologies. The first focuses on evaluating the volumes of social media messages, search engine queries, and Wikipedia hits and edits. The second methodology focuses on endeavors to be ahead of trends in financial markets through the quantitative evaluation of the content of social media messages, known as sentiment analysis (Zheludev, Smith & Aste, 2014).

Social media analytics tools are evolving further, both general and those specialized for financial institutions. This chapter proposes a general framework for the adoption of social media and social media analytics tools in the financial sector.

THE SOCIAL MEDIA ANALYTICS PROCESS

Since the beginnings of the use of Web 2.0 technologies in general, especially of social media or Web 2.0 applications that allow live interaction, the number of users has increased significantly. Nowadays, crowds of people use social media, whether only to browse the posted contents or to actively participate, post contents, share, like, comment, etc. Besides, the amount of contentsbeing operated on a daily basis is almost unimaginable. If we sum how much each user Facebook daily use Facebook, it turns out that approximately one billion Facebook's active users spend circa 20,000 years online every single day. If it is calculated for Twitter, it turns out that circa 140 million active Twitter users send out more than 340 million tweets, has over 4 billion views per day. (Fan & Gordon, 2014).

Exactly for these reasons (i.e., a tremendous amount of users, contents, and activities), activities and contents, on social media need to be monitored and analyzed.

Like any other research process, the analysis of activities on social media involves a number of tasks linked to the process. As Fan and Gordon (2014) stated, the process of social media analysis involves three basic stages: *Capture*, *Understand,* and *Present* (Figure 1).

The first stage, stage *Capture* involves the analysis of available sources and collection of relevant data on various social media platforms, both on currently widely popular social networks, as Facebook, Twitter, LinkedIn, YouTube, and Google+, and on various blogs, forums, wikis, and similar tools. These

Figure 1. Stages of social media analytics process (Fan & Gordon, 2014)
Source: Fan & Gordon, 2014

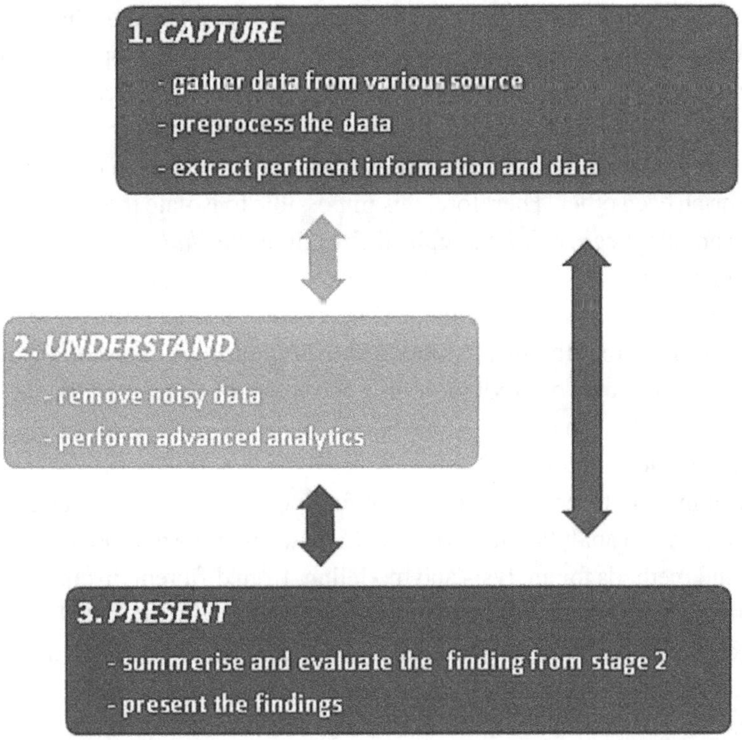

activities can run a company or can hire someone else. Since the goal is to satisfy all company's needs related to data and information, the result of this stage is an enormously large amount of data. In order to prepare a data set for the *Understand* stage, various preprocessing steps may be performed, including data modeling, data/record linking of data from different sources, stemming, part of speech tagging, feature extraction, and other syntactic and semantic operations that support analysis (Fan & Gordon, 2014).

Certainly, not all collected data are always usable, therefore what inevitably follows is the *Understand* stage, which is intended to identify only what is important, reject the "junk", and create a set of quantifiable and meaningful data and information. This process uses different techniques: rule-based text classifiers, sophisticated classifiers trained on labeled data, various statistical methods and other techniques derived from text and data mining, natural language processing, machine translation, and network analysis (Fan & Gordon, 2014).

The *Present* stage is a logical extension to the U*nderstand* stage. The results from different analytics in the *Understand* stage will be summarized, evaluated, and shown to users in an easily comprehensible format. Therefore, this stage uses different methods to visualize the results, especially dashboard tools that provide customized views for all types of users. They help make sense of large volumes of information, including patterns that are more apparent to people than machines (Fan & Gordon, 2014).

Upon examination of the basic characteristics of each stage, it is easy to conclude that the *Understand* stage is the keyphase because it creates an information base for making business decisions. Naturally, also the other two stages are crucial, but applying wrong methods in the *Understand* stage, or in the data cleaning and manipulation stage, may result in wrong conclusions and decisions.

What is important for the social media analytics process is the property of iterativeness. Namely, after one cycle the process is necessarily repeated because social media is a "live community" that grows every day. The results obtained from one cycle of social media analysis (passing through these three stages) are only a general clue for further activities, not a strong base for the adoption of long-term plans and strategies. The social media analytics process does not function as a classical life cycle that is "blamed" the most of not having a way back to thecompletion of one stage and shift to another stage.

Also, an important feature is the fact that the stages are connected and intertwined; they overlap, complement, and enrich each other. Therefore, it is impossible to isolate the stages fully or to distinguish where one ends and another begins. For example, the result of the *Understand* stage "helps" the *Capture* stage. By understanding and analyzing the collected data, it is visualized what is desired to be achieved during the analysis of data from social media, and that is the starting point for the data collection and retrieval stage. If it is found that the results obtained in stage *Present* are not adequate and interesting or do not have a satisfactory level of prediction, it is necessary to go back to the previous stage (*Understand* and *Capture)* and make some corrections (check incoming data, check the adequacy of selected methods, tune the parameters, and so on.)

By briefly describing the three stages of the social media analytics process, reference is made to some specific techniques and analytic methods used for data and information manipulation. In general, a variety techniques and methods for analysis and modeling, from different disciplines and fields, are used during the social media analytics process. According to Fan and Gordon (2014), the most used analytical methods and techniques for understanding, analyzing, and presenting large amounts of social media data are opinion mining or sentiment analysis, topic modeling, social network analysis, trend analysis, and visual analytics. These techniques can be used in the basic stages during the analysis process of data from different social media. For any method or technique is a characteristic that is primarily usable in a single stage, or some may be used in other stages. So, in the stage of understanding (Understand stage) can be used sentiment analysis and trend analysis. In the Understand stage can be used topic modeling and social network analysis. These two methods also can support the other two stages, stage Capture and Present stage. Visual analytics, however, can be used in the Understand and the Present stages.

The presented social media analytics process tries to cover the most of the activities/tools on social media, but it cannot cover all of them. Some tools have limitations in the information they can offer to their user or do not cover all the social media that are relevant for the user. Therefore, the scope of monitoring social media, or what will be analyzed and how it is determined according to every enterprise's business activities and needs, is crucial. The social media analytics compass is created (Figure 2) for the purpose of a more straightforward decision-making on what will be analyzed and how that.

As Figure 2 shows, the compass contains eight essential domains that should be analyzed on social media (Cleary, 2016):

- Audience profile.
- Audience size.
- Content analysis.
- Competitive benchmarking.
- Community responsiveness.
- Sentiment analysis.
- Traffic.
- Reach & engagement.

Figure 2. Social media analytics compass (Cleary, 2016)
Source: Cleary, 2016

Audience profile and *audience size*, as suggested by their titles, apply to all interested parties of an organization with which it interacts through social media. Namely, every organization needs to continuously monitor the number of its followers/friends on social media and examine whether the tool that it uses for social media analysis can cover the magnitude of the audience. Besides, not only is it important to cover all the audience, but it is also important to analyze their characteristics-whether they are enterprises or private persons, what their domains of interest are, etc.

Reach & engagement is the domainof social media analysis in which an organization tries to find out how far its activity on socially media reaches. In this matter, the aim is to answer two questions: 1) How much of the organization's audience are social media reaching? 2) How much audience are social media engaging with the organization's content? Answers to these questions allow an organization to find out how many people are paying attention to its posts, if they are aware of the organization, and how many of them "work" with the posted content. Literature usually refers to a company audience as consisting of three groups (Cleary, 2016):

- **Lurkers:** Users who follow the activities of the company on social networks, but do not interact with the company or its contents. These users most often account for the largest share of an organization's audience.
- **Influencers:** The so-called social media leaders, more precisely users, that have access to a larger audience and on some way they could influence the audience.
- **Engagers:** Users that are more active in an organization's community; as such, the organization will start recognizing some of their names.

If *Reach &engagement* are very low, it should be examined if the organization audience group consists of right people and what kind of content the organization posts, or why the postedcontents do not cause a response in the audience.

The domain called *Traffic* is closely connected with *Reach & engagement*. Namely, every action on social media is aimed to produce an action in the audience, so it is necessary to monitor the traffic of their reactions.

Creating an account and posting content on a large number of social media is free of charge, but in the case of large and professional organizations, preparing content can be relatively expensive. A large organization with a good reputation cannot afford to post any sorts of content because it can significantly affect its image and interaction with stakeholders. Therefore, it is very important to conduct *content analysis*, too, bearing in mind that preparing content for posting is often quite expensive. The *content analysis* involves getting answers to questions like (Cleary, 2016):

- Are videos, pictures, or text updates working best?
- Does the organization have the right mix of content?
- Is the organization getting engagement on its questions?
- What modificationson the platforms request the organization to change (e.g., changes to profile images)?

Content analysis is related to *sentiment analysis* which is intended to determine what the organization's audience "thinks" about it. *Sentiment analysis* entails a very large dose of risk because the expressed opinions often do not reflect people's true opinions and are not entirely credible. Nevertheless, the analysis can help the organization to realize that there is a problem (e.g., it is unlikely that all activists in the audience have the same, whether positive or negative, reaction to some content).

When analyzing all the defined important domains, the organization should always pay attention to its competition. For this reason, the domain of analysis called *competitive benchmarking* is indispensable in obtaining a true picture of the activities and success on social media. Every organization should always and repeatedly compare itself with its competitors to find out what it can learn from the competition on its way to success, and to establish what makes competitors much better and how the organization can improve.

The last domain of measurement in the social media analytics process according to Cleary (2016) is *Community Responsiveness*. Namely, the organization has to be very responsible to its community to ensure that the audience, or the community in which the organization exists, interacts with the company. In this way, the entity shows an interest in the community, ensuring a greater interaction with it, and this eventually leads to better results of the social media analysis.

SELECTION OF SOCIAL MEDIA ANALYTICS TOOLS

Tools for social media analytics can be perceived in very varied ways; further, literature offers different classification tools used in the social media analytics process. Namely, it is possible to speak of groups of tools that combine a number of techniques and methods applicable to individual stages of the social media analytics process. Thus, Batrinca and Treleaven (2015) specify three groups of tools:

- **Tools for Accessing to Data on Social Media**: Data services and tools for text data sourcing and scraping from social networking media, wikis, RSS feeds, news, etc.
- **Tools for Cleaning and Storage of Data from Social Media:** text data cleaning and storing tools.
- **Tools for Text Analysis:** Separate tools or collection of transformation and analysis tools for the analysis of scraped and cleaned data from the social media. These are simple tools capable of converting text data into other forms such as tables, charts, maps, more advanced analytics tools for social data analysis, connection identification, and network building.

Cleary (2016), however, identifies three types of tools:

- **Platform Analytics:** Free analytics tools offered by individual platforms (e.g. Facebook Insights or Twitter analytics).
- **Management Tool Analytics:** Analytics tools provided by social media management providers as part of their solution (for example, Agorapulse or SproutSocial).
- **Standalone Analytics:** Social media measurement tools that only provide functionality of social media analytics.

On the other hand, a large number of articles that can be found on the Web present, as social media analytics tools, a number of commercial and free applications that incorporate methods and techniques for all three stages of the social media analytics process. Different authors (Guido, 2016; Lee, 2014; Marvin & Behr 2016; Opitz, 2016), on their blogs or on specialized Websites, present tools, highlight their both strengths and weaknesses, and compare them against a number of technical and functional criteria, such as: company size, range of coverage referring to social networks, type of analysis that they support, frequency of alerts, CRM integration, support and training, real-time stream monitoring, geographic/language coverage, metrics and reporting, internal post and engagement metrics, free trial, integration with other applications, price, mobile apps, community analysis and demographics, and access to historical data.

Different recommendations for the selection of appropriate tools can be found by analyzing available texts (papers). This particularly applies to commercial tools, which are available in large numbers. In this regard, Ideya Ltd. made comparison of social media monitoring tools in November 2015 and found that at least 242 tools were available, as free, as payable (Chaffey, 2016).

However, in order to make the selection relatively easy, it is necessary to follow some guidance. One of the options is the social media analytics compass that was described in the previous section. This compass identifies what needs to be analyzed and measured and can be a reference for the selection of tools to conduct the analysis. Namely, knowing the importance of particular domains for its business, a company can pinpoint the appropriate tool for the analysis.

Also, as a good reference for the selection of social media platforms as well as social media analytics tools, the following criteria can be used (Tracx, 2015):

- An end-to-end integrated enterprise-wide platform that offers, at a minimum, the functionalities of listening, intelligence, advanced analytics, engagement, and monetization.
- Deep, data-driven, and actionable insights, and predictive and proactive guidance providing information for engagement and content strategies and strategic business decisions.

- Contextual insights (e.g., geo-spatial, behavioral, time of day), and how communities that discuss about brands are formed.
- Support for global brands, including multiple languages and a scalable architecture.
- Ability to interpret videos, images, and other non-text posts.
- Integration with other data sources and marketing platforms.

Undeniably, these criteria are quite general. Indeed, not only are they applicable for making decisions on tools for social media analysis, but they also allow to decide on the social media platform that the company will use for social media.

Once again, various lists of the best tools, sorted according to different criteria, are available on the Internet. However, more importantly, the basiccriterion that the company should follow is their business objective. Depending on this objective, key indicators will also be defined and used as a good filter for the selection of social media tools.

Issues, Controversies, Problems

As organizations have used social media more, their expectations, especially related to the fulfillment of social media promises, have become higher. Namely, social media promised companies that they would have become customer-centric and met all of their customers' needs if entities had used social media communication channels. Also, high growth of different social media analytics tools created the illusion that organizations would have been able to measure everything (Samuel & Reid, 2014). Unfortunately, so far social media analytics has failed to fulfill some of its promises, especially those related to full customer-centricity.

The following list summarizes the main social media analytics pitfalls of which their users should be aware:

- **Analytics Tools Cannot Reflect What Happens in Social Media:** Some of the recent research literature (Samuel & Reid, 2014) shows that a majority of social media users are relatively quiet, i.e., 85% of what social media analytics tools "hear" comes from less than 30% of social media audience, while the others are quiet, meaning they just listen (Samuel & Reid, 2014). Since social media analytics tools work with data gathered from about 30% of social media users, it is obvious that they cannot tell organizations what they need to know about their customers.
- **Social Media Users do not Reflect Organizations' Customers:** Social media users are not a representative pattern of the customer base. For example, the estimation is that 80% of the USA population is now on Facebook, but only 25% is on Twitter (Samuel & Reid, 2014).
- **Age and Geographic Bias:** Social media data contain a recognized bias that can significantly influence the output of social media analytics. People of younger age and in certain geographic locations use social media more frequently. As a result, some providers of social media analytics reduce these biases by normalizing their data. Nevertheless, it is important for marketing professionals to make allowances for this bias when making decisions. Indeed, if products are intended for younger urban population, this bias is positive, but if they are designed for more general groups, social media data can be observed only in regard of data from other sources that are free of these biases. It is important to stress this with social media having become a standard part of

standard commercial interactions, like websites, some of these biases are likely to dilute or dissolve (Petrocelli, 2013).

- **Amplification Issue:** Amplification, meaning content and message spreading by using social media network effects, makes the social media a desirable cost-effective marketing tool. However, amplification can bring serious drawbacks through message drift. Namely, people sometimes, instead of simply sharing a post and content, rephrase or shorten a message. In this way, they can change the basic meaning, sometimes into entirely new messages. It is hard to keep control of this process without continuous attention (Petrocelli, 2013).
- **Non-Textual Information:** Social media analytics tools highly rely on text data, especially when sentiment analysis tools are in question. However, it is impossible for these tools to directly analyze increasingly large amount of image, video, and audio content. The result is that the growing body of content contained in video blogs, video sharing (YouTube), photo sharing (Instagram and Pinterest), or podcasts, as well as the most part of the content on Facebook, do not yet have a prominent position in social media analysis (Petrocelli, 2013).
- **Inconsistent Dataset:** Substantial differences exist between social media analytics tools regarding filtering capabilities and access to Facebook and Twitter data. Also, crawlers and spam filters can affect dataset results (Etlinger & Li, 2011).
- **Language Limitations:** Social media analytics tools have many problems to cope with particular industry terms (e.g., wine-tasting notes "barnyardy", "wood smoke"), slangs and abbreviations, irony and sarcasm, emoticons (e.g., ☺), and especially with support for all global languages (Etlinger & Li, 2011).
- **Different Analytical Approaches by Social Media Analytics Tools Vendors:** Differences in the ways of data collection can affect final results. An approach based on a keyword is the simplest and cheap, but it is not accurate, as opposed to more advanced, but more costly, natural language processing and algorithmic approaches (Etlinger & Li, 2011).
- **Privacy and Security:** There are no absolute guarantees that customer and business information will not be compromised by online sharing or attacked by computer hackers.
- **Measuring Success and Monetization:** Although industry observers have noted that the lack of convincing evidence of the financial benefit of a social media strategy is an impediment to substantial investment in this area (Divol,Edelman & Sarrazin, 2012), there is also an emerging literature that researches the relation between social media and overall firm value or performance (Hitt,Jin &Wu, 2015).
- **Complaints and Bad Reviews Management:** If organizations are not prepared for complaints and bad reviews, negative publicity can seriously damage their reputations because customers in social media have very powerful tools for fast spreading both positive and negative comments.
- **Time Commitment:** Using social media as communication channels with customers requires the continuous engagement of organizational resources (human, technological, and financial) and full commitment of the whole organization. A social media marketing process is very iterative in comparison with traditional marketing campaigns has the ability to change and adapt at a faster rate. This adaptability requires platforms that marketing professionals can use to design, launch, and manage social media marketing campaigns in a proper way and conduct the social media analytics that provides deep customer understanding and monitoring for the effectiveness of these campaigns (Petrocelli, 2013).

Regardless of the open issues related to social media and social media analytics tools, the number of social media users has constantly grown, as the market for social media analytics tools has enlarged. The potential value of social media data analysis draws both research-oriented and practice-oriented professionals to invest more and more time, money, and effort to resolving the above mentioned pitfalls.

SOLUTIONS AND RECOMMENDATIONS

A Framework for the Adoption of Social Media Analytics in Finance

As the financial sector is one of the most regulated areas, financial institutions should take a disciplined approach to the adoption and implementation of social media analytics. Also, financial entities should aim at a multidisciplinary approach, with specialists in compliance, technology, information security, law, human resources, and marketing included in the process of reviewing and implementing social media analytics (Hansche & Chen, 2014). In order to achieve adequate coordination and integration of these different specialists, financial institutions need a defined framework for the adoption of social media analytics. The existence of this framework can ensure that a financial institution meets its goals for social media engagement, minimizes risk, and ensures compliance with existing and new laws and guidance that apply to its social media activities (Hansche & Chen, 2014).

Different sources (Abughosh, 2016; Deloitte, 2013; Gilfoil, Aukers & Jobs, 2015; Hansche & Chen, 2014) were consulted during the development of a framework for the adoption of social media analytics in finance. The proposed framework is based on the following layers (Figure 3):

- Strategic context.
- Legal and compliance context.
- Social media platform context.
- Integration of social media into a business model.
- Content distribution and users' engagement.
- Data collection context.
- Evaluation, risk, and control context.

The strategic context layer stresses that financial institutions need a social media strategy and vision that is harmonized with institutional strategy and defined business goals. The social media strategy should define:

- A social vision tailored to support the financial institution's business drivers, brand image, and corporate strategy (Deloitte, 2013).
- The scope and objectives of the social media strategy.
- The measurement of the effectiveness of the strategy through KPIs (Key Performance Indicators), such as total reach, volume by social media channels, positive, negative and neutral mentions, average response time, unique visitors, frequency of interactions, frequency of followers, frequency of active followers, number of frequency of leads, frequency of issues logged and issues resolved (Cognizant, 2014).
- Develop a strong plan for reducing risks before engaging in social platforms (Abughosh, 2016).

Figure 3. Framework for the adoption of social media analytics in finance
Source: Authors'own figure

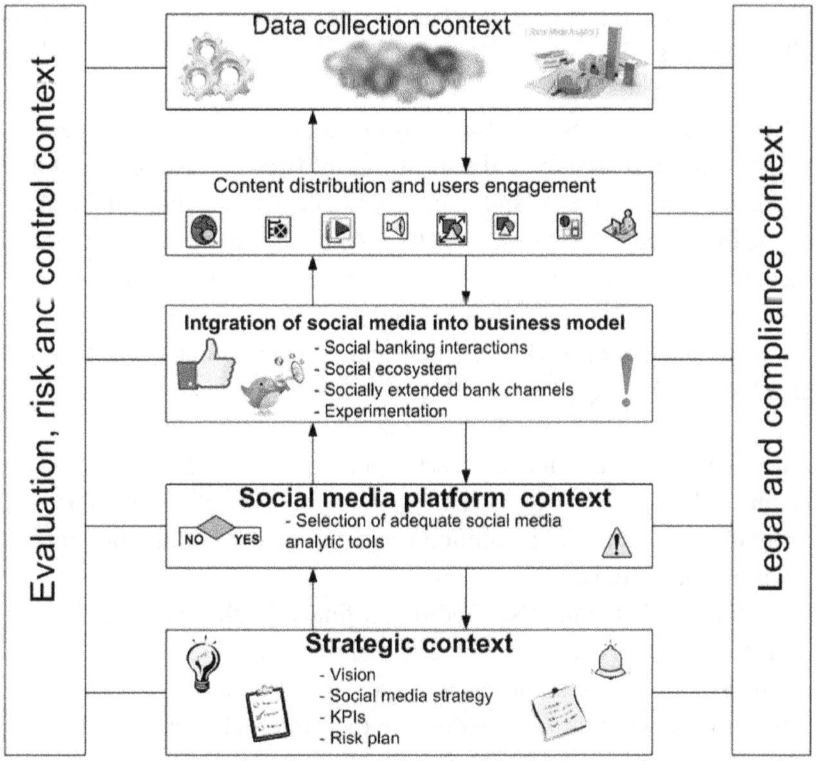

The legal and compliance context layer is closely relatedto all the other layers of the framework (Figure 3). As the FFIEC Guidance points out, even financial institutions not actively participating in social media will be at risk that must be evaluated, monitored, and dealt with in their social media policies (Federal Financial Institutions Examination Council, 2013). The adoption and implementation of a social media policy for employees are one of the possible ways for a financial institution to reduce some business and legal risks of using social media use.

The FFIEC Guidance recommends a financial institutions to adopt such a policy for their employees' social media use that is related to work, specifying what activities are prohibited, as well as a policy for employees' use that is unrelated to work, within the financial institution's social media governance policies and procedures (Federal Financial Institutions Examination Council, 2013).

The objectives of the policy should cover mitigating the risks of defamation and brand damage and of exposure of confidential customer and financial institution information.

The following issues should be addressed in a policy for the employees authorized by the financial institution to engage in social media activities on its behalf: establishing of adequate governance structure for posts approval; education of employees; tracking the use of personal and business electronic devices; protection of internal and external business information; derogatory comments about co-workers, bosses and/or clients, transparency - identifying oneself as an employee when posting about the financial institution (Hansche & Chen, 2014).

Also, the financial institution should develope general policies covering social media use by employees who do not participate in social media activities on behalf of the financial institution.

The social media platform context layer is related to the selection of adequate social media analytics tools (Figure 3). This process has been detailed in the previous section.

The integration of social media into a business model is the critical context in the proposed framework (Figure 3). Namely, the main reasons why financial institutions, or other organizations, decide to use social media are to ensure transparency and almost instant two-way interaction with their customers, to better respond to customers' requests, and to offer new services by channels their customers already used for other private or business activities. Nonetheless, if financial institutions want to be successful in using social media, they should integrate the use of social media into their overall business model and exploit these means to meet the goals defined in their business strategy.

In order to effectively integrate social media into their business model, financial institutions have to consider and define the following (Deloitte, 2013):

- **Social Banking Interactions:** Financial institutions have to discover how customers want to interact with them and how to engage customersin creating shared social value.
- **Social Ecosystem:** Each financial institution has to find and build the right mix of social channels to support their business goals.
- **Socially Extended Bank Channels:** Traditional financial channels should be transformed and expanded with social media channels enabling real two-way dialogue.
- **Experimentation:** Financial institutions first have to pilot their social concepts to refine understanding of customer's expectations and develop their internal capabilities.

The integration of social media into a business model is a very complex process. It means building the cross-functional capabilities needed to process insights from social channels, engage with customers, respond to their requests, and recognize and act on social opportunities (Deloitte, 2013). Obviously, this process of integration can affect an entire financial institution, asking for adoption of many changes in the institutional organization and behavior. A successful adoption of changesasks that financial institutions have answers to the following questions (Deloitte, 2013):

- Which groups will need to respond to customer service requests and inquiries?
- What types of requests and interactions will be received and supported?
- Which groups might be able to use the social insights being harvested?
- Where are the new connections between the functional areas needed to deliver on institutional vision?

The use of social media data should not be limited only to employees who work directly with the technology, but it should be used by the workers from different divisions of financial institutions. The reason for this lies in the fact that social media can provide signals about every part of the institutions' operation, so it is important to incorporate the signals learned from social media into the overall corporate business process. As users can directly interact with new financial institutions' product or service offerings through comments and reviews, financial institutions that can effectively manage these data is in a better position to predict future demands and improve their existing product or service lines. Signals learned from social media sentiment could feed directly into the product design, which, in turn, affects operations, marketing, and sales. Thus, tightly integrating social media data into financial institutions' operation and marketing efforts is critical (Ghose, Ipeirotis & Li, 2012). Especially when employees from various divisions of the financial institution can make sense of the social media data and effectively incorporate them into the institution's strategies, social media could have a much more profound effect on the financial institution than simply the marketing department. Using signals learned from social media can help guide the financial institution to flexibly adjust to changes in the business environment (Hitt, Jin & Wu, 2015).

Through the content distribution and users' engagement context (Figure 3), the financial institution should demonstrate that it can create or forward information that meets its target customers' needs, wants, or desires. Content can be defined as any information related to the particular financial institution, its products, and its service. The formats of content can be different: photos, video, display ads, blogs, tweets, emails, pop-up ads, white papers, and similar. In its social media strategy, a financial institution should define time schedules (daily, weekly, or monthly) and activities (e.g., content creation, content sharing, responding to comments and inquiries, spam deletion, enable effective tracking, review daily/weekly/monthly activities) related to content distribution and users' engagement.

The data collection context (Figure 3) should describe how a financial institution captures data from customers who responded in some way to the distributed content. Data should be generated by different social media channels (e.g., Facebook, Tweeter, blogs). Selected social media analytics tools are used for processing these data with the main goal of finding valuable information that the financial institution can use in its business.

The evaluation, risk, and control context stresses that a financial organization should continuously evaluate the activities described in the previous contexts and apply consistent controls across channels and departments engaged with or leveraging social media (Gilfoil, Aukers & Jobs, 2015). Continuous evaluations also means that the financial institution needs to make adjustments (e.g., replace platform, adopt new social media platform) on-the-fly, based on the analysis of social media metrics, such as number of members registered in the institution's social platform, number of interactions (user comments), number of times when institution social presence or post is visited, and similar elements. This context is closely related to all the other layers of the framework (Figure 3).

FUTURE RESEARCH DIRECTIONS

Social media analytics is still developing the field with many opportunities for further research exploration. Future research directions are divided into two categories:

- General social media analytics.
- Specific social media analytics for the financial sector.

Some of the main future research directions for general social media analytics can be summarized as follows:

- Achieving the full real real-time engagement, e.g. faster response times through improvements in social listening and automation software. Namely, as indicated by Search Engine Watch, 70% of

Twitter users anticipate a brand to respond to their tweets, and 53% expect it to do so within an hour, but this percentage is as high as 72% when a complaint is involved (Beese, 2016).
- Live streaming video, thanks to applications like Snapchat, Periscope, Facebook Live and similar, can enable social engagement with customers in an entirely new way.
- Mobile friendly – the majority of users of social media use them primarily over screens of smart mobile devices. In 2015, desktop traffic was surpassed by mobile traffic in 10 countries, including U.S. and Japan (Beese, 2016), so organizations' the primary interest is to ensure that their social media platform is at least mobile-friendly.
- Data-driven decisions. In the course of time, an increasingly important competitive edge will be in the ability of capturing, interpreting, and acting on signals from social media in the context of general enterprise data (Etlinger & Li, 2011). In the very near future, the ability to "speak data" will be a decisive skill for all those who work within the socially adaptive business. Namely, although machines will perform most of the processing-intensive analysis, the data interpretation ability will be fundamental to ensuring organizational agility.

The overall implications of data-driven business will prove to be disruptive to an even higher extent than the data itself. The businesses that can learn from disruption and use it to develop stronger and more reciprocal relationships with their customers will be successful in the age of data (Etlinger & Li, 2011).

- Dark social measurement - With 84% of what is globally shared in social media being dark to social media analytics (private sharing with close friends and family via peer-to-peer channels), there is a challenge to measure its efficiency in ways that sync with other social media measurement. The more concrete direction on this and collaboration between applications, networks, and platforms is necessary to make it meaningful (Odden, 2016).
- The content-based analysis should be more focused on including information on content that can provide important insights about the underlying social network. For example, the content at a given node may yield valuable clues on the expertise and interests of the corresponding party (Aggarwal, 2011).
- Social Chat Bots are recently offered by Facebook as a new kind of engagement. Since customers expect engagement in real time, it may be possible to satisfy basic customer service and information needs of brands by using bots. The result is that brands will need to invest in more interactive social experiences for their community (Odden, 2016).
- Social media automation features will grow to help brands with prospecting delivering content to the right customers at the right time and engagement–all integrated with a marketing dashboard for an end-to-end reporting of the impact social media has across the customer journey. However, similar to CRM, this is not a "plug and play" solution because organizations will need human expertise and a strategy to make the most out of their automation software investment (Odden, 2016).
- Temporal analysis, that is the inclusion of time-related development into network analysis, can significantly improve the quality of the results. Nonetheless, a significant amount of work has yet to be done on dynamic analysis of social networks which evolve rapidly in time (Aggarwal, 2011).
- Social media mining-the process of representing, analyzing, and extracting actionable patterns from social media data (Zafarani, Abbasi & Liu, 2014) - is becoming a more propulsive research

field. It discusses and integrates theories and methodologies from different fields, such as computer science, data mining, machine learning, social network analysis, network science, sociology, ethnography, statistics, optimization, and mathematics. It covers the tools for formal representation, measuring, modeling, and mining of meaningful patterns from large-scale social media data (Zafarani, Abbasi & Liu, 2014). Also, social media mining is cultivating a new type of data scientist who is proficient in social and computational theories, specialized for analysis of recalcitrant social media data, and skilled to help bridge the gap between what is known (social and computational theories) and what organizations want to know about the vast social media world using computational tools (Zafarani, Abbasi & Liu, 2014).

Some of the main future research directions for specific social media analytics for the financial sector can be summarized as follows (Greenfield, 2014):

- It is necessary to develop standards for international growth and methods optimized for mining non–Cashtag data.
- The increased amount of financial content has opened up possibilities for even more types of monitoring and analytics.
- With the advent of new data and tools for monitoring what is globally discussed and thought, it is on financial professionals to examine which ones of them would be best suited for their investment theses. Benefits will be drawn and information and profits made by those who prove capable of implementing them successfully.

CONCLUSION

The phrase *many-to-many* can be used to describe the situation related to social media. Many participants create an enormous quantity of content, making the *jungle of information* in which it is sometimes hard to find a right way without a good compass. Although social media analytics tools are pretending to be that compass, the huge number of different tools can additionally contribute to confusion and even make the whole situation more complex.

This chapter focused on social media analytics tools and the criteria for their selection. The chapter discusses main open issues and controversies, and finally proposes a general framework for the adoption of social media analytics as a possible solution for better coping with the complexity related to social media. The proposed framework is maybe general, but it recognizes necessary contexts and relations between them, and can be used as a compass for a better integration of social media into business processes.

Although social media analytics tools are necessary to ease organizations to cope with ever growing data from social media, it is important to stress that just tools (i.e., technology) are not enough. If social media analytics tools are not strategically aligned with existing business goals, if there is not a well-defined and aligned social media strategy, or, simply, if there is not an adequate framework for the adoption of social media analytics tools, organizations, including financial institutions, will continue to struggle to get their desired results.

Also, the proposed framework points out that the use of social media should not be limited just to employees who work directly with technology, but it should be spread to different departments in organizations because social media can provide signals about almost every part of organizations' operations. Namely, just knowing data about customers is not enough, without adequate business action, this knowledge has no sense. Social media analytics tools can assist users in exploiting customer information, but they cannot replace human creativity in building along-lasting relationship.

REFERENCES

Abughosh, S. (2016). *Social Media Analytics To Drive Business Advantage In Retail Banking*. Retrieved September 13, 2016, from https://www.linkedin.com/pulse/social-media-analytics-drive-business-advantage-suha

Aggarwal, C. C. (2011). An Introduction to Social Network Data Analytics, In C.C. Aggarwal (Ed.), Social Network Data Analytics (pp 1-16). New York: Springer Science+Business Media.

Batrinca, B., & Treleaven, P. C. (2015). Social media analytics: A survey of techniques, tools and platforms. *AI & Society*, *30*(1), 89–116. doi:10.1007/s00146-014-0549-4

Beese, J. (2016). 6 Social Media Trends That Will Take Over 2016. *Sprout Social*. Retrieved June 21, 2016 from http://sproutsocial.com/insights/social-media-trends/

Cleary, I. (2016). *Social Media Analytics Compass: What and How to Measure*. Retrieved September 22, 2016, from http://www.razorsocial.com/social-media-analytics-tools/

Cognizant. (2014). How Banks Can Use Social Media Analytics To Drive Business Advantage. *Cognizant 20-20 insights*. Retrieved September 22, 2016, from https://www.cognizant.com/Insights Whitepapers/How-Banks-Can-Use-Social-Media-Analytics-To-Drive-Business-Advantage.pdf

Deloitte. (2013). *Who says banks can't be social? Become a social bank, inside and out*. Retrieved May 2, 2016, from http://www2.deloitte.com/global/en/pages/financial-services/articles/banks-can-be-social.html

Divol, R., Edelman, D., & Sarrazin, H. (2012). Demystifying social media. *The McKinsey Quarterly*, *2*(12), 66–77.

Etlinger, S., & Li, C. (2011). *A Framework for Social Analytics Including Six Use Cases for Social Media Measurement.* Altimeter group. Retrieved August 16, 2016, from http://www.slideshare.net/Altimeter/altimeter-social-analytics-report

Facebook. (2016). *Most popular product brands on Facebook 2016.*Retrieved September 24, 2016, from https://www.statista.com/statistics/265657/leading-product-brands-with-the-most-fans-on-facebook/

Fan, W., & Gordon, M. D. (2014). The Power of Social Media Analytics. *Communications of the ACM*, *57*(6), 74–81. doi:10.1145/2602574

Federal Financial Institutions Examination Council. (2013). *Social Media: Consumer Compliance Risk Management Guidance*. Federal Financial Institutions Examination Council (December 11, 2013). Retrieved July 5, 2016, from https://www.ffiec.gov/press/PDF/2013_Dec%20Final%20SMG %20 attached%20to%2011Dec13%20press%20release.pdf

Financial Brand. (2015). Top 100 Banks on Facebook. *The Financial Brand*. Retrieved July 28, 2016, from https://thefinancialbrand.com/54734/power-100-2015-q3-facebook-banks/

Gartner. (2016). *Social Analytics*. Retrieved September 10, 2016, from http://www.gartner.com/it-glossary/social-analytics/

Ghose, A., Ipeirotis, P. G. & Li, B. (2012). Designing ranking systems for hotels on travel search engines by mining user-generated and crowd sourced content. *Marketing Science 31*(3), 493-520.

Gilfoil, D. M., Aukers, S. M., & Jobs, C. G. (2015). Developing And Implementing A Social Media Program While Optimizing Return On Investment – An MBA Program Case Study. *American Journal of Business Education*, *8*(1), 31–48.

Golesworthy, T. (2016). A Review of Social Media in The Banking Sector. *Customer THINK*. Retrieved September 20, 2016, fromhttp://customerthink.com/a-review-of-social-media-in-the-banking-sector/

Greenfield, D. (2014). *Social Media in Financial Markets: The Coming of Age...* GNIP (Whitepaper). Retrieved August 25, 2016, from http://stocktwits.com/research/social-media-and-markets-the-coming-of-age.pdf

Guido, M. (2016). *The List of the Top 25 Social Media Analytics Tools*. Retrieved September 14, 2016, from http://keyhole.co/blog/list-of-the-top-25-social-media-analytics-tools/

Hansche, H. L., & Chen, J. T. (2014). *Social Media Guide for Financial Institutions*. Chapman and Cutler LLP, USA. Retrieved July 29, 2016, fromhttp://www.chapman.com/insights-publications-Social_ Media _Financial_Institutions.html

He, W., Wu, H., Yan, G., Akula, V., & Shen, J. (2015). A novel social media competitive analytics framework with sentiment benchmarks. *Information & Management*, *52*(7), 801–812. doi:10.1016/j.im.2015.04.006

Hitt, L., Jin, F., & Wu, L. (2015). *Who Benefits More from Social Media: Evidence from Large-Sample Firm Value Analysis* (Preliminary). Retrieved August 28, 2016, from https://pdfs.semanticscholar.org/7a7c/36121c0c5fd6424ad7221ef2e958f03b7385.pdf

Holsapple, C., Hsiao, S.-H., & Pakath, R. (2014). Business Social Media Analytics: Definition, Benefits, and Challenges. In *Proceedings of 20th Americas Conference on Information Systems (AMCIS 2014): Smart Sustainability: The Information Systems Opportunity* (vol. 5, pp. 3703- 3714). Savannah, GA: Association for Information Systems (AIS).

Lee, K. (2014). *The Big List of The 61 Best Social Media Tools for Small Business*. Retrieved September 22, 2016, from https://blog.bufferapp.com/best-social-media-tools-for-small-business

Marvin, R., & Behr, A. (2016). *The Best Social Media Management & Analytics Tools of 2016*. Retrieved September 26, 2016, from http://www.pcmag.com/article2/0,2817,2491376,00.asp

Merriam-Webster. (2016). *Social media*. Retrieved September 25, 2016, from http://www.merriamwebster.com/dictionary/social%20media

Odden, L. (2016). *9 Social Media Marketing Trends That Could Make or Break Your Business in 2017*. Retrieved September 28, 2016, from http://www.toprankblog.com/2016/07/future-social-media-marketing/

Opitz, L. (2016). *5 Free Social Media Analytics Tools – With Recommendations from Experts*. Retrieved September 18, 2016, from https://www.talkwalker.com/blog/5-free-social-media-analytics-tools-experts

Petrocelli, T. (2013). *Market Landscape Report: Social Media Marketing and Analytics. The New Face of Customer Engagement*. Milford, MA: The Enterprise Strategy Group (ESG). Retrieved June 28, 2016, from http://www.oracle.com/us/corporate/analystreports/es-social-landscape-1936813.pdf

Samuel, A., & Reid, A. (2014). What Social Media Analytics Can't Tell You About Your Customers? *Vision Critical*. Retrieved June 12, 2016, from https://www.visioncritical.com/resources/socialcustomersreport/?utm_campaign=WSMACTY+Report&utm_medium=Blog&utm_source=Referral

Tracx. (2015). *A Buyer's Guide: Criteria for Selecting a Social Media Management Platform*. Retrieved July 11, 2016, from https://gdssummits.com/cmo/digital-eu/app/uploads/sites/72/2015/08/CMO-DML-EU-1-Tracx-BuyersGuide-Final.pdf

Zafarani, R., Abbasi, M. A., & Liu, H. (2014). *Social Media Mining, An Introduction* (draft version). Cambridge University Press. Retrieved August 17, 2016, fromhttp://dmml.asu.edu/smm/ SMM.pdf

Zheludev, I., Smith, R., & Aste, T. (2014). When Can Social Media Lead Financial Markets? *Scientific Reports, 4*, Article number 4213. Retrieved July 29, 2016, from http://www.nature.com/articles/srep04213

KEY TERMS AND DEFINITIONS

Amplification: The use of social media for spreading digital content and messages.

Cashtag: The special ($) tag associated to discussions about stock market (today financial issues generally) that enables easier tracking of that type of discussions on social media.

Community Responsiveness: The capability of an organization that readily reacts to suggestions, influences, appeals, or efforts of its customers and community.

Dark Social: The social sharing of content that can be measured by Web analytics programs (private sharing).

Sentiment Analysis: The computer identification, analysis, and categorization of opinions expressed in social media (usually in a piece of text) in order to determine whether the writer's attitude towards a particular topic or product is positive, negative, or neutral.

Social Chat Bots: The integration of artificial intelligence software (a chatbot) into social media (Facebook) to allow very sophisticated automated response (instead of real-life representative) to user queries.

Social Media: A collection of digital communication channels (e.g., blogs, forums, social networks) that enables interaction, collaboration, and sharing of content.

Social Media Analytics: The practice of gathering data from social media in order to analyze them and make business decisions.

Social Media Mining: The process of representing, analyzing, and extracting actionable patterns from social media data.

Chapter 13
Using Functional Link Artificial Neural Network (FLANN) for Bank Credit Risk Assessment

Saroj Kanta Jena
BML Munjal University, India

Maheshwar Dwivedy
BML Munjal University, India

Anil Kumar
BML Munjal University, India

ABSTRACT

Credit scoring is the most important and critical component conducted by the credit providers to decide whether to grant a loan to the applicant or not. Therefore credit scoring models are generally used to predict the potentiality of the loan applicant. A proper evaluation of the credit can help the service provider to determine whether to grant or to reject the credit. The objective of the study is to predict banking credit scoring assessment using a data mining technique i.e. Functional Link Artificial Neural Network (FLANN) classifier. Credit approval datasets: Australian credit and German credit have been used to do this analysis. The output of the study shows that the proposed model used for classification works better on credit dataset. Secondly, we have applied our proposed model on the two credit approval dataset to check the performance of the model for the classification accuracy. A proper evaluation of the credit using the proposed FLANN approach can help the service provider to accurately and quickly ascertain whether to grant credit or to reject.

INTRODUCTION

Classification technique is one the most difficult and complex task in the decision making process of human activity in business context. In the process of classification, a training set comprising of set of records can be generated, where each records of the training set consists of several attributes to provide the information about the record. Attributes, in general could be either continuous with reference to

DOI: 10.4018/978-1-5225-2148-8.ch013

ordered domain or categorical with reference to unordered domain. One class attribute included in the feature set specifically maps the records to the class it belongs. The objective of any classification related problem is to develop a model to classify feature (class) depending upon the remaining features of the record. Recently there have been several studies that focus on the complex task of classifying for prediction purpose. Several models have already been developed and proposed over the years. Majority of the models proposed fall into the following categories: statistical models, genetic models, neural networks and decision trees. Traditional methods to solve the classification problems aren't suitable given that in a classification problem, determining the optimal nonlinear boundary is a complicated task. Therefore, Artificial Neural Networks (ANNs) having non-linear learning capabilities could be utilized for solving many complex applications. However, there have been very limited studies from literatures available that utilize neural networks especially functional link artificial neural network (FLANN) for the purpose of classification in data mining.

Artificial Neural Networks (ANNs) are a set of powerful tools for its nonlinear learning capability. This tool is applied for the complex applications like functional approximation, unsupervised classification and optimization, identifying and controlling a nonlinear system. For solving the classification problem FLANN usually takes less time to optimize the weight vector than the traditional algorithms. In traditional algorithm the complexity increases as the no of layers of the neural network increases. Pao et al. (2008) is one of the first few studies that proposed the FLANN structure and have shown that, the structure can be used for functional approximation and pattern classification with a low computational load and with a faster convergence rate than the MLP (Multilayer perceptron) structure. The need of hidden layer is removed in this network structure so the learning algorithm used in this structure becomes very simple. The dimensionality of the input vector increases in the functional expansion and the output generated by the FLANN structure provide a better discrimination capability in the input pattern. Neural networks works better not only for classifying patterns but also for approximating complex nonlinear process dynamics. This model is a good candidate model for the nonlinear processes and exhibits some intelligent behaviour towards the nonlinearity processes. MLP, RBF (Radial basis function) and SVM (Support vector machine) are some of the popular types of NN Model widely reported in literature. It is found that these models reportedly perform well with improved prediction competency but with a greater computational cost. As, these models have hidden layers in their neural network it will predict with high computational cost. Structures like, PPN (polynomial perceptron network) and also the FLANN must be considered so as to decrease the computational cost of neural networks. In this paper we considered FLANN structure with three different polynomials. To train the network, we have used the back propagation (BP) algorithm.

LITERATURE REVIEW

Dawson &Wilby (2001) developed one approach by using ANNs to design the model for rainfall-runoff and to forecast the flood out of the rainfall. They have outlined the basic principles and structure of ANN model, and designed the training algorithms for the research purpose. They have discussed the themes of the data pre-processing techniques to validate the model; data normalization techniques; and different methods to evaluate the performance of the ANN model. The authors proposed a template to construct the ANN rainfall-runoff model after comparing the ANN model with the traditional statistical models. Finally, they suggested that research should focus not only on the properties of the ANN weights, but also on the evolution of typical performance measures for the complexity of the model. Corchado & Lees (2001) presented a research paper where they have tried to introduce the ANN method to analyse data as a simplification of traditional linear regression method. They have compared the function and structure of ANN with the existing linear models. The authors wanted to show that a back propagation ANN with one hidden layer will work as the universal function approximators. To reduce the dimensions of the data set, they have compared ANNs to the conventional Factor Analysis procedure. The authors have identified some problems for prediction in insurance sector with the application of both traditional statistical methods and ANN techniques. One major accusation of ANN is that the type of relationship among the dependent and the independent variable is not exposed. They also presented various methods for understanding the results of an ANN analysis, i.e., with imagining the usual form of the tailored function.

Buscema (2002) explained the concept and patterns of ANNs in his study. The use of ANNs in the process of data analysis was also the part of his study. He presented some multidimensional, complex, and dynamic phenomena that are uncontrollable and unpredictable with the outmoded "cause and effect" sense. In the same year, Behara et al. (2002) discussed on the development of ANN models to improve the analysis of service quality. They have developed a valid ANN model for service quality, and used the customer dataset from an auto dealership network of Netherlands generated out of the SERVEQUAL survey in the model. ANN approach has been used to model different definitions of service quality. In the process of predicting the service quality, the authors report that their perception minus expectation model predicted with lesser accuracy than the perception only model. Their study clearly shows that service quality measurement models involving expectation bereft of perception performed better than the other models.

Lin et al. (2003) assessed the usefulness of FNN (fuzzy neural network) method in the fraud detection process. They found that FNN performed better than the statistical and ANNs used in the previous studies. The performance of FNN compared with the Logit model was found better in predicting fraud cases. Basch et al. (2003) reported a method to predict the risk associated with the financial transaction. The predictive model executed for the authorization request on the associated data to generate a risk score. If the risk score is in the unacceptable range then the authorization request failed to complete the transaction. Malhotra & Malhotra (2003) likened the performance of MDA (Multiple Discriminant Analysis) and ANNs in categorising probable loan. They found that the ANN models always works better in comparison to MDA models in the process of categorising probable loans. They also cross validated their result with seven different dataset to improve the delinquent of bias with the training set and to check the performance of the ANN model in classifying the problem loans.

Nowadays, it is difficult to manage and use large amount of data in the decision making process. To overcome these challenges, some intelligent solutions generated from ANNs and GA (Genetic Algorithms) has been widely used and applied for such complicated problems. Metaxiotis & Psarras (2004) provided an overview of GA and ANN operations, and presented the applications of these techniques in the business domain. The main objective of their study was to focus and present the application of these techniques in the business domain. Finally, their study disclosed that ANN and GA techniques are providing practical benefits in their applications. Linder et al. (2004) investigated on targeting customers in the area of direct marketing and applied the most frequently used techniques like logistic regression (LR), classification trees (CTs) and ANNs to do such investigations. The objective of their study was to find the predictive performances of the techniques considered for the above investigation. It is found that the performance of all the technique rises with the size of the dataset. For the high complexity in the dataset the CTs and LR performed well than ANNs. If the sample size is small then ANNs performs better than the other two. Again LR outperformed than CTs for large sample size. It was concluded that the combination of these three models performed better in prediction even in the high complexity of the dataset.

Lee & Chen (2005) studied the credit scoring performance using ANN with a two-stage hybrid modelling procedure and MARS (multivariate adaptive regression splines). The justification under the studies is 1) To use MARS in building the credit scoring model, and 2) the achieved important variables are then functioned as the input nodes of the NNs model. They have considered housing loan dataset to test the efficiency and achievability of the projected model. They found that the model performed better using discriminant analysis, LR, ANNs and MARS and hence provides an alternative for the credit scoring analysis. Kumar & Bhattacharya (2006) proposed a comparative study of prediction performances of ANN model against the LDA model for forecasting corporate credit ratings. They found that the ANN model performed better than LDA model in both test dataset and training dataset. The ANN model found as a robust model in processing the dataset with missing values. Shen et al. (2007) studied the efficiency of classification models applied on fraud detection problems of credit analysis. They have tested three different models, i.e. NN, LR, and decision tree for the purpose of fraud detection. They have developed a framework to choose a best model to identify the fraud in credit analysis.

Angelini et al. (2008) described the application of NN models to assess the credit risk. They have developed two NN models, one special architecture network and one feed-forward network. In the same year, Abdou et al. (2008) investigated the ability of neural nets, such as probabilistic neural nets and, and conventional techniques such as, multi-layer feed-forward nets, logistic regression, probit analysis, and discriminant analysis in evaluating credit risk on personal loans' dataset. They found that NN models outperform all other models.

Jeatrakul & Wong (2009) presented the comparative study of five different NN models for binary classification problems. They have considered RBFNN (radial basis function neural network), PPN (probabilistic neural network), BPNN (back propagation neural network), GRNN (general regression neural network), and CMTNN (complementary neural network). They found that CMTNN performs better than other NN models for binary classification. Tsai & Chen (2010) also compared four different types of hybrid models. They found that 'Classification + Classification' hybrid model constructed on NNs and LR can provide the highest prediction accuracy which in return maximise the profit. Pacelli & Azzollini (2011) compared the ability of the ANN model and its architecture to forecast the credit risk on same panel of manufacturing companies for two different studies. They have tried to show the difference in the model output for the two different years.

Khashei et al. (2012) proposed an innovative hybrid ANN model in association with multiple linear regression models in order to get a new efficient model for classification problem. The proposed model performs better and with improved accuracy than the traditional ANN model. It is also found that the proposed model outperform in comparison to SVM, QDA, LDA, and KNN. Marques et al. (2012) focussed on evolutionary computing models of computational intelligence. They have summarised the latest developed evolutionary econometrics and computer science algorithms to credit scoring by reviewing several scientific articles available from 2000 to 2012. Wei et al. (2013) proposed an online banking fraud detection structure combining the appropriate resources using various innovative data mining methods. They have developed a contrast vector for customer's behaviour and their preference. They also have introduced the innovative Contrast-Miner algorithm to detect the fraudulent behaviour out of genuine behaviour. They found that it works better than the traditional fraud detection techniques.

Elsalamony (2014) considered different data mining techniques and summarized their application and analysis. The primary objective of their study was to observe the performance of MLPNN, LR, TAN, and C5.0 techniques on bank deposit subscription dataset. They have considered three different statistical measures; sensitivity, specificity, and classification accuracy to calculate the performances of these models. Their purpose was to increase the campaign by identifying the characteristics affect the success. Ogwueleka et al. (2015) proposed an ANN model with a six-step procedure. They have used back-propagation algorithm to train the ANN by changing its weights to minimise the error. They have conducted an evaluation process to find the acceptable result from the proposed model. White & Safi (2016) compared three different forecasting techniques Regression models, ANNs, and Autoregressive Integrated Moving Average (ARIMA). They found that ANNs performed better with auto-correlated errors in comparison to regression and ARIMA for nonlinear models.

METHODOLOGY

Data Set Information

We have considered two kinds of credit card applications. To protect the confidentiality of the records in the databases, we have changed the attribute names of the dataset to meaningless symbols. There is a good mix of attributes taken in this dataset – small number of values in continuous, nominal form, and larger numbers of values in continuous form. In this study, two types of data set have been used for credit classification: 1) German Credit Approval Data Set which classifies persons -described by a set of behavioural characteristics as good/ bad credit risks to lenders. This comes in two formats - all numeric and cost matrix form 2) Australian Credit Approval Data Set: This file agglomerates the credit card applications and provides the basis for the proposed credit card approval process. This database exists elsewhere in the data repository in a non-identical form.

Table 1. Credit approval data set Australian and German

Credit Approval Data Set		
Characteristics	**Australian**	**German**
Data Set Characteristics	Multivariate	Multivariate
Attribute Characteristics	Categorical, Integer, Real	Categorical, Integer
Associated Tasks	Classification	Classification
Number of Instances	690	1000
Number of Attributes	14	20
Missing Values	Yes	N/A
Area	Financial	Financial
Date Donated	N/A	N/A
Number of Web Hits	70829	182499

More information about data set (accessed date: 5/3/2016) is available at:
https://archive.ics.uci.edu/ml/datasets/Statlog+%28German+Credit+Data%29_
https://archive.ics.uci.edu/ml/datasets/Statlog+%28Australian+Credit+Approval%29_

Structure of Functional Link Artificial Neural Network (FLANN)

The FLANN structure was initially proposed by Pao [25], and is a powerful tool for performing complex decision making and is capable of generating complex nonlinear decision boundaries. In a FLANN structure, the requirement of hidden layer is removed from the structure. The linear weightage of the associated input patterns of the MLP is a complex task but the FLANN acts on the entire pattern by its functional link to generate a set of linearly independent functions easily. The functional expansion block of FLANN is made up of exponential type polynomials. Let, input to this structure is $X=[x_1, x_2]^T$. An increased pattern obtained by using this functional expansion is given by

$$X= [1, x_1T_2(x_1), \ldots.., x_2T_2(x_2), \ldots]'$$

The algorithm used to train the FLANN structure is simple and has a rapid convergence due to no hidden layer in the architecture. The performance of the single layer neural network can be compare with MLP network.

Functional Link Artificial Neural Network

A single layer feed forward architecture is used in the FLANN to perform better on non-linear relationship of the attributes. The neuron at the output layer of the neural network is computed by taking the weighted sum of the functional attributes of the dataset. The gradient descent method is employed to optimise the weights in the training process. It has been observed that the set of functions suited for functional expansion may not be sufficient to map the existing non-linearity of the given task. To avoid such cases few more new functions may be assimilated to the existing set of functions for the expansion of the input dataset. Further enhancement of the dimensions of the dataset may not be a right choice.

Figure 1. PPN structure

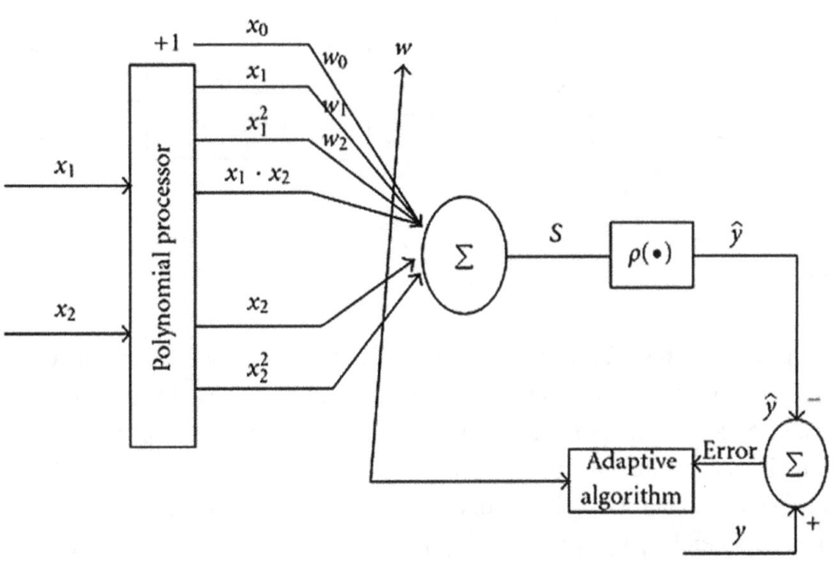

Figure 2. FLANN structure

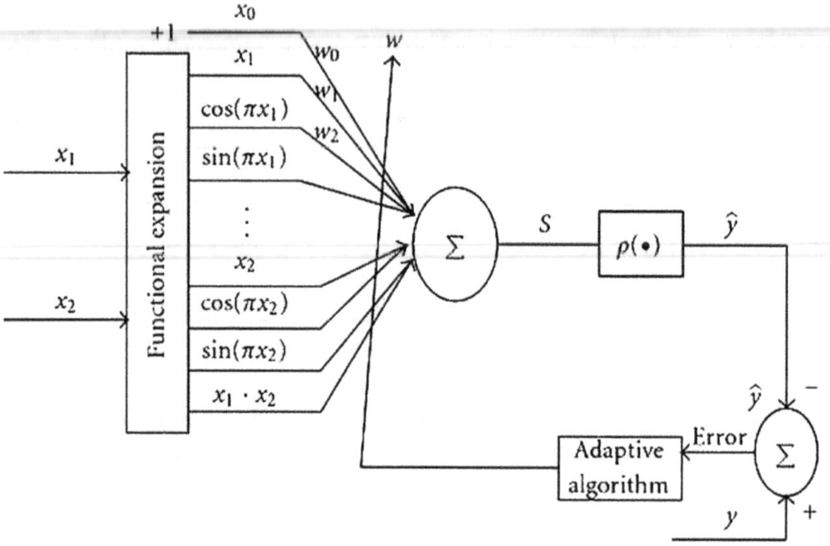

Figure 3. A Che. NN structure

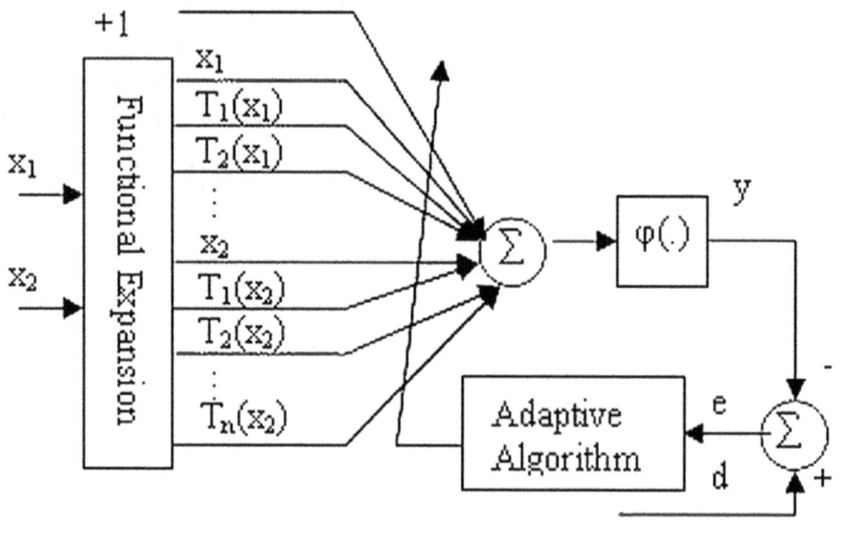

Proposed Method

In this work, we have used the general trigonometric function, Chebyshev expansion and exponential expansion for mapping the feature set from low to high dimension. The selection of the function depends on the data distribution and requires some prior domain knowledge of the process. We considered four trigonometric functions (two are sine and two are cosine) and one linear function (keeping the original form of the feature value) in our work. Here, in trigonometric function the range of the function is a real number and is lies between [-1, 1], where the domain is the feature values considered for the process.. The function can be expressed as

$$f : D \rightarrow R^{[-1,1] \cup x}$$

where D = $\{x_{i1}, x_{i2}, ..., x_{id}\}$, and d represents the total number of features in the domain. In general let us consider $f_1, f_2, ..., f_k$ be the number of functions applied to expand each feature value of the pattern. Therefore, each input pattern of the feature set can be illustrated as

$$\vec{X} = \{x_{i1}, x_{i2}, \ldots, x_{id}\} \rightarrow \{\{f_1(x_{i1}), f_2(x_{i1}), \ldots, f_k(x_{i1})\}, \ldots, \{f_1(x_{id}), f_2(x_{id}), \ldots, f_k(x_{id})\}\}$$
$$= \{\{y_{11}, y_{21}, \ldots, y_{k1}\}, \ldots, \{y_{1d}, y_{2d}, \ldots, y_{kd}\}\}$$

Trigonometric Functional Expansion

Here a functional model constitutes of a subset of orthogonal *sine* and *cosine* basis functions and the original pattern with its outer products are used for the functional expansion.

Consider a 2-D input pattern $X=[x_1, x_2]^T$, and the enhanced pattern of the feature set is obtained by applying a trigonometric functions as

$$x' = [x_1, cos\,(\delta x_1), sin\,(\delta x_1), cos\,(2\delta x_1), sin\,(2\delta x_1)]$$

The LMS algorithm was applied to train the network which makes the process easier given that there exists no hidden layer in the neural network.

Chebyshev Expansion

The Chebyshev polynomials are a set of orthogonal polynomials defined as the solution to the Chebyshev differential equation and denoted as $T_n(x)$. The first few Chebyshev polynomials are given by $T_0(x) = 1.0$, $T_1(x) = x$ and $T_2(x) = 2x^2 - 1$

The higher order Chebyshev polynomials can be produced by applying the recursive formula given by:

$$T_{n+1}(x) = 2xT_n(x) - T_{n-1}(x)$$

The initial few Chebyshev polynomials generated from the formula are given by

$$T_0(x) = 1.0,\ T_1(x) = x,\ T_2(x) = 2x^2 - 1,\ T_3(x) = 4x^3 - 3x,\ T_4(x) = 8x^4 - 8x^2 + 1, \text{ and}$$

$$T_5(x) = 16x^5 - 20x^3 + 5x$$

Exponential Expansion

For 2-D input patterns, the upgraded pattern can be found by utilizing exponential functions as given below:

$X_1 = [x_1, exp(x_1), exp(2\, x_1), exp(3\, x_1), ..., x_2, exp(x_2), exp(2\, x_2), exp(3\, x_2), exp(4\, x_2), ...]^T$.

It has been observed that this polynomial expansion would reduce the number of computations to a large extent and also implementing this scheme is very easy.

Computational Complexity

The computations of the sine and cosine functions using the FLANN structure are necessary for its functional expansion. However, in the traditional MLP method, the training as well as updation of the corresponding weights necessitates an extra computation due to presence of hidden layers. During error propagation, the MLP method requires the computation of the derivative of square error of each neuron from the hidden layer. Each of the training iterations can be broadly categorised into three phases, i.e.

1. The activation value of all the neurons of the entire network is computed in the forward calculation,
2. The square error derivatives are calculated through the back error propagation, and
3. The weights of the entire network are updated

Computational Model of a FLANN

Multilayer neural network remains the most popular amongst all other models for solving the complexities in classification. To date there exist several neural network algorithms that could be used to train the models. But, for models that are more involved and complex, there cannot be any single concrete algorithm that could claim to be the best for training especially in cases where there exist different levels of complexities in real life applications. Based on the nature and magnitude of the complexities, variables such as number of neurons and number of layers of the associated hidden layer need to be adjusted. Training the model becomes more complicated and cumbersome, as the number of neurons and the number of layers of the corresponding hidden layer increases. A single-layer neural network could be considered as a viable alternative approach, if the concern is to avoid or offset the complexities arising from multiple-layer neural network. The difficulty that arises with the single layer neural network models are that they being predominantly linear, often tend to underperform when used to solve complex real life problems. This being the case, and given that the classification task in most of the data mining process being non-linear, therefore, a single-layer NN will always fail to accomplish the classification accuracy. The FLANN architecture (Mishra and Dehuri, 2007; Pao, 2008) proposed a model with the motivation to address the gap between linear single layer NN and multi-layer NN. In hindsight, FLANN architecture could be construed as a non-linear network. The functional link of FLANN as opposed to the linear weighting of the input pattern acts on an element of a pattern or on the entire pattern by generating a set of linearly independent functions. These are then used to evaluate these functions with the pattern as the argument. The preceding section explains the pattern of a simple FLANN.

Let us consider a two dimensional input sample

$X=[x_1, x_2]^T$.

This sample is mapped to a higher dimensional space by functional expansion using trigonometric functions

$\Psi = [(x_1, sin\Pi x_1, sin2\Pi x_1, cos\Pi x_1, cos2\Pi x_1), (x_2, \sin\Pi x_2, sin2\Pi x_2, cos\Pi x_2, cos2\Pi x_2)]^T$

The weighted sum is defined by

$$\hat{y} = \sum_{i,j=1,2} w_i x_j + \sum_{i,j=1,2} w_i \sin i\pi x_j + \sum_{i,j=1,2} w_i \cos i\pi x_j \tag{1}$$

Here in the FLANN approach, Gradient descent algorithm is applied on the training samples to iteratively obtain the solution for W.

Using an approximating function $\Phi_w(X)$ we approximate or interpolate a continuous multivariate function $\Phi(X)$ during the learning phase. In the FLANN architecture, we use basis functions Ψ, together with a fixed number of weight parameters W to represent $\Phi_w(X)$. Based on the specific choice of set of basis functions Ψ, the new task then becomes to find the weight parameters W that can provide the best possible approximation of Ψ on the set of input-output samples. This can be achieved by iteratively updating W. For a complete theoretical exposition of the theory of FLANN classification scheme, one can refer to Mishra and Dehuri (2007).

Let k training patterns denoted by (x_i, y_i), $1 \leq i \leq k$ be applied to the FLANN and let the weight matrix be W. At the ith instant $1 \leq i \leq k$ the Q-dimensional input pattern and the FLANN output are given by

$X_i = (x_{i1}, x_{i2}, ..., x_{iQ})$, $1 \leq i \leq k$ and $\hat{Y}_i = [\hat{y}_i], 1 \leq i \leq k$

Hence $X = [X_1, X_2, ..., X_k]^T$. The augmented matrix of Q-dimensional input pattern and the FLANN output are given by:

$$(X, \hat{Y}) = \begin{Bmatrix} x_{1,1}\ x_{1,2} \cdots x_{1,Q} : \hat{y}_1 \\ x_{2,1}\ x_{2,2} \cdots x_{2,Q} : \hat{y}_2 \\ \cdots\cdots\cdots\cdots\cdots\cdots \\ x_{k,1}\ x_{k,2} \cdots x_{k,Q} : \hat{y}_k \end{Bmatrix} \tag{2}$$

As the dimension of the input pattern is increased from Q to Q' by a set of basis functions given by

$$\begin{aligned} \Psi(X_i) &= [\Psi_1(x_{i1}), \Psi_2(x_{i1}), ..., \Psi_1(x_{i2}), \Psi_2(x_{i2}), ..., \Psi_1(x_{iQ}), \Psi_2(x_{iQ}), ...] \\ &= [\Psi_1(x_{i1}), \Psi_2(x_{i2}), ..., \Psi_Q(x_{iQ})] \end{aligned}$$

The $k \times Q$ dimensional weight matrix is given by $W = [W_1, W_2, ..., W_k]^T$, where W_i is the weight vector associated with the ith output and is given by $W_1 = [W_{i1}, W_{i2}, ..., W_{iQ}]$. The ith output of the FLANN is given by

$$\hat{y}_i(t) = \varphi\left(\sum_{j=1}^{Q'} \Psi_j(x_{ij})(w_{ij})\right) = \varphi(W_i . \Psi^T(X_i)), \forall i$$

The error associated with the ith output is given by $e_i(t) = y_i(t) - \hat{y}_i(t)$. Using adaptive learning, weights of the FLANN can be updated as:

$$w_{ij}(t+1) = w_{ij}(t) + \mu.\Delta(t), \quad \Delta(t) = \delta_i(t).[\Psi(X_i)]$$

Where $\delta(t) = [\delta_1(t), \delta_2(t), ..., \delta_k(t)]$, and $\delta_i(t) = (1 - \hat{y}_i^2(t)e_i(t))$, where μ is called the learning parameter. Sometimes, when the choice of function considered for functional expansion cannot map the nonlinearity of the complex task, in such cases, additional functions have to be merged to the existing set of functions that are considered for expansion of the input data. This is easier said than done because at times dimensionalities of certain problems could be high and by further increasing the dimensionality should not be an appropriate choice. Therefore, it is sensible to select a smaller set of alternative functions, that is capable of mapping the concerned function to the preferred extent and which results in significant improvement in output.

CONFUSION MATRIX

The knowledge discovery process of the available data is an important process of determining valid and useful patterns of data. Data mining is considered to be an important step of KDD (Knowledge Discovery in Database). An exhaustive system of classification is a requiem to distinguish the variety of the systems generated by KDD and to identify the most useful system for the user. To identify a dataset wherein a small number of rules are applicable is the major hurdle of rule mining. The classifier for predicting the class of any recent instance will be these rules. It is important the classification algorithm is accurate, elegant and efficient. The algorithm will perform poorly on real world datasets as it is designed for a predefined distribution. To overcome this problem we need to divide the dataset into the following two parts.

- **Training Data Set:** It is the subset of the original dataset used to create the model.
- **Test Data Set:** It is the whole dataset which is then applied on the model tested through the training data set.
- **Confusion Matrix:** Is a known tool capable of measuring classification accuracy in data mining. Classification accuracy on a given test set can be measured as the % of test tuples that are accurately classified by the classifier.
- **A Confusion Matrix is Generally of the Form:** The performance accuracy of the model can be computed from different output of the confusion matrix designed for the model.

$$Accuracy = \frac{Number\ of\ tuples\ classified\ correctly}{Total\ number\ of\ tuples}$$

		Actual Class	
		Class 1	Class 0
Predicted Class	Class 1	TP	FN
	Class 0	FP	TN

TP: True Positive
TN: True Negative
FP: False Positive
FN: False Negative

$$Accuracy = \frac{TP + TN}{TP + TN + FP + FN} = \frac{TP + TN}{P + N}$$

where, $P = TP + FN \; and \; N = FP + TN$.

It is also important to find the error rate or misclassification rate of the classifier M.

Error rate (M) = 1- Accuracy (M), where Accuracy (M) is the accuracy of the classifier M. This also can be computed as

$$Error\ rate = \frac{FP + FN}{P + N}$$

The sensitivity & specificity measures can be computed and utilized to find the precise-ness of the model. Sensitivity is also referred to as the recognition rate, while specificity is the true negative rate.

$$Sensitivity = \frac{TP}{P}, and\ Specificity = \frac{TN}{N}$$

SIMULATION AND RESULT

In this model we have considered two different datasets, i.e., German credit dataset and Australian credit dataset. The datasets have been further divided into two categories, i.e., test set and training set. The data in the training set are trained with 1000 epochs and the weights are updated in each iteration. The average error is considered in each epoch shown in the following figure. We considered ten (10) different simulations and in each simulation randomly choosing the test and training data set to construct the confusion matrix for the two different datasets. From the confusion matrix we calculate the average of sensitivity, specificity, precision, and accuracy as shown in the figure below. The results shown in Table 2 to Table 5 are the confusion matrices of FLANNT model for both the datasets and SIM 1 to SIM 10 represents the 10 simulations taken to compute the performance of the model for classifying good credit and bad credit.

The different performance measures i.e. sensitivity, specificity, precision and accuracy have been computed by considering the values of Table 2 and Table 3 for test and training datasets respectively. The average performance of the different measures has been calculated for both test and training datasets of the German credit dataset. The graph (Figure 4) shows that the sensitivity of our model is more than 93% from the training set of the German credit dataset. The accuracy label of the model is more than

Table 2. Confusion matrix of FLANNT model for German credit test dataset

Simulation	SIM1	SIM2	SIM3	SIM4	SIM5	SIM6	SIM7	SIM8	SIM9	SIM10
True Positive	294	298	292	289	285	293	293	294	306	304
False Negative	52	43	51	67	61	53	60	53	46	48
False Positive	91	89	88	69	75	71	76	72	87	88
True Negative	63	70	69	75	79	83	71	81	61	60

Table 3. Confusion matrix of FLLANT model for German credit training dataset

Simulation	SIM1	SIM2	SIM3	SIM4	SIM5	SIM6	SIM7	SIM8	SIM9	SIM10
True Positive	336	313	323	339	332	283	332	343	348	234
False Negative	11	28	32	22	19	51	16	14	9	24
False Positive	53	48	46	40	48	34	47	42	66	34
True Negative	100	111	99	99	101	132	105	101	77	108

Table 4. Confusion matrix of FLANNT model for Australian Credit test dataset

Simulation	SIM1	SIM2	SIM3	SIM4	SIM5	SIM6	SIM7	SIM8	SIM9	SIM10
True Positive	121	117	139	128	122	123	123	130	121	112
False Negative	46	34	20	32	25	18	27	27	28	32
False Positive	12	27	35	23	27	34	15	32	30	21
True Negative	166	167	151	162	171	170	180	156	166	180

Table 5. Confusion matrix of FLANNT model for Australian credit training dataset

Simulation	SIM1	SIM2	SIM3	SIM4	SIM5	SIM6	SIM7	SIM8	SIM9	SIM10
True Positive	147	142	135	151	140	142	162	143	136	138
False Negative	13	15	18	13	14	16	11	19	13	15
False Positive	16	22	10	12	12	9	9	9	12	14
True Negative	169	166	182	169	179	178	163	174	184	178

84% with the training dataset. The model classifies "good credit" applicant as a "good credit" for the loan approval process. The potential customer is accepted by the model for the credit with 93% probability. Similarly, we can compute different performance measures for Australian Credit dataset from Table 4 and Table 5. The graph (Figure 5) shows that the sensitivity is more than 90% from the training set of the Australian credit dataset. The accuracy label of the model is more than 92% with the training dataset. Here the specificity is more than 93% calculated from the training set .The model classifies "bad credit" applicant as a "bad credit" for the loan approval process. The potential customer is accepted by the model for the credit with 90% probability. The bad credit customer is rejected by the model for the credit with 93% probability.

Figure 4. FLANNT on German credit data

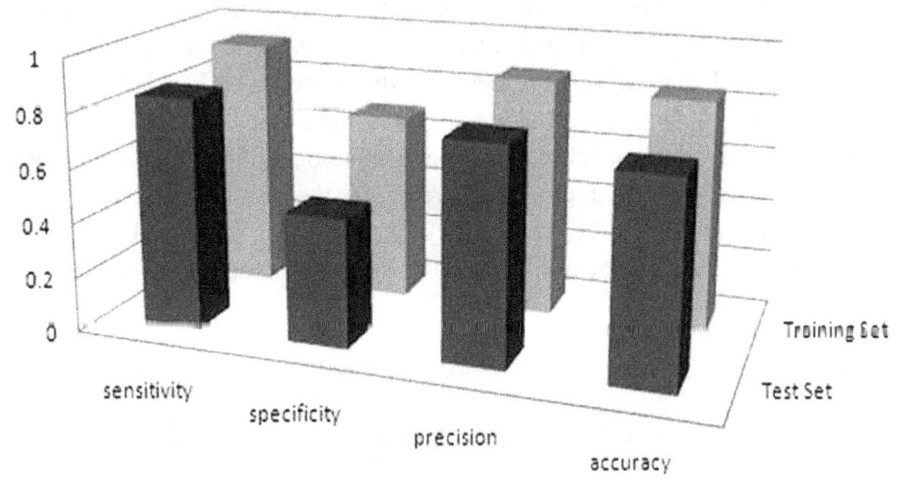

	sensitivity	specificity	precision	accuracy
Test Set	0.8467	0.4691	0.7857	0.732
Training Set	0.9324	0.6915	0.8747	0.8432

Figure 5. FLANNT on Australian credit data

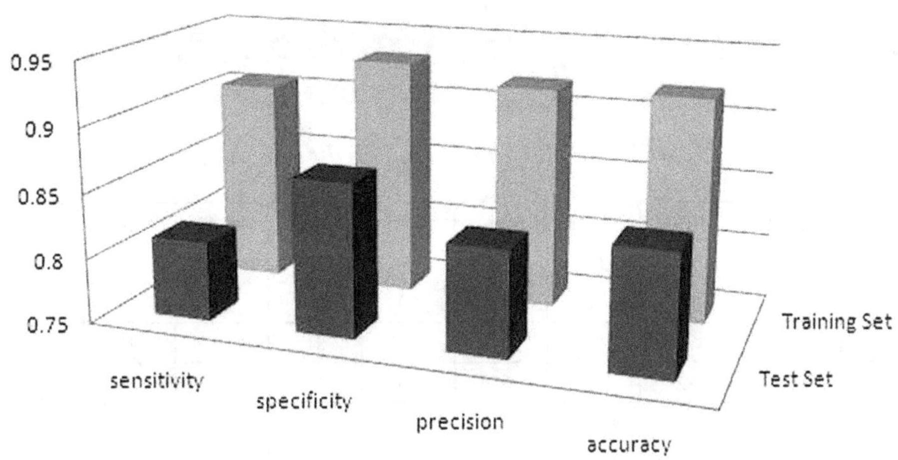

	sensitivity	specificity	precision	accuracy
Test Set	0.8113	0.8673	0.8308	0.842
Training Set	0.9067	0.9331	0.9201	0.9211

The difference between the intended output and the actual output is the error and it is calculated for each epoc. The graph (Figure 6) shows the error convergence pattern. In case of Australian credit dataset the error is less than 0.07 (7%) and in case of German credit data the error is less than 0.14 (14%).

The results shown in Table 6 to Table 9 are the confusion matrices of FLANNC model for both the datasets. The graph (Figure 10) shows that the sensitivity is more than 92% from the training set of the German credit dataset. The accuracy label of the model is more than 85% with the training dataset. The model classifies "good credit" applicant as a "good credit" for the loan approval process. The potential customer is accepted by the model for the credit with 92% probability. The graph (Figure 8) shows that the sensitivity is more than 89% from the training set of the Australian credit dataset. The accuracy label

Figure 6. Average error convergence of FLANNT for Australian and German credit data

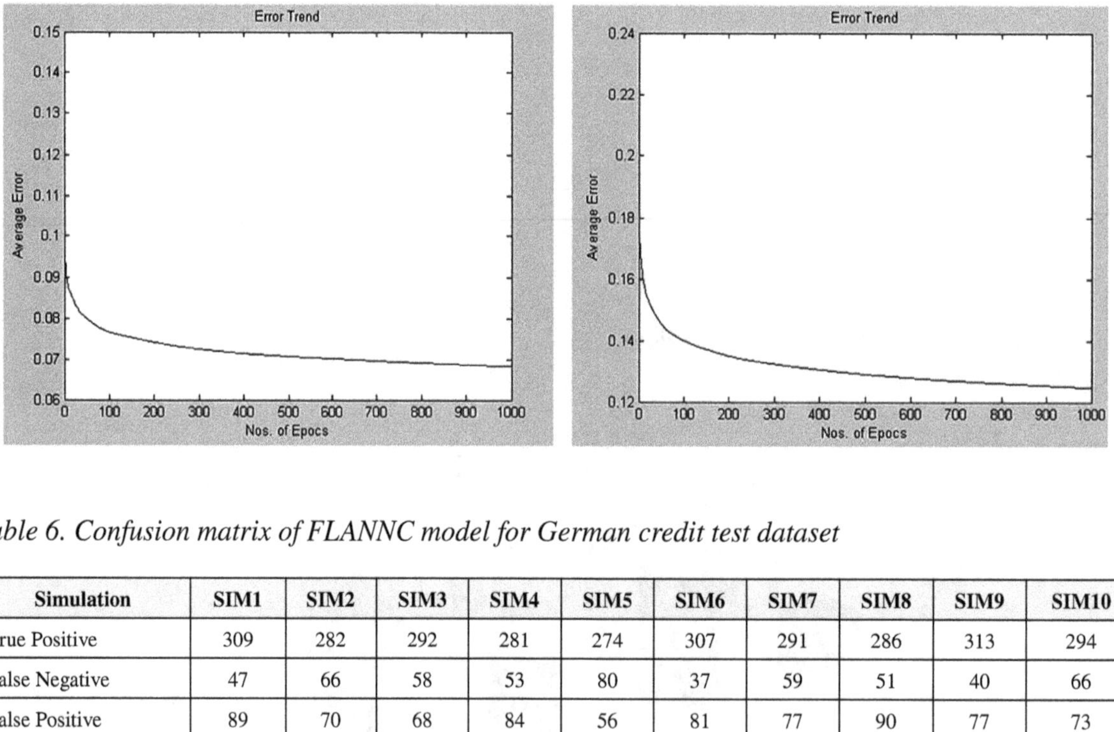

Table 6. Confusion matrix of FLANNC model for German credit test dataset

Simulation	SIM1	SIM2	SIM3	SIM4	SIM5	SIM6	SIM7	SIM8	SIM9	SIM10
True Positive	309	282	292	281	274	307	291	286	313	294
False Negative	47	66	58	53	80	37	59	51	40	66
False Positive	89	70	68	84	56	81	77	90	77	73
True Negative	55	82	82	82	90	75	73	73	70	67

Table 7. Confusion matrix of FLANNC model for German credit training dataset

Simulation	SIM1	SIM2	SIM3	SIM4	SIM5	SIM6	SIM7	SIM8	SIM9	SIM10
True Positive	330	343	334	302	315	323	326	331	335	312
False Negative	25	17	20	53	27	34	21	27	20	38
False Positive	49	41	38	43	25	50	48	37	48	51
True Negative	96	99	108	102	133	93	105	105	97	99

Table 8. Confusion matrix of FLANNC model for Australian credit test dataset

Simulation	SIM1	SIM2	SIM3	SIM4	SIM5	SIM6	SIM7	SIM8	SIM9	SIM10
True Positive	120	131	119	126	100	114	127	117	124	114
False Negative	23	28	40	34	58	47	34	37	35	28
False Positive	34	20	17	22	16	19	21	24	21	24
True Negative	168	166	169	163	171	165	163	167	165	179

Table 9. Confusion matrix of FLANNT model for Australian credit training dataset

Simulation	SIM1	SIM2	SIM3	SIM4	SIM5	SIM6	SIM7	SIM8	SIM9	SIM10
True Positive	150	127	137	144	158	136	128	134	134	139
False Negative	15	15	23	9	9	15	24	18	13	16
False Positive	17	16	12	24	16	13	12	15	9	12
True Negative	163	187	173	168	162	181	181	178	186	178

Figure 7. FLANNC on German Credit

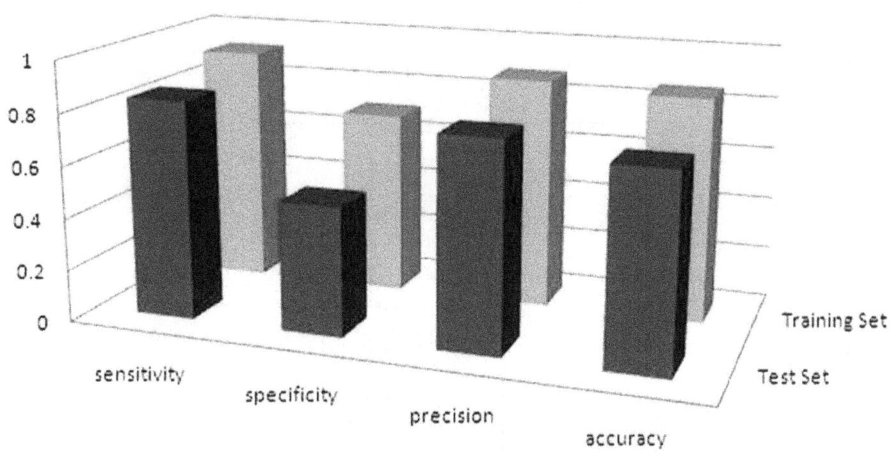

	sensitivity	specificity	precision	accuracy
Test Set	0.8403	0.4948	0.7935	0.7356
Training Set	0.9201	0.7059	0.8834	0.8576

of the model is more than 91% with the training dataset. Here the specificity is more than 92% calculated from the training set. The bad credit customer is rejected by the model for the credit with 92% probability.

The graph (Figure 9) shows the error convergence pattern for FLANNC. In case of German credit dataset the error is 0.12 (12%) and in case of Australian credit data the error is less than 0.09 (9%).

Figure 8. FLANNC on Australian Credit

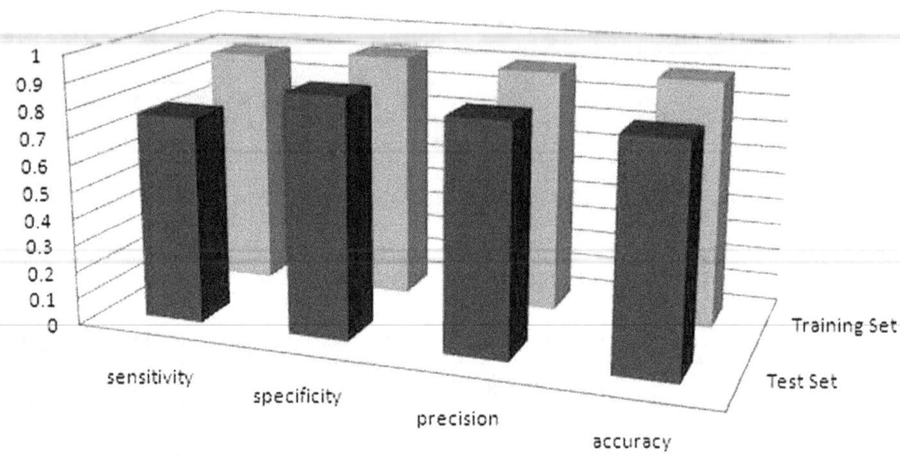

	sensitivity	specificity	precision	accuracy
Test Set	0.7671	0.8854	0.8461	0.8313
Training Set	0.8979	0.923	0.9054	0.9113

Figure 9. Average Error convergence of FLANNC for German and Australian Credit data

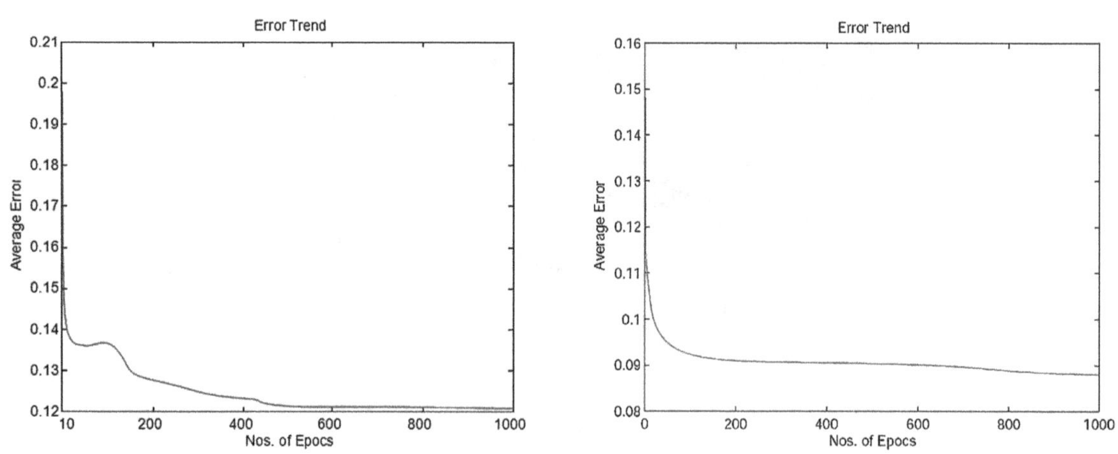

The results shown in Table 10 to Table 13 are the confusion matrices of FLANNE model for both the datasets. The graph (Figure 10) shows that the sensitivity is around 89% from the training set of the German credit dataset. The accuracy label of the model is more than 76% with the training dataset. The model classifies "good credit" applicant as a "good credit" for the loan approval process. The potential customer is accepted by the model for the credit with 89% probability. The graph (Figure 11) shows that the sensitivity is more than 89% from the training set of the Australian credit dataset. The accuracy label

Table 10. FLANNE model for German credit test dataset

Simulation	SIM1	SIM2	SIM3	SIM4	SIM5	SIM6	SIM7	SIM8	SIM9	SIM10
True Positive	309	277	305	327	326	309	281	280	229	280
False Negative	34	77	47	25	26	48	53	72	129	77
False Positive	94	52	91	106	99	76	80	67	29	65
True Negative	63	94	57	42	49	67	86	81	113	78

Table 11. FLANNE model for German credit training dataset

Simulation	SIM1	SIM2	SIM3	SIM4	SIM5	SIM6	SIM7	SIM8	SIM9	SIM10
True Positive	326	297	347	314	351	320	350	281	303	195
False Negative	22	56	10	30	2	22	6	47	40	139
False Positive	81	57	102	73	137	85	117	58	63	39
True Negative	71	90	41	83	10	73	27	114	94	127

Table 12. FLANNE model for Australian credit test dataset

Simulation	SIM1	SIM2	SIM3	SIM4	SIM5	SIM6	SIM7	SIM8	SIM9	SIM10
True Positive	126	145	132	131	144	142	146	141	145	138
False Negative	19	7	9	11	8	13	14	16	10	12
False Positive	38	40	43	43	44	45	38	33	39	38
True Negative	162	153	161	160	149	145	147	155	151	157

Table 13. FLANNE model for Australian credit training dataset

Simulation	SIM1	SIM2	SIM3	SIM4	SIM5	SIM6	SIM7	SIM8	SIM9	SIM10
True Positive	113	137	133	145	141	136	150	138	141	143
False Negative	53	14	19	10	14	16	9	9	13	15
False Positive	29	37	40	39	35	36	38	41	37	44
True Negative	150	157	153	151	155	157	148	157	154	143

of the model is more than 84% with the training dataset. Here the specificity is more than 80% calculated from the training set. The bad credit customer is rejected by the model for the credit with 80% probability.

The graph (Figure 12) shows the error convergence pattern for FLANNE. In case of German credit dataset, the error is less than 0.2 (20%) and in case of Australian credit data the error is less than 0.15 (15%).

Figure 10. FLANNE German credit data

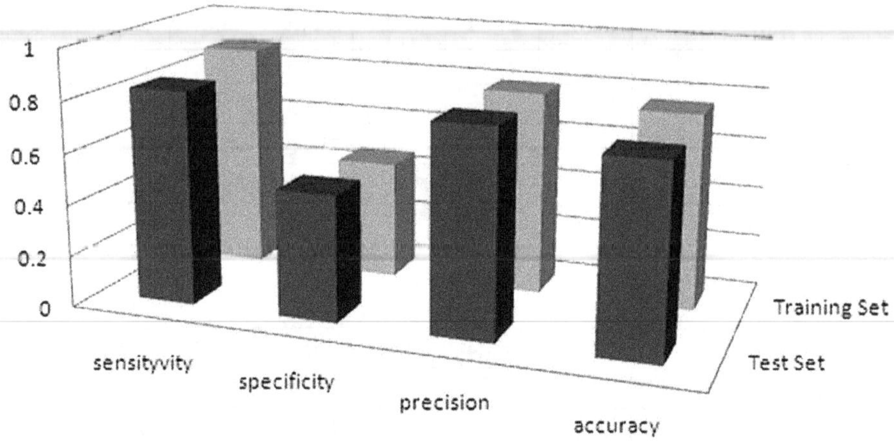

	sensityvity	specificity	precision	accuracy
■ Test Set	0.8331	0.492	0.7988	0.7306
▒ Training Set	0.8899	0.4642	0.7973	0.7628

Figure 11. FLANNE Australian credit data

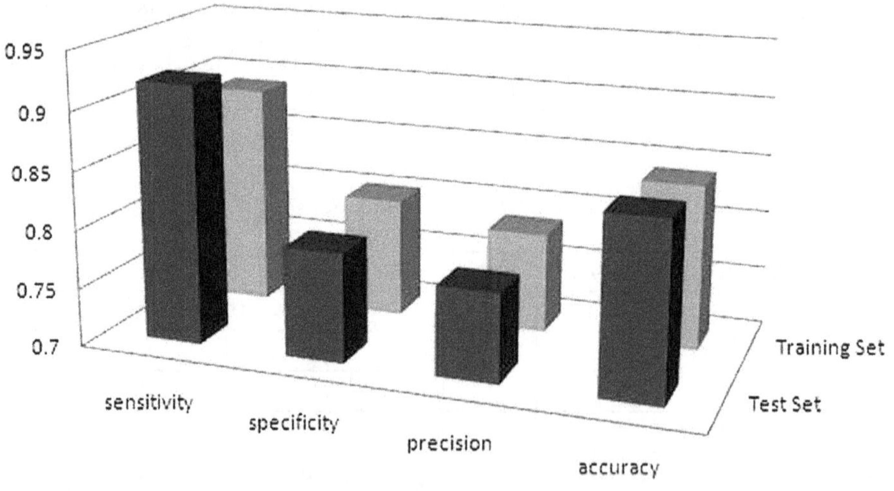

	sensitivity	specificity	precision	accuracy
■ Test Set	0.9211	0.7934	0.776	0.8492
▒ Training Set	0.8905	0.8023	0.7857	0.8411

Figure 12. Average error convergence of FLANNE for German and Australian credit data

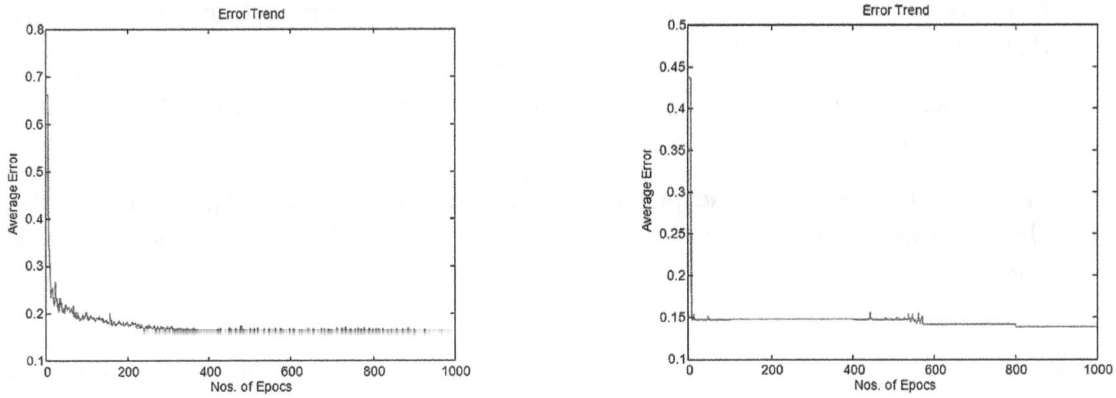

CONCLUSION

The credit datasets were tested as per the proposed FLANN architecture. We have used three different variants for the proposed architecture: trigonometric, chebyshev and exponential approximations. The accuracy of all the three models were compared and summarized in the sections above. It was found from our computations that FLANNT performed better so far as classification of the German credit data is concerned for good and bad credit. However, so far as accuracy is concerned, the model FLANNT showed better convergence for Australian credit data.

REFERENCES

Abdou, H., Pointon, J., & El-Masry, A. (2008). Neural nets versus conventional techniques in credit scoring in Egyptian banking. *Expert Systems with Applications*, *35*(3), 1275–1292. doi:10.1016/j.eswa.2007.08.030

Abdou, H. A. (2009). An evaluation of alternative scoring models in private banking. *The Journal of Risk Finance*, *10*(1), 38–53. doi:10.1108/15265940910924481

Angelini, E., di Tollo, G., & Roli, A. (2008). A neural network approach for credit risk evaluation. *The Quarterly Review of Economics and Finance*, *48*(4), 733–755. doi:10.1016/j.qref.2007.04.001

Basch, C. A., Bruesewitz, B. J., Siegel, K., & Faith, P. (2003). *U.S. Patent No. 6,658,393*. Washington, DC: U.S. Patent and Trademark Office.

Becchetti, L., & Sierra, J. (2003). Bankruptcy risk and productive efficiency in manufacturing firms. *Journal of Banking & Finance*, *27*(11), 2099–2120. doi:10.1016/S0378-4266(02)00319-9

Behara, R. S., Fisher, W. W., & Lemmink, J. G. (2002). Modelling and evaluating service quality measurement using neural networks. *International Journal of Operations & Production Management*, *22*(10), 1162–1185. doi:10.1108/01443570210446360

Binner, J. M., Bissoondeeal, R. K., Elger, T., Gazely, A. M., & Mullineux, A. W. (2005). A comparison of linear forecasting models and neural networks: an application to Euro inflation and Euro Divisia. *Applied Economics, 37*(6), 665-680.

Buscema, M. (2002). A brief overview and introduction to artificial neural networks. *Substance Use & Misuse, 37*(8-10), 1093–1148. doi:10.1081/JA-120004171 PMID:12180558

Corchado, J. M., & Lees, B. (2001). Adaptation of cases for case based forecasting with neural network support. In *Soft computing in case based reasoning* (pp. 293–319). Springer London. doi:10.1007/978-1-4471-0687-6_13

Crone, S. F., & Finlay, S. (2012). Instance sampling in credit scoring: An empirical study of sample size and balancing. *International Journal of Forecasting, 28*(1), 224–238. doi:10.1016/j.ijforecast.2011.07.006

Dawson, C. W., & Wilby, R. L. (2001). Hydrological modelling using artificial neural networks. *Progress in Physical Geography, 25*(1), 80–108. doi:10.1191/030913301674775671

Elsalamony, H. A. (2014). Bank Direct Marketing Analysis of Data Mining Techniques. *International Journal of Computers and Applications, 85*(7).

Fenton, N., & Neil, M. (2012). *Risk assessment and decision analysis with Bayesian networks*. CRC Press.

Francis, L. (2001, March). Neural networks demystified. *Casualty Actuarial Society Forum*, 253-320.

Holopainen, M., & Sarlin, P. (2015). Toward robust early-warning models: A horse race, ensembles and model uncertainty. *Bank of Finland Research Discussion Paper*, (6).

Jeatrakul, P., & Wong, K. W. (2009, October). Comparing the performance of different neural networks for binary classification problems. In *Natural Language Processing, 2009. SNLP'09. Eighth International Symposium on* (pp. 111-115). IEEE. doi:10.1109/SNLP.2009.5340935

Khashei, M., Hamadani, A. Z., & Bijari, M. (2012). A novel hybrid classification model of artificial neural networks and multiple linear regression models. *Expert Systems with Applications, 39*(3), 2606–2620. doi:10.1016/j.eswa.2011.08.116

Khashman, A. (2010). Neural networks for credit risk evaluation: Investigation of different neural models and learning schemes. *Expert Systems with Applications, 37*(9), 6233–6239. doi:10.1016/j.eswa.2010.02.101

Khashman, A. (2011). Credit risk evaluation using neural networks: Emotional versus conventional models. *Applied Soft Computing, 11*(8), 5477–5484. doi:10.1016/j.asoc.2011.05.011

Koh, H. C., Tan, W. C., & Peng, G. C. (2004). Credit scoring using data mining techniques. *Singapore Management Review, 26*(2), 25.

Kumar, K., & Bhattacharya, S. (2006). Artificial neural network vs linear discriminant analysis in credit ratings forecast: A comparative study of prediction performances. *Review of Accounting and Finance, 5*(3), 216–227. doi:10.1108/14757700610686426

Kumar, K., & Haynes, J. D. (2003). Forecasting credit ratings using an ANN and statistical techniques. *International Journal of Business Studies.*

Lee, T. S., & Chen, I. F. (2005). A two-stage hybrid credit scoring model using artificial neural networks and multivariate adaptive regression splines. *Expert Systems with Applications*, *28*(4), 743–752. doi:10.1016/j.eswa.2004.12.031

Leong, C. K. (2015). Credit risk scoring with bayesian network models. *Computational Economics*, 1–24.

Lin, J. W., Hwang, M. I., & Becker, J. D. (2003). A fuzzy neural network for assessing the risk of fraudulent financial reporting. *Managerial Auditing Journal*, *18*(8), 657–665. doi:10.1108/02686900310495151

Lin, S. L. (2009). A new two-stage hybrid approach of credit risk in banking industry. *Expert Systems with Applications*, *36*(4), 8333–8341. doi:10.1016/j.eswa.2008.10.015

Linder, R., Geier, J., & Kölliker, M. (2004). Artificial neural networks, classification trees and regression: Which method for which customer base? *The Journal of Database Marketing & Customer Strategy Management*, *11*(4), 344–356. doi:10.1057/palgrave.dbm.3240233

Maes, S., Tuyls, K., Vanschoenwinkel, B., & Manderick, B. (2002, January). Credit card fraud detection using Bayesian and neural networks.*Proceedings of the 1st international naiso congress on neuro fuzzy technologies*, 261-270.

Malhotra, R., & Malhotra, D. K. (2003). Evaluating consumer loans using neural networks. *Omega*, *31*(2), 83–96. doi:10.1016/S0305-0483(03)00016-1

Marques, A. I., García, V., & Sanchez, J. S. (2012). A literature review on the application of evolutionary computing to credit scoring. *The Journal of the Operational Research Society*, *64*(9), 1384–1399. doi:10.1057/jors.2012.145

Metaxiotis, K., & Psarras, J. (2004). The contribution of neural networks and genetic algorithms to business decision support: Academic myth or practical solution? *Management Decision*, *42*(2), 229–242. doi:10.1108/00251740410518534

Mezei, J., & Sarlin, P. (2016). *RiskRank: Measuring interconnected risk*. arXiv preprint arXiv:1601.06204

Misra, B. B., & Dehuri, S. (2007). Functional Link Artificial Neural Network for Classification Task in Data Mining. *J. Comput. Sci.*, *3*(12), 948–955. doi:10.3844/jcssp.2007.948.955

Ogwueleka, F. N., Misra, S., Colomo-Palacios, R., & Fernandez, L. (2015). Neural network and classification approach in identifying customer behavior in the banking sector: A case study of an international bank. *Human Factors and Ergonomics in Manufacturing & Service Industries*, *25*(1), 28–42.

Oreski, S., Oreski, D., & Oreski, G. (2012). Hybrid system with genetic algorithm and artificial neural networks and its application to retail credit risk assessment. *Expert Systems with Applications*, *39*(16), 12605–12617. doi:10.1016/j.eswa.2012.05.023

Pacelli, V., & Azzollini, M. (2011). An artificial neural network approach for credit risk management. *Journal of Intelligent Learning Systems and Applications*, *3*(2), 103–112. doi:10.4236/jilsa.2011.32012

Pao, H. T. (2008). A comparison of neural network and multiple regression analysis in modeling capital structure. *Expert Systems with Applications*, *35*(3), 720–727. doi:10.1016/j.eswa.2007.07.018

Phua, C., Lee, V., Smith, K., & Gayler, R. (2010). *A comprehensive survey of data mining-based fraud detection research.* arXiv preprint arXiv:1009.6119

Shen, A., Tong, R., & Deng, Y. (2007, June). Application of classification models on credit card fraud detection. In *Service Systems and Service Management, 2007 International Conference on* (pp. 1-4). IEEE. doi:10.1109/ICSSSM.2007.4280163

Singh, P., & Borah, B. (2013). Indian summer monsoon rainfall prediction using artificial neural network. *Stochastic Environmental Research and Risk Assessment*, *27*(7), 1585–1599. doi:10.1007/s00477-013-0695-0

Sun, J., Li, H., Huang, Q. H., & He, K. Y. (2014). Predicting financial distress and corporate failure: A review from the state-of-the-art definitions, modeling, sampling, and featuring approaches. *Knowledge-Based Systems*, *57*, 41–56. doi:10.1016/j.knosys.2013.12.006

Tang, T. C., & Chi, L. C. (2005). Neural networks analysis in business failure prediction of Chinese importers: A between-countries approach. *Expert Systems with Applications*, *29*(2), 244–255. doi:10.1016/j.eswa.2005.03.003

Triki, I. (n.d.). *Credit Scoring Models for a Tunisian Microfinance Institution: Comparison between Artificial Neural Network and Logistic Regression*. Academic Press.

Tsai, C. F., & Chen, M. L. (2010). Credit rating by hybrid machine learning techniques. *Applied Soft Computing*, *10*(2), 374–380. doi:10.1016/j.asoc.2009.08.003

Tsakonas, A., Dounias, G., Doumpos, M., & Zopounidis, C. (2006). Bankruptcy prediction with neural logic networks by means of grammar-guided genetic programming. *Expert Systems with Applications*, *30*(3), 449–461. doi:10.1016/j.eswa.2005.10.009

Wei, W., Li, J., Cao, L., Ou, Y., & Chen, J. (2013). Effective detection of sophisticated online banking fraud on extremely imbalanced data. *World Wide Web (Bussum)*, *16*(4), 449–475. doi:10.1007/s11280-012-0178-0

West, J., & Bhattacharya, M. (2016). Intelligent financial fraud detection: A comprehensive review. *Computers & Security*, *57*, 47–66. doi:10.1016/j.cose.2015.09.005

White, A. K., & Safi, S. K. (2016). The Efficiency of Artificial Neural Networks for Forecasting in the Presence of Autocorrelated Disturbances. *International Journal of Statistics and Probability*, *5*(2), 51. doi:10.5539/ijsp.v5n2p51

Xu, X., Zhou, C., & Wang, Z. (2009). Credit scoring algorithm based on link analysis ranking with support vector machine. *Expert Systems with Applications*, *36*(2), 2625–2632. doi:10.1016/j.eswa.2008.01.024

Yeung, D. S., Ng, W. W., Chan, A. P., Chan, P. P., Firth, M., & Tsang, E. C. (2007). A multiple intelligent agent system for credit risk prediction via an optimization of localized generalization error with diversity. *Journal of Systems Science and Systems Engineering*, *16*(2), 166–180. doi:10.1007/s11518-007-5048-4

Zhang, G. P. (2004). Business forecasting with artificial neural networks: An overview. *Neural Networks in Business Forecasting*, 1-22.

Chapter 14
Vehicular Traffic Forecasting in Filling Station

Peeyush Pandey
IIM Indore, India

Tuhin Sengupta
IIM Indore, India

ABSTRACT

Forecasting is the one of the important part of decision making process. It helps managers to identify short term and long term future trends in the business activities. It may help in forecasting demand in retail store, predicting customer traffic at the petrol pump, calculation of probable population in upcoming years etc. There are plenty of studies published on forecasting techniques which are just introductory or highly mathematical and lacks in providing managerial perspective of solving business problems to the students. This chapter elucidates various forecasting techniques and its application in the field of management. In addition, various examples of real life problems are solved and analyzed with multiple forecasting techniques. Through this chapter students will have a clear understanding of the various nuances of different forecasting models in one single data set. Students will be able to identify future trend and seasonality in real life data set and evaluate more appropriate forecasting technique for the decision-making process.

1. LEARNING OBJECTIVES

- This chapter will help students to learn two different forecasting techniques of stationary time series and its applications in service sector
- With the learning provided through the chapter, students will be able to identify the best forecasting technique for the dataset in hand.
- This chapter will help students in problem solving and identifying future trends in various domains of service industry.

DOI: 10.4018/978-1-5225-2148-8.ch014

Intended Audience

1. MBA/Post Graduate Students specializing in the area of Operations Management, Information Systems & Quantitative Techniques who are interested in learning forecasting techniques and its applications.
2. Faculty members in the area of Operations Management, Information Systems & Quantitative Techniques can use this chapter as a guideline in preparing their forecasting teaching pedagogy.
3. Corporate Practitioners who are looking for simple forecasting techniques with its applications in the Service Sector

2. INTRODUCTION

Forecasting is the process of predicting future trends based on historical data. companies nowadays look for better forecasting techniques so that they can plan their activities in advance. For example a petrol pump owner can reduce his operational cost by forecasting number of vehicles that may arrive for the purpose of oil filling, a product manufacturer can harness maximum profit by forecasting product's demand, manager in the retail store can reduce his operational cost by assigning optimal number of employees which satisfies forecasted customer traffic. Forecasting can also help in getting future trends of economy, population, pollution, weather and traffic etc.

With rising competition in the market and to remain competitive, companies nowadays started to focus on better forecasting techniques to plan and schedule their activities. Since the success of any business depends heavily on how well its management can predict future trends and can devise appropriate strategies. The management can utilize forecasting to determine how to allocate their budgets or plan for anticipated expenses for an upcoming period. This is typically based on the projected demand for the goods and services they offer. The inappropriate forecasting strategies of a company can lead to bankruptcy due to shortage or excess of inventory, unnecessary labor expenses and lack of technological advancement.

There are ample of forecasting techniques developed in recent years but their use largely depends on the context requirement. It is the responsibility of forecaster to select efficient forecasting technique considering its use and data handling flexibility for particular application. The more appropriate forecasting technique will give the more accurate results and future trend In this way, the selection of best forecasting technique is based on many factors like: available historical data, time available for analysis, cost benefit analysis, context of the problem and desirable accuracy of the forecaster. These factors must be evaluated and analyzed on various level while selecting a better forecasting technique. For example, a forecaster should select a technique that fully utilizes the available data. The trade-off between available data and accuracy of forecast must be analyzed carefully. There can be multiple techniques which may provide accurate forecast but for those techniques the requirement of historical of data may be large. Therefore the forecaster must first identify the product for which forecasting is to be made and it's; life cycle stage, available historical data, factors effecting the production of the product and desirable accuracy of the forecast etc.

There are basically two types of forecasting techniques i.e qualitative forecasting techniques and quantitative forecasting techniques. The first one refers to the opinions and judgment of experts, consumers and senior level managers on the basis of their past experience. This type of forecasting techniques are used when no numerical data is available to analyze the past trend. These techniques are usually applied for the long term planning and decision making.

Whereas quantitative forecasting techniques uses the historical numerical data to forecast the future trend. The underlying assumption of these type of techniques is that the future data will continue to follow existing trend.

In addition, casual models are also used for the complex forecasting problems for better accuracy of forecasts. It uses historical data, special events, refined and specific information about relationships between system elements for forecasting purpose. These models are beyond the scope of this chapter as our main focus is to provide students an overview of various forecasting techniques. A detailed description of both qualitative and quantitative forecasting techniques is shown in the following section.

In this way, this chapter shows an overview of various forecasting techniques and its applications in real life problem. It gives the audience an understanding of selecting best forecasting technique for the problem in hand. Through this students will be able to analyze benefits and shortcoming of various forecasting techniques for a real life problem.

3. QUALITATIVE FORECASTING TECHNIQUES

Qualitative forecasting refers to estimation techniques that uses experts opinion, intuitions and experience rather than numerical analysis. In real life there can be multiple scenarios in which quantitative information is not available or the quantitative forecasting techniques cant not be applied. Therefore, in those situation, qualitative forecasting techniques plays a vital role. For example, when a new product is introduced in the market then the company has no historical data of its consumption. Therefore the demand forecasting for the product is basically based on many experts opinion and judgment. The qualitative forecasting technique brings together the experience, judgment and human ratings logically to relate the factors being estimated. Such techniques are frequently used in the case when historical data is not available and the product is just came out form the R & D. Qualitative forecasting techniques can be useful in formulating short-term forecasts. The most popular qualitative forecasting techniques are described as follows:

Manager's Opinion

In this forecasting technique, managers find out the forecasted quantity on the basis of real life data or on the basis of her past experience. This is the most informal of the methods, because it simply involves a single manager using his or her best judgment to make the forecast.

Jury of Executive Opinion

This technique is different from the earlier one in a way that it requires a group of high level experts in the process of decision making. Under this forecasting technique, the relevant opinions of multiple experts are taken, combined and averaged to reach at a single forecast. This method is used for the critical decisions in which responsibility is divided among the several executives. The executives are asked to participate and generate new ideas that can later be evaluated and used for the decision making.

Sales Force Composite

In this forecasting method, sales people are known to be more reliable source of information for the demand forecast as they are in close proximity to the customers. It is a bottom up approach in which sales figures from different territory are combined to form a corporate sales forecast. The basic assumption of this method is that the sales force has significant insights regarding the state of the future market which may not be true in all case. For example, the overly optimistic sale force may inflate the size of demand in the expectation of bigger event which may not be the case in real life.

Consumer Market Survey

In this method, companies conduct their own survey which consist a set of question that are asked to the potential consumers of the product and services. The questions are about the consumer's purchase plan, their response for the additional feature in the product, future needs which help in developing initial forecast of the companies sale. The companies usually collect the responses of consumers through telephone, personal interview and promotional activities and the statistical analysis is performed to test the hypothesis of consumers behavior.

Delphi Method

The Delphi method originally developed by Rank Corporation in 1969 for forecasting military events. It is the extended version of the jury of executive opinion method. In this approach. a panel of experts are questioned individually to extract their opinions about the future event. the responses are then analyzed and summarized presented back in front of panel by the third party for further consideration. All the responses are anonymous so that the experts do not get influenced by others. This process is repeated until a consensus is obtained. This type of method is very useful in long term forecasting. The method removes the disadvantage of group think since the responses are anonymous. The only drawback of this method is the low reliability of the method and the lack of consensus in some cases.

4. QUANTITATIVE FORECASTING TECHNIQUES

Quantitative forecasting techniques extract the meaningful statistics and predict future values based on observed numerical data points. It uses the historical data points stored in the format of time series. Whereas Time Series is a series of past data points graphed in equal interval of time. if X_i is the variable of interest at different point of time $i = 1, 2, \ldots t$ then the observed values $\{X_1, X_2, \ldots X_t\}$ of variable X_i are known as the time series. for example, the number of vehicles arrived in a petrol pump for the purpose of oil filling at different point of time is a time series shown in Figure 1.

In this way to forecast the number of vehicles in the next hour, the historical data is analyzed and a mathematical model is postulated to represent the process of vehicle arrival. So time series forecasting is the use of a model to predict future values based on previously observed values. Some time in real life, when we do not have complete knowledge of exact model that fits best to the forecasting, an approximate model should be used. Under the quantitative forecasting techniques, several pattern of time

Figure 1.

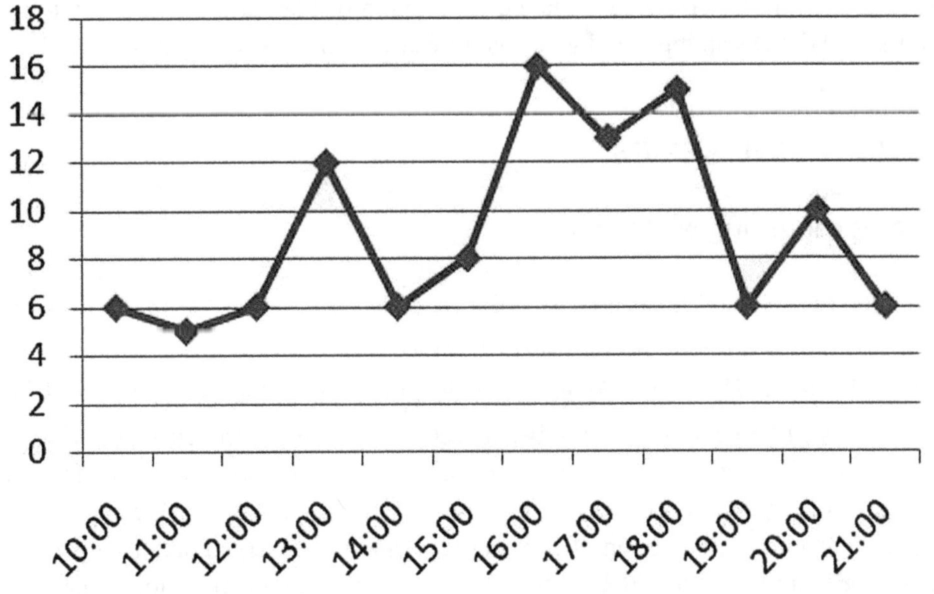

series can be seen in Figure 2. Figure 2a shows the number of vehicles arrived at the petrol pump at different point of time, the arrival is generated through constant level process (stationary time series) with random fluctuation, Figure 2b shows the generation of number of vehicle by a linear trend with fluctuation superimposed, Figure 2c displays the seasonal effect in the generation of number of vehicles with constant level model and random fluctuation.

Once the pattern of historical data is identified, a mathematical model to forecast future values is constructed. For example, for a stationary time series as illustrated in Figure 2a, the mathematical model can be represented as $X_t = B + error(t)$, where X_t represents the observed value at time t, B is the constant level and $error(t)$ is the random error with mean zero and constant variance. The forecast F_{t+1} for the period $t+1$ must depend in the historical data ($X_1, X_2, \dots X_t$).

Figure 2.

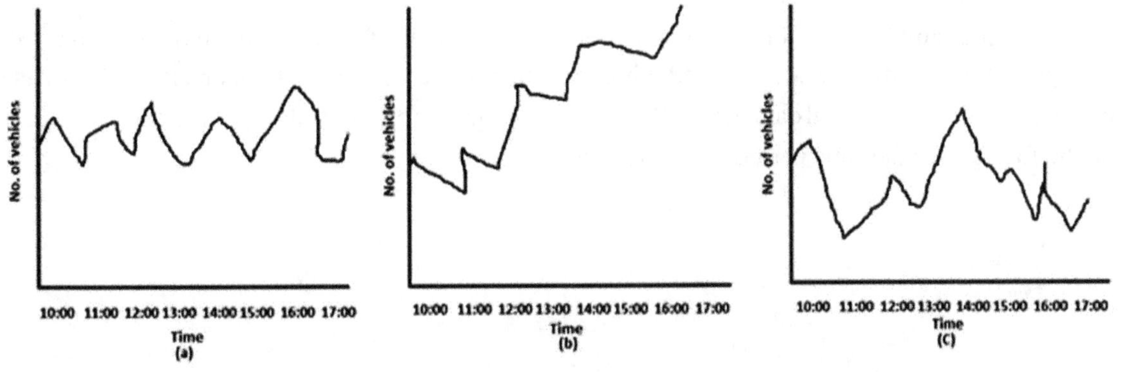

There are two type quantitative forecasting techniques presented in this section i.e. stationary time series and trend based time series. The detailed description of both are shown following which takes observed numerical data as an input and gives the forecast for the upcoming time period.

5. STATIONARY TIME SERIES

Last-Value Forecasting Method

Last value forecasting method uses the data point recently observed in the time series to predict the future value. If t is the current time and value observed at time t is X_t then the forecasted value for time period $t+1$ will be $F_{t+1} = X_t$. For example, the number of vehicles arriving on the petrol pump in the next period will be equal to the number of vehicles arrived in the current period according to last- value forecasting method. This method has a disadvantage of providing imprecise information about the future because of large variance due to sample size of one. This will provide true information only if 1) the model violates the assumption of constant level and the observed data changes so rapidly that anything available before time period t is meaningless or irrelevant or 2) It violate the law of constant variance and variance at time t is much smaller and as compared to the time periods before period t. So this method works well when the conditions changes rapidly and the information available before the time period t is irrelevant and meaningless. This is also known as naive method because it just uses the sample of size one for predicting the future values when additional relevant information is available.

- **Example 1:** A petrol pump situated in a central India faces the irregular vehicular traffic for the purpose of oil filling at different point of time. The manager wants to find out the expected number of vehicles that may arrive in the next day, so that he can plan and schedule the activities accordingly. Since the operational cost incurred at the petrol pump plays an important role in generating profit. Table 1 shows the vehicular arrival pattern of one week during the opening hours at petrol pump.

The last column in Table 1 shows the forecast for next day obtained with help of last- value forecasting method.

Averaging Forecasting Method

Instead of using sample size of one as shown in earlier method, this forecasting method uses all the data points present in the time series. for predicting the value in the next period, this method simply takes the average of all the historical data points. If $X_1, X_2, \ldots X_t$ are the observed data point at time $i = 1,2,\ldots t$ then the forecast for the time period $t+1$ will be

$$F_{t+1} = \sum_{i=1}^{t} X_i / t$$

Table 1. Vehicular traffic of one week at petrol pump

Observed data								LV
	1	2	3	4	5	6	7	8
Date →	MON	TUE	WED	THUR	FRI	SAT	SUN	MON
Time	No. of vehicles arrived in petrol pump							
10:00	5	12	18	18	12	11	8	8
11:00	9	15	19	12	13	10	22	22
12:00	20	20	18	20	19	23	20	20
13:00	18	22	23	8	13	23	15	15
14:00	16	20	17	18	12	7	9	9
15:00	10	22	23	10	22	23	15	15
16:00	22	23	23	22	22	20	10	10
17:00	23	20	18	25	23	23	14	14
18:00	21	23	8	20	20	12	11	11
19:00	11	23	2	15	1	8	3	3
20:00	6	0	3	8	10	3	1	1
21:00	1	2	4	3	9	3	3	3
AVERAGE	**14**	**17**	**15**	**15**	**15**	**14**	**11**	**11**

This estimate is an excellent one if the process is entirely stable, i.e., if the assumptions about the underlying model are correct. However, the process may not be stable for the longer time period and this model uses all the data points available in the time series. So this method is best suitable for the young processes as compared to the old one.

- **Example 2:** Table 2 presents the same example, described in example 1. It shows the forecast of vehicles for the next day obtained from averaging method.

Moving-Average Forecasting Method

Instead of using all the data points available in the time series as shown in the earlier method, this method uses the n data points recently observed in the time series. Since the process may not behave same for the longer period, this method works well in that case. If $X_1, X_2, \ldots X_t$ are the observed data points at time period $i = 1,2,\ldots t$ and n is the number of recent data points those are used to find the forecast of time period $t+1$. Then

$$F_{t+1} = \sum_{i=t-n+1}^{t} X_i \,/\, n$$

Table 2. Forecasting with averaging method

	Observed data							Averaging
	1	2	3	4	5	6	7	8
Date →	MON	TUE	WED	THUR	FRI	SAT	SUN	MON
Time	No. of vehicles arrived in petrol pump							
10:00	5	12	18	18	12	11	8	12
11:00	9	15	19	12	13	10	22	14
12:00	20	20	18	20	19	23	20	20
13:00	18	22	23	8	13	23	15	17
14:00	16	20	17	18	12	7	9	14
15:00	10	22	23	10	22	23	15	18
16:00	22	23	23	22	22	20	10	20
17:00	23	20	18	25	23	23	14	21
18:00	21	23	8	20	20	12	11	16
19:00	11	23	2	15	1	8	3	9
20:00	6	0	3	8	10	3	1	4
21:00	1	2	4	3	9	3	3	4
AVERAGE	**14**	**17**	**15**	**15**	**15**	**14**	**11**	**14**

The method can be easily updated in each time period. For forecasting the value (F_{t+1}) in next period it drops the older data point and adds the recent one for the better accuracy. The moving-average estimator works on the basis of recency effect in which the forecasted value more likely to follow the recent trend. The disadvantage of this method is that, it places the same weight for all the historical data point it considers to forecast the value, whereas it may be different in multiple cases. A good method should place higher weight on the recent observations as compared to the older one as they are less representative of current conditions.

- **Example 3:** The problem described in the example 1, is solved with the help of moving average forecasting method. It is the common practice used by many practitioners which considers last four periods observation. After the forecast of the next period, the observation of first period is dropped and the recent observation is taken into consideration for calculating the average. The last column in table 3 shows the forecast obtained through moving average method by taking the recent four observations into consideration.

Exponential Smoothing Forecasting Method

This is the most popular forecasting technique to produce smoothed time series. Instead of assigning similar weights for the observed data as in moving average forecasting technique, this method assigns exponentially decreasing weights as the observations get older. In other words, the recent observations get relatively higher weight in forecasting as compared to the older one. The simplest of exponentially

Table 3. Forecasting with moving average method

	Observed data							MA
	1	**2**	**3**	**4**	**5**	**6**	**7**	**8**
Date →	MON	TUE	WED	THUR	FRI	SAT	SUN	MON
Time	**No. of vehicles arrived in petrol pump**							
10:00	5	12	18	18	12	11	8	12
11:00	9	15	19	12	13	10	22	14
12:00	20	20	18	20	19	23	20	21
13:00	18	22	23	8	13	23	15	15
14:00	16	20	17	18	12	7	9	12
15:00	10	22	23	10	22	23	15	18
16:00	22	23	23	22	22	20	10	19
17:00	23	20	18	25	23	23	14	21
18:00	21	23	8	20	20	12	11	16
19:00	11	23	2	15	1	8	3	7
20:00	6	0	3	8	10	3	1	6
21:00	1	2	4	3	9	3	3	5
AVERAGE	**14**	**17**	**15**	**15**	**15**	**14**	**11**	**14**

smoothing method is called 'simple exponential smoothing'. This method is best suitable for the data with no trend or seasonal pattern. In exponential smoothing, there can be multiple smoothing parameters which can be used to determine the weights of observations. The forecasted value in time period $t+1$ with the help of exponential smoothing can be shown as follows:

$$F_{t+1} = \alpha * x_t + (1-\alpha) * F_t$$

Where α $(0 < \alpha < 1)$ is a smoothing parameter, x_t is the observation in time period t and F_t is the forecast obtained in time period t. From the above formula, we can see that the forecasting function is recursive in nature which depends on the previous forecasted value and observed value. The extended formula for the F_{t+1} can be represented as:

$$F_{t+1} = \alpha * x_t + \alpha * (1-\alpha) * x_{t-1} + \alpha * (1-\alpha)^2 * x_{t-2} + \ldots$$

It can be seen from the above equation that the exponential smoothing method assigns the higher weight to the recent observation and exponentially decreasing weights to the older observations. Furthermore, the first equation shows that to forecast in time period t the data prior to period *t* need not be retained; all that is required is x_t and the previous forecast F_t.

the main drawback of exponential smoothing is that it is difficult to find out appropriate smoothing parameter α. if α is chosen to be small then the response to the change will be slow and if α is chosen to be large then the response the change will be fast, with large variability in output. Another disadvantage of this method is that it lags behind a continuing trend; i.e., if the constant-level model is incorrect and the mean is increasing steadily, then the forecast will be several periods behind.

- **Example 4:** In exponential smoothing, we assign a smoothing parameter α which essentially signifies the importance of latest observation on the forecasted value. If the forecaster feels that the latest observation has a considerable impact on the forecasted observation for next period then he must assign a larger value of $alpha$ for the recent observation. the last column in table 4 shows the forecast for the next period obtained through exponential smoothing with $\alpha = 0.9$

Comparison of Forecasting Techniques for Stationary Time Series

Mean absolute deviation (MAD) is the difference between average forecasted value and the average observed value for the forecasted period. It is one of the popular approach to find better forecasting method. The lesser the MAD value, better the forecast will be. The MAD for a particular forecasting technique can be shown as follows:

Table 4. Forecasting with Exponential smoothing method

	Observed data							**ES**
	1	**2**	**3**	**4**	**5**	**6**	**7**	**8**
Date →	MON	TUE	WED	THUR	FRI	SAT	SUN	MON
Time	**No. of vehicles arrived in petrol pump**							
10:00	5	12	18	18	12	11	8	8
11:00	9	15	19	12	13	10	22	21
12:00	20	20	18	20	19	23	20	20
13:00	18	22	23	8	13	23	15	15
14:00	16	20	17	18	12	7	9	10
15:00	10	22	23	10	22	23	15	15
16:00	22	23	23	22	22	20	10	11
17:00	23	20	18	25	23	23	14	15
18:00	21	23	8	20	20	12	11	12
19:00	11	23	2	15	1	8	3	4
20:00	6	0	3	8	10	3	1	1
21:00	1	2	4	3	9	3	3	3
AVERAGE	**14**	**17**	**15**	**15**	**15**	**14**	**11**	**11**

$$\text{MAD} = \frac{\sum_{i=1}^{N} \left| A_i - F_i \right|}{\text{N}}$$

Where A_i is the actual realized observation day i, F_i is the forecasted value of day i and N is the total number of observations forecasted for day i.

Table 5 shows the comparison of various forecasting techniques. First column in this table shows the actual values observed in the next period which is used to find better forecast by calculating the mead absolute deviation of forecasted values with this value. Since the best value of α is not known in advance, we find the MAD for different values of α i.e. $\alpha = 0.1, 0.5 \text{ and} 0.9$. Result shows that for $\alpha = 0.1$ the MAD value is minimum for exponential smoothing which is 6.39.

On calculating the average MAD value corresponding to all forecasting techniques, we found that moving average gives the best forecast in this case, since the average MAD value is minimum in this method as compared to other forecasting techniques. In another way we can say moving averages are best used for forecasting purposes when the variable in consideration has lower fluctuations and is relatively stable.

6. TREND BASED TIME SERIES

Double Exponential Smoothing

A typical grocery items in a retail store may have demand patterns where it may be observed that the monthly level is gradually increasing (or decreasing) in a steady manner. This shows that the time series

Table 5. Comparison of various forecasting techniques

Actual observed value	Forecasted Value						MAD Value					
				Exponential Smoothing						Exponential Smoothing		
	Last Value	Averaging Method	Moving Average	Alpha = 0.9	Alpha = 0.1	Alpha = 0.5	Last Value	Averaging	Moving Average	Alpha = 0.1	Alpha = 0.5	Alpha = 0.9
3	8	12	12.25	8.47	12.20	10.33	5	9	9	9	7	5
4	22	14	14.25	21.10	13.90	17.50	18	10	10	10	14	17
10	20	20	20.5	20.00	20.00	20.00	10	10	11	10	10	10
10	15	17	14.75	15.28	17.55	16.42	5	7	5	8	6	5
5	9	14	11.5	9.60	14.40	12.00	4	9	7	9	7	5
8	15	18	17.5	15.33	18.00	16.67	7	10	10	10	9	7
23	10	20	18.5	11.20	20.80	16.00	13	3	5	2	7	12
23	14	21	21.25	14.80	21.20	18.00	9	2	2	2	5	8
23	11	16	15.75	11.63	16.70	14.17	12	7	7	6	9	11
3	3	9	6.75	3.70	9.30	6.50	0	6	4	6	4	1
1	1	4	5.5	1.40	4.60	3.00	0	3	5	4	2	0
4	3	4	4.5	3.07	3.60	3.33	1	0	1	0	1	1
Average MAD value							7	6.42	6.08	6.39	6.66	6.93

data has a trend. A normal forecasting model attempting to predict a trend based time series will in most probability generate forecasts which are biased. For example, exponential smoothing only allows one to emphasize the importance of new observations with the respect to the old observations (Gardner, 1985). This importance is characterized by alpha (damping factor). A lower value of alpha signifies that the model is stable and the forecaster gives very little weightage to the new observations. Such a model can only be predicted by either linear regression or double exponential smoothing. Both these models have two coefficients, namely, 'a' and 'b', where 'a' is the intercept and b is the slope. Linear regression forecast model generates a straight line fit through the most recent N history demands giving equal weight to each demand. The trend smoothing forecast model revises the forecast coefficients as each new demand entry becomes available. The model has two parameters, α and β, that are used to revise the trend coefficients, (a, b), at each month (LaViola, 2003). Linear regression as a methodology is common and hence it is intentionally excluded from the scope of this chapter. We will now explain the double exponential smoothing in detail with the help of an example.

We will assume that the data has a seasonality issue. We attempt to treat the dual problem of seasonality issue and trend analysis by Centered Moving Average followed by Double Exponential Smoothing

However, we would like to highlight that if the data did not had any trend in it, we would have gone for Centered Moving Average followed by Linear Exponential Smoothing. We will now discuss the steps involved in the former case, i.e., Centered Moving Average followed by double exponential smoothing.

Table 6 provides an illustrative example of consumption of engine oil (in litre) at different point of time in petrol pump. The manager wants to calculate seasonal adjusted data so that better planning and scheduling decision can be taken in advance.

For this seasonal adjusted data works as an input when we start the double exponential smoothing process. The step by step procedure for calculating the seasonal adjusted values is shown as follows (also see Figure 3).

- **Step 1:** Column 1 and Column 2 are already given as a problem. Column 2 represents the numerical data sequentially arranged in a time series and Column 1 represents the period number. We first calculate the cycle length (T). Here since the data represents the demand for all six days of a week slot, we take T=6
- **Step 2:** Determine the centered moving average values (Column 3)

$$CMA(6)_t = \frac{1}{6} * \left(\frac{D_{t-3}}{2} + D_{t-2} + D_{t-1} + D_t + D_{t+1} + D_{t+2} + \frac{D_{t+3}}{2} \right)$$

- **Step 3:** Calculate the seasonality ratio (Column 4)

$$Seasonality\,Ratio = Demand_t \,/\, CMA_t$$

- **Step 4:** Calculate the de-normalized seasonality Index for each cell (Column 5)

$$De - normalized\,seasonality\,index =$$
$$Average\ (Sesasonality\,Ratio_t + Seasonality\,Ratio_{t+6} + Seasonality\,Ratio_{t+6+6}$$

Table 6. Explanation of calculating the seasonality index and seasonally adjusted data using centered moving average

CENTERED MOVING AVERAGE - SEASONALITY						
Periods	**Demand**	**CMA(6)**	**Seasonality Ratio (Demand/CMA(6)**	**Unnormalized Seasonality Index**	**Normalized Seasonality Index**	**Seasonal Adjusted Data (De-seasonalized Data)**
1	2.93			1.30	1.29	2.27
2	4.19			1.47	1.46	2.86
3	3.27			1.00	1.00	3.28
4	2.82	3.78	0.75	0.65	0.65	4.36
5	3.13	4.34	0.72	0.64	0.64	4.90
6	4.62	4.80	0.96	0.97	0.96	4.79
7	6.36	5.06	1.26	1.30	1.29	4.92
8	7.51	5.23	1.44	1.47	1.46	5.13
9	5.43	5.53	0.98	1.00	1.00	5.45
10	3.76	6.04	0.62	0.65	0.65	5.81
11	4.30	6.67	0.64	0.64	0.64	6.74
12	7.02	7.21	0.97	0.97	0.96	7.28
13	10.03	7.50	1.34	1.30	1.29	7.76
14	11.46	7.62	1.50	1.47	1.46	7.83
15	7.93	7.79	1.02	1.00	1.00	7.96
16	4.73	8.16	0.58	0.65	0.65	7.31
17	4.84	8.68	0.56	0.64	0.64	7.58
18	8.45			0.97	0.96	8.76
19	13.11			1.30	1.29	10.15
20	14.56			1.47	1.46	9.95

- **Step 5:** Calculate the normalized seasonality index for each cell (Column 6)

We would normalize these averages since we would want the seasonal coefficients to sum up to cycle length.

$$Normalized\,seasonality\,index = \frac{De - normalized\,seasonality\,index * T}{\sum_{i=1}^{i=T} De - normalized\,seasonality\,index}$$

- **Step 6:** Calculate the De-Seasonalized data or the Seasonally Adjusted Data

$$De - Seasonalized\,Demand_t = \frac{Demand_t}{Normalized\,Seasonality\,index_t}$$

Now we show how double exponential smoothing (Refer Table 7 and Figure 3) that can be applied to the seasonally adjusted data

- **Step 7:** Column 1 and Column 2 are self explanatory as it has been taken forward from the previous example. We need to first initialize the parameter a and b. Let us take the value of a=2 since the seasonal adjusted data for period 1 has a value of 2.27. Although any initialization could have served the purpose as it would have adjusted along the time series. We assume the slope b=0.5. The forecast value F is the sum of a and b.
- **Step 8:** We can take any value of α and β for the time being as the optimized value of α and β will be calculated later by Excel Solver
- **Step 9:** Calculate the value of a and b for the second period onwards

$$a_t = \alpha * \left(De - seasonalized\,Data_t\right) + \left(1 - \alpha\right) * \left(a_{t-1} + b_{t-1}\right)$$

$$b_t = \beta * \left(a_t - a_{t-1}\right) + \left(1 - \beta\right) * b_{t-1}$$

Table 7. Double exponential smoothing with seasonal adjusted data

Centered Moving Average		Double Exponential Smoothing					
Periods	Seasonal Adjusted Data (De-seasonalized Data)	a	b	F	DES Error	Sq. Error	Re-seasonalized Forecast
1	2.27	2.00	0.50	2.50	-0.23	0.05	3.23
2	2.86	2.86	0.50	2.50	0.36	0.13	3.66
3	3.28	3.28	0.50	3.36	-0.08	0.01	3.35
4	4.36	4.36	0.50	3.78	0.58	0.33	2.45
5	4.90	4.90	0.50	4.86	0.04	0.00	3.10
6	4.79	4.79	0.50	5.40	-0.61	0.37	5.21
7	4.92	4.92	0.50	5.29	-0.37	0.14	6.84
8	5.13	5.13	0.50	5.42	-0.29	0.08	7.93
9	5.45	5.45	0.50	5.63	-0.18	0.03	5.61
10	5.81	5.81	0.50	5.95	-0.14	0.02	3.85
11	6.74	6.74	0.50	6.31	0.42	0.18	4.03
12	7.28	7.28	0.50	7.24	0.04	0.00	6.98
13	7.76	7.76	0.50	7.78	-0.02	0.00	10.05
14	7.83	7.83	0.50	8.26	-0.43	0.18	12.09
15	7.96	7.96	0.50	8.33	-0.37	0.14	8.30
16	7.31	7.31	0.50	8.46	-1.15	1.32	5.47
17	7.58	7.58	0.50	7.81	-0.23	0.05	4.99
18	8.76	8.76	0.50	8.08	0.68	0.46	7.79
19	10.15	10.15	0.50	9.26	0.88	0.78	11.97
20	9.95	9.95	0.50	10.65	-0.69	0.48	15.57

- **Step 10:** Calculate the DES error for each period and Squared Error

$$DES\,Error = De - Seasonalized\,Data - F$$

$$Squared\,Error = DES\,Error^2$$

- **Step 11:** Calculate the Re-Seasonalized forecast

$$Re - Seasonalized\,Forecast = F * Normalized\,Seasonality\,Index$$

- **Step 12:** Optimize the value of alpha and beta

$$Min\left(Squared\,Error\right)$$

$$Subject\,to \qquad 0 \le \alpha \le 1, 0 \le ^2 \le 1$$

Figure 3 depicts the graph between the actual demand and the re-Seasonalized demand obtained from double exponential smoothing.

We would not discuss the application of linear regression in great in this chapter as it is beyond the scope of the book. Forecasting techniques using regression analysis requires a deeper treatment and hence it has been intentionally left out. We present a brief introduction to linear regression and summary of the basic functional difference in using a double exponential smoothing with respect to linear regression.

Figure 3.

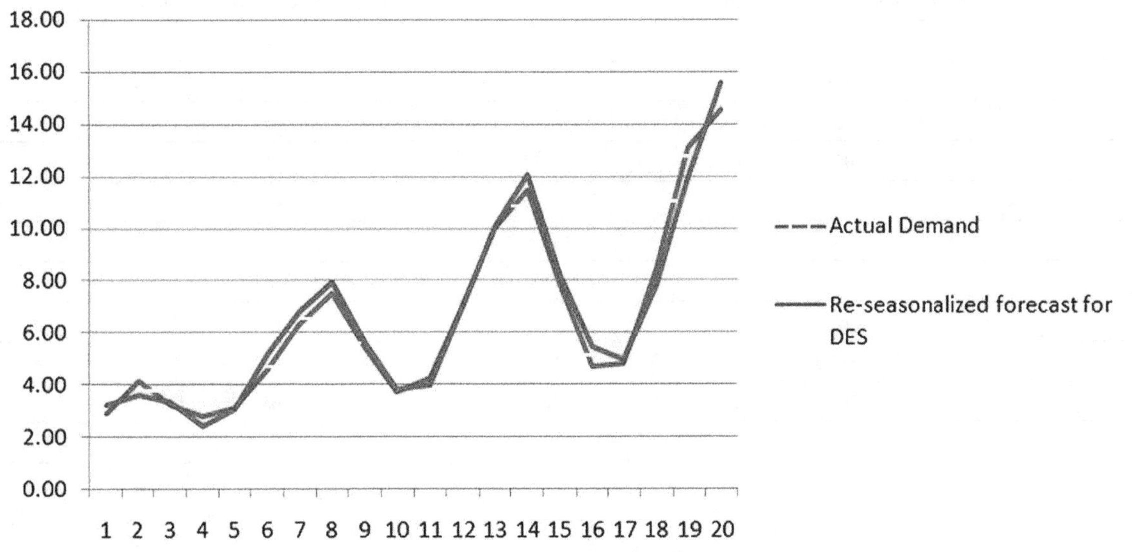

Linear Regression

As we already know, linear regression is a statistical technique which fits the mean beat fit line given the data points of the predictor. In some cases, the variable to be forecasted (dependent variable) has a direct relationship with a set of variables (independent variable). This kind of forecasting is sometimes known as causal forecasting. The basic regression equation is given below

$$Y = \beta_0 + \beta_1 X_1 + \beta_2 X_2 + \beta_3 X_3 + \ldots + \beta_n X_n + \epsilon$$

Here, Y is the dependent variable and X's are the independent variables.

Let me take a simple example to illustrate your point. Suppose, the manager of a filling station perceives that the sale of one of its engine oil is a function of advertising expenses. Table 8 shows the total sale and the advertising cost of engine oil at different point of time.

Below is the regression output of the example stated above. We see that the coefficient β is 1.44 which indicates that advertising cost has a positive relationship with the sale of engine oil. However due to limited size of data, the predictors are found to be non-significant. This was just an introductory example to show how predictor variables predict the dependent variable. If we substitute the coefficient into the main regression equation we get the following value.

$$Y = 362.3616 + 1.445*X$$

So, when the advertising cost of engine oil is Rs. 500 thousands (say), then expected sale of engine oil will be Rs. 1084 thousand. Table 9 shows the summary statistics of the regression model.

Table 8. Sale and advertising cost of engine oil

Sale of engine oil (In thousands)	Advertising Cost (In thousands)
1200	400
1400	450
950	480
600	400
800	420
975	620
1357	650
1367	600
1317	620
1396	680
1289	675

Table 9. Statistics of regression model

SUMMARY OUTPUT								
Regression Statistics								
Multiple R	0.601559							
R Square	0.361873							
Adjusted R Square	0.29097							
Standard Error	231.8727							
Observations	11							
ANOVA								
	df	*SS*	*MS*	*F*	*Significance F*			
Regression	1	274404.4347	274404.4347	5.10378002	0.050245961			
Residual	9	483884.4744	53764.9416					
Total	10	758288.9091						
	Coefficients	*Standard Error*	*t Stat*	*P-value*	*Lower 95%*	*Upper 95%*	*Lower 95.0%*	*Upper 95.0%*
Intercept	362.3616	355.6229923	1.018948628	0.334835131	-442.1135376	1166.837	-442.114	1166.837
X Variable 1	1.445375	0.639785732	2.259154714	0.050245961	-0.001920921	2.892671	-0.00192	2.892671

7. COMPARISON BETWEEN DOUBLE EXPONENTIAL SMOOTHING (DES) AND LINEAR REGRESSION (LR)

See Table 10.

8. FUTURE RESEARCH DIRECTIONS

The following future research directions can be explored within the scope of this chapter:

1. Forecasting in Tourism industry has been limited. Given the dynamic nature of the industry and the unique constraints it carries, we feel there is a scope of ample research in this sector especially in countries like India. This is because, tourism and hospitality industry has all the characteristics which demands the use of exponential smoothing, double exponential smoothing and triple exponential smoothing. Some of the characteristics are: seasonality in demand patterns which itself is a function of demography features such as location, climate, sightseeing and proximity to nearest airport, railway station etc., huge competition among players makes it a difficult business to survive given information technology revolution, trend index of location brand as a independent variable to the successive period forecasted demand. There is also an opportunity to explore advanced techniques such as non-linear smooth transition regression, non-parametric singular spectrum analysis, mixed-frequency modeling technique etc.

Table 10. Comparison of double exponential smoothing and linear regression

	Comparison between DES and LR	
	Double Exponential Smoothing	**Linear Regression**
1	Initialization Part is Tricky. Different forecasters use different ways to initialize	No need to initialize
2	Computations are easy. It can be easily be computed in EXCEL	Computations are cumbersome. If the observations are low, EXCEL can be used but it is desirable that other statistical software's such as SPSS, R, SAS be utilized for better analysis
3	It works with small data set	Larger data set is desirable for variance explanation
4	Decreasing weights as we move from old observations to new observations	Equal weights for all observations
5	No such additional variable required	Requires additional independent variable for better model fit

2. There is a growing need from managers that academic forecasting techniques involve more of data and less of firm-specific factors and environmental specific factors. For example, let us assume that we are trying to predict the demand of a set of generic drug for a medical store in a sub-urban town in India. The owner of the shop may have given us an historical data for the past five years. But, we must learn that there are many factors which heavily influence the forecast of a particular shop in such places. One of such factors is doctor's recommendation of similar medicines and proximity of such shops close to the doctor's chambers. Second, competition among different medical stores within that broad locality. Third, the ability to cater to various sections of the population (elderly and youth) effectively. Aged-people would like to have a store nearby who can provide them with all the medicines irrespective of the price. On the contrary, less aged people may have the incentive to deviate to other medical stores in search of discounts.
3. A promising area of research may be to forecast energy demand from residential buildings in India. This is because of two reasons, one, energy consumption has been increasing at a very steady rate in residential buildings due to the emergence of tier-2 and tier-3 cities. Due to the huge influx of workforce in metropolitans, many tier-1 cities are going to expansion to accommodate this influx. Hence this study would prove to be beneficial to energy policy makers in India and other such developing countries. Various advanced techniques are being used such as artificial neural network (ANN), support vector regression (SVR), Gaussian mixture models (GMM) etc.
4. Similar research can be carried out in fashion industry where the demand is highly uncertain and the product is perishable beyond a certain range. Let us discuss this issue in brief. Suppose FabIndia launches a kurta in August specifically designed for the winter season. Therefore, the stock needs to be sold at most in the winter season. This means that the product is kept for a specific period beyond which the price of the product drops drastically. This is because of two reasons: one, this attire is not suitable for other seasons. Therefore, once the winter season ends, fashion apparel customers would like to buy dresses for the upcoming seasons. Second, a counter argument could be stated that the particular dress may be sold in the next winter season. The answer to this argument is NO. This is because; the uniqueness of fashion industry is that the products do not get repeated for the next period. Hence the opportunity cost of lost sales due to seasonality is very high. A good

research context can be derived from this industry. Interesting questions such as the reasons behind keeping a FabIndia showroom in Ahmadabad and not Baroda can be an interesting problem.

5. A unique problem context may arise from the construction sector. Almost all construction projects involve ordering of fasteners for fixing various structures involved in the design. However, the dimensions of each fastener may be different. And also, such fasteners are always required in large numbers for a medium-level construction project. A typical construction planning engineer under the supervision of the Project Manager would select a vendor which would first satisfy quality and then time. It has been observed from author's own experience that there are occasions where a third variable comes into play which very few people speak of. This variable is known as "capacity constraint". Fasteners suppliers have low margin for their products and as a result do not keep a large inventory in its stockpile. The suppliers may be very trustworthy in terms of timely delivery and quality products but due to its limited capacity, he may not be awarded the contract. If we try to solve this problem from the perspective of the suppliers, we need to keep in mind one thing. The commencement of construction projects are extremely uncertain and are an independent factor of the location of the supplier's warehouse. Due to this uncertainty, these suppliers typically keep common fasteners for day-day activities in the neighboring region. As manufacturing of such products involve semi-skilled to skilled laborers, it has been observed that there are lot of options in terms of selecting a suitable supplier for a construction project. Such suppliers tend to avoid large stockpile of specialized fasteners with the apprehension that another supplier may get a contract and he may have to forego the entire stock. In view of this, the fastener market remains unorganized. This has led to the formation of informal coordination between established contractors and selected suppliers. Due to this lack of information, only certain suppliers are able to supply the entire demand of such projects and thereby earning a larger share of profits. The contractor has no choice but to establish such relationships so that timely delivery of quality products are ensured for smooth functioning of the projects. The question is "How can forecasters help suppliers who have the capacity but are reluctant to produce the stock in advance?"

9. CONCLUSION

This chapter focuses on to provide understanding of various forecasting techniques in different applications of management. It will help students to evaluate and analyze various forecasting technique and through this they will be able to select better forecasting technique that will efficiently use available historical data for the prediction of better future trends. In this chapter emphasizes on qualitative and quantitative forecasting techniques which further divided in multiple approaches. Some the approaches are: Delphi's method, Last - value method, Averaging method, Moving Average, Exponential Smoothing, Double Exponential Smoothing and linear regression. The basic idea of this chapter is three fold: to give an introductory treatment of how moving average and exponential smoothing can be treated in similar data set, to explain to the readers how the issue of trend and seasonality can be tackled by extending the concept of linear exponential smoothing to double exponential smoothing and triple exponential smoothing, and to give them real life dataset for better appreciation of such forecasting techniques. The limitations of this chapter is twin fold: this chapter does not discuss about various advanced techniques such as ARMA, ARIMA, ANN, SVR models and this chapter intentionally refrains from discussing the mathematical interpretations/derivations of various forecasting techniques with the motive of catering to the practitioners and the end users at large.

REFERENCES

Armstrong, J. S. (Ed.). (2001). *Principles of forecasting: a handbook for researchers and practitioners* (Vol. 30). Springer Science & Business Media. doi:10.1007/978-0-306-47630-3

Batty, M. (1969). Monitoring an exponential smoothing forecasting system. *The Journal of the Operational Research Society*, *20*(3), 319–325. doi:10.1057/jors.1969.76

Gardner, E. S. (1985). Exponential smoothing: The state of the art. *Journal of Forecasting*, *4*(1), 1–28. doi:10.1002/for.3980040103

Holt, C. C. (2004). Forecasting seasonals and trends by exponentially weighted moving averages. *International Journal of Forecasting*, *20*(1), 5–10. doi:10.1016/j.ijforecast.2003.09.015

LaViola, J. J. (2003, May). Double exponential smoothing: an alternative to Kalman filter-based predictive tracking. In *Proceedings of the workshop on Virtual environments 2003* (pp. 199-206). ACM. doi:10.1145/769953.769976

KEY TERMS AND DEFINITIONS

Auto Correlation: When the error term at time t is correlated with the error term at time (t-1), we say that the regression model has an auto-correlation issue.

Auto Regressive Process: Auto-regressive process AR(r) is a process of order r where the dependent variable at time t is a function of independent variables of time (t-1) to (t-r). Here the word 'regressive' is used to denote the regression of the dependent variable with the independent variables.

First Difference: If the value at time t of a stationary data is M and the value at time (t+1) is N, then the first difference is known as (N-M). When the first difference is stationary and completely random, it is called a random walk.

Non Stationary: A non-stationary time series is characterized by trends, cycles, seasonality or random walk.

Random Walk: A sequence of time series data where the mean and variance of the data change with time. Therefore, this process is known as non-stationary process but the first difference is stationary.

Stationary: A stationary time series is defined by a sequence of numerical data whose statistical properties such as mean, variance, skewness, auto-correlation remains constant over time. Most of the statistical forecasting models assume time series data to be stationary.

Time Series: A time series is defined as a group or sequence of data organized according to a specific timeline. Each item refers to a numerical value for that particular instant of time.

Compilation of References

Abdou, H. A. (2009). An evaluation of alternative scoring models in private banking. *The Journal of Risk Finance*, *10*(1), 38–53. doi:10.1108/15265940910924481

Abdou, H., Pointon, J., & El-Masry, A. (2008). Neural nets versus conventional techniques in credit scoring in Egyptian banking. *Expert Systems with Applications*, *35*(3), 1275–1292. doi:10.1016/j.eswa.2007.08.030

Abrate, G., & Viglia, G. (2016). Strategic and tactical price decisions in hotel revenue management. *Tourism Management*, *55*, 123–132. doi:10.1016/j.tourman.2016.02.006

Abughosh, S. (2016). *Social Media Analytics To Drive Business Advantage In Retail Banking*. Retrieved September 13, 2016, from https://www.linkedin.com/pulse/social-media-analytics-drive-business-advantage-suha

Acker, O., Blockus, A., Pötscher, F. (2013). *Benefiting from Big Data: A new approach for the telecom industry.* Strategy & Formerly Booz & Company.

Aggarwal, C. C. (2011). An Introduction to Social Network Data Analytics, In C.C. Aggarwal (Ed.), Social Network Data Analytics (pp 1-16). New York: Springer Science+Business Media.

Agovino, M., Ferrara, M., & Garofalo, A. (2016). An exploratory analysis on waste management in Italy: A focus on waste disposed in landfill. *Land Use Policy*, *57*, 669–681. doi:10.1016/j.landusepol.2016.06.027

Agrawal, Agrawal, & Singh. (2010). *Demand Chain Management*. Macmillan.

Agrawal, D. K. (2012). Demand chain management: Factors enhancing market responsiveness capabilities. *Journal of Marketing Channels*, *19*(2), 101–119. doi:10.1080/1046669X.2012.667760

Agrawal, R., Imielinski, T., & Swami, A. (1993), Mining Association Rules Between Sets Of Items In Large Databases. *Proceedings of the ACM SIGMOD International Conference on Management of data*, 207-216. doi:10.1145/170035.170072

Agrawal, R., & Shafer, J. C. (1996). Parallel Mining of Association Rules. *IEEE Transactions on Knowledge and Data Engineering*, *8*(6), 962–969. doi:10.1109/69.553164

Ahsan, S. N., Ferzund, J., & Wotawa, F. (2009, September). Automatic software bug triage system (BTS) based on Latent Semantic Indexing and Support Vector Machine. In *Software Engineering Advances, 2009. ICSEA'09. Fourth International Conference on* (pp. 216-221). IEEE.

Akhavan, R. M., & Beckmann, M. (2016). A configuration of sustainable sourcing and supply management strategies. *Journal of Purchasing and Supply Management*. doi:10.1016/j.pursup.2016.07.006

Al-Maolegi, M., & Arkok, B. (2014). An Improved Apriori Algorithm for Association Rules. *International Journal on Natural Language Computing*, *3*(1), 21–29. doi:10.5121/ijnlc.2014.3103

Alvandi, M., Fazli, S., & Abdoli, F. S. (2012). K-Mean clustering method for analysis customer lifetime value with LRFM relationship model in banking services. *International Research Journal of Applied and Basic Sciences*, *3*(11), 2294–2302.

Amaro, S., Duarte, P., & Henriques, C. (2016). Travelers use of social media: A clustering approach. *Annals of Tourism Research*, *59*, 1–15. doi:10.1016/j.annals.2016.03.007

Anderson, J. C., & Narus, J. A. (1998). Business marketing: Understand what customers value. *Harvard Business Review*, *76*, 53–67. PMID:10187246

Andrenacci, N., Ragona, R., & Valenti, G. (2016). A demand-side approach to the optimal deployment of electric vehicle charging stations in metropolitan areas. *Applied Energy*, *182*, 39–46. doi:10.1016/j.apenergy.2016.07.137

Angelini, E., di Tollo, G., & Roli, A. (2008). A neural network approach for credit risk evaluation. *The Quarterly Review of Economics and Finance*, *48*(4), 733–755. doi:10.1016/j.qref.2007.04.001

Anvik, J. (2006, May). Automating bug report assignment. In *Proceedings of the 28th international conference on Software engineering* (pp. 937-940). ACM.

Anvik, J., Hiew, L., & Murphy, G. C. (2005, October). Coping with an open bug repository. In *Proceedings of the 2005 OOPSLA workshop on Eclipse technology eXchange* (pp. 35-39). ACM. doi:10.1145/1117696.1117704

Anvik, J., Hiew, L., & Murphy, G. C. (2006, May). Who should fix this bug? In *Proceedings of the 28th international conference on Software engineering* (pp. 361-370). ACM.

Anvik, J., & Murphy, G. C. (2011). Reducing the effort of bug report triage: Recommenders for development-oriented decisions. *ACM Transactions on Software Engineering and Methodology*, *20*(3), 10. doi:10.1145/2000791.2000794

Arias, M. B., & Bae, S. (2016). Electric vehicle charging demand forecasting model based on big data technologies. *Applied Energy*, *183*, 327–339. doi:10.1016/j.apenergy.2016.08.080

Armstrong, A. J., Garrett-Mayer, E. S., Yang, Y. C. O., de Wit, R., Tannock, I. F., & Eisenberger, M. (2007). A contemporary prognostic nomogram for men with hormone-refractory metastatic prostate cancer: A TAX327 study analysis. *Clinical Cancer Research*, *13*(21), 6396–6403. doi:10.1158/1078-0432.CCR-07-1036 PMID:17975152

Armstrong, J. S. (Ed.). (2001). *Principles of forecasting: a handbook for researchers and practitioners* (Vol. 30). Springer Science & Business Media. doi:10.1007/978-0-306-47630-3

Bae, E., & Bailey, J. (2006). COALA: A Novel Approach for the Extraction of an Alternate Clustering of High Quality and High Dissimilarity.*The Sixth IEEE International Conference on Data Mining* (pp. 53-62). IEEE. doi:10.1109/ICDM.2006.37

Baeza-Yates, R., & Ribeiro-Neto, B. (1999). *Modern information retrieval* (1st ed.). New York Press.

Balabanović, M., & Shoham, Y. (1997). Fab: Content-based, collaborative recommendation. *Association for Computing Machinery*, *40*(3), 66–72. doi:10.1145/245108.245124

Balešentis, T., Balešentis, A., & Brauers, W. K. (2011). Multi–Objective Optimization of Well–Being in the European Union Member States. *Economic Research-Ekonomska Istraživanja*, *24*(4), 1–15. doi:10.1080/1331677X.2011.11517485

Baležentis, A., Valkauskas, R., & Baležentis, T. (2010). Evaluating situation of Lithuania in the European Union: structural indicators and MULTIMOORA method. *Technological and Economic Development of Economy*, (4), 578-602.

Baležentis, T., & Baležentis, A. (2011). A multi-criteria assessment of relative farming efficiency in the European Union Member States. *Žemės ūkio mokslai, 18*(3), 125-135.

Baležentis, T., & Baležentis, A. (2014). A Survey on Development and Applications of the Multi-criteria Decision Making Method MULTIMOORA. *Journal of Multi-Criteria Decision Analysis*, *21*(3-4), 209–222. doi:10.1002/mcda.1501

Bandyopadhyay, S., Mukhopadhyay, A., & Maulik, U. (2007). An improved algorithm for clustering gene expression data. *Bioinformatics (Oxford, England)*, *23*(21), 2859–2865. doi:10.1093/bioinformatics/btm418 PMID:17720981

Barranco, M. J., & Martínez, L. (2010). A method for weighting multi-valued features in content-based filtering.Lecture Notes in Computer Science, 6098(3), 409–418. doi:10.1007/978-3-642-13033-5_42

Basch, C. A., Bruesewitz, B. J., Siegel, K., & Faith, P. (2003). *U.S. Patent No. 6,658,393*. Washington, DC: U.S. Patent and Trademark Office.

Batrinca, B., & Treleaven, P. C. (2015). Social media analytics: A survey of techniques, tools and platforms. *AI & Society*, *30*(1), 89–116. doi:10.1007/s00146-014-0549-4

Batty, M. (1969). Monitoring an exponential smoothing forecasting system. *The Journal of the Operational Research Society*, *20*(3), 319–325. doi:10.1057/jors.1969.76

Becchetti, L., & Sierra, J. (2003). Bankruptcy risk and productive efficiency in manufacturing firms. *Journal of Banking & Finance*, *27*(11), 2099–2120. doi:10.1016/S0378-4266(02)00319-9

Bedeley, R. T., & Iyer, L. S. (2014). Big Data opportunities and challenges: the case of banking industry.*Proceedings of the Southern Association for Information Systems Conference*, 1-7.

Beese, J. (2016). 6 Social Media Trends That Will Take Over 2016. *Sprout Social*. Retrieved June 21, 2016 from http://sproutsocial.com/insights/social-media-trends/

Behara, R. S., Fisher, W. W., & Lemmink, J. G. (2002). Modelling and evaluating service quality measurement using neural networks. *International Journal of Operations & Production Management*, *22*(10), 1162–1185. doi:10.1108/01443570210446360

Bettenburg, N., Just, S., Schröter, A., Weiss, C., Premraj, R., & Zimmermann, T. (2008, November). What makes a good bug report? In *Proceedings of the 16th ACM SIGSOFT International Symposium on Foundations of software engineering* (pp. 308-318). ACM. doi:10.1145/1453101.1453146

Bhattacharya, P., & Neamtiu, I. (2010, September). Fine-grained incremental learning and multi-feature tossing graphs to improve bug triaging. In *Software Maintenance (ICSM), 2010 IEEE International Conference on* (pp. 1-10). IEEE. doi:10.1109/ICSM.2010.5609736

Bhattacharya, P., Neamtiu, I., & Shelton, C. R. (2012). Automated, highly-accurate, bug assignment using machine learning and tossing graphs. *Journal of Systems and Software*, *85*(10), 2275–2292. doi:10.1016/j.jss.2012.04.053

Bholat, D. (2015). *Big Data and central banks*. Retrieved September 28, 2016, from http://www.bankofengland.co.uk/research/Documents/ccbs/bigdatawriteup.pdf

Binner, J. M., Bissoondeeal, R. K., Elger, T., Gazely, A. M., & Mullineux, A. W. (2005). A comparison of linear forecasting models and neural networks: an application to Euro inflation and Euro Divisia. *Applied Economics, 37*(6), 665-680.

Boudet, H. S., Flora, J. A., & Armel, K. C. (2016). Clustering household energy-saving behaviours by behavioural attribute. *Energy Policy*, *92*, 444–454. doi:10.1016/j.enpol.2016.02.033

Bouguessa, M. (2013). Clustering categorical data in projected spaces. *Data Mining & Knowledge Discovery, Springer*, *1*(29), 3–38.

Brauers, W. K., & Ginevičius, R. (2013). How to invest in Belgian shares by MULTIMOORA optimization. *Journal of Business Economics and management, 14*(5), 940-956.

Brauers, W. K., Ginevicius, R., & Podviezko, A. (2012). Evaluation of performance of Lithuanian commercial banks by multi-objective optimization. *The 7th International Scientific Conference Business and Management*, 1042-1049. doi:10.3846/bm.2012.133

Brauers, W. K. M., Ginevicius, R., & Podvezko, A. (2014b). Ranking of the Lithuanian Banks During the Recession of 2008-2009 by the MULTIMOORA Method. *Annals of Management Science*, *3*(1), 1–28.

Brauers, W. K. M., Ginevicius, R., & Podviezko, A. (2014a). Development of a methodology of evaluation of financial stability of commercial banks. *Panoeconomicus*, *61*(3), 349–367. doi:10.2298/PAN1403349B

Brauers, W. K. M., Kildienė, S., Zavadskas, E. K., & Kaklauskas, A. (2013). The construction sector in twenty European countries during the recession 2008–2009–country ranking by MULTIMOORA. *International Journal of Strategic Property Management*, *17*(1), 58–78. doi:10.3846/1648715X.2013.775194

Brauers, W. K. M., & Zavadskas, E. K. (2006). The MOORA method and its application to privatization in a transition economy. *Control and Cybernetics*, *35*(2), 445.

Brauers, W. K. M., & Zavadskas, E. K. (2010). Project management by MULTIMOORA as an instrument for transition economies. *Technological and Economic Development of Economy*, *16*(1), 5–24. doi:10.3846/tede.2010.01

Brauers, W. K. M., & Zavadskas, E. K. (2011). MULTIMOORA optimization used to decide on a bank loan to buy property. *Technological and Economic Development of Economy*, *17*(1), 174–188. doi:10.3846/13928619.2011.560632

Brauers, W. K. M., & Zavadskas, E. K. (2012). Robustness of MULTIMOORA: A method for multi-objective optimization. *Informatica*, *23*(1), 1–25.

Burke, R. (2000). Knowledge-based recommender systems. Encyclopedia of Library and Information Systems, 69, 175–186.

Burke, R. (2002). Hybrid recommender systems: Survey and experiments. User Modeling and User-Adapted Interaction, 12, 331-370.

Burke, R. (2007). Hybrid web recommender systems. In *The AdaptiveWeb.* Springer.

Burke, R. (2002). Hybrid recommender systems: Survey and experiments. *User Modeling and User-Adapted Interaction*, *12*(4), 331–370. doi:10.1023/A:1021240730564

Buscema, M. (2002). A brief overview and introduction to artificial neural networks. *Substance Use & Misuse*, *37*(8-10), 1093–1148. doi:10.1081/JA-120004171 PMID:12180558

Capgemini global insurance Centre of excellence. (2015). *Big Data Analytics in Life Insurance*. Retrieved September 29, 2016, from http://www.slideshare.net/sahoodk/big-data-analytics-for-life-insurers-a

Cerquitelli, T., Servetti, A., & Masala, E. (2016). Discovering users with similar internet access performance through cluster analysis. *Expert Systems with Applications*, *64*, 536–548. doi:10.1016/j.eswa.2016.08.025

Chakrapani, C. (2004). *Statistics in market research*. London: Arnold Publisher.

Chen, C., Duh, L., & Liu, C. (2004). A personalized courseware recommendation system based on fuzzy item response theory.*IEEE International Conference on e-Technology, e-Commerce and e-Service* (pp. 305–308.). IEEE. doi:10.1109/EEE.2004.1287327

Cheng, E. W., Li, H., & Yu, L. (2005). The analytic network process (ANP) approach to location selection: A shopping mall illustration. *Construction Innovation*, *5*(2), 83–97. doi:10.1108/14714170510815195

Chen, L., & Pu, P. (2010). Critiquing-based recommenders: Survey and emerging trends. *User Modeling and User-Adapted Interaction Journal*, *22*(1-2), 125–150. doi:10.1007/s11257-011-9108-6

Chen, T. H., Nagappan, M., Shihab, E., & Hassan, A. E. (2014, May). An empirical study of dormant bugs. In *Proceedings of the 11th Working Conference on Mining Software Repositories* (pp. 82-91). ACM.

Chen, Z. S., Jang, J. S. R., & Lee, C. H. (2011). A kernel framework for content based artist recommendation system in music. *IEEE Transactions on Multimedia*, *13*(6), 1371–1380. doi:10.1109/TMM.2011.2166380

Chesley, P., Vincent, B., Xu, L., & Srihari, R. (2006). Using Verbs and Adjectives to Automatically Classify Blog Sentiment.*Proceedings of the AAAI-2006 Spring Symposium on Computational Approaches to Analyzing Weblogs*.

Chin, H. B., Sipe, T. A., Elder, R., Mercer, S. L., Chattopadhyay, S. K., Jacob, V., & Chuke, S. O. et al. (2012). The effectiveness of group-based comprehensive risk-reduction and abstinence education interventions to prevent or reduce the risk of adolescent pregnancy, human immunodeficiency virus, and sexually transmitted infections: Two systematic reviews for the Guide to Community Preventive Services. *American Journal of Preventive Medicine*, *42*(3), 272–294. doi:10.1016/j.amepre.2011.11.006 PMID:22341164

Christopher, M., & Ryals, L. J. (2014). The supply chain becomes the demand chain. *Journal of Business Logistics*, *35*(1), 29–35. doi:10.1111/jbl.12037

Cios K.J., Pedrycz, W., Swiniarski, R.W., & Kurgan, L.A. (2012). *Data mining: A knowledge discovery approach*. Springer.

Cleary, I. (2016). *Social Media Analytics Compass: What and How to Measure*. Retrieved September 22, 2016, from http://www.razorsocial.com/social-media-analytics-tools/

Clore, G. L., Ortony, A., & Foss, M. A. (1987). The psychological foundations of the affective lexicon. *Journal of Personality and Social Psychology*, *53*(4), 751–766. doi:10.1037/0022-3514.53.4.751

Cognizant. (2014). How Banks Can Use Social Media Analytics To Drive Business Advantage. *Cognizant 20-20 insights*. Retrieved September 22, 2016, from https://www.cognizant.com/Insights Whitepapers/How-Banks-Can-Use-Social-Media-Analytics-To-Drive-Business-Advantage.pdf

Cohen, W. W. (1995, July). Fast effective rule induction.*Proceedings of the twelfth international conference on machine learning*, 115-123.

Corchado, J. M., & Lees, B. (2001). Adaptation of cases for case based forecasting with neural network support. In *Soft computing in case based reasoning* (pp. 293–319). Springer London. doi:10.1007/978-1-4471-0687-6_13

Cornelis, C., Guo, X., Lu, J., & Zhang, G. (2005). A fuzzy relational approach to event recommendation.*Proceedings of 2nd Indian International Conference on Artificial Intelligence*, 2231–2242.

Cowie, R., Douglas-Cowie, E., Tsapatsoulis, N., Votsis, G., Kollias, S., Fellenz, W., & Taylor, J. (2011). Emotion recognition in human-computer interaction. *IEEE Signal Processing Magazine*, *18*(1), 32–80. doi:10.1109/79.911197

Crisp, M. A., & Chen, L. (2014). Global supply of health professionals. *The New England Journal of Medicine*, *370*(10), 950–957. doi:10.1056/NEJMra1111610 PMID:24597868

Croitoru, A., Wayant, N., Crooks, A., Radzikowski, J., & Stefanidis, A. (2015). Linking cyber and physical spaces through community detection and clustering in social media feeds. *Computers, Environment and Urban Systems*, *53*, 47–64. doi:10.1016/j.compenvurbsys.2014.11.002

Crone, S. F., & Finlay, S. (2012). Instance sampling in credit scoring: An empirical study of sample size and balancing. *International Journal of Forecasting*, *28*(1), 224–238. doi:10.1016/j.ijforecast.2011.07.006

Cubranic, D., & Murphy, G. (2004). Automatic bug triage using text categorization.*Proceedings of the Sixteenth International Conference on Software Engineering & Knowledge Engineering.*

Daie, P., & Li, S. (2016). Hierarchical clustering for structuring supply chain network in case of product variety. *Journal of Manufacturing Systems*, *38*, 77–86. doi:10.1016/j.jmsy.2015.10.002

Dang, X. H., & Bailey, J. (2010). A hierarchical information theoretic technique for the discovery of non linear alternative clusterings.*16th ACM SIGKDD International Conference on Knowledge Discovery and Data Mining* (pp. 573-582). New York: ACM. doi:10.1145/1835804.1835878

Dardac, N., & Boitan, I. A. (2009). A Cluster Analysis Approach for Banks' Risk Profile: The Romanian Evidence. *European Research Studies*, *12*(1), 109.

Data Query System of the Banks Association of Turkey. (n.d.). Retrieved July 13, 2016, from https://www.tbb.org.tr/tr/bankacilik/banka-ve-sektor-bilgileri/veri-sorgulama-sistemi/illere-ve-bolgelere-gore-bilgiler/73

Davidson, I., & Qi, Z. (2008). Finding alternative clusterings using constraints.*The Eightth IEEE International Conference on Data Mining* (pp. 773-778). IEEE.

Dawson, C. W., & Wilby, R. L. (2001). Hydrological modelling using artificial neural networks. *Progress in Physical Geography*, *25*(1), 80–108. doi:10.1191/030913301674775671

De Treville, S., Shapiro, R. D., & Hameri, A. P. (2004). From supply chain to demand chain: The role of lead time reduction in improving demand chain performance. *Journal of Operations Management*, *21*(6), 613–627. doi:10.1016/j.jom.2003.10.001

Delias, P., Doumpos, M., Grigoroudis, E., Manolitzas, P., & Matsatsinis, N. (2015). Supporting healthcare management decisions via robust clustering of event logs. *Knowledge-Based Systems*, *84*, 203–213. doi:10.1016/j.knosys.2015.04.012

Deloitte. (2013). *Who says banks can't be social? Become a social bank, inside and out.* Retrieved May 2, 2016, from http://www2.deloitte.com/global/en/pages/financial-services/articles/banks-can-be-social.html

Deshmukh, A. K., & Mohan, A. (2012). Role of relationship marketing in demand chain collaboration. In Exploring Consumer Dynamics: A Relationship and Behavioral Approach. New Delhi: Himalaya Publishing House.

Deshmukh, A. K., & Mohan, A. (2016). Demand Chain Management (DCM): The Marketing and Supply Chain Interface Redefined. *The IUP's Journal of Supply Chain Management*, *13*(1), 20–36.

Dey, L., Afroz, N., & Nath, R. P. D. (2014) Emotion extraction from real time chat messenger. *Proceedings of 3rd International Conference on Informatics, Electronics & Vision*, 1-5. doi:10.1109/ICIEV.2014.6850785

Divol, R., Edelman, D., & Sarrazin, H. (2012). Demystifying social media. *The McKinsey Quarterly*, *2*(12), 66–77.

do Carmo, C. M. R., & Christensen, T. H. (2016). Cluster analysis of residential heat load profiles and the role of technical and household characteristics. *Energy and Building*, *125*, 171–180. doi:10.1016/j.enbuild.2016.04.079

Dong, L., Wang, L., Khahro, S. F., Gao, S., & Liao, X. (2016). Wind power day-ahead prediction with cluster analysis of NWP. *Renewable & Sustainable Energy Reviews*, *60*, 1206–1212. doi:10.1016/j.rser.2016.01.106

Dung & Cao. (2012). *A high-order hidden Markov model for emotion detection from textual data.* Springer Berlin Heidelberg.

Ekman, P. (1992). An argument for basic emotions. *Cognition and Emotion*, *6*(1), 169–200. doi:10.1080/02699939208411068

Elsalamony, H. A. (2014). Bank Direct Marketing Analysis of Data Mining Techniques. *International Journal of Computers and Applications*, *85*(7).

Erfani Joorabchi, M., Mirzaaghaei, M., & Mesbah, A. (2014, May). Works for me! characterizing non-reproducible bug reports. In *Proceedings of the 11th Working Conference on Mining Software Repositories* (pp. 62-71). ACM. doi:10.1145/2597073.2597098

Erlikh, L. (2000). Leveraging legacy system dollars for e-business. *IT Professional*, *2*(3), 17–23. doi:10.1109/6294.846201

Ernst, & Young. (2013). *Advanced analytics for insurance*. Retrieved September 29, 2016, from http://www.ey.com/Publication/vwLUAssets/Advanced_analytics_for_insurance/$FILE/Adv-analytics_insurance_AUNZ00000335.pdf

Etlinger, S., & Li, C. (2011). *A Framework for Social Analytics Including Six Use Cases for Social Media Measurement.* Altimeter group. Retrieved August 16, 2016, from http://www.slideshare.net/Altimeter/altimeter-social-analytics-report

Facebook. (2016). *Most popular product brands on Facebook 2016.*Retrieved September 24, 2016, from https://www.statista.com/statistics/265657/leading-product-brands-with-the-most-fans-on-facebook/

Fan, W., & Gordon, M. D. (2014). The Power of Social Media Analytics. *Communications of the ACM*, *57*(6), 74–81. doi:10.1145/2602574

Farmer, A. E., McGuffinb, P., & Spitznagelc, E. L. (1983). Heterogeneity in schizophrenia: A cluster-analytic approach. *Psychiatry Research*, *8*(1), 1–12. doi:10.1016/0165-1781(83)90132-4 PMID:6572983

Farzan, R., & Brusilovsky, P. (2006). Social navigation support in a course recommendation system. Springer. doi:10.1007/11768012_11

Fayyad, U., Piatetsky-Shapiro, G., & Smyth, P. (1996). Knowledge discovery and data mining: Towards a unifying framework.*2nd ACM International Conference on Knowledge Discovery and Data Mining (KDD)* (pp. 82-88). Portland, OR: AAAI.

Federal Financial Institutions Examination Council. (2013). *Social Media: Consumer Compliance Risk Management Guidance.* Federal Financial Institutions Examination Council (December 11, 2013). Retrieved July 5, 2016, from https://www.ffiec.gov/press/PDF/2013_Dec%20Final%20SMG %20 attached%20to%2011Dec13%20press%20release.pdf

Fedoseeva, S., & Zeidan, R. (2016). A dead-end tunnel or the light at the end of it: The role of BRICs in European exports. *Economic Modelling*, *59*, 237–248. doi:10.1016/j.econmod.2016.07.016

Felfernig, A., & Burke, R. (2008), Constraint-based Recommender Systems: Technologies and Research Issues. *ACM International Conference on Electronic Commerce*, 17-26. doi:10.1145/1409540.1409544

Felfernig, A., Friedrich, G., Jannach, D., & Zanker, M. (2006). An integrated environment for the development of knowledge-based recommender applications. *International Journal of Electronic Commerce*, *11*(2), 11–34. doi:10.2753/JEC1086-4415110201

Fenton, N., & Neil, M. (2012). *Risk assessment and decision analysis with Bayesian networks.* CRC Press.

Feranata, R. (2014). *Managing information explosion 'is it challenge or gold mine? How does banks response?* Retrieved September 29, 2016, from http://www.slideshare.net/RullyFeranata/bi-big-data-use-case-for-banking-by-rully-feranata

Financial Brand. (2015). Top 100 Banks on Facebook. *The Financial Brand.* Retrieved July 28, 2016, from https://thefinancialbrand.com/54734/power-100-2015-q3-facebook-banks/

Fox, B., Dam, R. V. D., & Shockley, R. (2013). *Analytics: Real-world use of Big Data in telecommunications, How innovative communications service providers are extracting value from uncertain data.* IBM Global Business Services Business Analytics and Optimization. Retrieved September 29, 2016, from http://www-935.ibm.com/services/multimedia/Anaytics.pdf

Francis, L. (2001, March). Neural networks demystified. *Casualty Actuarial Society Forum*, 253-320.

Gabay, G. & Moore, D. (2015). Antecedents of patient trust in health-care insurers. S*ervices Marketing Quarterly, 36*(1), 77-93.

Gabay, G. (2016b). Does loyalty of patients to their physicians predict loyalty to the healthcare insurer? *Health Marketing Quarterly, 33*(2).

Gabay, G., & Moskowitz, H. R. (2016). Reducing congestive heart failure patient re-admissions. In M. Prince & C. V. Priporas (Eds.), Market Sensing and Marketing Research. Academic Press.

Gabay, G. (2015). Perceived control over health, communication and patient-physician trust. *PEC, 98*(12), 1550–1557. PMID:26187177

Gabay, G. (2016a). Exploring perceived control and self-rated health in re-admissions among younger adults: A retrospective Study. *Patient Education and Counseling, 99*(5), 800–806. doi:10.1016/j.pec.2015.11.011 PMID:26626068

Gabay, G., & Moskowitz, H. R. (2015a). Extending Psychophysics Methods to Evaluating Potential Social Anxiety Factors in Face of Terrorism. *Jahrbuch für Psychologie und Psychotherapie, 4*(6), 167–176.

Gabay, G., & Moskowitz, R. H. (2015b). Mind Genomics: What profesisonal conduct enhances the emotional wellbeing of teens at the hospital. *Journal of Psychological Abnormalities in Children, 4*(3). doi:10.4172/2329-9525.1000147

Gardner, E. S. (1985). Exponential smoothing: The state of the art. *Journal of Forecasting, 4*(1), 1–28. doi:10.1002/for.3980040103

Garg, S. (2016). *The new frontier for the Pharmaceutical and Life Sciences Industry: Real Big Value from Big Data.* TATA Consultancy Services. Retrieved September 29, 2016, from http://www.tcs.com/SiteCollectionDocuments/White%20 Papers/Pharmaceutical-Industry-Big-Data-1113-2.pdf

Garg, P. (2010). Critical success factors for enterprise resource planning implementation in Indian retail industry: An exploratory study. *Int. J. Comput. Sci. Inf. Secur, 8*(2), 358–363.

Gartner. (2016). *Social Analytics*. Retrieved September 10, 2016, from http://www.gartner.com/it-glossary/social-analytics/

Gegick, M., Rotella, P., & Xie, T. (2010, May). Identifying security bug reports via text mining: An industrial case study. In *2010 7th IEEE Working Conference on Mining Software Repositories (MSR 2010)* (pp. 11-20). IEEE.

Ghaemmaghami, H., Dean, D., Sridharan, S., & van Leeuwen, D. A. (2016). A study of speaker clustering for speaker attribution in large telephone conversation datasets. *Computer Speech & Language, 40*, 23–45. doi:10.1016/j.csl.2016.03.005

Ghazi, D., Inkpen, D., & Szpakowicz, S. (2010). Hierarchical versus flat classification of emotions in text.*Proceedings of the NAACL HLT 2010 workshop on computational approaches to analysis and generation of emotion in text*, 140-146.

Ghose, A., Ipeirotis, P. G. & Li, B. (2012). Designing ranking systems for hotels on travel search engines by mining user-generated and crowd sourced content. *Marketing Science 31*(3), 493-520.

Ghosh, G., Banerjee, S., & Yen, N. Y. (2016). State transition in communication under social network: An analysis using fuzzy logic and Density Based Clustering towards big data paradigm. *Future Generation Computer Systems, 65*, 207–220. doi:10.1016/j.future.2016.02.017

Gilfoil, D. M., Aukers, S. M., & Jobs, C. G. (2015). Developing And Implementing A Social Media Program While Optimizing Return On Investment – An MBA Program Case Study. *American Journal of Business Education*, *8*(1), 31–48.

Golesworthy, T. (2016). A Review of Social Media in The Banking Sector. *Customer THINK*. Retrieved September 20, 2016, fromhttp://customerthink.com/a-review-of-social-media-in-the-banking-sector/

Gölz, S., & Hahnel, U. J. (2016). What motivates people to use energy feedback systems? A multiple goal approach to predict long-term usage behaviour in daily life. *Energy Research & Social Science*, *21*, 155–166. doi:10.1016/j.erss.2016.07.006

Gondek, D., & Hofmann, T. (2003). Conditional information bottleneck clustering. *Third International Conference on Data Mining, Work-shop on Clustering Large Datasets* (pp. 36-42). Citeseer.

Gondek, D., & Hofmann, T. (2005). Non-redundant clustering with conditional ensembles.*11th ACM International Conference on Knowledge Discovery and Data Mining (SIGKDD)* (pp. 70-77). Chicago: ACM.

Gong, S. (2010). A collaborative filtering recommendation algorithm based on user clustering and item clustering. *Journal of Software*, *5*(7), 745–752. doi:10.4304/jsw.5.7.745-752

Gorakala, S. K., & Michele, U. (2015). *Building a recommendation system with R*. Packt Publishing.

Görener, A., Dincer, H., & Hacioglu, U. (2016). Application of multi-objective optimization on the basis of ratio analysis (MOORA) method for bank branch location selection. *International Journal of Finance & Banking Studies, 2*(2), 41-52.

Goyal, P., Rahman, Z., & Kazmi, A. A. (2015). Identification and prioritization of corporate sustainability practices using analytical hierarchy process. *Journal of Modelling in Management*, *10*(1), 23–49. doi:10.1108/JM2-09-2012-0030

Green, P. E., Krieger, A. M., & Wind, Y. (2001). Thirty years of conjoint analysis: Reflections and prospects. *Interfaces, 31*(3), S56-S73.

Greenfield, D. (2014). *Social Media in Financial Markets: The Coming of Age...* GNIP (Whitepaper). Retrieved August 25, 2016, from http://stocktwits.com/research/social-media-and-markets-the-coming-of-age.pdf

Green, P. E., & Srinivasan, V. (1978). Conjoint analysis in consumer research: Issues and outlook. *The Journal of Consumer Research*, *5*(2), 103–123. doi:10.1086/208721

Gu, F., Hall, P., & Miles, N. (2016). Development of composites based on recycled polypropylene for injection moulding automobile parts using hierarchical clustering analysis and principal component estimate. *Journal of Cleaner Production*, *137*, 632–643. doi:10.1016/j.jclepro.2016.07.028

Guido, M. (2016). *The List of the Top 25 Social Media Analytics Tools*. Retrieved September 14, 2016, from http://keyhole.co/blog/list-of-the-top-25-social-media-analytics-tools/

Guo, X., & Lu, J. (2007). Intelligent e-government services with personalized recommendation techniques. *International Journal of Intelligent Systems*, *22*(5), 401–417. doi:10.1002/int.20206

Gutierrez, D. D. (2016). *InsideBigData guide to Big Data for finance*. Retrieved September 29, 2016, from https://www.em360tech.com/wp-content/files_mf/1427803213insideBIGDATAGuidetoBigDataforFinance.pdf

Hafezalkotob, A., & Hafezalkotob, A. (2015). Comprehensive MULTIMOORA method with target-based attributes and integrated significant coefficients for materials selection in biomedical applications. *Materials & Design*, *87*, 949–959. doi:10.1016/j.matdes.2015.08.087

Hafezalkotob, A., Hafezalkotob, A., & Sayadi, M. K. (2016). Extension of MULTIMOORA method with interval numbers: An application in materials selection. *Applied Mathematical Modelling*, *40*(2), 1372–1386. doi:10.1016/j.apm.2015.07.019

Hair, J. F., Black, W. C., Babin, B. J., Anderson, R. E., & Tatham, R. (2010). *Multivariate Data Analysis*. Pearson Education.

Haldar, N. A. H., Khan, F. A., Ali, A., & Abbas, H. (2016). Arrhythmia Classification using Mahalanobis Distance based Improved Fuzzy C-Means Clustering for Mobile Health Monitoring Systems. *Neurocomputing*.

Hall, M., Frank, E., Holmes, G., Pfahringer, B., Reutemann, P., & Witten, I. H. (2009). The WEKA Data Mining Software: An Update. *SIGKDD Explorations*, *11*(1), 10–17. doi:10.1145/1656274.1656278

Handl, J., & Knowles, J. (2007). An evolutionary approach to multiobjective clustering. *Evolutionary Computation IEEE Transaction*, *11*(1), 56–76. doi:10.1109/TEVC.2006.877146

Han, J., Kamber, M., & Pei, J. (2011). *Data mining: concepts and techniques*. San Francisco: Morgan Kaufmann.

Han, J., & Lee, H. (2015). Adaptive landmark recommendations for travel planning: Personalizing and clustering landmarks using geo-tagged social media. *Pervasive and Mobile Computing*, *18*, 4–17. doi:10.1016/j.pmcj.2014.08.002

Han, J., Pei, J., & Yin, Y. (2003). Mining Frequent Patterns without Candidate Generation.*ACM SIGMOD Intl. Conference on Management of Data*, 54-87.

Hansche, H. L., & Chen, J. T. (2014). *Social Media Guide for Financial Institutions*. Chapman and Cutler LLP, USA. Retrieved July 29, 2016, fromhttp://www.chapman.com/insights-publications-Social_Media_Financial_Institutions.html

Hartigan, J. (1985). Statistical theory in clustering. *Journal of Classification*, 63-76.

Heikkilä, J. (2002). From supply to demand chain management: Efficiency and customer satisfaction. *Journal of Operations Management*, *20*(6), 747–767. doi:10.1016/S0272-6963(02)00038-4

Herlocker, J. L., Konstan, J. A., Borchers, A., & Riedl, J. (1999). An algorithmic framework for performing collaborative filtering. In *Proceedings of the 22nd Annual International ACM SIGIR Conference on Research and Development in Information Retrieval - SIGIR '99* (pp. 230–237). New York: ACM Press. doi:10.1145/312624.312682

Herlocker, J. L., Konstan, J. A., Terveen, L. G., & Riedl, J. T. (2004). Evaluating collaborative filtering. *ACM Transactions on Information Systems*, *22*(1), 5–53. doi:10.1145/963770.963772

Herp, J., Pedersen, N. L., & Nadimi, E. S. (2016). Wind turbine performance analysis based on multivariate higher order moments and Bayesian classifiers. *Control Engineering Practice*, *49*, 204–211. doi:10.1016/j.conengprac.2015.12.018

Herrera-Restrepo, O., Triantis, K., Seaver, W. L., Paradi, J. C., & Zhu, H. (2016). Bank branch operational performance: A robust multivariate and clustering approach. *Expert Systems with Applications*, *50*, 107–119. doi:10.1016/j.eswa.2015.12.025

He, W., Wu, H., Yan, G., Akula, V., & Shen, J. (2015). A novel social media competitive analytics framework with sentiment benchmarks. *Information & Management*, *52*(7), 801–812. doi:10.1016/j.im.2015.04.006

Hewett, R., & Kijsanayothin, P. (2009). On modeling software defect repair time. *Empirical Software Engineering*, *14*(2), 165–186. doi:10.1007/s10664-008-9064-x

Hilletofth, P., & Ericsson, D. (2007). Demand chain management: Next generation of logistics management. *Conradi Research Review*, *4*(2), 1–18.

Hitt, L., Jin, F., & Wu, L. (2015). *Who Benefits More from Social Media: Evidence from Large-Sample Firm Value Analysis* (Preliminary). Retrieved August 28, 2016, from https://pdfs.semanticscholar.org/ 7a7c/36121c0c5fd6424ad7221ef2e958f03b7385.pdf

Hokkanen, J., Jacobson, T., Skingsley, C., & Tibblin, M. (2015). The risk-bank's future information supply in light of Big Data. *Economic Commentaries*, *17*, 1–5.

Holopainen, M., & Sarlin, P. (2015). Toward robust early-warning models: A horse race, ensembles and model uncertainty. *Bank of Finland Research Discussion Paper*, (6).

Holsapple, C., Hsiao, S.-H., & Pakath, R. (2014). Business Social Media Analytics: Definition, Benefits, and Challenges. In *Proceedings of 20th Americas Conference on Information Systems (AMCIS 2014): Smart Sustainability: The Information Systems Opportunity* (vol. 5, pp. 3703- 3714). Savannah, GA: Association for Information Systems (AIS).

Holt, C. C. (2004). Forecasting seasonals and trends by exponentially weighted moving averages. *International Journal of Forecasting*, *20*(1), 5–10. doi:10.1016/j.ijforecast.2003.09.015

Hosseini, H., Nguyen, R., & Godfrey, M. W. (2012, March). A market-based bug allocation mechanism using predictive bug lifetimes. In *Software Maintenance and Reengineering (CSMR), 2012 16th European Conference on* (pp. 149-158). IEEE. doi:10.1109/CSMR.2012.25

Hsu, W.-Y. (2017). Clustering-based compression connected to cloud databases in telemedicine and long-term care applications. *Telematics and Informatics*, *34*(1), 299–310. doi:10.1016/j.tele.2016.05.010

Hua Lu, M., Madu, C. N., Kuei, C. H., & Winokur, D. (1994). Integrating QFD, AHP and benchmarking in strategic marketing. *Journal of Business and Industrial Marketing*, *9*(1), 41–50. doi:10.1108/08858629410053470

Hunyadi. (n.d.). Performance comparison of Apriori and FPGrowth algorithms in generating association rules. *Proceedings of the European Computing Conference*, 376-381.

IDC. (2011). *IDC's Digital Universe study*. Retrieved from http://idcdocserv.com/1142

Internet Live Stats. (2016). Retrieved from http://www.internetlivestats.com/

Irving Fisher Committee on Central Bank Statistics. (2015). *Central banks' use of and interest in "Big Data"*. Retrieved September 28, 2016, from http://www.bis.org/ifc/publ/ifc-report-bigdata.pdf

Izard, C. E. (1977). *Human emotions*. New York: Plenum Press. doi:10.1007/978-1-4899-2209-0

Jacobs, D. (2006). The promise of demand chain management in fashion The promise of demand chain management in fashion. *Journal of Fashion Marketing and Management*, *10*(1), 84–96. doi:10.1108/13612020610651141

Jain, A. K., & Dubes, R. C. (1988). Algorithms for clustering data. Upper Saddle River, NJ: Academic Press.

Jain, V. K., & Kumar, S. (2015). An Effective Approach to Track Levels of Influenza-A (H1N1) Pandemic in India Using Twitter. *Procedia Computer Science*, *70*(1), 801–807. doi:10.1016/j.procs.2015.10.120

Jain, V. K., Kumar, S., Jain, N., & Verma, P. (2016). A novel Approach to Track Levels public emotions related to epidemics in multilingual data. *2nd International conference and Youth School Information technology and Nanotechnology,* 883-889.

Jannach, D. (2004). Preference-based treatment of empty result sets in product finders and knowledge-based recommenders. *Proceedings of the 27th Annual German Conference on Artificial Intelligence*, 145–159.

Jeatrakul, P., & Wong, K. W. (2009, October). Comparing the performance of different neural networks for binary classification problems. In *Natural Language Processing, 2009. SNLP'09. Eighth International Symposium on* (pp. 111-115). IEEE. doi:10.1109/SNLP.2009.5340935

Jee, C. (2016, January 18). *Top software failures 2015/2016: The worst software glitches this year*. Retrieved July 23, 2016, from http://www.computerworlduk.com/galleries/infrastructure/top-10-software-failures-of-2014-3599618/

Jeong, G., Kim, S., & Zimmermann, T. (2009, August). Improving bug triage with bug tossing graphs. In *Proceedings of the 7th joint meeting of the European software engineering conference and the ACM SIGSOFT symposium on The foundations of software engineering* (pp. 111-120). ACM. doi:10.1145/1595696.1595715

Jin, H., Huang, J., Xie, X., & Zhang, Q. (2006). Using Classification Techniques to Improve Replica Selection in Data Grid. On the Move to Meaningful Internet Systems 2006: CoopIS.DOA.GADA. and ODBASE. *Lecture Notes in Computer Science*, *4276*, 1376–1387. doi:10.1007/11914952_24

Jony, R. I. (2013). *Preprocessing solutions for telecommunication specific Big Data use cases* (Master's Dissertation). Aalto University, Finland.

Jüttner, U., Christopher, M., & Baker, S. (2007). Demand chain management-integrating marketing and supply chain management. *Industrial Marketing Management*, *36*(3), 377–392. doi:10.1016/j.indmarman.2005.10.003

Jüttner, U., Peck, H., & Christopher, M. (2003). Supply chain risk management: Outlining an agenda for future research. *International Journal of Logistics: Research and Applications*, *6*(4), 197–210. doi:10.1080/13675560310001627016

Kanwal, J., & Maqbool, O. (2012). Bug prioritization to facilitate bug report triage. *Journal of Computer Science and Technology*, *27*(2), 397–412. doi:10.1007/s11390-012-1230-3

Khashei, M., Hamadani, A. Z., & Bijari, M. (2012). A novel hybrid classification model of artificial neural networks and multiple linear regression models. *Expert Systems with Applications*, *39*(3), 2606–2620. doi:10.1016/j.eswa.2011.08.116

Khashman, A. (2010). Neural networks for credit risk evaluation: Investigation of different neural models and learning schemes. *Expert Systems with Applications*, *37*(9), 6233–6239. doi:10.1016/j.eswa.2010.02.101

Khashman, A. (2011). Credit risk evaluation using neural networks: Emotional versus conventional models. *Applied Soft Computing*, *11*(8), 5477–5484. doi:10.1016/j.asoc.2011.05.011

Khoshnevisan, B., Rafiee, S., Omid, M., Mousazadeh, H., Shamshirband, S., & Ab Hamid, S. H. (2015). Developing a fuzzy clustering model for better energy use in farm management systems. *Renewable & Sustainable Energy Reviews*, *48*, 27–34. doi:10.1016/j.rser.2015.03.029

Knotek, P. (2014). Banking sectors in EMU-cluster analysis. *European Scientific Journal, 10*(34).

Kohane, I. S., Drazen, J. M., & Campion, E. W. (2012). A glimpse of the next 100 years in medicine. *The New England Journal of Medicine*, *367*(26), 2538–2539. doi:10.1056/NEJMe1213371 PMID:23268669

Koh, H. C., Tan, W. C., & Peng, G. C. (2004). Credit scoring using data mining techniques. *Singapore Management Review*, *26*(2), 25.

Korhonen, P., Huttunen, K., & Eloranta, E. (1998). Demand chain management in a global enterprise-information management view. *Production Planning and Control*, *9*(6), 526–531. doi:10.1080/095372898233777

Kotu, V., & Deshpande, B. (2014). *Predictive analytics and data mining: concepts and practice with rapidminer*. Morgan Kaufmann.

Kouser & Sunita. (2013). A comparative study of K Means Algorithm by Different Distance Measures. *International Journal of Innovative Research in Computer and Communication Engineering,* 2443-2447.

KPMG Report. (2014). *Indian Retail: The next growth story*. Available at: https://www.kpmg.com/IN/en/IssuesAndInsights/ArticlesPublications/Documents/BBG-Retail.pdf

Kriegel, H.-P., & Zimek, A. (2010). Subspace clustering, ensemble clustering, alternative clustering, multiview: what can we learn from each other? *MultiClust:First International Workshop on Discovering, Summarizing and Using Multiple Clusterings Held in Conjunction with KDD 2010.*

Kumar, K., & Haynes, J. D. (2003). Forecasting credit ratings using an ANN and statistical techniques. *International Journal of Business Studies.*

Kumar, K., & Bhattacharya, S. (2006). Artificial neural network vs linear discriminant analysis in credit ratings forecast: A comparative study of prediction performances. *Review of Accounting and Finance*, *5*(3), 216–227. doi:10.1108/14757700610686426

Kumar, M. V., Chaitanya, M. V., & Madhavan, M. (2012). Segmenting the banking market strategy by clustering. *International Journal of Computers and Applications*, *45*, 10 15.

Kundakcı, N. (2016). Combined Multi-Criteria Decision Making Approach Based On Macbeth And Multi-MOORA Methods. *Alphanumeric Journal*, *4*(1), 17–26. doi:10.17093/aj.2016.4.1.5000178402

Kuo, R., Mei, C., Zulvia, F., & Tsai, C. (2016). An application of a metaheuristic algorithm-based clustering ensemble method to APP customer segmentation. *Neurocomputing*, *205*, 116–129. doi:10.1016/j.neucom.2016.04.017

Lamkanfi, A., Demeyer, S., Soetens, Q. D., & Verdonck, T. (2011, March). Comparing mining algorithms for predicting the severity of a reported bug. In *Software Maintenance and Reengineering (CSMR), 2011 15th European Conference on* (pp. 249-258). IEEE. doi:10.1109/CSMR.2011.31

Lamkanfi, A., Demeyer, S., & Giger, E. (2010, May). Predicting the severity of a reported bug. In *Proceedings of the International working conference on mining software repositories* (pp. 1-10). ACM. doi:10.1109/MSR.2010.5463284

Laney, D. (2001). *3D Data management: controlling data volume, velocity, and variety.* Retrieved September 29, 2016, from https://blogs.gartner.com/doug-laney/files/2012/01/ad949-3D-Data-Management-Controlling-Data-Volume-Velocity-and-Variety.pdf

Langabeer, J., & Rose, J. (2002). Is the supply chain still relevant? *Logistics Manager*, (March), 11-13.

LaViola, J. J. (2003, May). Double exponential smoothing: an alternative to Kalman filter-based predictive tracking. In *Proceedings of the workshop on Virtual environments 2003* (pp. 199-206). ACM. doi:10.1145/769953.769976

Le Cam, M., Daoud, A., & Zmeureanu, R. (2016). Forecasting electric demand of supply fan using data mining techniques. *Energy*, *101*, 541–557. doi:10.1016/j.energy.2016.02.061

Lee, K. (2014). *The Big List of The 61 Best Social Media Tools for Small Business.* Retrieved September 22, 2016, from https://blog.bufferapp.com/best-social-media-tools-for-small-business

Lee, C.-H. (2012). Mining spatio-temporal information on microblogging streams using a density-based online clustering method. *Expert Systems with Applications*, *39*(10), 9623–9641. doi:10.1016/j.eswa.2012.02.136

Lee, C., Hallak, R., & Sardeshmukh, S. R. (2016). Drivers of success in independent restaurants: A study of the Australian restaurant sector. *Journal of Hospitality and Tourism Management*, *29*, 99–111. doi:10.1016/j.jhtm.2016.06.003

Lee, T. S., & Chen, I. F. (2005). A two-stage hybrid credit scoring model using artificial neural networks and multivariate adaptive regression splines. *Expert Systems with Applications*, *28*(4), 743–752. doi:10.1016/j.eswa.2004.12.031

Leong, C. K. (2015). Credit risk scoring with bayesian network models. *Computational Economics*, 1–24.

Liebowitz, J. (2010). *Business Analytics An Introduction.* Boca Raton, FL: PressCRC

Lin, C., Cho, Y.-R., Hwang, W.-C., Pei, P., & Zhang, A. (2007). Clustering methods in a protein–protein interaction network. In X. Hu & Y. Pan (Eds.), *Knowledge Discovery in Bioinformatics: Techniques, Methods, and Applications*. Chichester, UK: John Wiley & Sons, Inc. doi:10.1002/9780470124642.ch16

Linder, R., Geier, J., & Kölliker, M. (2004). Artificial neural networks, classification trees and regression: Which method for which customer base? *The Journal of Database Marketing & Customer Strategy Management*, *11*(4), 344–356. doi:10.1057/palgrave.dbm.3240233

Lin, J. W., Hwang, M. I., & Becker, J. D. (2003). A fuzzy neural network for assessing the risk of fraudulent financial reporting. *Managerial Auditing Journal*, *18*(8), 657–665. doi:10.1108/02686900310495151

Lin, S. L. (2009). A new two-stage hybrid approach of credit risk in banking industry. *Expert Systems with Applications*, *36*(4), 8333–8341. doi:10.1016/j.eswa.2008.10.015

Liu, Y., Xu, C., & Cheung, S. C. (2014, May). Characterizing and detecting performance bugs for smartphone applications. In *Proceedings of the 36th International Conference on Software Engineering* (pp. 1013-1024). ACM. doi:10.1145/2568225.2568229

Lu, S., Park, S., Seo, E., & Zhou, Y. (2008, March). Learning from mistakes: a comprehensive study on real world concurrency bug characteristics. In ACM Sigplan Notices (Vol. 43, No. 3, pp. 329-339). ACM. doi:10.1145/1346281.1346323

Lu, J. (2004). Personalized e-learning material recommender system.*Proc. of the International Conf. on Information Technology for Application*, 374-379.

Lukins, S. K., Kraft, N. A., & Etzkorn, L. H. (2010). Bug localization using latent Dirichlet allocation. *Information and Software Technology*, *52*(9), 972–990. doi:10.1016/j.infsof.2010.04.002

Ma, C., Smith, H. W., Chu, C., & Juarez, D. T. (2015). Big Data in pharmacy practice: Current use, challenges, and the future. *Integrated Pharmacy Research and Practice*, *4*, 91–99. doi:10.2147/IPRP.S55862

Madu, C., Kuei, C., & Madu, A. (1991). Establishing priorities for the information technology industry in Taiwan: A Delphi approach. *Long Range Planning*, *24*(5), 105–118. doi:10.1016/0024-6301(91)90256-N

Mäenpää, K. (2006). Clustering the consumers on the basis of their perceptions of the Internet banking services. *Internet Research*, *16*(3), 304–322. doi:10.1108/10662240610673718

Maes, S., Tuyls, K., Vanschoenwinkel, B., & Manderick, B. (2002, January). Credit card fraud detection using Bayesian and neural networks.*Proceedings of the 1st international naiso congress on neuro fuzzy technologies*, 261-270.

Malhotra, R., & Malhotra, D. K. (2003). Evaluating consumer loans using neural networks. *Omega*, *31*(2), 83–96. doi:10.1016/S0305-0483(03)00016-1

Margret, J. J., & Sreenivasan, S. (2013). Implementation of Data Mining in Medical Fraud Detection. *International Journal of Computers and Applications*, *69*(5), 1–4. doi:10.5120/11835-7556

Marques, A. I., García, V., & Sanchez, J. S. (2012). A literature review on the application of evolutionary computing to credit scoring. *The Journal of the Operational Research Society*, *64*(9), 1384–1399. doi:10.1057/jors.2012.145

Marvin, R., & Behr, A. (2016). *The Best Social Media Management & Analytics Tools of 2016*. Retrieved September 26, 2016, from http://www.pcmag.com/article2/0,2817,2491376,00.asp

Matter, D., Kuhn, A., & Nierstrasz, O. (2009, May). Assigning bug reports using a vocabulary-based expertise model of developers. In *2009 6th IEEE International Working Conference on Mining Software Repositories* (pp. 131-140). IEEE doi:10.1109/MSR.2009.5069491

McAfee, A., & Brynjolfsson, E. (2012). Big data *The management revolution. Harvard Business Review*, *90*, 61–67. PMID:23074865

McAfee, A., Brynjolfsson, E., Davenport, T. H., Patil, D., & Barton, D. (2012). Big data. *The management revolution. Harvard Business Review*, *90*(10), 61–67. PMID:23074865

McCarthy, K., Salem, Y., & Smyth, B. (2010). Experience-Based Critiquing. *Reusing Critiquing Experiences to Improve Conversational Recommendation, ICCBR*, *10*, 480–494.

McEachan, R. R. C., Conner, M., Taylor, N. J., & Lawton, R. J. (2011). Prospective prediction of health-related behaviors with the theory of planned behaviour: A meta-analysis. *Health Psychology Review, 5*(2), 97-144.

Menon, A., & Jain, A. (2014). *Analytics in Pharma and Life Sciences*. Everest Group Research. Retrieved September 29, 2016, from http://www.genpact.com/docs/default-source/resource-/analytics-in-pharma-and-life-sciences

Mentzer, J.T. (2001). *Supply Chain Management: Strategy, Planning & Operation*. New Delhi: Response Books/ Sage India.

Menzies, T., & Marcus, A. (2008, September). Automated severity assessment of software defect reports. In *Software Maintenance, 2008. ICSM 2008. IEEE International Conference on* (pp. 346-355). IEEE. doi:10.1109/ICSM.2008.4658083

Merriam-Webster. (2016). *Social media*. Retrieved September 25, 2016, from http://www.merriamwebster.com/dictionary/social%20media

Metaxiotis, K., & Psarras, J. (2004). The contribution of neural networks and genetic algorithms to business decision support: Academic myth or practical solution? *Management Decision*, *42*(2), 229–242. doi:10.1108/00251740410518534

Mezei, J., & Sarlin, P. (2016). *RiskRank: Measuring interconnected risk.* arXiv preprint arXiv:1601.06204

Miguel, P., Gonçalves, J., Neves, L., & Martins, A. G. (2016). *Using clustering techniques to provide simulation scenarios for the smart grid.* Sustainable Cities and Society.

Mihalcea, R., & Strapparava, C. (2005). Making Computers Laugh: Investigations in Automatic Humor Recognition. *Proceedings of the Joint Conference on Human Language Technology/Empirical Methods in Natural Language Processing*, 531-538.

Miner, G., Elder, I. V. J., Fast, A., Hill, T., Nisbet, R., & Delen, D. (2012). *Practical Text Mining and Statistical Analysis for Non-structured Text Data Applications*. Academic Press.

Miner, L., Bolding, P., Hilbe, J., Goldstein, M., Hill, T., Nisbet, R., & Miner, G. (2014). *Practical Predictive Analytics and Decision Systems for Medicine: Informatics Accuracy and Cost-Effectiveness for Healthcare Administration and Delivery Including Medical Research*. Academic Press.

Miranda, T., Claypool, M., Gokhale, A., & Sartin, M. (1999). Combining contentbased and collaborative filters in an online newspaper.*Proceedings of ACM SIGIR Workshop on Recommender Systems.*

Misra, B. B., & Dehuri, S. (2007). Functional Link Artificial Neural Network for Classification Task in Data Mining. *J. Comput. Sci.*, *3*(12), 948–955. doi:10.3844/jcssp.2007.948.955

Moin, A., & Neumann, G. (2012, November). Assisting bug triage in large open source projects using approximate string matching.*Proc. 7th Int. Conf. on Software Engineering Advances.*

Mythili, M. S., & Mohamed Shanavas, A. R. (2013). Performance Evaluation of Apriori and FP-Growth Algorithms. *International Journal of Computers and Applications*, *79*(10), 34–37. doi:10.5120/13779-1650

Narver, J. C., & Slater, S. F. (1990). The effect of a market orientation on business profitability. *Journal of Marketing, 54*(4), 20–35. doi:10.2307/1251757

Neviarouskaya, A., Prendinger, H., & Ishizuka, M. (2007). Analysis of affect expressed through the evolving language of online communication.*Proceedings of the 12th International Conference on Intelligent User Interfaces,* 278-281. doi:10.1145/1216295.1216346

Newman, A. J., & Cullen, P. (2002). *Retailing: environment & operations*. Cengage Learning EMEA.

Niknafs, A., Denzinger, J., & Ruhe, G. (2013). A systematic literature review of the personnel assignment problem. *Proceedings of the International Multiconference of Engineers and Computer Scientists.*

Nistor, A., Jiang, T., & Tan, L. (2013, May). Discovering, reporting, and fixing performance bugs. In *Proceedings of the 10th Working Conference on Mining Software Repositories* (pp. 237-246). IEEE Press.

Niyagas, W., Srivihok, A., & Kitisin, S. (2006). Clustering e-banking customer using data mining and marketing segmentation. *ECTI Transactions on Computer and Information Technology*, *2*(1), 63–69.

Odden, L. (2016). *9 Social Media Marketing Trends That Could Make or Break Your Business in 2017*. Retrieved September 28, 2016, from http://www.toprankblog.com/2016/07/future-social-media-marketing/

Ogwueleka, F. N., Misra, S., Colomo-Palacios, R., & Fernandez, L. (2015). Neural network and classification approach in identifying customer behavior in the banking sector: A case study of an international bank. *Human Factors and Ergonomics in Manufacturing & Service Industries*, *25*(1), 28–42.

Önay, O. (2016). Multi-Criteria Assessment of Better Life via TOPSIS and MOORA Methods. *International Journal of Business and Social Science*, *7*(1), 225–234.

Önay, O., & Yıldırım, B. F. (2016). Evaluation of NUTS Level 2 Regions of Turkey by TOPSIS, MOORA and VIKOR. *International Journal of Humanities and Social Science*, *6*(1), 212–221.

Opitz, L. (2016). *5 Free Social Media Analytics Tools – With Recommendations from Experts*. Retrieved September 18, 2016, from https://www.talkwalker.com/blog/5-free-social-media-analytics-tools-experts

Ordoñez, H., Corrales, J. C., Cobos, C., Wives, L. K., Thom, L. H., & Ordoñez, A. (2016). Grouping of business processes models based on an incremental clustering algorithm using fuzzy similarity and multimodal search. *Expert Systems with Applications.*

Oreski, S., Oreski, D., & Oreski, G. (2012). Hybrid system with genetic algorithm and artificial neural networks and its application to retail credit risk assessment. *Expert Systems with Applications*, *39*(16), 12605–12617. doi:10.1016/j.eswa.2012.05.023

Ormazabal, M., & Puga-Leal, R. (2016). An exploratory study of UK companies taxonomy based on environmental drivers. *Journal of Cleaner Production*, *133*, 479–486. doi:10.1016/j.jclepro.2016.06.011

Ortony, A., Clore, G. L., & Collins, A. (1988). *The Cognitive Structure of Emotions*. Cambridge University Press. doi:10.1017/CBO9780511571299

Osgood, C. E., Succi, G. J., & Tannenbaum, P. H. (1957). *The Measurement of Meaning*. Urbana, IL: University of Illinois Press.

Özbek, A. (2015). Efficiency Analysis of Foreign-Capital Banks in Turkey by OCRA and MOORA. *Research Journal of Finance and Accounting*, *6*(13), 2222–1697.

Pacelli, V., & Azzollini, M. (2011). An artificial neural network approach for credit risk management. *Journal of Intelligent Learning Systems and Applications*, *3*(2), 103–112. doi:10.4236/jilsa.2011.32012

Pang, B., & Lee, L. (2008). Opinion mining and sentiment analysis. *Foundations and Trends in Information Retrieval*, *2*(1), 1–135. doi:10.1561/1500000011

Pao, H. T. (2008). A comparison of neural network and multiple regression analysis in modeling capital structure. *Expert Systems with Applications*, *35*(3), 720–727. doi:10.1016/j.eswa.2007.07.018

Park, J.-Y., & Jang, S. (2013). Confused by too many choices? Choice overload in tourism. *Tourism Management, 35*, 1-12. doi:10.1016/j.tourman.2012.05.004

Parvatiyar, A., & Sheth, J. N. (2001). Customer relationship management: Emerging practice, process, and discipline. *Journal of Economic and Social Research*, *3*(2), 1–34.

Pazzani, M. J., & Billsus, D. (2007). Content-based recommendation systems. *The Adaptive Web, LNCS*, *4321*, 325–341. doi:10.1007/978-3-540-72079-9_10

Pei, J., & Han, J. (2004). Mining Sequential Patterns by Pattern Growth: The Prefix Span Approach. *IEEE Transactions on Knowledge and Data Engineering*, *16*(10), 1–17.

Pereira, R., Fagundes, A., Melício, R., Mendes, V., Figueiredo, J., Martins, J., & Quadrado, J. (2016). A fuzzy clustering approach to a demand response model. *International Journal of Electrical Power & Energy Systems*, *81*, 184–192. doi:10.1016/j.ijepes.2016.02.032

Perikos, I., & Hatzilygeroudis, I. (2013). *Recognizing emotions present in Natural Language Sentences*. University of Patras.

Petrocelli, T. (2013). *Market Landscape Report: Social Media Marketing and Analytics. The New Face of Customer Engagement*. Milford, MA: The Enterprise Strategy Group (ESG). Retrieved June 28, 2016, from http://www.oracle.com/us/corporate/analystreports/es-social-landscape-1936813.pdf

Petrovic, M., Stefanova, E., Ziropadja, L., Stojkovic, T., & Kostic, V. S. (2016). Neuropsychiatric symptoms in Serbian patients with Parkinsons disease. *Journal of the Neurological Sciences*, *367*, 342–346. doi:10.1016/j.jns.2016.06.027 PMID:27423616

Phua, C., Lee, V., Smith, K., & Gayler, R. (2010). *A comprehensive survey of data mining-based fraud detection research*. arXiv preprint arXiv:1009.6119

Plutchik, R. (1980). A General Psycho evolutionary Theory of Emotion. In Emotion: Theory, Research and Experience: Theories of Emotions (vol. 1). New York: Academic.

Pohl, D., Bouchachia, A., & Hellwagner, H. (2016). Online indexing and clustering of social media data for emergency management. *Neurocomputing*, *172*, 168–179. doi:10.1016/j.neucom.2015.01.084

Porcel, C., & Herrera-Viedma, E. (2010). Dealing with incomplete information in a fuzzy linguistic recommender system to disseminate information in university digital libraries. *Journal Knowledge-Based Systems, 23*(1), 32–39.

Pukkhem, N. (2013). Ontology-based semantic approach for learning object recommendation. *ACEEE International Journal on Information Retrieval, 3*(4). Retrieved from http://hal.archives-ouvertes.fr/hal-00942526/

PwC Report. (2015). *Total Retail 2015: Retailers and the age of disruption*. Available at: https://www.pwc.in/assets/pdfs/publications/2015/retailers-and-the-age-disruption.pdf

Qi, Z., & Davidson, I. (2009). A principled and flexible frameworkfor finding alternative clusterings. *The15th ACM SIGKDD International Conference on Knowledge Discovery and Data Mining* (pp. 717–726). ACM.

Raghavan, V. (1967). *The Number of Rasa-S*. Theosophical Publishing House.

Raghupathi, W., & Raghupathi, V. (2014). Big Data analytics in healthcare: Promise and potential. *Health Information Science and Systems, 2*(3), 1–10. PMID:23823667

Rahman, M. M., Sohan, S. M., Maurer, F., & Ruhe, G. (2010, September). Evaluation of optimized staffing for feature development and bug fixing. In *Proceedings of the 2010 ACM-IEEE International Symposium on Empirical Software Engineering and Measurement* (p. 42). ACM. doi:10.1145/1852786.1852841

Rainbird, M. (2004). Demand and supply chains : The value catalyst. *International Journal of Physical Distribution & Logistics Management, 34*(3), 230–250. doi:10.1108/09600030410533565

Rao, S., & Gupta. R. (2012). Implementing Improved Algorithm Over APRIORI Data Mining Association Rule Algorithm. *International Journal of Computer Science And Technology,* 489-493.

Rao, S., & Kak, A. (2011, May). Retrieval from software libraries for bug localization: a comparative study of generic and composite text models. In *Proceedings of the 8th Working Conference on Mining Software Repositories* (pp. 43-52). ACM. doi:10.1145/1985441.1985451

Raymond, E. S. (1998). The cathedral and the bazaar. *First Monday, 3*(3).

Read, J., Hope, D., & Carroll, J. (2007). Annotating expressions of Appraisal in English.*Proceedings of the ACL-2007 Linguistic Annotation Workshop*, 93-100.

Renda, M., & Straccia, U. (2005). A personalized collaborative digital library environment: A model and an application. *Information Processing & Management, 41*(1), 5–21. doi:10.1016/j.ipm.2004.04.007

Report of The Banks Association of Turkey. (n.d.). *Distribution of selected indicators of banking system according to cities and regions in the Turkey*. Retrieved July 13, 2016, from https://www.tbb.org.tr/tr/bankacilik/banka-ve-sektor-bilgileri/4

Report, E. Y. (2015). *India — pulse of retail and consumer markets What does a changing consumer mean for the sector?* Available at: http://www.ey.com/Publication/vwLUAssets/EY-india-a-pulse-on-the-consumer-products-market-march-2015.pdf/$FILE/EY-india-a-pulse-on-the-consumer-products-market-march-2015.pdf

Resnick, P., Varian, H. R., & Editors, G. (1997). Recommender systems mende tems. *Communications of the ACM, 40*(3), 56–58. doi:10.1145/245108.245121

Ricci, F., Rokach, L., & Shapira, B. (2010). *Recommender systems handbook*. New York: Springer-Verlag New York, Inc.

Rid, W., Ezeuduji, I. O., & Pröbstl-Haider, U. (2014). Segmentation by motivation for rural tourism activities in The Gambia. *Tourism Management, 40*, 102–116. doi:10.1016/j.tourman.2013.05.006

Rise, J., Kovac, V., Kraft, P., & Moan, I. S. (2008). Predicting the intention to quit smoking and quitting behaviour: Extending the theory of planned behaviour. *British Journal of Health Psychology, 13*(2), 291–310. doi:10.1348/135910707X187245 PMID:17535498

Ruotsalo, T. (2010). *Methods and applications for ontology-based recommender systems. science and technology*. Retrieved December 12, 2015, from http://lib.tkk.fi/Diss/2010/isbn9789526031514/

Russom, P. (2011). *Big data analytics*. TDWI Best Practices Report, Fourth Quarter.

Saad, G. H. (2001). Strategic performance evaluation: Descriptive and prescriptive analysis. *Industrial Management & Data Systems, 101*(8), 390–399. doi:10.1108/EUM0000000006169

Saaty, T. L. (1977). A scaling method for priorities in hierarchical structures. *Journal of Mathematical Psychology, 15*(3), 234–281. doi:10.1016/0022-2496(77)90033-5

Saaty, T. L. (1980). *The Analytic Hierarchy Process*. New York, NY: McGraw-Hill.

Saha, M., & Mitra, P. (2014). VLGAAC: Variable length genetic algorithm based alternative clustering. *ICONIP, 8835*, 194–202.

Saha, R. K., Khurshid, S., & Perry, D. E. (2015). Understanding the triaging and fixing processes of long lived bugs. *Information and Software Technology, 65*, 114–128. doi:10.1016/j.infsof.2015.03.002

Saha, R. K., Lawall, J., Khurshid, S., & Perry, D. E. (2015, May). Are these bugs really normal? In *Proceedings of the 12th Working Conference on Mining Software Repositories* (pp. 258-268). IEEE Press.

Salter, J., & Antonopoulos, N. (2006). Recommender agent: Collaborative and content-based filtering. *Analysis, 21*(February), 35–41.

Samuel, A., & Reid, A. (2014). What Social Media Analytics Can't Tell You About Your Customers? *Vision Critical.* Retrieved June 12, 2016, from https://www.visioncritical.com/resources/ socialcustomersreport/?utm_campaign=WSMACTY+Report&utm_medium=Blog&utm_source=Referral

Santos, J. B., & DAntone, S. (2014). Reinventing the wheel? A critical view of demand-chain management. *Industrial Marketing Management, 43*(6), 1012–1025. doi:10.1016/j.indmarman.2014.05.014

Sathi, A., Harken, R., Eunice, T., & Thomas, M. (2013). *Advanced analytics platform deep dive components, patterns, architecture decisions ISA-3637*. Retrieved September 29, 2016, from http://www.slideshare.net/arvindsathi/big-data-analytics-27981097

Schmöller, S., Weikl, S., Müller, J., & Bogenberger, K. (2015). Empirical analysis of free-floating carsharing usage: The Munich and Berlin case. *Transportation Research Part C, Emerging Technologies, 56*, 34–51. doi:10.1016/j.trc.2015.03.008

Selen, W., & Soliman, F. (2002). Operations in todays demand chain management framework. *Journal of Operations Management, 20*(6), 667–673. doi:10.1016/S0272-6963(02)00032-3

Shah, Khandakar & Abu. (2008). Reverse Apriori Algorithm for Frequent Pattern Mining. *Asian Journal of Information Technology*, 524-530.

Shaheen, S., El-Hajj, W., Hajj, H., & Elbassuoni, S. (2014). Emotion Recognition from Text Based on Automatically Generated Rules. *2014 IEEE International Conference on Data Mining Workshop*, 383-382. doi:10.1109/ICDMW.2014.80

Shapiro, B. P. (1977). Can marketing and manufacturing co-exist. *Harvard Business Review, 55*(5), 104.

Shen, A., Tong, R., & Deng, Y. (2007, June). Application of classification models on credit card fraud detection. In *Service Systems and Service Management, 2007 International Conference on* (pp. 1-4). IEEE. doi:10.1109/ICSSSM.2007.4280163

Shmueli, G., Patel, N. R., & Bruce, P. C. (2007). *Data mining for business intelligence: concepts, techniques, and applications in Microsoft Office Excel with XLMiner*. John Wiley & Sons.

Shokripour, R., Kasirun, Z. M., Zamani, S., & Anvik, J. (2012, November). Automatic bug assignment using information extraction methods. In *Advanced Computer Science Applications and Technologies (ACSAT), 2012 International Conference on* (pp. 144-149). IEEE. doi:10.1109/ACSAT.2012.56

Shokripour, R., Anvik, J., Kasirun, Z. M., & Zamani, S. (2013, May). Why so complicated? simple term filtering and weighting for location-based bug report assignment recommendation. In *Proceedings of the 10th Working Conference on Mining Software Repositories* (pp. 2-11). IEEE Press. doi:10.1109/MSR.2013.6623997

Shokripour, R., Anvik, J., Kasirun, Z. M., & Zamani, S. (2015). A time-based approach to automatic bug report assignment. *Journal of Systems and Software*, *102*, 109–122. doi:10.1016/j.jss.2014.12.049

Siegel, E., & Davenport, T. H. (2013). *Predictive Analytics. The Power to Predict Who Will Click, Buy, Lie, or Die Hardcover*. Wiley.

Singh, A., Yadav, A., & Rana, A. (2013). K-means with Three different Distance Metrics. *International Journal of Computers and Applications*, *67*(10), 13–17. doi:10.5120/11430-6785

Singh, P., & Borah, B. (2013). Indian summer monsoon rainfall prediction using artificial neural network. *Stochastic Environmental Research and Risk Assessment*, *27*(7), 1585–1599. doi:10.1007/s00477-013-0695-0

Sinha, P. K., & Uniyal, D. P. (2008). *Managing Retailing*. Oxford University Press.

Sinwar & Kaushik. (2014). Study of Euclidean and Manhattan Distance Metrics using Simple K- Means Clustering. *International Journal for Research in Applied Science and Engineering Technology,* 270-274.

Soliman, F., & Youssef, M. (2001). The impact of some recent developments in e-business on the management of next generation manufacturing. *International Journal of Operations & Production Management*, *21*(5/6), 538–564. doi:10.1108/01443570110390327

Soltanolkotabi, M., Elhamifar, E., & Candès, E. J. (2014). 05 23). Robust subspace clustering. *Annals of Statistics*, *42*(2), 669–699. doi:10.1214/13-AOS1199

Somasundaram, K., & Murphy, G. C. (2012, February). Automatic categorization of bug reports using latent dirichlet allocation. In *Proceedings of the 5th India software engineering conference* (pp. 125-130). ACM. doi:10.1145/2134254.2134276

Spolsky, J. (2000). *Painless Bug Tracking*. Retrieved July 23, 2016, from http://www.joelonsoftware.com/articles/fog0000000 029.html

Stankevičienė, J., Sviderskė, T., & Miečinskienė, A. (2014). Dependence of sustainability on country risk indicators in EU Baltic Sea region countries. *Journal of Business Economics and Management*, *15*(4), 646–663. doi:10.3846/1611 1699.2014.965555

Steinbach, M., Tan, P.-N., Kumar, V., Klooster, S., & Potter, C. (2003). Discovery of climate indices using clustering. *The Ninth ACM SIGKDD International Conference on Knowledge Discovery and Data Mining* (pp. 446-455). New York: ACM. doi:10.1145/956750.956801

Stewart, A., Ledingham, R., & Williams, H. (2017). Variability in body size and shape of UK offshore workers: A cluster analysis approach. *Applied Ergonomics*, *58*, 265–272. doi:10.1016/j.apergo.2016.07.001 PMID:27633221

Strapparava, C., Valitutti, A., & Stock, O. (2006). The affective weight of lexicon.*Proceedings of the Fifth International Conference on Language Resources and Evaluation,* 423–426.

Strehl, A., & Ghosh, J. (2002). Cluster ensembles- a knowledge reuse framework for combining multiple partition. *Journal of Machine Learning Research*, 583–617.

Sun, J., Li, H., Huang, Q. H., & He, K. Y. (2014). Predicting financial distress and corporate failure: A review from the state-of-the-art definitions, modeling, sampling, and featuring approaches. *Knowledge-Based Systems*, *57*, 41–56. doi:10.1016/j.knosys.2013.12.006

Sureka, A. kumar Singh, H., Bagewadi, M., Mitra, A., & Karanth, R. A Decision Support Platform for Guiding a Bug Triager for Resolver Recommendation Using Textual and Non-Textual Features. *3rd International Workshop on Quantitative Approaches to Software Quality*, 25.

Suresh & Ramanjaneyulu. (2013). Mining Frequent Itemsets Using Apriori Algorithm. *International Journal of Computer Trends and Technology, 4*(4), 760-764.

Su, Y. M. (2011). Real-time anomaly detection systems for Denial-of-Service attacks by weighted k-nearestneighbour classifiers. *Expert Systems with Applications, 38*(4), 3492–3498. doi:10.1016/j.eswa.2010.08.137

Tamrawi, A., Nguyen, T. T., Al-Kofahi, J., & Nguyen, T. N. (2011, May). Fuzzy set-based automatic bug triaging: NIER track. In *2011 33rd International Conference on Software Engineering* (pp. 884-887). IEEE.

Tang, T. C., & Chi, L. C. (2005). Neural networks analysis in business failure prediction of Chinese importers: A between-countries approach. *Expert Systems with Applications, 29*(2), 244–255. doi:10.1016/j.eswa.2005.03.003

Tan, P.-N., Kumar, V., & Srivastava, J. (2004). Selecting the right objective measure for association analysis. *Information Systems, 29*(4), 293–313. doi:10.1016/S0306-4379(03)00072-3

Tian, Y., Lo, D., & Sun, C. (2012, October). Information retrieval based nearest neighbor classification for fine-grained bug severity prediction. In *2012 19th Working Conference on Reverse Engineering* (pp. 215-224). IEEE. doi:10.1109/WCRE.2012.31

Todde, G., Murgia, L., Caria, M., & Pazzona, A. (2016). A multivariate statistical analysis approach to characterize mechanization, structural and energy profile in Italian dairy farms. *Energy Reports, 2*, 129–134. doi:10.1016/j.egyr.2016.05.006

Tokito, S., Kagawa, S., & Nansai, K. (2016). Understanding international trade network complexity of platinum: The case of Japan. *Resources Policy, 49*, 415–421. doi:10.1016/j.resourpol.2016.07.009

Tomkins, S. S. (1962). *Affect, imagery, consciousness. In The positive affects* (pp. 20–31). New York: Springer.

Tracx. (2015). *A Buyer's Guide: Criteria for Selecting a Social Media Management Platform*. Retrieved July 11, 2016, from https://gdssummits.com/cmo/digital-eu/app/uploads/sites/72/2015/08/CMO-DML-EU-1-Tracx-BuyersGuide-Final.pdf

Triki, I. (n.d.). *Credit Scoring Models for a Tunisian Microfinance Institution: Comparison between Artificial Neural Network and Logistic Regression*. Academic Press.

Truong, D. T., & Battiti, R. (2012). A cluster-oriented genetic algorithm for alternative clustering. *IEEE 12th International Conference on Data Mining (ICDM)* (pp. 1122 - 1127). Brussels: IEEE.

Tsai, C. F., & Chen, M. L. (2010). Credit rating by hybrid machine learning techniques. *Applied Soft Computing, 10*(2), 374–380. doi:10.1016/j.asoc.2009.08.003

Tsakonas, A., Dounias, G., Doumpos, M., & Zopounidis, C. (2006). Bankruptcy prediction with neural logic networks by means of grammar-guided genetic programming. *Expert Systems with Applications, 30*(3), 449–461. doi:10.1016/j.eswa.2005.10.009

Turban, E., Sharda, R., & Delen, D. (2011). Decision Support and Business Intelligence Systems (9th ed.). Upper Saddle River, NJ: Prentice hall.

Udo, G. G. (2000). Using analytic hierarchy process to analyze the information technology outsourcing decision. *Industrial Management & Data Systems, 100*(9), 421–429. doi:10.1108/02635570010358348

Uygurtürk, H. (2015). Evaluating internet branches of banks using fuzzy MOORA method. *Int.*[Turkish]. *Journal of Management Economics and Business, 11*(25), 115–128.

Valdivia Garcia, H., & Shihab, E. (2014, May). Characterizing and predicting blocking bugs in open source projects. In *Proceedings of the 11th working conference on mining software repositories* (pp. 72-81). ACM. doi:10.1145/2597073.2597099

Vega-Pons, S., & Ruiz-Shulcloper, J. (2011). A survey of clustering ensemble algorithms. *International Journal of Pattern Recognition and Artificial Intelligence*, *25*(03), 337–372. doi:10.1142/S0218001411008683

Vergados, D. J., Mamounakis, I., Makris, P., & Varvarigos, E. (2016). Prosumer clustering into virtual microgrids for cost reduction in renewable energy trading markets. *Sustainable Energy. Grids and Networks*, *7*, 90–103.

Vinh, N. X., & Epps, J. (2010). minCEntropy: A novel information theoretic approach for the generation of alternative clusterings. *IEEE 10th International Conference on Data Mining (ICDM)* (pp. 521 - 530). Sydney: IEEE.

Vollmann, T. E., & Cordon, C. (1998). Building Successful Customer Supplier Alliances. *Long Range Planning*, *31*(5), 684–694. doi:10.1016/S0024-6301(98)00073-9

Walters, D. W., & Rainbird, M. (2007). *Strategic Operations Management: A Value Chain Approach*. Basingstoke, UK: Palgrave.

Wang, R.-Q., & Kong, F.-S. (2007). Semantic-enhanced personalized recommender system. *Sixth International Conference on Machine Learning and Cybernetics*, 19–22. doi:10.1109/ICMLC.2007.4370858

Wang, M., Zuo, W., & Wang, Y. (2016). An improved density peaks-based clustering method for social circle discovery in social networks. *Neurocomputing*, *179*, 219–227. doi:10.1016/j.neucom.2015.11.091

Watson, D., & Tellegen, A. (1985). Towards a consensual structure of mood. *Psychological Bulletin*, *98*(2), 219–235. doi:10.1037/0033-2909.98.2.219 PMID:3901060

Wei, W., Li, J., Cao, L., Ou, Y., & Chen, J. (2013). Effective detection of sophisticated online banking fraud on extremely imbalanced data. *World Wide Web (Bussum)*, *16*(4), 449–475. doi:10.1007/s11280-012-0178-0

Wen, H., & Song, L. (2015). A demand chain design for Chinese oatmeal companies. *Journal of Industrial Engineering and Management*, *8*(2), 335–348. doi:10.3926/jiem.1316

West, J., & Bhattacharya, M. (2016). Intelligent financial fraud detection: A comprehensive review. *Computers & Security*, *57*, 47–66. doi:10.1016/j.cose.2015.09.005

White, A. K., & Safi, S. K. (2016). The Efficiency of Artificial Neural Networks for Forecasting in the Presence of Autocorrelated Disturbances. *International Journal of Statistics and Probability*, *5*(2), 51. doi:10.5539/ijsp.v5n2p51

Wong, S. C., & Huang, C. Y. (2014). A Factor– Cluster Approach to Understanding Hong Kong Hotel Employees Symptom-management-related Coping Behavior Towards Job Stress. *Asia Pacific Journal of Tourism Research*, *19*(4), 469–491. doi:10.1080/10941665.2012.749929

Wu, W., Zhang, W., Yang, Y., & Wang, Q. (2011, December). Drex: Developer recommendation with k-nearest-neighbor search and expertise ranking. In *2011 18th Asia-Pacific Software Engineering Conference* (pp. 389-396). IEEE.

Wu, C. R., Chang, H. Y., & Wu, L. S. (2008). A framework of assessable mutual fund performance. *Journal of Modelling in Management*, *3*(2), 125–139. doi:10.1108/17465660810890117

Wu, L. L., Xie, B., Kaiser, G. E., & Passonneau, R. (2011). BugMiner: Software reliability analysis via data mining of bug reports? In *Proceedings of the International Conference on software engineering and knowledge engineering* (pp. 95-100).

Xuan, J., Jiang, H., Ren, Z., Yan, J., & Luo, Z. (2010, July). Automatic Bug Triage using Semi-Supervised Text Classification. SEKE, 209-214.

Xuan, J., Jiang, H., Hu, Y., Ren, Z., Zou, W., Luo, Z., & Wu, X. (2015). Towards effective bug triage with software data reduction techniques. *IEEE Transactions on Knowledge and Data Engineering*, *27*(1), 264–280. doi:10.1109/TKDE.2014.2324590

Xu, X., Zhou, C., & Wang, Z. (2009). Credit scoring algorithm based on link analysis ranking with support vector machine. *Expert Systems with Applications*, *36*(2), 2625–2632. doi:10.1016/j.eswa.2008.01.024

Yabing, J. (2013). Research of an Improved Apriori Algorithm in Data Mining Association Rules. *International Journal of Computer and Communication Engineering*, *2*(1), 25–27. doi:10.7763/IJCCE.2013.V2.128

Yang, C., & Huang, J. B. (2000). A decision model for IS outsourcing. *International Journal of Information Management*, *20*(3), 225–239. doi:10.1016/S0268-4012(00)00007-4

Yeung, D. S., Ng, W. W., Chan, A. P., Chan, P. P., Firth, M., & Tsang, E. C. (2007). A multiple intelligent agent system for credit risk prediction via an optimization of localized generalization error with diversity. *Journal of Systems Science and Systems Engineering*, *16*(2), 166–180. doi:10.1007/s11518-007-5048-4

Yeung, K., Haynor, D., & Ruzzo, W. (2001). Validating clustering for gene expression data. *Bioinformatics (Oxford, England)*, *17*(4), 309–318. doi:10.1093/bioinformatics/17.4.309 PMID:11301299

Yıldırım, B. F., & Önay, O. (2013). Ranking cloud storage technology firms using FUZZY AHP – MOORA method. *YÖNETİM: İstanbul Üniversitesi İşletme İktisadı Enstitüsü Dergisi*, *24*(75), 59–81.

Yu, L., Tsai, W. T., Zhao, W., & Wu, F. (2010, November). Predicting defect priority based on neural networks. In *International Conference on Advanced Data Mining and Applications* (pp. 356-367). Springer Berlin Heidelberg. doi:10.1007/978-3-642-17313-4_35

Yuan, T. I. A. N., David, L. O., & Chengnian, S. U. N. (2013). DRONE: Predicting Priority of Reported Bugs by Multi-factor Analysis.*29th IEEE International Conference on Software Maintenance*, 200-209.

Zafarani, R., Abbasi, M. A., & Liu, H. (2014). *Social Media Mining, An Introduction* (draft version). Cambridge University Press. Retrieved August 17, 2016, fromhttp://dmml.asu.edu/smm/ SMM.pdf

Zahedi, F. (1986). The analytic hierarchy process-a survey of the method and its applications. *Interfaces, 16*(4), 96-108.

Zaiane, O. (2002). Building a recommender agent for e-learning systems.*Proceedings of the International Conference on Computers in Education* (vol. 51, pp. 55–59). Washington, DC: IEEE Computer Society. doi:10.1109/CIE.2002.1185862

Zaki, M. J. (2000). Scalable algorithms for association mining. *IEEE Transactions on Knowledge and Data Engineering*, *1*(2), 372–390. doi:10.1109/69.846291

Zanetti, M. S., Scholtes, I., Tessone, C. J., & Schweitzer, F. (2013, May). Categorizing bugs with social networks: a case study on four open source software communities. In *Proceedings of the 2013 International Conference on Software Engineering* (pp. 1032-1041). IEEE Press. doi:10.1109/ICSE.2013.6606653

Zeithaml, V. A. (1988). Consumer perceptions of price, quality, and value: A means-end model and synthesis of evidence. *Journal of Marketing*, *52*(3), 2–22. doi:10.2307/1251446

Zhang, G. P. (2004). Business forecasting with artificial neural networks: An overview. *Neural Networks in Business Forecasting*, 1-22.

Zheludev, I., Smith, R., & Aste, T. (2014). When Can Social Media Lead Financial Markets? *Scientific Reports, 4*, Article number 4213. Retrieved July 29, 2016, from http://www.nature.com/articles/srep04213

Zhou, B., Neamtiu, I., & Gupta, R. (2015, April). Predicting concurrency bugs: how many, what kind and where are they? In *Proceedings of the 19th International Conference on Evaluation and Assessment in Software Engineering* (p. 6). ACM. doi:10.1145/2745802.2745807

Zikopoulos, P., & Eaton, C. (2011). *Understanding Big Data: Analytics for Enterprise Class Hadoop and Streaming Data*. McGraw Hill Professional.

About the Contributors

Rajendra Sahu is a Professor at the institute. Dr. Sahu has done his Ph.D from IIT, Kharagpur after completing his M.Sc (Engg.) and MIM. He has been associated with the teaching profession for the past 20 years, and has been closely involved with industrial consultancy projects, and as an external Consultant for IIT, Kharagpur. Management Consultancy has been his forte. He has been associated with prestigious projects in the past, and has also published about 90 papers in his areas of proficiency and interest. His primary areas of interest are Systems Approach to Management, Business Process Management, Business Analytics, e-Commerce, and IT enabled Services. He is currently the Secretary of Systems Dynamics Society of India.

Manoj Kumar Dash earned his M.A. with specialization in Econometrics, M.Phil. with specialization in Econometrics, Ph.D. in Economics on topic 'Econometrics of Complete Demand System' and M.B.A. in Marketing from Berhampur University, Berhampur (Orissa). He had published more than 63 research paper in various journals of International and National repute. He is the author of three books titled 'Managerial Economics', 'Applied Demand Analysis' and "Think New-Think Better: A case study of Entrepreneurship" and edited five books till date. He received several prizes in the Research Paper presentation competitions in both National and International Seminar/Conferences. He was involved as Chair Member in International Conference of Arts and Science held at Harvard University, Boston (USA), Member of Steering Committee in International Conference on ESTD 2014 held at ABV- Indian Institute of Information Technology and Management Gwalior. He had conducted 22 Faculty Development Pogramme sponsored by AICTE, MHRD and IIITM on Multivariate Analysis, Econometrics, Research Methodology, Mulch-Criteria Optimization, Multivariate analysis in Marketing, SPSS software etc. He introduced many course in Marketing such as Digital Marketing, New Product and Service Development, Multivariate Analysis in Marketing, Established Behavioural Economics and Experimental Laboratory at ABV- IIITM Gwalior. He visited two countries USA and Cyprus for presenting paper in international conferences. His area of interest are Multi-criteria Optimization, Behavioural Economics, Decision Making Modelling, Econometrics Modelling, and Marketing Research.

Anil Kumar is a member of the faculty of Operations Management and Quantitative Techniques in the School of Management at BML Munjal University. He has completed his Ph.D in Management Science from Indian Institute of Information Technology and Management, Gwalior (M.P), India. He has published in reputed national and international journals and presented in national/international conferences. He has more than 30 research papers/book chapters and 4 books to his credit. He is a member of many scientific societies like International Society on Multiple Criteria Decision Making (ISMCDM),

Production and Operation Management Society (POMS), Analytics Society of India (ASI) and Society of Information Sciences (SIS) etc. His research interest includes Marketing Analytics, Supply Chain Analytics, Multi-Criteria Decision Making, Fuzzy Multi-Criteria Decision Making, Fuzzy Optimization through Type-2 fuzzy, Generalizability of fuzzy set, Application of Soft-Computing and Econometrics Modeling in Marketing, Multi-Criteria Decision Making and Fuzzy applications in E-Commerce and M-Commerce, Multi-Criteria Decision Making and Fuzzy applications in Decision Making.

* * *

Sheik Abdullah A works as Assistant Professor, Department of Information Technology, Thiagarajar College of Engineering, Madurai, Tamil Nadu, India. He completed his B.E (Computer Science and Engineering), at Bharath Niketan Engineering College, and M.E (Computer Science and Engineering) at Kongu Engineering College under Anna University, Chennai. He has been awarded as gold medalist for his excellence in the degree of Post Graduate. He is pursuing his Ph.D in the domain of Medical Data Analytics, and his research interests include Medical Data Research, E-Governance and Big Data. He has handled various E-Governance projects such as automation system for tracking community certificate, birth and death certificate, DRDA and income tax automation systems. He has published research articles in various reputed journals and International Conferences. He has been assigned as an reviewer in Various reputed journals such as European Heart Journal, Proceedings of the National Academy of Sciences, Physical Sciences (NASA) and so on. He has received the Honorable chief minister award for excellence in E-Governance for the best project in E-Governance. Currently he is working towards the significance of the medical data corresponding to various diseases and resolving its implications through the development of various algorithmic models.

Omer Beyca is an Assistant Professor in the Industrial Engineering Department at Istanbul Technical University, Turkey. He received his B.S. degree from Fatih University and PhD. degree from Oklahoma State University in Industrial Engineering and Management. His research interests machine learning applications, data mining and statistical modeling.

Ramya C holds a B.E degree in Computer Science and Engineering from K.L.N. College of Engineering, Madurai. She is currently pursuing M.E. in Computer Science and Information Security at Thiagarajar College of Engineering, Madurai.

Nidhi Dadhich received his Bachelor of Engineering in Electronics and Communication Engineering from Rajeev Gandhi Technical University, Bhopal, India and his Masters of Technology degree in Future Studies and Planning from Devi Ahilya University, Indore, India.

Arun Kumar Deshmukh is PhD Research Scholar and UGC- Senior Research Fellow (UGC-JRF) at Faculty of Management Studies (FMS), Banaras Hindu University (BHU), Varanasi. His research interests are Demand/ Supply Chain Management, and Distribution & Channel Management, Relationship Marketing and Retailing. He has authored several research papers presented in international / national conferences, published in journals and as book chapters. He is the recipient of three national level research fellowships from agencies such as Indian Council of Social Science Research (ICSSR). University Grants Commission (UGC), and Ministry of Human Resource Development (MHRD) during his doctoral research.

Maryam Ebrahimi was born in 1980 in Iran. She is affiliated as a Visiting Scholar to Portland State University for the purpose of applying modeling and simulation techniques in the areas of technology management and renewable energy. She was a postdoctoral fellow at the Alexander von Humboldt Foundation –Georg Forster Research Fellowship in the field of Information Systems Management at Bayreuth University, Germany. Her Postdoctoral research was about "designing a fuzzy multi-agent system for renewable energy technology strategy planning in SMEs". She works also as a lecturer in Azad University – electronic campus in the fields of IT management and industrial management. Her interests are modeling and simulation, technology management, strategic planning, SMEs, and energy studies. A few of her publications are "hybrid simulation approach for technological innovation policy making in developing countries", and "multi-method approach for the comparative analysis of solar and wind energy industry structures in Germany and Iran.

Gillie Gabay is a systems science expert. She studies health psychology, the study of psychological and behavioral processes in health, illness and healthcare. Ms. Gabay studies patient-physician trust, patient-insurer trust, public trust in physicians, physicians-top management trust, promotion of medication adherence, reduction of hospital re-admissions, patient-physician communication and the enhancement of value for patients and physicians in hospitals. She promotes a systemic integrated approach where multiple views are accounted for: The view of the health system, the view of the patient and the view of the clinician. She is the previous head of the organizational developement Graduate program at the College of Management in Israel (COLMAN) and the past Chair of the Systemic Organizational Consulting Graduate Program at COLMAN.

Dražena Gašpar is a Full-time Professor on Faculty of Economics, the University of Mostar in the field of Business Informatics (Data Bases, Programming, Accounting Information Systems, Business Information Systems, Business Intelligence, Software Engineering). Almost 20 years of experience in the software industry as the software developer, project manager and manager of software departments in several companies. Since 2001 co-founder and co-owner of the software company HERA Mostar. Research interests: Information technology in education, Information technology in business, Databases, Data Warehouse, Business Intelligence, Programming, Methodology for the development of Information Systems, Software development, and Software project management.

Anjali Goyal is a research scholar in Jaypee Institute of Information Technology. Her interest areas include decision making, optimisation techniques and mining software repositories.

Vinay Kumar Jain received his Bachelor's Degree in 2009 from Rajiv Gandhi Proudyogiki Vishwavidyala, Bhopal, India and received his Master's Degree from Jaypee University of Engineering and Technology, India in 2012. Now, he is pursuing his Ph.D. degree from Jaypee University of Engineering and Technology, Guna, M.P., India.

Shishir Kumar is working as Professor & HOD. Dr. Shishir has completed his Ph. D. in 2005. His work area of Ph.D. was Load balancing strategies of Internet Servers. He has joined this organization in July 2005 as Assistant Professor. He has sixteen years of teaching experience in various organizations of repute for PG & UG courses of Computer Science & IT. Many students of various UG and PG courses of Computer Science and IT had developed their projects under his guidance. He is associated with many International Conferences as a reviewer, Technical Program Committee member etc. To name a few are ICACT (IEEE Phoenix Park, Korea), SETIT (Tunisia; IEEE France Section), ICIECA (Harbin, China), AIC (Athens, Greece), SIGCOM (ACM Kyoto, Japan), MIC-CNIT (Jordan Amman), IEEE SMC (Texas USA) etc. He is also associated with many renowned International Journals as reviewer / editorial board member. He is also in a panel of reviewer for IEEE Communication Society. He is also working as honorary advisor to SETEPS-India for various academic and literary activities.

Mirela Mabić is an Assistant on Faculty of Economics, University of Mostar in the field of Business Informatics (Business Informatics, Business Information Systems, Databases, Accounting Information Systems, Business Intelligence, Internet Marketing). Research interests: Business Information Systems, Practical Application of Software and Web Technologies both in Business and in Education, Real-Life Experience in IT Management, Quality of Higher Education and Applied Statistics.

Ashutosh Mohan did his Master's in Business Administration from Faculty of Management Studies (FMS), Banaras Hindu University, Varanasi in 2000 with top honors. He worked as Senior Research Fellow at Faculty of Management Studies (FMS), University of Delhi, for three years after clearing the UGC-JRF examination and received Doctorate Degree. He is a recipient of AICTE's Career Award for Young Teachers (CAYT). He completed a major project of ICSSR, New Delhi and is working on a major project funded by AICTE. He has published more than 10 papers in referred journals and presented more than 30 papers at various international and national forums including the paper presentation in prestigious IPSERA conference at University of San Diego, USA, 7th SMEs Conference at Kuching, Malaysia. He is also a recipient of CAPS Fellowship, University of Arizona, USA. He is serving as member of Review Board from India (one out of two members from India) of esteemed journal titled as Journal of Supply Chain Management, USA and Associated Editor of BHU Management Review. He provided guidance to three doctoral research candidates and more than 50 master's dissertations. He widely traveled throughout the world for his academic endeavors covering USA, European Union, UAE, Russia and East Asian countries. He conducted and / or served as resource person at various forums such as MDP of GAIL & Apollo Hospital, AICTE – QIP Programmes, TSM, FMS-DU, IIT-D, UGC-Refresher and Orientation Courses etc. He coordinated two National Conference, three Executive Development Programmes (EDP) and three Quality Improvement Programmes sponsored by AICTE. He worked as faculty at Centre for Management Studies, Jamia Millia Islamia, New Delhi for two years. Presently, he has been in teaching, research and consultancy as Asstt. Professor at Faculty of Management Studies (FMS), Banaras Hindu University (BHU), Varanasi, and is currently focusing on the Supply Chain Management (SCM) practices and its collaboration with Customer Relationship Management (CRM) in Retailing and SMEs.

Howard Moskowitz graduated from Harvard University in 1969 with a Ph.D. in experimental psychology. Prior to that he graduated Queens College (New York), Phi Beta Kappa, with degrees in mathematics and psychology. He has written/edited 26 books, has published well over 300 articles, and serves on the editorial board of major journals. Moskowitz won the Scientific Director`s Gold Medal for outstanding research at the U.S. Army Natick Laboratories, and the 2001 and 2003 awards from ESOMAR (World Society Of Market Research). In 2004, Dr. Moskowitz was elected as an IFT Fellow, and also was awarded the "David R. Peryam Award", from ASTM, in recognition of outstanding contributions to the field of basic and applied sensory science. Moskowitz has been the recipient of numerous awards, including the ARF Research Innovation Award, the David R. Peryam lifetime achievement award by the American Society for Testing and Materials, and the Charles Coolidge Parlin Award from the American Marketing Association, considered to be the 'Nobel Prize' of market research. The latter was awarded for Moskowitz's lifetime contributions to the field, ranging from product work to the optimization of consumer concept and package designs. Dr. Howard Moskowitz has been selected to receive the 2010 Walston Chubb Award for Innovation, presented annually by Sigma Xi, The Scientific Research Society. The Chubb award recognizes and promotes creativity in science. For the development of the science of Mind Genomics Dr. Moskowitz was awarded the 2012 Edison Award.

Avinash Navlani received his Bachelor of Engineering in Information Technology from Rajeev Gandhi Technical University, Bhopal, India and his Masters of Technology degree in Future Studies and Planning from Devi Ahilya Univeristy, Indore, India. He is now pursuing a Ph.D. degree in Data Science at Devi Ahilya Univeristy. His research areas are in Data Mining, Cloud Computing, and Information Security.

Onur Önay is a teaching and research assistant in the Business School at the Istanbul University. He holds PhD in quantitative decision making methods. His areas of interest and research are operations research, mathematical modeling, quantitative methods and applications of the decision making methods in business. He has published several papers in various journals.

Steven Onufrey (deceased) was a founding partner of Mind Genomics Advisors. Steve was the Chief Implementation Officer, with the responsibility to plan, create and implement the different faces of the Customer Experience for Mind genomics. Steve created the vision of applying Mind Genomics to the banking and health sectors. Finally, with Dr. Howard Mokowitz, Steve developed the Personal ViewPoint Identifier™ and the Digital Viewpoint Identifier™, allowing the user of Mind Genomics to assign new people to the appropriate mind-set segments, and by so doing ensure that their experience was optimal for their mind-set.

Başar Öztayşi is a full time Associate Professor at Industrial Engineering Department of Istanbul Technical University (ITU). His research interests include multiple criteria decision making, data mining and intelligent systems. He has 25 articles, 32 conference papers and 10 book chapters. He has edited a book on Supply Chain Management which is published by Springer. Başar Öztayşi teaches courses on data management, information systems management and business intelligence and decision support systems.

Peeyush Pandey is a doctoral student in the area of Operations Management & Quantitative Techniques at IIM Indore. His research interests lies in the area Retail Operations, Sustainable Supply chain and Fuzzy set theory. He has good exposure in Mathematical Modeling, Optimization and Meta -heuristics.

Stephen D. Rappaport is a researcher and marketing consultant specializing in consumer-centered business strategy. Stephen holds a B.A from Stony Brook University and is a senior fellow at Wharton's SEI Center for Advanced Studies in Management.

Nilanjan Ray is from Kolkata, India. He has obtained his M.Com (Mktg), MBA (Mktg), STC FMRM (IIT-Kgp), PhD (Management) from The University of Burdwan Department of Business Administration). He has 8 years teaching experience in BBA, MBA, BCom and 6 years Research experience and guided around 56 Post Graduate students' project . Dr. Ray has contributed over 30 research papers in reputed National and International Referred, Peer Reviewed Journals and Proceedings. He has contributed 10 book Chapters and also Chief Editor of 4 Edited Book Volumes of IGI Global USA. He has also associated himself as a reviewer of Journal of Business and Economics, Research Journal of Business and Management Accounting and Journal of Service Marketing Emerald Group Publishing Limited, Research Journal of Business and Management Accounting, and as an Editorial Board Member of several referred Journals. He has also chaired in a technical session at IJAS Conference 2012, at Harvard University, Boston, USA. Dr. Ray is a life-member of the International Business Studies Academia.

Scott Robinson has been an enterprise technology consultant in the United States for more than 20 years, advising corporations and government agencies in collaborative methodologies, systems interface, data-sharing and the application of analytics. In addition, he has done research in neuropsychology and early brain development, and currently studies the relationship between brain components and socio-political bias.

Selvakumar S is Professor in Computer Science & Engineering, G.K.M College of Engineering and Technology, Chennai. His research interests includes in the domain of Knowledge & Data Engineering, Software Engineering, and Information Security. He has published more that 35 reputed journals and in various National and International conferences. He completed his Doctorate from Anna University, Chennai. He has over 20 years of teaching experience with interests towards various fields such as software testing, programming, data science and engineering, data warehousing and mining, and design methods.

Neetu Sardana is an Assistant Professor (Senior Grade) in the Department of Computer Science in Jaypee Institute of Information Technology, Noida. She has more than 14 years of teaching experience. She has published papers in many national and international conferences and journals. Her research interest is in the area of Mining Software Repositories, Social Network Analysis and Web Mining. She has many research papers in peer reviewed Journals & Conferences. She had supervised several M.Tech Thesis and B.Tech Major Projects. Currently she is guiding four PhD's. She is also serving as a PC member of IC3 conference which is held every year in JIIT-Noida.

İbrahim Yazici earned BSc in industrial engineering from Kocaeli University in 2011, MSc in industrial engineering from İstanbul Technical University in 2015. He is currently doing doctorate at İstanbul Technical University. His research areas are data mining, multi-criteria decision making and statistical decision making.

Selim Zaim has been professor in industrial engineering department at İstanbul Technical University for 3 years. His research areas are simulation and system modelling, multivariate statistical analysis, multi-criteria decision making and data mining.

Index

N

O

P

Q

R

S

T

V

Purchase Print + Free E-Book or E-Book Only*

Purchase a print book through the IGI Global Online Bookstore and receive the e-book for free or purchase the e-book only! Shipping fees apply.

www.igi-global.com

Recommended Reference Books

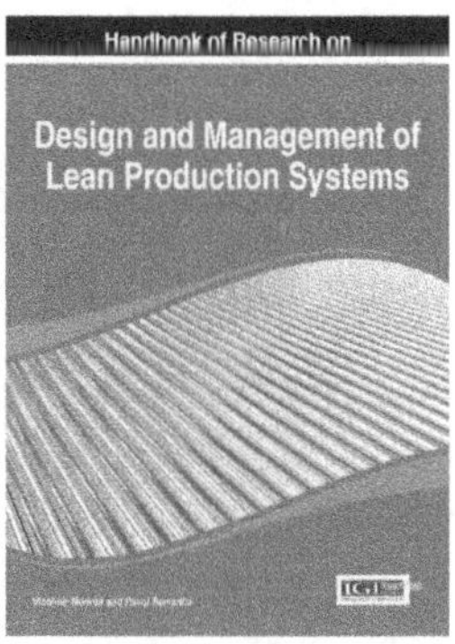

ISBN: 978-1-4666-5039-8
© 2014; 487 pp.
List Price: $260

ISBN: 978-1-4666-7476-9
© 2015; 508 pp.
List Price: $212

ISBN: 978-1-4666-6182-0
© 2014; 325 pp.
List Price: $180

ISBN: 978-1-4666-4474-8
© 2014; 735 pp.
List Price: $276

ISBN: 978-1-4666-5950-6
© 2014; 290 pp.
List Price: $156

ISBN: 978-1-4666-6595-8
© 2015; 406 pp.
List Price: $156

*IGI Global now offers the exclusive opportunity to receive a free e-book with the purchase of the publication in print, or purchase any e-book publication only. You choose the format that best suits your needs. This offer is only valid on purchases made directly through IGI Global's Online Bookstore and not intended for use by book distributors or wholesalers. Shipping fees will be applied for hardcover purchases during checkout if this option is selected.

Should a new edition of any given publication become available, access will not be extended on the new edition and will only be available for the purchased publication. If a new edition becomes available, you will not lose access, but you would no longer receive new content for that publication (i.e. updates). The free e-book is only available to single institutions that purchase printed publications through IGI Global. Sharing the free e-book is prohibited and will result in the termination of e-access.

Publishing Information Science and Technology Research Since 1988

IGI GLOBAL DISSEMINATOR OF KNOWLEDGE

www.igi-global.com | Sign up at www.igi-global.com/newsletters | facebook.com/igiglobal | twitter.com/igiglobal

www.ingramcontent.com/pod-product-compliance
Lightning Source LLC
LaVergne TN
LVHW060425300926
849162LV00006B/1532
* 9 7 8 1 5 2 2 5 2 1 4 8 8 *